The Savage
in Judaism

The Savage in Judaism

An Anthropology of
Israelite Religion
and Ancient Judaism

Howard Eilberg-Schwartz

INDIANA UNIVERSITY PRESS

Bloomington and Indianapolis

Chapter 5 originally appeared in *Journal of Ritual Studies* 2:1 (1988), 1–30. An earlier version of chapter 9 appeared in *History of Religions* 26:4 (1987), 357–381. They are included here by permission of the original publishers.

The paper used in this publication meets the minimum requirements of American National Standard for Information Sciences—Permanence of Paper for Printed Library Materials, ANSI Z39.48-1984.
⊗™

Manufactured in the United States of America

Library of Congress Cataloging-in-Publication Data

Eilberg-Schwartz, Howard.
The savage in Judaism : an anthropology of Israelite religion and ancient Judaism / Howard Eilberg-Schwartz.
p.   cm.
Includes bibliographical references.
ISBN 0-253-31946-3 — ISBN 0-253-20591-3 (pbk.)
1. Judaism—Origin. 2. Religion, Primitive. 3. Religion, Primitive—Palestine. 4. Symbolism in the Bible. 5. Rites and ceremonies in the Bible. 6. Purity, Ritual—Biblical teaching.
I. Title.
BM534.E54 1990
296'.09'01—dc20   89-45919
                                                                            CIP

1 2 3 4 5 94 93 92 91 90

To Skip and Eda Lou
For Serenity, Courage, and the Wisdom to Know the Difference
and
To Penina
for the gift of childhood, hers and mine

Contents

Conclusion: Savaging Judaism: *Anthropology of Judaism as
Cultural Critique*

Preface

The argument of this book is contained in its title. *The Savage in Judaism* exposes and challenges the opposition between Judaism and "savage" religions that has shaped the conceptualization of Judaism in the discourses of modernity. Since the Enlightenment, Judaism has typically been regarded as superior to other religions, with the single exception of Christianity. Although inferior to Christianity, "the absolute religion," Judaism was not considered sufficiently primitive to be classified with the religion of savages. This judgment gave rise to the conviction that interpreters of Judaism had little if anything to learn from either the discipline of anthropology or comparative inquiry. Since anthropology has traditionally made "primitive societies" its object of analysis, the questions, theories, and insights generated within that discipline as well as ethnographic literature have generally been assumed irrelevant for understanding the religion of the Jews.

This book, by contrast, aligns itself with a growing trend that is seeking to collapse the distinction between Judaism and savage religions. It does so in two different ways. By way of background, it recounts the history of that opposition, how it emerged, how it functioned, and what its consequences have been. In revealing the prejudices that until recently have made an anthropology of Judaism inconceivable, this historical argument calls for a fundamental reassessment of how Judaism is studied and the standard interpretations those methods of study generate. This historical argument is followed by several chapters that subject specific practices from Israelite religion and ancient Judaism to anthropological inquiry. These studies show how differently Judaism appears when it is passed under the gaze of anthropological inquiry and cross-cultural analysis.

The idea for this book began to emerge seven years ago when I was a rabbinical student at the Jewish Theological Seminary of America. I originally turned to anthropology as the result of growing dissatisfaction with the models of interpretation through which I was taught to think about the history of Judaism. From the very beginning, I found that those interpretive models either did not provide answers to the kinds of questions in which I was interested or the answers they offered were not particularly satisfying. At a friend's recommendation, I began reading Lévi-Strauss's *The Savage Mind*, my first introduction to anthropology. Although I did not entirely understand that book at the time, I already sensed that the kinds of questions that were engaged and the types of answers that were offered spoke more directly to my own concerns. After Lévi-Strauss, I read Douglas, Durkheim, Geertz, Radcliffe-Brown, Malinowski, Evans-Pritchard, Boas, Kroeber, Radin, and so on, eventually doing graduate work in anthropology at Brown University.

The immersion in anthropology provided me with interesting new angles on questions I had already begun to ask. At the same time, my way of thinking about Israelite religion and ancient Judaism was changing.

My first attempt to bring anthropology to bear on ancient Judaism was the occasion of a senior sermon, an address by graduating rabbinic students to the seminary community. For my sermon, I chose to subject the menstrual taboo in Judaism to anthropological analysis. My homiletics professor, who insisted on reviewing a sermon before its delivery, was enraged by the content of my sermon and threatened to fail me out of rabbinical school. My sermon, in his words, was as bad as "Romans fornicating in the streets." After protracted negotiation, we reached a compromise. He would tolerate the sermon if I deleted the word "semen." To this day, my talk is remembered by that community as the "semen sermon" and jokes are still made about it being a "seminal" address. A maturer version of that talk appears in this book (chapter 7).

At the time, I did not realize that I had touched a nerve not just of one man but of modern discourses on Judaism. The nervousness and anxiety stimulated by talk of menstrual blood reflected the ways that Jews had been taught to think about their tradition and their bodies, ways of thinking that were themselves products of modern discourses that presupposed a distinction between Judaism and savage religions. This book represents an attempt to do away with that problematic opposition and to see what the consequences might be for the conceptualization of Israelite religion and ancient Judaism.

Because I am neither an anthropologist nor a biblical scholar by training, I am particularly grateful to those anthropologists (Mary Douglas, Shlomo Deshen, James Fernandez, Nancy Jay, Harvey Goldberg, Riv-Ellen Prell, and Walter Zenner) and scholars of Hebrew Bible (Gary Anderson, James Ackerman, Jo Ann Hackett, Ron Hendel, Bernhard Lang, Jacob Milgrom, and Robert Wilson) who were kind enough to tolerate and encourage my incursions into their areas of expertise. While they by no means agree with everything I have said, they have offered invaluable help in thinking through the concerns I have taken up. With their help, I have nuanced my arguments in ways that would otherwise have been impossible. Originally, this book was to include a third part that would have brought the discussion of rationality, as it has emerged in anthropological inquiry, in contact with the study of rabbinic logic. Initial thoughts on this issue will or already have appeared in other contexts (Eilberg-Schwartz 1987a; 1987b; forthcoming). I hope to develop this issue more fully in a future context.

Countless friends and colleagues have supported this project. Most important have been my close friends and colleagues Louis Newman, Martin Jaffee, Paul Lauritzen, and Riv-Ellen Prell. Each has been involved in this project at every stage. As friends they have nurtured me through the difficult and painful process of deciding what this project was about and bringing it to completion. They were there on the phone whenever the self-doubts and anxieties took control. As colleagues, they pushed me further in my thinking than I could have gone on my own. This book would never have seen the light of day without their unyielding support, friendship, and honesty. They have helped me to believe in myself.

Special thanks to Alan Londy for introducing me to the work of Lévi-Strauss, to George Hicks and David Murray for my first formal introduction to anthropology, and to Sherry Saggers and Pat Symonds for socializing me in the anthropology department. Thanks also to Wendell Dietrich for grounding me in European intellectual history.

I am also particularly grateful to my former colleagues in the Religious Studies department at Indiana University. They did everything they could to cultivate me as a young scholar. They enabled me to take a semester of paid leave without which I could never have finished this project. Several of the chapters in this book were critiqued at departmental colloquia. In particular, I wish to thank James Ackerman, Judith Berling, Jo Ann Hackett, Luke Johnson, Richard Miller, Samuel Preuss, and Jane Rubin for critically reading several individual chapters. Judith Berling's encouragement to conceptualize this project as a book rather than as discrete articles came at a crucial moment in my own intellectual and personal development. Jim Ackerman and Jo Ann Hackett provided invaluable encouragement and criticism of my work on Israelite religion. Special thanks also to Richard Miller, Jane Rubin, and Greg Schopen for those wonderful debates over pizza. Those were the days! Michael Morgan, my former colleague in Jewish Studies, was also an important conversation partner during the time this project was in progress.

While writing this book, I participated in a series of colloquia on Religion(s) in Culture and History at the University of Chicago Divinity School. These conversations had an important impact on my thinking and their effects are dispersed throughout the various chapters of this book. Thanks especially to Frank Reynolds for giving a junior colleague a chance.

Without my new colleague, David Watt, the momentum of this project would never have continued after my move to Temple University. His support and friendship during the past year sustained me. Larry Hoffman's encouragement from afar also rescued me from self-doubt at crucial moments. Several graduate students also deserve thanks: Mark Pitts and William Guinee for legwork in the library, and Irene Riegner for her close proofreading of the final manuscript.

Numerous friends sustained me and my family during the past three and a half years. Thanks to Larry, Debby, Jacob, and Aaron for a home away from home, to Jeff, Marcie, and Tali for an oasis in a desert, and to Lisa, Fred, and Yael for being there during some rough times.

My wife Amy is the midwife to this project. She, more than anyone else, helped me breathe during the birth pangs that delivered this book. How she tolerated the possessed person she sometimes had to live with is difficult to fathom. The past three years have been growing times, sometimes painful, sometimes exciting, always important. I am grateful for her love, devotion, and support and for the opportunity to share our experiences together. She has enriched my life in countless ways.

Finally, to the people to whom this book is dedicated. To Skip and Eda Lou for gifts no book could ever have given. And to Penina, my daughter, whose curiosity, laughter, and wisdom have opened my eyes to life.

The Savage
in Judaism

INTRODUCTION

❧

The Savage in Judaism

Savages are no more exempt from human folly than civilized
men, and are no doubt equally liable to the error of thinking
they . . . can do what in fact cannot be done. But this error is
not the essence of magic, it is a perversion of magic. And we
should be careful how we attribute it to the people we call
savages who will one day rise up and testify against us.

Collingwood 1958

In intellectual discourse these days, the term "savage" is passé, and properly
so. The term is a pejorative that implies a judgment of superiority by the
person who applies the term to another group. Rather than pass judgment on
others, present interpreters of culture and religion wish to understand or
come to terms with the culture and religion of others. They operate on the
assumption that difference does not imply inferiority. In short, the current
generation of interpreters has discovered no savages. It has explored the highlands of New Guinea, the outbacks of Australia, the forests of the Congo and
found that they are populated with a variety of intriguing peoples who differ
from Westerners in a number of ways that are worth thinking about and exploring. But these people are not "savages" whose cultural and religious
practices are inferior to those of the West.

There was a period of time, however, when savages did exist, when travelers
were discovering them in many parts of the world and intellectuals were writing incessantly about them. Ironically, these travelers and writers were looking in the same places and talking about the same people as the current
generation of interpreters. But what they saw were undeveloped, simple peoples who had not yet advanced up the evolutionary ladder to the point
achieved by Western society. The savage, therefore, was a creation of another
generation, a generation that was not only confident of the difference between its own culture and the ones it was discovering, but certain also of its
own superiority. I am of course referring to the late nineteenth- and early
twentieth-century students of culture and religion who routinely invoked the
adjective "savage" to describe various societies.

In retrospect, we can see that the twentieth century represents a period of reaction, when the superiority of Western civilization was gradually called into question and the ethnocentric bias of scholarly discourse became a problem that had to be addressed. Numerous factors contributed to the changing tenor of discourse on culture and religion, including, among other things, the increasing problems of colonization, the growing understanding of other cultures through ethnographic study, the gradual loss of faith in the progress of science, and the paradoxical realization that the modern forms of life we have created have generated a more inhumane world than those of the so-called savages.

Whatever the reasons, as Western thinkers lost confidence in the superiority of their own culture, the "savage" gradually became extinct. As twentieth-century anthropology developed, the emphasis was on dismantling one by one the differences that previously had been relied upon to distinguish the "savage" from us. All the convenient ways of distinguishing between the societies of the West and the small face-to-face societies of New Guinea, Australia, or Africa proved to be impositions of the Western scholar.

This process is not yet complete. There are still important discourses that presuppose the category of the savage. This book is about one of those discourses, the scholarly study of Judaism. Only recently have interpreters begun to overcome the artificial and problematic opposition between Judaism and primitive or savage religions that was bequeathed to them by European thinkers of the previous three centuries (see chapters 1 and 2). This new trend, initially stimulated by the studies of Mary Douglas (1966) and Edmund Leach (1969), is now acquiring a momentum of its own.[1]

But for much of the twentieth century, interpreters avoided comparisons between Judaism and those religions that previously were considered primitive, a prejudice already pointed out by Leach (1969, 109–10), Feeley-Harnik (1982, 99), and Goldberg (1987, 7–10), among others. Since anthropology has traditionally made primitive society its domain of inquiry, few interpreters of Judaism have been willing to turn to that discipline for either a theoretical framework or substantive insight. For similar reasons, ethnographic literature and cross-cultural studies have been generally ignored. To be sure, there have been some notable exceptions, for example, the work of William Robertson Smith, James G. Frazer, Sidney Hooke, Theodor Gaster, Raphael Patai, and most recently Mary Douglas and Edmund Leach.[2] But on the whole the use of ethnographic data or anthropological theory to illuminate beliefs and practices of Judaism has been a marginal enterprise in the twentieth century until only recently.

This book argues that the suppression of the savage has had an important impact on the picture of Judaism that is created and sustained by scholarly discourse. There is, of course, no stable object called Judaism that scholars think and write about. It is a shifting, constantly changing abstraction that is created even as it is written about. It is as much a product of intellectual discourse as an object of it. Consequently, the Judaism that is talked about and examined is itself a product of certain assumptions that are taken for granted by the people doing the talking. In the past three hundred years, one of those crucial assumptions has been the presumed difference between Judaism and the religions of primitive societies.

That assumption leads to one picture of Judaism. It determines that certain kinds of questions are asked rather than others, that particular types of comparisons are considered fruitful while others are treated as uninteresting or irrelevant, and that certain methods are adopted to answer the questions interpreters deem important. It is not surprising that the picture that is created confirms the original impression, namely, that the comparison of Judaism and primitive societies is not very interesting and the subjection of Judaism to anthropological inquiry is not very important. This book questions that impression. It is my assertion that the opposition between Judaism and savage religions has become problematic and without overcoming it, a variety of interesting questions about Judaism cannot even be imagined.

There are two related reasons for the longstanding hostility toward anthropology and the comparative study of Judaism. The first of these reasons is obvious. Passing Judaism under the anthropological gaze represents a tacit admission that Judaism has important commonalities with primitive religions. Many interpreters have been unwilling to make such a concession. As I will show in some detail in chapters 1 and 2, the impulse to radically differentiate Judaism and savage religions was part of an ongoing attempt to protect the privileged status of Judaism, and by extension, Christianity. This motivation informed the work of both Jewish and Christian interpreters from the Enlightenment until the present day.

It is self-evident why Jewish interpreters would want to deny any basic similarities between Judaism and the religion of savages. But such a stance was also naturally adopted by many who wanted to protect the superior status of Christianity, since Christianity grounds its own truth claims on the Scriptures of Judaism. For example, the idea that Jesus is the Messiah is justified in terms of the prophecies of the Hebrew Bible. For the claim to be true, the authority of the prophecies must not be questioned. Since Christianity is entangled in Judaism in this way, the equation of Judaism and savage religions inevitably posed a problem for the authority and status of Christianity as well. Consequently, those thinkers who wished to protect Christianity often sought ways of opposing Judaism and savage religions. These motivations continue to influence interpretations of Judaism throughout the twentieth century.

But this defensive posturing does not explain everything. Not all twentieth-century interpreters have felt the need to privilege Judaism. On the contrary, many viewed their scholarship as posing a challenge to the view that Judaism is unique. Nonetheless, these same interpreters have also ignored anthropology and mistrusted the comparative study of Judaism. As I shall argue below, the theoretical commitments that these interpreters inherited had been for-

mulated, at least in part, by their predecessors who assumed a radical
difference between Judaism and savage religions. Although subsequent interpreters had no stake in perpetuating a distinction between Judaism and the
religion of primitives, they inadvertently did so by not questioning the received framework in which research on Judaism is carried out.

In this introduction, I show how these prejudices operate in one set of
twentieth-century scholarly traditions, those that interpret Israelite religion
and ancient Judaism. It is a scholarly convention to distinguish "Israelite religion" from "ancient Judaism." "Israelite religion" typically refers to the religious cultures of Israelites from at least the advent of the Israelite monarchy
in the tenth century B.C.E. to the Babylonian exile in the sixth century B.C.E.
"Ancient Judaism" generally refers to those religious cultures that developed
in the centuries following the return of Israelites (now Jews) from the Babylonian exile.³ In this period, a variety of important changes occurred in the
religion of Israel as a result, in part, of the exile and subsequent contact with
Persian, Hellenistic, and then Roman cultures. As the above terminology indicates, Israelite religion is not conceptualized as part of Judaism. But that
was not always the case. From the Enlightenment until well into the nineteenth century, the religion of ancient Israel was identified by a variety of
interchangeable terms, including "Mosaic Legislation," "the religion of the
Jews," or simply "Judaism." In what follows, I generally preserve the terminological distinction between "Israelite religion" and "ancient Judaism."
But when generalizing, as at the end of this chapter, and when referring to
discourses that do not make this distinction, as in part 1, I simply refer to
both traditions as "Judaism."

As we shall see, the prejudice against savages contributed to the emerging
hostility toward anthropology and comparative inquiry in twentieth-century
interpretations of Israelite religion. This state of affairs, as I suggest in part 1,
replicates strategies operating long ago in earlier discourses that equated Israelite religion with "Judaism."

Anthropology, Israelite Religion, and the Religions of Savages

The fact that interpreters of Israelite religion have generally ignored anthropology has been noted by Mendenhall (1961, 35), Gottwald (1979, 293),
Feeley-Harnik (1982, 99) and R. Wilson (1984, 25).⁴ As Gottwald puts it,
"After W. R. Smith and J. Wellhausen studied the applicability of bedouin
tribalism to early Israelite tribalism, so headstrong was the retreat away from
any further sustained anthropological and sociological studies of Israel that
biblical study has been almost totally divorced from the social sciences for
half a century."

I am suggesting that the retreat from anthropological studies in particular
has stemmed from a desire to oppose Israelite and primitive religions. That is

not to deny that certain conceptions of primitive cultures and religions have entered twentieth-century discourse on the religion of Israel (Rogerson 1978).[5] But one rarely finds interpreters of Israelite religion appealing to studies of other religions apart from those of the ancient Near East. The following quotation, taken from H. Ringgren's *Israelite Religion* (1966, 1), is symptomatic of the larger opposition between Israelite and primitive religions that has operated in biblical studies in the twentieth century:

> A different methodological problem has to do with the use of extrabiblical comparative material to explain religious phenomena in Israel. . . . First, in many details remarkable similarities can be observed between the Israelite religion and other ancient Near Eastern religions. . . . Israel by no means developed in a religious vacuum, but stood in close relationship to its neighbors in the religious as well as in the cultural domain. Second, our sources do not provide a complete picture of the Israelite religion. Many details that are difficult to understand on the basis of Israelite material alone can often be explained when comparative material is brought to bear on the question. . . . Ideas only alluded to in the Old Testament appear in their proper context in the light of comparative material. . . . What we have said shows that the comparative method is both desirable and necessary.

Ringgren insists that Israelite religion be considered in "comparative" framework. But for Ringgren, as for more interpreters of Israelite religion, "comparative" and "extrabiblical" simply mean seeing Israelite religion against the background of other religions in the same geographical area. Extrabiblical material does not include studies of the Nuer, the Dinka, the Samoans, the Plains Indians, or the Trobriand Islanders. Although Ringgren is willing to use Assyrian myths to illuminate Israelite ones, he ignores the myths of peoples who were not geographically and temporally contiguous with ancient Israel. Ringgren's work is illustrative of a general presumption in biblical studies that contextualizing Israelite religion in its ancient Near Eastern setting is more illuminating and, perhaps, less fraught with difficulties than comparing the religion of ancient Israel to religions in other parts of the world. Those writers who have situated Israelite religion in a broader context by invoking comparisons to primitive religions have been at the margins of biblical studies or have come from outside the field altogether and hence their work has been treated as less than serious.

Since comparisons between Israelite religion and non–Near Eastern religions have been unthinkable for mainstream interpreters of ancient Israel in the twentieth century, the ideas of scholars who worked on other religions, such as Durkheim, Hubert and Mauss, Malinowski, Radcliffe-Brown, Evans-Pritchard, Boas, Mead, Kroeber, and Benedict, to name only a few, rarely influenced the study of Israelite religion in any significant way. Only since the mid-sixties, when Mary Douglas (1966) compared Israelite food avoidances with the practices of "primitive" cultures and Edmund Leach (1969) applied the structuralism of Lévi-Strauss to Israelite religious narratives, has an anthropological approach emerged in the study of Israelite religion. Since their essays appeared, there has been a growing tendency to use anthropological data to illuminate aspects of Israelite religion and even to speak of anthropological approaches to the Hebrew Bible (Culley 1985). In chapter 3, I will consider the reasons for this recent interest of anthropologists in Israelite religion.

A similar resistance to anthropological inquiry has been evident in the study of ancient Judaism, particularly among interpreters of rabbinic Judaism. In discussions of these traditions, little appeal has been made to ethnographic literature or anthropological theory. Generally, the study of ancient Judaism, like the interpretation of Israelite religion, has been dominated by textual analysis or by studies which contextualize a cultural element in its historical setting. Numerous attempts have been made to see rabbinic Judaism in interaction with Greco-Roman culture or Christianity (e.g., Daube 1949; Lieberman 1950; Fischel 1977). In this case, too, there have been a few noteworthy exceptions, such as the work of Max Kadushin (1952), which relied to some extent on the anthropology of Lévy-Bruhl. More recently, under the influence of Mary Douglas, Jacob Neusner (1979) has pointed out the importance of anthropology for the study of talmudic literature. For Neusner, anthropology primarily contributes the insight that religions are orderly and coherent systems in which "the character of the way of life and the conceptions of the world mutually illuminate and explain one another" (1979, 3). Furthermore, Neusner finds anthropology helpful because anthropologists have learned how to discern the larger issues of a culture from the minute details of a given way of life. This insight, Neusner notes, is particularly useful for the interpreter of rabbinic literature, a literature which dwells on what appear to be trivial details. Other interpreters (Eilberg-Schwartz 1986, 190–200; and forthcoming; Hoffman 1987; Lightstone 1988) have begun to follow Neusner's lead in turning to anthropology for insight about rabbinic Judaism. But despite the importance of anthropology for his research program, Neusner has remained committed to seeing Judaism in interaction with its cultural neighbors (e.g., Neusner 1986b). Indeed, Neusner has condemned cross-cultural comparisons that do not involve the comparison of cultural wholes (Neusner 1978), a position that effectively rules out cross-cultural comparisons altogether (Smith 1982).

In sum, in the study of Israelite religion and ancient Judaism there has been a strong tendency to ignore anthropological theory, ethnographic literature, and cross-cultural studies. Instead, there has been a fixation with historical contextualization, which either leads to a denigration of comparison altogether or at most seeks comparisons between contiguous religions and cultures. When comparisons are tolerated, they are almost all of the metonymic variety, that is, between cultures and religions that are in a single geographical area and hence "in contact." But there is a lack of interest in, and even hostility toward, metaphoric comparisons, comparisons that are drawn between religions and cultures that are similar in some respect but are separated in place and perhaps also in time.

The Untold Story: Why Biblical Studies Rejected Anthropology and Metaphoric Comparisons

Robert Wilson has suggested that the resistance among interpreters of ancient Israel to the use of anthropological methods and comparative data is in part a reaction against "the comparative method" of late nineteenth- and early twentieth-century interpreters of religion who, from the perspective of their successors, moved too glibly from society to society in seeking comparisons. Those who used "the comparative method" compared anything and everything in their expectation of finding a universal evolutionary scheme in the development of religion, culture, and mind. Their approach was labeled "conjectural history" since they attempted to reconstruct the specific history of a given religion on the basis of a postulated evolutionary scheme. Primitive societies provided evidence of the stages through which more advanced cultures had already moved. Since such interpreters were "armchair anthropologists" and did not examine a given cultural trait "in context," their interpretations were ludicrous from the perspective of persons who were more familiar with the societies in question. Consequently, when those using the comparative method compared items from various cultures, they were comparing one misinterpretation with another. That, at any rate, has been the judgment of subsequent interpreters of religion and culture. For interpreters of Israelite religion, these abuses were particularly evident in the works of William Robertson Smith and James G. Frazer, the most important figures to use the comparative method to understand Israelite religion. In Wilson's words,

> Like the sociologists and anthropologists whose work they used, [the late nineteenth- and early twentieth-century] Old Testament critics often wrenched the comparative material out of its social context and then embedded it in a comprehensive social theory that was frequently dominated by an evolutionary perspective. The theory and its accompanying evidence were then imposed on the Old Testament, which was interpreted so as to produce the desired results. . . . When biblical scholars finally began to recognize these problems, they reacted by curtailing their use of anthropological and sociological material. (1984, 25)

Instead of ranging far and wide over the religions of the world, biblical scholars reacted against the comparative method by insisting on understanding Israelite religion against the backdrop of other ancient Near Eastern religions. As Sayce (1889, 357–58) puts it in his review of Robertson Smith's *Lectures on the Religion of the Semites,* "I must enter a protest against the assumption that what holds good of Kaffirs or Australians held good also for the primitive Semite. The students of language have at last learnt that what is applicable to one family of speech is not necessarily applicable to another, and it would be well if the anthropologist would learn the same lesson." If one takes this lesson seriously and treats cultures as analogous to languages, then it makes no sense to make cross-cultural comparisons.[6] The only relevant comparisons are between families of cultures, cultures that have a common ancestry. Hence one must see Israelite religion in the context of neighboring religions.

Scholars of Israelite religion also noted a second advantage to seeing Israelite religion against the backdrop of other ancient Near Eastern religions. In so doing, the interpreter would have at hand empirical evidence for the historical unfolding of religions. No longer would the historian of ancient Israel have to import an a priori evolutionary framework or rely on reconstruction of the prehistory of Israelite religion, as the advocates of the comparative method had done. Now the actual history of Israelite religion was directly available from literary and archaeological remains. In the words of William Albright (1942, 77), one of the most important archaeologists of the ancient Near East and an influential historian of Israelite religion, "Archaeology makes it increasingly possible to interpret each religious phenomenon and movement of the Old Testament in the light of its *true background and real sources,* instead of forcing its interpretation into some preconceived historical mold" (emphasis supplied). Situating Israelite religion against the background of other ancient Near Eastern religions would thus avoid the perceived abuses of the comparative method, particularly as applied to Israelite religion by Robertson Smith and Frazer. The commitment to contextualization was thus reinforced by a desire to escape the evolutionary framework and speculative comparisons of late nineteenth- and early twentieth-century anthropology.

Persuasive as this argument may have been, it is not the whole story. It masks deeper, more powerful motives at work in the repudiation of the comparative method and in the subsequent obsession with the ancient Near East. One of those motives was the desire to oppose Israelite and primitive religions, a desire that permeated European thought for three centuries before our own. This is one of the reasons that the work of Frazer and Robertson Smith proved so problematic to subsequent interpreters of ancient Israelite religion. In their hands, the comparative method demonstrated provocative similarities between the religions of savages and Israelites and, consequently, threatened to undermine the privileged status of the latter. To be sure, Robertson Smith and Frazer both qualify their interpretations in various ways. In his prefatory remarks to *Folklore in the Old Testament* (1919, x), Frazer claims that "the scope of my work has obliged me to dwell chiefly on the lower side of ancient Hebrew life revealed in the OT, on the traces of savagery and superstition which are to be found in its pages. . . . the revelation of the baser elements which underlay the civilization of ancient Israel serves rather as a foil to enhance by contrast the glory of a people which, from such dark depths of ignorance and cruelty, could rise to such bright heights of wisdom and virtue." Robertson Smith makes similar remarks throughout his *Lectures*.

Such qualifications notwithstanding, the work of these writers could not help but impress their readers with the many similarities between Israelite and savage religions. In this respect, Robertson Smith and Frazer were more radical than their contemporaries who used the comparative method. Edward Tylor, for example, in his *Primitive Culture* (1958 [1871]), 49) mentions the Semites only three times. He neglects the "Semitic Family, which represents one of the oldest known civilizations of the world," because "this family takes in some rude tribes but none which would be classed as savages." Tylor gives the impression that the savage is temporally anterior to ancient Israel and that consequently the study of primitive religion is irrelevant to the study of ancient Judaism. But in Robertson Smith's and Frazer's works, that distance is reduced and almost eliminated. The primitive is no longer safely ensconced "behind," "before," or "under" Israelite religion but threatens to appear at its very heart and thus within striking distance of Christianity as well.[7]

That this was one of the implications of Frazer's and Robertson Smith's work is evident from their writing as well as from the reactions of critics. Robertson Smith relies heavily on information from savage societies in his *Kinship and Marriage in Early Arabia* (1903 [1885]) and *Lectures on the Religion of the Semites* (1927 [1889]). In the latter work, he argues that a large number of Hebrew practices, including rules about uncleanness and holiness, derived from a savage stage of religious development. "The fact that all the Semites have rules of uncleanness as well as rules of holiness, that the boundary between the two is often vague, and that the former as well as the latter present the most startling agreement in point of detail with savage *taboo*, leaves no reasonable doubt as to the [savage] origin and ultimate relations of the idea of holiness" (1927 [1889], 153). Robertson Smith also goes so far as to suggest that the Hebrew sacrificial institution had developed from the primitive institution of totemism, in which a kin group communed with its god by eating an animal that it thought of as one of its kin (1927 [1889], 289). As one opponent of Smith put it, his doctrine of sacrifice represented "a new theory of the essential character of the Old Testament religion," one which "cut away the basis on which the whole doctrine of salvation rests" (quoted in Black and Chrystal 1912, 417). To be sure, Robertson Smith, like Frazer, periodically reminds his readers that Hebrew religion was much more sophisticated than the primitive religions to which he was comparing it. Nonetheless, his work points to far more commonalities than most cared to admit.

It was this feature of Robertson Smith's work that Frazer highlights in his obituary for his teacher and friend. "Another important province in the history of religion which Robertson Smith was the first to explore is the religion of pastoral tribes. The conclusions which he arrived at, mainly from an analysis of Semitic sacrificial ritual, are strikingly confirmed by an induction from the facts of pastoral life as observed among rude pastoral tribes in various parts of the world, especially in Africa" (1967 [1894], 289). Frazer also points out that Robertson Smith was one of the first to show that sacramental sacrifices

> are not confined to Christianity, but are common to it with heathen and even savage religions. Whether he was right in tracing their origin to totemism may be questioned: the evidence thus far does not enable us to pronounce decisively. But that religious ideas and observances of this type are world-wide, and that they originated, not in an advanced, but in a low stage of society and in a very crude phase of thought, is not open to question. . . . Among the many questions which it raises, the one which will naturally interest Christians most deeply is "How are we to explain the analogy which it reveals between the Christian Atonement and Eucharist on the one side, and the mystical or sacramental sacrifices of the heathen religions on the other." (1967 [1894], 288–89)

Similarly, Stanley Cook (1902, 413–48), in his review of the debate over Israelite totemism, notes that Robertson Smith's work implies that "the curious rite of the Ordeal of Jealousy, the superstitious fear of iron in holy places, ritual dances, scapegoats, speaking trees, and stars imbued with life, are among the indications that Israel was no different to other primitive peoples."

The same impulses were even more pronounced in the work of Frazer. In his letter to the publisher George Macmillan offering him *The Golden Bough,* Frazer writes that "the resemblance of many of the savage customs and ideas to the fundamental doctrines of Christianity is striking. But I make no reference to this parallelism leaving my readers to draw their own conclusions, one way or the other" (Downie 1970, 53). As this statement makes clear, one of Frazer's objectives was to inscribe the savage at the very heart of the "Judeo-Christian" tradition (Ackerman 1987, 164–97; Strathern 1987). Just before publishing the second edition of *The Golden Bough,* Frazer wrote to his close friend Solomon Schechter, a well-known rabbi and talmudist. "I trust," he writes, "that you will approve of the book in its new and enlarged form. There are things in it which are likely to give offence both to Jews and Christians, but especially, I think to Christians. You see I am neither the one nor the other, and don't mind knocking them impartially" (Ackerman 1987, 169–70). Most provocative is Frazer's discussion of corn spirits. Frazer notes the custom among many peoples of eating new corn as if it were the body of a corn spirit. This primitive notion of transubstantiation led Frazer to comment that "on the whole it would seem that neither the ancient Hindoos nor the ancient Mexicans [i.e., Aztecs] had much to learn from the most refined mysteries of Catholic theology" (Downie 1970, 52).

The implication of comparing primitive religions to classic traditions of the West was not lost on a number of writers. Reflecting on the impact of *The Golden Bough* on the study of classics, Stanley Casson writes,

> *The Golden Bough* marked a turning point in anthropological studies, for it forced the scholars of the literary traditions to enlarge their vision, to realize the implications of ancient Greek and Roman customs which they had failed to analyse, and to accustom themselves to the new contributions which anthropological research could make to what had hitherto been a purely literary appreciation of ancient authors. Here was the inner mind of the two great ancient civilisations being revealed intimately to scholars who had hitherto examined only the surface. Dark and mysterious rites and survivals, magic and superstition which would be normal in Polynesia or Australia, were seen to have been working in the background of the most civilised periods of the ancient world. (Downie 1970, 58)

Equally provocative was Frazer's *Folklore in the Old Testament* (1919). Custom after custom in the Old Testament became the occasion for extensive citations of parallel customs among primitive societies. Despite Frazer's disclaimers, this work created the impression that almost all aspects of Israelite religion were survivals from savagery.

Whether intentional or not, Frazer's and Robertson Smith's works collapsed the longstanding dichotomy between Israelite and savage religions. For this reason, there was a distinct advantage to be gained by rejecting the comparative method. If the method turned out to be problematic, the resemblances between Israelite and savage religions could be safely ignored. Thus while biblical scholars had some legitimate dissatisfactions with the first attempts to subject Israelite religion to anthropological inquiry, some questionable motives also contributed to the growing hostility toward anthropology and the comparative study of Israelite religion.

At least one reviewer of Frazer's work complained about his contemporaries' unwillingness to admit analogies between primitive religions and ancient Judaism. Thus in his review of Frazer's *Folklore of the Old Testament,* H.J.D. Astley (1929, 104) writes,

> Old-fashioned students of this [Old Testament] literature, hallowed by so many religious associations, are likely to be shocked by the suggestion that within its pages are contained tales and descriptions of customs that can in any way be attached to the category of folk-lore. They feel inclined to exclaim: "Hands off! Defile not the holy thing with profane touch; this is sacred ground, and must be approached only by those from whose feet the shoes have been reverently put off."

Some interpreters of Israelite religion frankly acknowledged having such sentiments. In critiquing the work of Robertson Smith and Frazer, Snaith (1944, 17) urges:

If there are no distinctive elements in Christianity, then, in the name of whatever gods there then may be, let us be realistic and sensible. Let us dismiss the
whole affair to its proper home in the limbo of the dead illusions of mankind.
. . . On the other hand, if Christianity does contain distinctive elements, both
in common with Judaism and against the rest of religions . . . then, in the
Name of the One God, let us examine them, and let us be very sure indeed of
what precisely they are. No institution, be it religious or secular, has any right to
continue to exist unless it has, and can show in all the market-places of the
world, a special and distinct reason for its separate existence.

Snaith is representative of a larger impulse within biblical studies to defend the
uniqueness of Israelite religion, an impulse particularly evident in the biblical
theology school (Oden 1987; Childs 1970, 47–50; Dever 1980, 1–14).

But what is so interesting and paradoxical is how the same purpose was
achieved in the shift from the comparative method of Robertson Smith and
Frazer to the enterprise of studying Israelite religion in the context of other
ancient Near Eastern religions, a labor that has dominated twentieth-century
study of Israelite religion. As noted above, this shift in emphasis is frequently
thought of as a result of theoretical dissatisfactions with the comparative
method. Instead of comparing elements from cultures separated in time and
place, the new comparative method studied Israelite religion in the context of
contiguous traditions. But the newly emerging comparative method served
another purpose. It replicated the very evolutionary framework that biblical
scholars found so problematic in the anthropologists' method of comparative inquiry.[8] Ironically, then, in repudiating anthropological inquiry, biblical interpreters perpetuated the old dichotomy between Israelite and savage
religions.

Note, for example, how Albright (1942, 4) rejects the comparative method
while at the same time reaffirming the idea of an evolutionary sequence of
humankind.

But the gap between savage mentality and the mind of modern man is too great
to be easily bridged by direct observation, and the attempt [by anthropologists]
to fill the gap by studying the ideas of half-savage peoples of today is nearly
always vitiated by the fact that these peoples have been strongly influenced by
more highly developed civilizations, virtually all of which reflect a post-Hellenic
stage of progress. . . . In such cases, we can seldom be sure about the aboriginal
character of a given cultural element. The only way in which we can bridge this
gap satisfactorily is by following the evolution of the human mind in the Near
East itself, where we can trace it from the earliest times through successive archaeological ages to the flowering of the Greek spirit. . . . What we have in
mind is nothing less than the ultimate reconstruction, as far as possible, of the
route which our cultural ancestors traversed in order to reach Judaeo-Christian
heights of spiritual insight and ethical monotheism. In this book we are concerned with the religion of the Old Testament, of which the religion of the New
was only the extension and the fulfillment.

Albright believed the study of religious development in the ancient Near Eastern cultures would reveal the evolutionary sequence of the human mind, by showing how the religion of the Old and New Testaments represents a superior stage of moral and spiritual insight. "In this book," he writes, "I have tried to emphasize the fact that Israelite faith was much closer to Christianity and to rabbinic Judaism than to the basically prelogical religions of the ancient Near East" (1942, 177). "No matter where we turn in the extant literature of Israel, we find sobriety and consistency beyond anything known in older cultures. Israel discarded almost all proto-logical thinking" (1964 [1940], 53).

Paradoxically, the repudiation of the comparative method within biblical studies did not involve a rejection of an evolutionary framework, as it did in anthropology. On the contrary, it enabled interpreters of Israelite religion to rejuvenate an evolutionary framework that had already been placed in jeopardy by the work of Robertson Smith and Frazer. Now biblical interpreters could produce empirical historical evidence for the fundamental antithesis between primitive religion and the religion of Israel. When Israelite religion was seen against the background of other ancient Near Eastern religions, the dichotomy between ancient Judaism and primitive religions seemed to arise "out of the data." What disturbed Albright, therefore, was not the evolutionary assumptions that informed the comparative method. What bothered him was the fact that such assumptions did not have empirical support. "No great historian or philologian is likely to construct his system in a vacuum; there must be some body of external data or some plane of reference by the aid of which he can redeem his system from pure subjectivity" (Albright 1964 [1940], 136). The way to prove an evolutionary development was not by roaming over the world as Robertson Smith and Frazer had done but by tracing the history of thought in the ancient Near East. "There is no road from primitive and savage thought to Europe which does not pass directly through the ancient Orient" (1960 [1940], 122).

This evolutionary impulse is not limited to the work of Albright. Throughout the twentieth century the emphasis on contextualizing ancient Israelite religion in the ancient Near East served similar polemical purposes for both Jewish and Christian scholars. "It is only within the setting of its environment in the ancient East that the special character of the Israelite religion emerges clearly, and only then that one can begin to understand her own distinctive place in that story" (J. Hehn quoted in Vriezen 1967, 23). Or, as Kaufmann (1972 [1937–56], 21) puts it,

We designate as pagan all the religions of mankind from the beginnings of recorded history to the present, excepting Israelite religion and its derivatives, Christianity and Islam. This distinction assumes that, on the one hand, there is something unique about Israelite religion that sets it off from all the rest, and on the other, that there is an essential common aspect to all other religions which gives them their pagan character.

Other interpreters have shared similar sentiments (Vriezen 1967, 11; Wright 1950, 13).

Subsequent writers continued to repeat the assertion that Israelite religion reflected a fundamental development in religious mentality. "It would seem that the Hebrews, no less than the Greeks, broke with the mode of speculation which had prevailed up to their time. . . . This conception of God represents so high a degree of abstraction that, in reaching it, the Hebrews seem to have left the realm of mythopoeic thought" (H. and H. A. Frankfort 1971 [1946], 241–44). "Long before the history of Israel began, the ancient Near East had left any stage of animism or dynamism far behind" (Wright 1950, 16). The same argument continues to find noteworthy adherents (Sarna 1970, xxviii).

Along with this fundamental rupture in religious consciousness appeared an equally significant development in moral insight. This is particularly evident when Israelite religion is compared with that of the Canaanites. "The sexual emphasis of Canaanite religion was certainly extreme and at its worst could only have appealed to the baser aspects of man. Religion as commonly practiced in Canaan, therefore, must have been a rather sordid and degrading business, when judged by our standards, and so, it seems, it appeared to religious circles of Israel" (Wright 1957, 13). When scholarship exposes the mythological and polytheistic context out of which Israelite religion emerged, "one cannot marvel enough at the power which made it possible for Israel to break away from this world of ideas and speak about the relationship of God to the world in quite a different way" (von Rad 1976, 65). Quotations such as these could be readily multiplied. What they show is how often the desire to situate Israelite religion against the background of the ancient Near East has served a defensive posturing and evolutionary agenda.

In this respect different motives operated in the rejection of the comparative method within biblical studies from the ones that operated in anthropology. To be sure, anthropologists, like interpreters of ancient Israel, also voiced doubts about wrenching items out of their cultural contexts. For this reason, American anthropology, like biblical studies, reacted against the comparative method by turning to studies of cultural diffusion among peoples in contiguous geographical areas. But the central motivation for criticizing the comparative method within anthropology was its evolutionary assumptions. For Boas and his students in the American tradition, as well as Malinowski, Radcliffe-Brown, and their students in the British school, the repudiation of the comparative method was part of an attack on evolutionary theory. In the study of Israelite religion, by contrast, an opposite impulse is evident. The emphasis on history, context, and diffusion clearly fed an evolutionary polemic. Once Israelite religion was set in its ancient Near Eastern context, a historical scheme emerged that was not altogether different from the evolutionary schemes postulated in the nineteenth century. Israelite religion appeared to arise out of and in reaction to the polytheistic religions of the Canaanites, Sumerians, Assyrians, and Babylonians. This historical orientation highlighted the unique aspects of Israelite religion, especially the development of monotheism and the repudiation of mythology. From this perspective, Israelite religion appears as a historical, rational, moral, and monotheistic religion in contrast to the mythological, irrational, ahistorical, and morally degrading religions that surrounded it. In sum, the rejection of anthropology and the comparative method and the increasing emphasis on archaeology, history, diffusion, and context had the effect, if not the intended consequence, of preserving the opposition between Israelite religion and savage religions.

This is not to deny that important theoretical issues were also at stake in the rejection of the comparative method. As noted above, critics of the comparative method raised some legitimate questions about the wisdom of taking cultural items out of their context. Moreover, not all interpreters of Israelite religion shared the biases exposed above. Indeed, some viewed the attempt to study Israelite religion in the context of other ancient Near Eastern religions as a way to challenge the ideology of Israel's uniqueness. When placed in the context of the ancient Near East, one discovered striking similarities between Israelite religion and the religious traditions of contiguous cultures. These similarities showed that Israelite religion was not a revealed religion that had dropped from the sky but a historical one that had developed out of its historical background and had absorbed many important ideas and institutions from its cultural neighbors.

Still, one wonders what would have happened in biblical studies if the impulse to differentiate Israelite and savage religions had not also been present. Clearly, these prejudices helped achieve the almost unquestioned consensus that anthropology and comparative inquiry were problematic. As often happens, a scholarly consensus once achieved turns into a foundational axiom that is passed from teacher to student. Students who did not necessarily share the prejudices of their teachers nonetheless inherited certain theoretical commitments that were shaped in part by their teachers' biases. In concentrating their efforts on situating Israelite religion against the background of other Near Eastern religions, they perpetuated an opposition that they had no stake in preserving.

Without these prejudices operating, it is conceivable that biblical studies could have responded to the comparative method differently. Interpreters of Israelite religion made the hasty judgment that since this comparative method was problematic, all cross-cultural inquiry is problematic. But as I argue in chapter 4, that conclusion is not warranted. The failure of the comparative method stemmed from its evolutionary assumptions and its disregard for the larger cultural contexts in which specific elements found their place. It would have been equally reasonable to conclude that a more judicious sort of comparative method, one that attended to elements in their cultural context and one that operated without evolutionary assumptions, would prove more compelling.

This at any rate was the conclusion within the nascent British school of anthropology, which has harbored a strong comparative thrust despite its repudiation of the comparative method as practiced by Robertson Smith and Frazer. For Radcliffe-Brown, as for many students in that tradition, the goal of fieldwork was to see whether the insights derived from studying tribe x could be generalized to tribe y. For example, Radcliffe-Brown attempted to formulate a theory of kinship that could explain kinship systems in diverse contexts. In the British tradition, the failure of the comparative method did not mean that comparisons across cultures were inherently problematic.[9]

In retrospect, it is ironic that interpreters of Israelite religion, suspicious of the comparative method, so enthusiastically took up the study of other ancient Near Eastern traditions. As subsequent reflection has shown, comparisons between religions in the same geographical area are fraught with the same kinds of theoretical problems as comparisons between religions in different geographical areas. As Fohrer puts it in his *History of Israelite Religion* (1972, 25),

> When using this comparative [Near Eastern] material, we must of course be careful to observe and maintain the unique features of Israelite religion. Something that sounds like a feature of another religion need not have the same meaning it has in the other religion. Religious concepts or customs can have different meanings and purposes in two different religions, even when these religions are close neighbors geographically and historically. The ancient Near Eastern material must therefore always be employed with caution.

Other interpreters have expressed similar reservations (Anderson 1951, 285, 291; Frankfort 1951; Sarna 1970, xxvii; Vriezen 1967, 23).

In any comparative study, the same kind of interpretive difficulties present themselves: What should be compared and why? Is the comparison of two traits valid? What are the criteria for deciding? How can one be sure that parallel traits in two contiguous cultures have the same meanings in their respective cultural systems? It is appropriate that biblical scholars referred to their new approach as "the comparative method," for it has a number of the same interpretive difficulties as "the comparative method" employed by the late nineteenth- and early twentieth-century anthropologists. Interpreters of Israelite religion were deceived in thinking they had developed a more objective method for interpreting religion. They had not.

The thrust of this argument is not to deny the importance of diffusion as a cultural process, the importance of a historical perspective, or the usefulness of seeing Israelite religion against the background of the ancient Near East. Without a doubt, our understanding of Israelite religion has been enriched by the project of comparing it to contiguous traditions. The point is simply that things could have been other than they were. The impulse to study Israelite religion in the context of the ancient Near East did not have to dominate biblical studies to the exclusion of other kinds of interests. Alongside the concern with context and diffusion, biblical studies could have nourished a tradition of cross-cultural comparison, one that attended to theoretical developments within anthropology while at the same time taking account of the results achieved by students of ancient Near Eastern cultures. At the very least, this discussion reopens the question of whether cross-cultural inquiry and anthropological theory can further our understanding of Israelite religion. This book is a wager that they can.

Judaism and Savage Religions in Anthropology

If biblical interpreters have been guilty of perpetuating an opposition between Israelite religion and primitive religions, a similar story has to be told about the discipline of anthropology. Apart from Frazer's *The Golden Bough* and *Folklore in the Old Testament,* there had been no attempt by anthropologists to make Israelite religion or ancient Judaism a serious focus of inquiry until the work of Mary Douglas (1966) and Edmund Leach (1969).[10] Thanks to Douglas's work, the Israelite dietary restrictions have entered anthropological discourse and have had an important impact on anthropological theory (e.g., Bulmer 1967; Tambiah 1969). To be sure, references to Israelite religion are found in anthropological writings before Douglas's work. But such references are episodic and generally serve as a rhetorical device. By referring to practices or conceptions of the Israelites, the anthropologist domesticated the alien practice or belief by pointing to an analogous practice that was recognizable but not too familiar. The following statement from the preface to Evans-Pritchard's *Nuer Religion* (1956, vii) is symptomatic of the role played by Israelite religion and ancient Judaism in twentieth-century anthropological writings. "When, therefore, I sometimes draw comparisons between Nuer and Hebrew conceptions, it is no mere whim but is because I myself find it helpful, and I think others may do so too, in trying to understand Nuer ideas to note this likeness to something with which we are ourselves familiar without being too intimately involved in it." Within anthropology, episodic references to Israelite religion served to illuminate primitive religions, but Israelite religion itself was not considered a legitimate object of inquiry.

The tendency among anthropologists to ignore Israelite religion and ancient Judaism, like the prejudice among biblical scholars against studies of primitive societies, was partially a reaction to the comparative method of the late nineteenth- and early twentieth-century anthropologists. Within anthropology, dissatisfactions with the comparative method and "armchair anthropology" produced an emphasis on fieldwork that involved living for an extended period of time among the people under study.[11] Ethnography seemed to avoid the abuses of the comparative method. Not only did participant-observation sidestep the problem of postulating a people's history, but it enabled anthropologists to view cultural items as part of a larger cultural and social system within which they operated. As noted above, in the American tradition the retreat from the comparative method also led to an interest in the interrelationships among cultures and religions in contiguous geographical areas. Since a rejection of the comparative method produced an emphasis on intensive fieldwork and face-to-face interaction with the people under study, anthropologists lost interest in religious cultures such as Judaism that could only be investigated through historical sources. The conjectural history of the comparative method was replaced by a study of real historical and social processes. As Evans-Pritchard (1951, 74) later puts it, "Formerly the anthropologist, like the historian, regarded documents as the raw material of his study. Now the raw material was social life itself." In other words, in rejecting the nineteenth-century comparative method, twentieth-century anthropology repudiated the model of anthropologist as classicist.[12] In its place emerged another model, the anthropologist as traveler and visitor among alien peoples.

While all of these factors were no doubt at work in the diminishing interest in Judaism among anthropologists, this still is not the whole story. A strong interest in intensive studies actually predated the demise of the comparative method (Stocking 1983). For this reason, the shift from anthropologist as classicist to anthropologist as fieldworker cannot be completely attributed to growing dissatisfactions with the comparative method. The assumption of a fundamental distinction between primitive and civilized peoples also contributed to this development. Not only was this opposition already in place before anthropologists discovered the importance of fieldwork, but the very emphasis on fieldwork was in part a result of anthropology's commitment to the study of primitive society.

This opposition is evident in the work of late nineteenth-century anthropologists who ignored Israelite religion. As noted previously, Edward Tylor does not include the Semites in his *Primitive Culture* (1958 [1871], 49) because "this family takes in some rude tribes but none which would be classed as savages." Similarly, in his *Anthropology and the Classics* (1966 [1908], 3) R. R. Marett writes,

> Anthropology and the Humanities—on verbal grounds one might suppose them coextensive; yet in practice they divide the domain of human cultures between them. The types of human culture are, in fact, reducible to two, a simpler and a more complex, or, as we are wont to say (valuing our own achievements, I doubt not, rightly), a lower and a higher. By established convention anthropology occupies itself solely with culture of a simpler and lower kind. The Humanities, on the other hand . . . concentrates on whatever is most constitutive and characteristic of the higher life of society.

The task of anthropology as it was articulated in the late nineteenth century was to understand the origin and development of religion, culture, and the human mind. To understand the origin of these phenomena necessitated looking at primitive cultures which were thought to reflect the early history of humankind. Primitive societies were living fossils, relics of a distant past which European culture had long ago transcended. The religion and culture of higher civilizations could shed no light on the early history of religion, culture, and humanity.

An opposition between Israelite religion and primitive religions was contained in this larger distinction between primitive and civilized peoples. This is why the religion of Israel fell outside the purview of anthropological inquiry. Although it retained survivals from a primitive past, Israelite religion had largely transcended and thus obscured its primitive origins. The study of Israelite religion could not contribute to an understanding of how religion began, the issue at the center of anthropological attention.

The operation of this opposition is evident, for example, if one compares the work of Emile Durkheim and Max Weber. Durkheim, whose work provides the foundation for several traditions within anthropology, formulated his theories by studying the Australian aborigines. These societies, Durkheim assumed, were the most primitive and simplest available for study. Studying them would enable him to understand the origin and function of religion in a way that was not possible when studying religion in complex and developed societies (Durkheim 1965 [1915], 13–20; Lukes 1985, 455–57). By contrast, Weber, whose work especially influenced sociology, developed his theories through an explication of the "world religions" (*Weltreligionen*), that is, Confucianism, Buddhism, Hinduism, Judaism, Christianity, and Islam (Parsons 1968, 2:539; Lukes 1985, 457). As anthropology and sociology emerged as recognizable and distinctive disciplines, an opposition between world and primitive religions was presupposed and preserved.

That the disciplinary divisions reflected this ideological opposition was both evident and embarrassing to those working within anthropology. As early as 1931, Radcliffe-Brown (1958 [1931], 45) notes in a presidential address to the British Association for the Advancement of Science that

> anthropology as now organized includes as a third field the study of the languages and cultures of non-European peoples, and particularly of those peoples who have no written history. This separation of the people of the world into two groups, one of which is studied by the anthropologist, while the other is left to historians, philologists and others, is obviously not justifiable by any logical coordination of studies, and is no longer fully justified by practical considerations, as it was when it first arose.

But anthropology did not change. Although the ideological basis of these dichotomies had long since been called in question, the disciplinary commitments had already been formed. Anthropologists would continue to study small face-to-face societies; historians, philologists, and theologians would continue to study Israelite religion and ancient Judaism.

As is now evident, strong motives for ignoring the study of Judaism existed within anthropology before the discipline's emerging hostility toward history and growing interest in intensive fieldwork. Ironically, then, the developing emphasis on ethnography is better understood as the result rather than the cause of the lack of interest in classical traditions. Since anthropology had already designated primitive societies as its objects of inquiry, it had to develop an appropriate method for studying these societies. Since nonliterate folk seemed like "people without history," the only way to understand them was by living and talking with them.

The connection among these factors is evident in Malinowski's methodological introduction to *Argonauts of the Western Pacific,* the work often credited with articulating the theoretical justification for ethnography. "In our society," writes Malinowski (1961 [1922], 12),

> every institution has its intelligent members, its historians, and its archives and documents, whereas in a native society there are none of these. After this is realised an expedient has to be found to overcome this difficulty. This expedient for an Ethnographer consists in collecting concrete data of evidence and drawing the general inferences for himself. This seems obvious on the face of it, but was not found out or at least practised in Ethnography till field work was taken up by men of science.

The method of study was partially determined by the choice of subject matter. Had anthropology not already repudiated the classics, fieldwork may not have become the *sine qua non* of anthropology. It is not surprising, therefore, that in the past few decades as anthropology has begun to widen its own horizon and take an interest in complex and literate societies, history has emerged once more as a valuable tool (e.g., Sahlins 1981; 1985).

As in the case of biblical studies, one wonders how anthropology might have been different had the opposition between primitive and civilized not had such a significant impact on the formation of the discipline. Without such an opposition it is possible to imagine that Israelite religion and ancient Judaism, among other classical traditions, could have remained more central in anthropology's repertoire. In ignoring these traditions, the practice of twentieth-century anthropology was paradoxically influenced by one of the assumptions that it had officially rejected, the assumption of a fundamental difference between higher and lower religions. The lack of interest among twentieth-century anthropologists in Judaism is itself a "survival" of an older attitude of the nineteenth century which viewed such religious cultures as fundamentally different from those of savages.

Given that such an opposition has been operative both among interpreters of Judaism and anthropologists, it is not surprising that that dichotomy was eventually institutionalized in the university: the study of Judaism and the religions of "primitive" societies are housed in different departments; the former takes place in departments of religious studies, Near Eastern languages, oriental or Jewish studies, the latter in departments of anthropology. As I suggest in chapter 3, the recent interest in Judaism by anthropologists such as Douglas and Leach is the consequence of a growing dissatisfaction with this division.

As anthropology overcomes this original opposition, the anthropologist can once again became a classicist and the classicist an anthropologist. In retrospect it is clear that the difference between doing ethnography and studying a people through their textual remains is by no means as sharp as early ethnographers once thought. The metaphor of culture as text, initially formulated by Clifford Geertz, has proven invaluable for cultural analysis (see Scholte 1987). To be sure, when an ethnographer lives with a group, she or he questions informants and therefore has an experience that is unlike the activity of interpreting texts. But the operations by which that experience is turned into an ethnography are similar to those used in interpreting texts (Clifford and Marcus 1986; Clifford 1988). The ethnography that is produced is generally written after returning from the field and may take months or even years to write. In giving an account of religion or culture, the ethnographer relies on "fieldnotes" or a text that has been taken from its original context. No matter how intensive or thorough the fieldwork, the ethnographer must intervene to produce a coherent, logical account. In Geertz's (1973, 9) now classic formulation, "What we call our data are really our own constructions of other people's constructions of what they and their compatriots are up to." This recent understanding of ethnography as a form of writing requires a reevaluation of the assumed differences between doing fieldwork and studying classics and thus helps put in question the longstanding opposition between anthropology and classical studies.

The Savage Within

As the opposition between Judaism and savage religions is obliterated, one can expect to find the savage reinscribed within Judaism. By this I mean that some traits originally assumed to be characteristic of primitive peoples alone will turn out on reflection to be characteristics of Judaism itself. In saying this, I am anticipating that the same process which has already taken place within the disciplines of anthropology and philosophy will also finally occur within the study of Judaism. As anthropologists and philosophers dismantled the opposition between savagery and civilization, they began to realize that what they had originally seen in the savage was in fact a shadowy version of ourselves that we had failed to recognize.

My argument regarding the savage is similar to Hayden White's argument about the "Wild Man." White (1978, 7) suggests that the concept of "Wild Man" helped to sustain Western cultural myths by serving as a negative point of reference. As this concept and others like it were unmasked, they were interiorized.

> From biblical times to the present, the notion of the Wild Man was associated
> with the idea of the wilderness—the desert, forest, jungle, and mountains—
> those parts of the physical world that had not yet been domesticated or marked
> out for domestication in any significant way. As one after another of these wil-
> dernesses was brought under control, the idea of the Wild Man was progres-
> sively despatialized. This despatialization was attended by a compensatory
> process of psychic interiorization.

A similar process of interiorization has taken place in the case of the savage. But in contrast to the "Wild Man," the savage has undergone what might be called a cultural interiorization. Characteristics of savages have been absorbed into Western culture's understanding of its own practices.

As an example, consider the way in which qualities once ascribed to the savage mind were gradually incorporated into the characterization of the Western mind. Lévy-Bruhl (1985 [1910]), for example, describes the savage mind as "impervious to experience," by which he means that natives fail to notice when experience proves certain beliefs and practices to be fallacious. According to Lévy-Bruhl, this characteristic of primitive thought explains why natives continue to perform magical rites, such as throwing grain in the air to produce rainfall, even though such rites regularly fail to produce the desired effect. The primitive mind simply does not take account of disconfirming evidence because it is based on a kind of logic different from our own, a logic rooted in emotional connections rather than logical ones. For Lévy-Bruhl, therefore, the savage is irrational, at least when compared to the scientist who takes note of disconfirming evidence. Indeed, science is the paradigmatic rational activity, because science progresses by subjecting hypotheses to empirical tests and by relinquishing them when they are refuted by evidence.

Lévy-Bruhl was not alone in this characterization of the savage mind. Tylor and Frazer, although working from different assumptions, also note the way that primitive thought protects its practices from disconfirming evidence (Evans-Pritchard 1933; 1934). It does this by elaborating secondary rationalizations and by giving ad hoc explanations that will account for the failure of a rite. For example, if throwing grain into the air does not produce rain, a native might blame the failure of the rite on the neglect of one of the proper procedures or taboos. Alternatively, a native can always blame its failure on hostile forces believed to undermine the magical act. When the weight of tradition stands behind a practice, disconfirming evidence cannot undermine the confidence that natives have in its efficacy.

Malinowski (1961 [1922]; 1954 [1925]; 1978 [1935]), among others, attempts to undo the opposition Lévy-Bruhl, Tylor, and Frazer created between the impervious savage and the rational scientist. Based on intensive field-work, he argues that the native is in fact sensitive to experience and understands a great deal about nature. Malinowski points to the sophisticated technology developed by the Trobriand Islanders for coping with their environment, including their methods of cultivating and raising crops and their techniques for building and sailing boats. The success of the Trobrianders in these activities presupposes a great deal of knowledge about the environment. The Trobrianders know very well that seeds will not grow if they are not planted during the proper season and in the proper kinds of soil. Moreover, they understand certain principles of buoyancy; otherwise, it would be impossible for them to construct canoes. The presence of such technology, therefore, indicates that natives have experimented with nature and learned certain lessons. Malinowski moves beyond the opposition created by his predecessors by arguing that the savage is sensitive to experience and therefore as rational as a scientist. In Malinowski's judgment, the only difference between a native and a scientist is the respective quantity of empirical information that their cultures have each accumulated.

The collapse of any sharp dichotomy between the savage and civilized mind eventually had the consequence of allowing those qualities originally associated with primitive thought to reappear as traits of scientific thinking. Polanyi (1958), Kuhn (1970), Feyerabend (1975; 1978), and Lakatos (1970), among others, have suggested that the scientific community itself is in some sense impervious to experience and protects its own theories against disconfirmation. Opposing the view of the scientific community as continually looking for evidence to test current theories, Kuhn, for example, draws attention to the way that scientists devote themselves to the puzzles that a given paradigm has created. Normal science is the attempt to make nature fit into the box provided by the paradigm within which scientists are working. According to this view, the scientific community (at least during the activity of normal science) attempts to protect the paradigm against refuting evidence. It does this, Kuhn argues, by pushing out of sight the evidence that would undermine the paradigm with which it is currently working. In addition, scientists elaborate secondary interpretations and ad hoc answers to protect the paradigm against a seemingly recalcitrant fact. Kuhn suggests that all the puzzles on which scientists work can, from another point of view, be seen as problems that undermine the theories to which scientists are committed. Yet, most of the time those problems are treated as puzzles that test scientists' ingenuity, not facts that threaten scientific theories.

For the present purposes, it does not matter that Kuhn's understanding of science has been criticized in some quarters. What is significant is how the collapse of the distinction between the savage and scientific mind resulted in the interiorization of "savage" traits within Western self-understandings. In short, if nineteenth-century and early twentieth-century intellectuals discovered the savage in distant places, subsequent thinkers gradually learned that if savagery is to be found anywhere, it is at home among us. In this sense, the study of the savage has proved to be a learning process about ourselves.[13]

The Savage in Judaism

As the opposition between Judaism and savage religions continues to give way, a process similar to the one described above will occur. Traits once associated with the savage will be recognized as part of Judaism itself. The investigations in this book are intended to contribute to this process. They focus on some of the practices of Israelite religion and ancient Judaism that have been marginalized for being associated with primitive religions, such as circumcision and the menstrual taboo as well as more general rules governing the purity and impurity of objects. In addition, I examine a number of rules governing animal husbandry and agriculture, such as the prohibitions against boiling a kid-goat in its mother's milk, sacrificing an animal before it is eight days old, taking a mother bird and her fledglings from the nest, sacrificing an animal and its offspring on the same day, mating two different kinds of animals, eating land animals that do not chew their cud and have cloven hooves, cutting the corners of one's field, and planting two different crops in a single field. It is no accident that such practices have received scant attention by comparison with other problems, such as the idea of covenant, God, or the divine-human relationship. The denial of the savage in Judaism requires that such practices be suppressed because they invariably remind interpreters of primitive religions. The suppression of primitive elements is accomplished in two ways: either they are ignored or, when they are mentioned, they are trivialized as either "survivals" from "primitive" religious forms or as degenerated practices from an even earlier and once sophisticated form of religion. Either way the invocation of a temporal sequence effectively denies that such practices are essential to Judaism. Moreover, when such practices are discussed, their similarity to parallel practices in primitive traditions is typically denied. As our embarrassment in the face of such similarities subsides, however, practices once marginalized can be rediscovered, and their role within Judaism more fairly estimated.

The willingness to set Judaism on equal footing with "savage" religions will also further the growing rapprochement between biblical and Judaic studies on the one hand and anthropology on the other. A turn toward the anthropological tradition will provide a fresh set of questions to ask about Judaism and new ways of answering those questions. For example, since Durkheim's and Mauss's *Primitive Classification* (1963 [1903]) one of the recurring projects within anthropology has been to understand the diverse ways societies classify their world and the criteria by which they do so. In fact, some anthropologists have gone so far as to suggest that differences in cultures boil down to differences in classificatory schemes. While understanding such schemes is traditionally an anthropological concern, it does bear on the study of Israelite religion and ancient Judaism, as I have attempted to show in chapters 8 and 9. Recent ethnographies have also examined the way in which root metaphors shape social practices. The attention to this issue within anthropology alerted me to the way in which certain root metaphors provided a foundation for rituals and narratives of ancient Israel (chapter 5).

Anthropology, of course, uses numerous interpretive lenses. This book by no means exhausts the possibilities. It stems from a particular tradition within anthropology, namely, the one that emerges from the work of Durkheim and is carried forward by the British social anthropologists, particularly Radcliffe-Brown, Evans-Pritchard, Douglas, and Turner, as well as the work of Lévi-Strauss. In appropriating this tradition, however, I have also tried to take account of the criticisms that have been leveled against it. I am aware, for example, of the problems of functionalism (Hempel 1968; Merton 1967; Penner 1971), as well as the criticisms made of the structuralist perspective of both Radcliffe-Brown and Lévi-Strauss (Harris 1968; Hayes and Hayes 1970; Moore and Olmstead 1952; Rossi 1974). While the influences of these approaches are evident in my own work, I move beyond the limitations of those traditions in various ways.

It is for this reason that numerous other voices are heard throughout this book. I have tried, for example, to take account of the increasing impact of literary criticism on the discipline of anthropology. Consequently, symbolic and cultural anthropology, as exhibited particularly in the work of Geertz and Fernandez, have influenced my conception of cultural analysis, as has work on the cultural construction of gender and sexuality (e.g., Rosaldo and Lamphere 1974; Ortner and Whitehead 1981). Finally, postfoundational discussions within philosophy (Rorty 1982; Gadamer 1975), literary criticism (Fish 1980; Johnson 1980), history (Foucault 1973a; 1977; White 1978), and history and philosophy of science (Kuhn 1970; Feyerabend 1975; 1978) have all shaped my thinking in various ways. These voices by no means set the agenda for this book, but they do hover in the background and make their clearest statement in this Introduction and the first two chapters. In particular, the work of deconstructive critics (Culler 1982; Johnson 1980) and Foucault (1973a) has taught me that the key to a tradition often lies in what it excludes. My reading of these writers drew my attention to the way the primitive has been marginalized in modern discourses on Judaism.

But it is the anthropologists who are my primary interlocutors. Conversations with their works have been particularly illuminating in my own quest to make some sense of particularly unusual aspects of Judaism. These writers taught me to look for certain connections that I otherwise would not have seen. From Douglas and Lévi-Strauss, I learned to attend to relationships between eating and sexual practices and to homologies between rules governing animal husbandry and those governing social relations. Durkheim and Radcliffe-Brown showed me how the structure of social relationships has an impact upon a person's experience of social life, an experience that is in turn reflected in other discursive and nondiscursive practices. Turner, Geertz, and Fernandez impressed me with the importance of symbols and metaphors in the performance of rituals.

From this tradition as a whole, I have also derived a particular understanding of what it means to interpret a social practice. According to all these writers, the interpretation of a practice emerges when its relationship to various other social activities is determined. According to this view, cooking styles, kinship rules, sexual prohibitions, bodily cleanliness, and theological assertions intersect and overlap in interesting ways. The role of the interpreter is to see how these various domains reinforce, reflect, or stand in tension with one another. While interpreters of Israelite religion and ancient Judaism have been attentive to the integrative tendencies of culture, rarely have studies been produced that attend to the relationship among the specific cultural codes that have interested anthropologists.

It is this view of culture that allows me to arrive at interpretations of given practices that would in some instances be unacceptable to the people whose practices I am interpreting. I take for granted that the connections among social practices are not always self-evident to members of a given society. While the interpreter is not omniscient, she or he may see things that people within a given culture cannot see for themselves. An anthropologist makes claims about social practices analogous to those a literary critic makes about a given work of literature. The interpreter of a text is able to see features of it that were not necessarily evident to the author. To be sure, an author always has a number of explicit goals and reasons for writing a given work in a particular way. But language also has a way of controlling the writer. Although the author may give one reason for having chosen a particular phrase or theme, the critic is perfectly entitled to come along and show additional ways that a phrase or theme links up with other parts of the work. The critic unpacks connections that an author often does not realize are there.

This view also makes sense when applied to culture and social practice. The meaning of a practice is contained in the total set of connections it makes with other discursive and nondiscursive practices that constitute the cultural system. It is this understanding of culture that allows me to say, for example, that a rule about not boiling a kid-goat in its mother's milk is parallel to the rule prohibiting incest between an Israelite boy and his mother (chapter 5). I suspect that readers who have not read widely in anthropological literature will find interpretations such as this one somewhat far-fetched. But if it does not surprise anyone that social rules are linked to certain conceptions of God, why should it seem so absurd that practices and conceptions related to food and sex are also enmeshed in one another? In one sense, adopting an anthropological perspective means learning to look for connections between such specific domains as cooking and sex.

In offering such accounts of ancient Israelite practices, I by no means intend to suggest that my interpretations are the only ones possible. Given the conception of culture just presented, I take for granted that a given practice may have more than one meaning, function, or homology. The prohibition about seething a kid-goat in its mother's milk may be interpreted otherwise than as homologous to an incest prohibition. Since a given practice is related to numerous others, the task of interpretation, which has to be shared by numerous interpreters, involves seeking all of these various connections. Indeed, in my view what gives individuals in a community a sense that a given practice is efficacious (or even ordained by God) is the fact that practices intersect with one another in numerous ways within a given culture. In other words, the more connections a given practice makes with other social activities, the more individuals experience its power.

Consider again an analogy from literature. When a writer struggles to perfect a line or verse, she eventually finds "just the right word" even though she cannot always say why that word "works" better than others. What makes that word work, as critics routinely point out, is the way that word links up in numerous ways with other words, sounds, and themes in the adjoining sentences and in the work as a whole. A similar collective process is at work in culture. The sense that one practice is better than another, that it is right, efficacious, or divinely sanctioned, often has to do with the powerful ways that this practice links up with others.

Finally, it is important to acknowledge that the kind of historical anthropology attempted here has to surmount difficulties foreign to the anthropologist in the field. Since the historical anthropologist cannot question natives about the meaning of practices, she or he is in the position of doing cultural archaeology, a mode of interpretation that involves imagining what practices meant from incomplete and partial remains. These unstated meanings can often be detected from symbolic artifacts such as metaphors, which point to larger complexes of unarticulated meaning. Cross-cultural studies are also crucial to the process of reconstructing the larger cultural system. Such studies point to meanings and functions of a practice only hinted at in the literary remains of an ancient tradition. Comparison thus emerges as a tool for imagining the unspoken meanings and correspondences that once constituted a cultural system (see chapter 4).

Having specified the agenda of this book as a whole, let me explain the strategy by which my argument unfolds. In order to make an anthropology of Judaism compelling, it is first necessary to relinquish the distinction between Judaism and savage religions. To do so necessitates understanding why that opposition has had such a grip on intellectual discourse about religion. It is to this historical question that I first turn in part 1. In this context, I explore the factors that produced and sustained the opposition between Judaism and savage religion in European scholarship from the seventeenth to nineteenth centuries. I then consider the impulses that have recently called that opposition into question. Once those factors are exposed, I take on the criticisms aimed at cross-cultural comparison. I argue that metonymic comparisons (those between cultures or religions in juxtaposition) are not inherently better than metaphoric comparisons (those between cultures and religions separated by time or place). Consequently, studies that place Israelite religion or ancient Judaism against the background of ancient Near East, Greco-Roman, or Christian contexts are not necessarily superior to those that move across time and space. In part 1, then, I try to overcome the opposition between Judaism and savage religions by exposing and challenging the assumptions on which it has rested.

Part 2 represents substantive contributions to an anthropology of Judaism. Here, certain practices of ancient Israel's religious cultures are examined in light of anthropological studies of "primitive" societies. As mentioned above, part 2 focuses on practices that have been marginalized in biblical studies, including circumcision, menstrual taboos, and other rules about impurity and animals. These essays join the growing number of studies that use anthropological theory and comparative ethnography to illuminate aspects of Israelite religion and ancient Judaism.[14] In addition, I explore the ways that Israelite practices are historically transformed as they are appropriated by subsequent communities that have different social structures and hence provide individuals with different experiences of the world. I am especially interested in the transformations that occur as the religious practices and conceptions of Israelite priests are inherited by other groups such as the Dead Sea community, the early rabbis, and Christians.

The Conclusion brings together the various arguments of this book, drawing particular attention to the political implications of passing Judaism under the anthropological gaze. I argue that the anthropology of Judaism is one logical and necessary conclusion of the anthropological tradition itself. One important goal of that tradition has been to dismantle the opposition between savage and civilized traditions. But that goal cannot be accomplished until the effects of that opposition are eradicated. As long as the anthropological lens is focused on some traditions and not others, the old prejudices continue to operate. The subjection of Judaism to anthropological inquiry, therefore, represents an attempt to carry the relativistic critique contained within twentieth-century anthropology to its logical conclusions. At the same time, the anthropological study of Judaism releases a savage critique of Judaism itself.

In sum, the present book is a conversation I have fabricated between a particular group of anthropologists and their heirs, on the one hand, and the religious culture of ancient Judaism, on the other. I hope that this conversation will be enlightening to some and will stimulate other colloquies of a similar kind.

Part I

Judaism and
Savage Religions
Archaeology of an Opposition

1.

The Literature of Travel and the Enlightenment Critique

I have not limited myself to learning the characteristics of the Indian and informing myself about their customs and practices, I have sought in these practices and customs, vestiges of the most remote antiquity. I have read carefully [the works] of the earliest writers who treated the customs, laws and usages of the peoples of whom they had some knowledge. I have made a comparison of these customs with each other. I confess that, if the ancient authors have given me information on which to base conjectures about the Indians, the customs of the Indians have given me information on the basis of which I can understand more easily and explain more readily many things in the ancient authors. Perhaps, by bringing my thoughts to light, I shall open to those interested in the reading of these authors, some paths of investigation that they will be able to follow further. Perhaps, I shall be fortunate enough to uncover the veins of a mine which will become rich in their hands. I hope that, surpassing me, they may go still further and be willing to give an exact form, a fair dimension to many things of which I shall only skirt the surface in passing.

Père François Lafitau 1974 (1724)

The twentieth century did not invent the opposition between Judaism and savage religions. That opposition developed and was nourished within modern discourses on religion and thus has a history that extends back for at least three centuries.[1] The motivations that produced and sustained this dichotomy are obvious and have already been noted. Positing a fundamental difference between the religion of ancient Jews and savages protected the privileged status of both ancient Judaism and Christianity. Nonetheless, the story of how this opposition arose and how it expressed itself in the discourses of modernity is of interest in its own right.

The story begins in the sixteenth and seventeenth centuries when the concept of the savage initially emerged as a critical category in European thought (Fairchild 1961; George 1958; Hanke 1970; Hodgen 1964; Manuel 1959; 1983). At this time, voyagers, missionaries, conquerors, and commercial expansion pushed back the borders of the unknown world. Such travels produced a voluminous literature that provided increasingly detailed information about the beliefs and practices of alien peoples living in, among other places, North and South America, Africa, and New Guinea. This literature in turn stimulated a European discussion both popular and philosophic about the nature of savages and their place in the scheme of things.

The literature on the savage is fascinating in a number of respects. From the standpoint of this inquiry, one is startled to find that in this literature the opposition between the religions of Jews and savages had not yet won its victory. The following discussion focuses on those writers who recognized and felt compelled to account for the numerous resemblances between Judaism and the religions of the peoples indigenous to North and South America, although a similar story could be told about the early writings on the religion of African aborigines (Patai 1962; Hodgen 1964, 338). Spanish writers including Juan Suárez de Peralta, Diego Durán, and Gregorio García, English writers such as Thomas Thorowgood, John Eliot, and John Spencer, and French writers including Marc Lescarbots and Père François Lafitau pondered the commonalities between the religion of the first Jews and the "aborigines" of America. Some of these writers were so startled by the similarities between ancient Jewish practices and those of the savages of the New World that they actually believed the latter were the ten lost tribes of Israel.

Defending this view, Garcia notes that the Indians appeared to keep certain parts of the Mosaic Code (Huddleston 1967, 70–71). The Incas had a ceremony resembling Passover; the Yucatecan Indians practiced circumcision; the Mexicans and Incas kept eternal fires burning on their altars just like the Jews. Other tribes respected many of the same rules that Israelites had observed regarding women. Such tribes prohibited women from entering into the temples, forbade men from having sexual relations with women after childbirth, and prohibited men and women from wearing clothes of the opposite sex. In addition, widows were required to marry their nearest male relatives. All of these rules have striking if not exact parallels in the laws of ancient Israel (Lev. 6:9; 12:1–8; Deut. 22:5; Gen. 38:8; Deut. 25:5–10; Ruth 4:5, 8–10).[2] Following a similar line of reasoning, John Eliot in *A Brief Narrative of the Progress of the Gospel amongst the Indians in New England in the Year 1670* espouses the view that the Indians are descendants of the ancient Jews, because, like the ancient Jews, the Indians sequestered women who were menstruating, mourned grievously for the dead, reckoned time by nights and months, and gave dowries for wives (Wasserman 1954, 459–60; Huddleston 1967, 134).

To win public support for Eliot's missionary activity among the Indians,

Thomas Thorowgood published *Iews in America, or Probabilities That the Americans Are of That Race* (1650). Influenced by millenarian expectations, Thorowgood believed that the second coming could be hastened by converting the Jews to Christianity. Eliot's work of seeking the conversion of the "American Jews" would help inaugurate the end of days (Glaser 1973, 33–35; Huddleston 1967, 130–34; Wolf 1901, xiv–xv; Hyamson 1903, 660–67). Thorowgood (1650, 3–10) argues that the Indians must be descendants of ancient Jews because "the rites, fashions, ceremonies, and opinions of the Americans [Indians] are in many things agreeable to the custome of the Jewes, not onely prophane and common usages, but such as be called solemn and sacred."³

Thorowgood goes on to list some fifty points of resemblance between the ancient Jews and Indians. In terms of "prophane customes," he notes that like the Jews, the Indians "constantly and strictly separate their women in a little Wigwam by themselves in their feminine seasons"; they annoint their heads as did the Jews; they "wash themselves often, twice or thrice in the day . . . and the Jewes were frequent in this, Mar. 7.3, 4. Io. [=Job] 2.6"; "they eat no swine flesh tis hateful to them, as it was among the Jewes, Levit. 11.7"; "they wash strangers feet, and are very hospitall to them, and this was the known commendation of old Israell"; they "compute their times by nights an use which Laet confesseth they had from the Hebrews"; "the Indian women are easily delivered of their children, without Midwives, as those in Exod. I.19." Thorowgood also compares the Indian kinship terminology to that of the ancient Jews. "As the Jewes were wont to call them fathers and mothers, that were not their naturall parents, so the Indians give the same appellation to Unkle and Aunts."

In addition to similarities in the "prophane customes," Thorowgood (1650, 6–10) cites numerous commonalities between their "solemn and sacred" practices. In addition to circumcision, Thorowgood notes that

2. The Indians worship that God they say, who created the Sun, Moon, and all invisible things, who gives them also all that is good. 3. They knew of that floud which drowned the world, and that it was sent for the sin of man, especially for unlawfull lust, and that there shall never be such a deluge againe. 4. It is affirmed by them neverthelesse that after many yeers, fire shall come down from above and consume all. 5. They beleeve the immortality of the soule, and that there is a place of joy, another of torment after death, whither they shall goe that kill, lie, or steale, which place they call Popoguffo, a great pit, like the expression, Num. 16.33 and Rev. 19.1 & c. but they which do no harme shall be received into a good place, and enjoy all manner of pleasure. 6. The Americans have in some parts an exact form of King, Priest, and Prophet, as was aforetime in Canaan. . . . 8. The Temples wherein they worship, sing, pray and make their Offerings, are fashioned and used as with the Jewes; at Mexico they were built foure square, and sumptuous as Ezek. 40.47. . . . 10. They had places also therein, which none might enter into but their Priests. Heb. 9.6, 7. . . . 12. They

had almost continuall fire before their Idols, and took great care lest the fire before the Altar should dye, they call that the Divine Harth, where there is fire continually, like that in Leviticus 6:9. **13**. None may intermeddle with their Sacrifices but the Priests, who were also in high estimation among them as they were among the Jewes. . . . **15**. In their necessities they always sacrificed, which done, they grew hopefull and confident. **16**. They burnt Incense, had their Censars, and cake Oblations, as Ier. [=Jer.] **7.18**. **17**. The first fruits of their corne they offered, and what they gat by Hunting and fishing. . . . **19**. In all of Peru they had but one Temple, which was most sumptuous, Consecrated to the Maker of the world; yet they had foure other places also for Devotion, as the Jews had severall Synagogues, beside that their glorious Temple. . . . **21**. A yeare of Jubile did they observe, as did Israel also.

If the idea of the Indians' descent from the Jews seems far-fetched today, it is interesting to note that Manasseh ben Israel, a well-known rabbi from Amsterdam, also argued that the ten lost tribes had managed to settle in the New World and had influenced the religious beliefs and practices of its inhabitants. Manasseh invokes this argument in his attempt to persuade the Parliament of England to readmit the Jews to England. Speaking to the messianic expectations of the Puritans and Anglicans in England, he notes that according to the Bible the Messiah would come when the Jews were scattered to all corners of the earth. The fact that Jews had been found in the New World meant that the arrival of the Messiah was imminent. The readmittance of the Jews to England, the last end of the earth, was a final and necessary event prior to the Messiah's arrival (Glaser **1973**, 33–43; Glassman **1975**, 109–33; Huddleston **1967**, 128–33; Roth **1945**; Wolf **1901**).

To support his views, Manasseh points to the numerous similarities between the Indians and ancient Israelites.

> For he that will compare the Lawes and Customes of the Indians and the Hebrewes together, shall finde them agree in many things; whence you may easily gather, That the Indians borrowed those of the Hebrewes (who lived among them) before, or after they went to the unknowne Mountaines. The Indians of Yucatan, and the Acuzainitenses doe circumcise themselves. The Totones of New Spaine, and Mexicans . . . rend their garments, if there happen any sudden misfortune or the death of any. . . . The Mexicans, and Totones . . . kept continually fire upon their Altars, as God commands in Leviticus. Those of Peru doe the same, in their Temples dedicated to the Sun. The Nicaraguazenses doe forbid their women who were lately brought a bed, to enter their Temples, till they are purified. The inhabitants of Hispaniola thinke those doe sin, who lye with a woman a little after her childe-birth. And the Indians of new Spaine doe severely punish Sodomie. Many of the Indians doe bury their dead on the Mountaines; which also is the Jewish custome; and Garcias saith, the name Chanan is found in those Countries. You may wonder at this, that the Indians doe every fifty yeares celebrate a Jubilee. . . . Also that on the Sabbath day all are bound to be present in the Temple, to perform their Sacrifices, and Ceremo-

nies. They also were divorced from their wives, if they were not honest. The Indians of Peru, New-Spaine, and Guatemala did marry the Widdowes of their dead Brethren. May not you judge from these things, that the Jewes lived in those places, and that the Gentiles learned such things of them? Adde also to what hath been said, that the knowledge which the Indians had, of the Creation of the world, and of the universall Flood, they borrowed from the Israelites. (Glaser 1973, 22)

Not everyone accepted the theory of Jewish origin for the inhabitants of the New World. But those writers who rejected this theory nonetheless recognized and felt compelled to account for the striking similarities between the ancient Jews and the savages of the New World. In response to Thorowgood's book, for example, Hamon L'Estrange wrote *Americans No Iewes, or Improbabilities That the Americans Are of That Race* (1652). In dismissing Thorowgood's argument, L'Estrange does not deny the parallels. Rather he notes that the same practices were in use among other peoples who clearly were not descendants of Israelites.[4] Similarly, Lescarbots (1914 [1611], 200), who believed that Noah populated North America, nonetheless points out several striking parallels between the practices of the ancient Jews and the Indians. "Our savage women after they have brought forth the fruit of this exercise [childbirth], by I know not what practices, observe, without law, that which was commanded in the law of Moses concerning purification (Lev. 12). For they shut themselves up apart, and do not know their husbands for thirty, or even forty days."

Lafitau's work *Moeurs des sauvages amériquains comparées aux moeurs des premier temps* (1724) (Customs of the American Indians Compared with the Customs of Primitive Times) represents the culmination of this tradition of comparing ancient Jewish and savage practices. Lafitau argues that the American savages separated from the original stock of humanity before the revelation to Moses. In his view, the commonalities between the ancient Jews and the American Indians constitute evidence of a common original religion of Adam from which both Indian and Hebrew religion derived (Fenton and Moore 1974; Chinard 1913, 319, 323; Healy 1958, 160–62; Hodgen 1964, 312–14; Manuel 1959, 19; Pagden 1982, 198–209). Lafitau intended his discussion to counter the arguments of writers such as Fontenelle who claimed that earliest humanity did not have any religion. Such atheists based their view on the reports that travelers had encountered primitive peoples who had no religion. On the basis of such reports, some philosophers inferred that the first humans had no belief in God and no religious practices. Lafitau sets out to refute this argument by attempting to reconstruct the religion of Adamic culture. He argues that one could assume that the religious conceptions and practices the ancient Jews and American savages had in common must have derived from the original religion of humanity.

Anthropologists and ethnologists have already emphasized the way in which Lafitau anticipated many crucial developments in the emergence of their disciplines. Radcliffe-Brown, for example, writes that Lafitau's "attempt to illuminate the customs of antiquity by comparing them with similar customs of the American Indians marks him as one of the precursors of social anthropology" (Fenton and Moore 1974, xxix). From the standpoint of this inquiry, Lafitau's work clearly anticipates an anthropology of Judaism. He goes well beyond the other writers of his day in recognizing all sorts of similarities between ancient Judaism and primitive religions.

He compares, for example, the practice of celibacy among Indian priests and the Jewish Essenes, the Hebrew practice of circumcision and the Indian customs of piercing ears and nose, and the Hebrew and the Iroquois custom of having a widow marry her former husband's brother (1974 [1724], 177, 339). In considering the way the Indians sequester women during their menstrual periods, Lafitau writes that "they are quite rigourous in America where huts are made apart for them, such as were made for lepers among the Jews" (1974, 178). Writing about the Indian feast for a young hunter's first kill, Lafitau notes the "rather clear resemblance to the [Israelite] sacrifice of the first fruits (of all things) to God, a feast required by the written law and, perhaps, also by the natural law" (1974, 316). During this feast, everything has to be consumed and "if they do not finish it all they have to throw what remains into fire as the Jews did with the Pascal lamb" (1974, 316). While describing the Indian practice of offering tobacco to their gods, Lafitau refers to the Israelite practice of offering to God only those animals which are considered clean. "It seems," he writes, "that, whether among the Israelites or the gentiles, all that was useful for ordinary nourishment, especially the flesh of animals was offered to God, or indeed, to idols" (1974, 138).

But it is not only the readiness to see similarities between savage religion and ancient Judaism that makes Lafitau's work so fascinating. He also goes so far as to use the practices of Indians to illuminate aspects of Israelite religion. In one instance, for example, Lafitau appeals to the customs of the Indians to support an interpretation of a contradictory set of passages in Genesis that deal with the nature of the relationship between Sarah and Abraham. In one scriptural passage, Sarah is described as the half-sister of Abraham because they share the same father Terah (Gen. 20:12). Elsewhere, however, Sarah is called Terah's daughter-in-law (Gen. 11:31). Following other commentators, Lafitau concludes that "among the Jews, it was the general rule for relatives in the collateral lines in any degree of relationship whatever to call each other brothers and sisters when they could trace back, on both sides, to a common ancestor" (1974, 335). In Lafitau's view, Sarah is the daughter of Nahor and hence Abraham's niece. Since she is his collateral relative, she is called Abraham's sister. Lafitau supports this interpretation by citing the Iroquois and Huran practice of classifying all their mother's sisters as "mothers," and all their father's brothers as "fathers," a practice that has come to be known in anthropological writings as a classificatory system of kinship terminology. Lafitau argues that

Scripture is reflecting such a system when it refers to Sarah both as Abraham's sister and as the daughter-in-law of Abraham's father (1974, 335).

It is not important here whether Lafitau's interpretation is plausible. What is significant is his willingness to rely on knowledge of savage religions, particularly their kinship terminology, to understand the practices of ancient Israelite culture. In doing so, Lafitau anticipates the recent work of Andriolio (1973), Donaldson (1981), Gottwald (1979, 293–337), Jay (1985; 1988), Leach (1969), Oden (1987, 106–30), Prewitt (1981), and Schapera (1955), among others, who use anthropological studies of kinship to attempt a reconstruction of early Israelite kinship systems and a clarification of biblical passages dealing with kinship relations.

In retrospect, it is surprising that these late sixteenth- and early seventeenth-century writers were so attentive to the similarities between ancient Judaism and the religion of the American "aborigines." The question naturally arises as to why these writers were willing and able to see these commonalities and find them interesting. To put it somewhat differently, what factors were involved in clearing the space within European discourse for the emergence of this incipient anthropology of Judaism?

Savage and Jew: A Shared Stereotype

The ability to see resemblances between ancient Judaism and savage religions was a result, at least in part, of the overlapping stereotypes of savages and contemporary Jews in the European imagination. Sifting through the writings on Judaism and heathenism during the sixteenth and seventeenth centuries, one finds striking similarities between the European conceptions of the Jew and the savage. As a Christian anti-type, both were pictured as less than fully human, falling somewhere in the great chain of being between human and ape. The savage and the Jew presented similar problems to Christians. In what ways could these peoples be rescued from their idolatrous practices and converted to the true faith? Not surprisingly, European writers relied on the same vocabulary and images to describe the religious practices of their Jewish contemporaries and the savages discovered in the New World. Jews trafficked with the Devil; they practiced ritual murder, especially the murder of innocent children (Fisch 1971; Glassman 1975; Trachtenberg 1945). Europeans leveled similar accusations at savages. Missionary and travel literature routinely described savage religious practices as devil worship and frequently reported the practice of cannibalism and child sacrifice (Bissell 1924, 6, 370–73; Chinard 1911; Kennedy 1950; Pearce 1950; Hanke 1965; 1970; Wasserman 1954). Judaism and savage religions both lacked any redeeming moral qualities.

For these reasons, Europeans used similar language to describe Jewish and savage religious practices. This shared vocabulary is evident, for example, if one compares the seventeenth-century voyage literature on the savage with a similar sort of travel literature on Jews and Judaism. This "travel" literature on Jews and Judaism emerged in England during the early seventeenth century, when virtually no Jews were living in that country. Jews had been expelled from England in 1290, and only a relatively small number of Jews had entered England before the seventeenth century. English travelers who went abroad to other European countries brought back stories of their exotic visits to Jewish synagogues. Even after the Jews were readmitted to England in the mid-seventeenth century, numerous English writers report their visits to the local but still exotic synagogues. These reports are similar in tone and attitude to European accounts of savage religion. Compare, for example, Lescarbot's description of Brazilian religion in 1609 with some English accounts of Judaism from the same century:

> As for the Brazilians, I find by the account of Jean de Léry, that not only are they like our savages, without any form of religion or knowledge of God, but that they are so blinded and hardened in their cannibalism that they seem to be in no wise capable of the Christian doctrine. Also they are visibly tormented and beaten by the devil. . . . When one tells the Brazilians that they must believe in God, they fully agree, but by and by they forget their lesson and return to their own vomit, which is a strange brutishness, not to be willing at the least to redeem themselves from the devil's vexation by religion. (1914 [1611], 100–101)

In 1636, John Weemse, an Englishman, writes about the Jews that "many of them who have beene compelled to bee baptized have fallen backe againe to their vomit of Iudaisme." In 1659, Samuel Pepys visited a synagogue during Simhat Torah, a lighthearted Jewish holiday. He has the following to say about that occasion: "But, Lord! to see the disorder, laughing sporting and no attention, but confusion in all their service, more like brutes than knowing the true God, would make a man forswear ever seeing them more: and indeed I never did see so much, or could have imagined there had been any religion in the whole world so absurdly performed as this." In 1662, John Greenhalgh also had occasion to visit a synagogue and remarks in a letter to Reverend Thomas Crompton that "the Jews with their taleisim [i.e., prayer shawls] over their heads presented to the observer a strange, uncouth, foreign and . . . barbarous sight" (Glassman 1975, 96, 139–40).

The fact that Jews and savages were similarly stereotyped in the European imagination helped nourish the theory that the American Indians were originally of Jewish stock. Diego Durán, for example, concludes that the Indians must be descended from the Jews because of the similarities in their "way of life, ceremonies, rites, and superstitions, omens and hypocrisies." Durán also writes that "that which most forces me to believe that these Indians are of Hebrew lineage is the strange pertinacity they have in not casting away their idolatries and superstitions, living by them as did their ancestors, as David said in the 105th Psalm." In a similar argument for their common ancestry,

Garcia notes that both peoples were timid, liars, and prone to ceremony and idolatry (Huddleston 1967, 38–39, 70).

It is not surprising that European "travelers" described the religion of the Jews and savages in similar terms. After all, both savage religion and Judaism served as objects of contrast for European self-understandings, a technique that Hayden White (1978, 151) has called ostensive self-definition by negation. When "the need for positive self-definition asserts itself but no compelling criterion of self-identification appears, it is always possible to say something like: 'I may not know the precise content of my own felt humanity, but I am most certainly *not* like that.' " In European thought, Judaism and savage religion were often the "thats" in the landscape to which one pointed.

The secondary literature on European views of both savages and Jews emphasizes how each served as foils for European views of Christianity:

> The Indian whom the sixteenth century voyagers came to know was, more than anything else, a creature whose way of life showed Englishmen what they might be were they not civilized and Christian, did they not fully partake of the divine idea of order. . . . The Indian became important for the English mind, not for what he was in and of himself, but rather for what he showed civilized men they were not and must not be. (Pearce 1967, 4–5)

> The stories containing references to Jews, which in many instances were carried over from earlier centuries, could be used to point out the superiority of Christianity over Judaism and to strengthen the faith of Christians who questioned the teachings of the church. The Jews, shrouded in legend, were an excellent foil, and the clerics used them often in their sermons. Thus, if they did not exist in the flesh, their imaginary spirits were resurrected to enhance the power of the church in the eyes of the faithful. (Glassman 1975, 29)

Given the overlapping stereotypes of the Jew and the savage and the similar use to which such stereotypes were put, it is not surprising that numerous writers recognized commonalities between Judaism and savage religions. But there were other factors as well that enabled this inchoate anthropology of Judaism to emerge. One of the most important of these was the Bible itself.

The Principle of Monogenesis

According to the biblical account of creation, all humanity derived from Adam, the original human entity whom God had created. All peoples, including even the savages in the Americas, were direct descendants of Adam and Adamic culture. The majority of Europeans who wrote on savage religions, including those discussed above, upheld this biblical premise of monogenesis. Consequently, European writers expected to find similarities between the religion of the savages and the religion of the ancients. Since savages were descendants of the original stock of humankind, savage religion contains traces of the original culture and religion. Indeed, it was only by finding such similarities that these writers believed they could identify the point in time when the separation and dispersion of various peoples had occurred. Such parallels and similarities, therefore, did not pose theological problems for these writers. On the contrary, they confirmed the veracity of the biblical story that all peoples derived from one original stock of humankind.

Writers did disagree on the precise moment in history when the savages of the New World had lost contact with the original human society. Those who believed the separation had occurred after the Jewish revelation treated savage practices and beliefs as corrupted but nonetheless recognizable derivatives of Mosaic law. Other writers believed the American savages had lost contact with original humanity before the Jewish revelation and consequently the parallels in practice and belief could not be explained as a result of an earlier historical connection. To explain the similarities, these writers repeated the argument used by the early church fathers to explain the commonalities between Christianity and the pagan religions of antiquity. The similarities were the work of the Devil who was actively worshiped by the savages. In competing with God for the allegiance of humankind, the Devil had aped the practices of the divinely revealed religion. The savages' vile and abominable practices and beliefs were bastardizations of the true religion of Jews and Christians. Lescarbot, for example, offers this explanation for why the savages of New France, like the ancient Hebrews, performed certain religious practices following the birth of a child: "They can render no reason for this [i.e., forcing the infant to swallow grease or oil], but that it is a custom of long continuance: whereupon I conjecture that the devil, who hath always borrowed ceremonies from the Church, as well in the ancient as in the new law, wished that his people, as I call them that believe not in God, and are out of the communion of saints, should be anointed like to God's people, which unction he hath made to be inward, because the spiritual unction of the Christian is so" (1914 [1611], 3:80).

It is now evident why a space in European discourse momentarily opened for an inquiry into the commonalities between ancient Judaism and savage religions. Such parallels did not yet pose a danger to the privileged status of revealed religion. The stock explanations available were sufficient to account for the similarities between ancient Judaism and heathenism without undermining the assumption that the Jewish religion had been revealed. These similarities were either the survivals of revealed religion that had been nearly obliterated by the human tendency to superstition, error, and sin, or the work of the Devil who seduced humanity away from God by inventing perverted versions of divine religion.

These first anthropologists of Judaism had no way of anticipating the use to which reason would put their comparisons. They had no way of knowing that they had helped prepare the ground for an all-out attack on the privileged status of Judaism and Christianity. Yet, in pointing to the commonalities between ancient Judaism and contemporary heathenism, these writers had unknowingly fashioned what would shortly prove to be one of the greatest weapons in the rationalist attack on revealed religion (Frantz 1967; Gay 1968, 15). Such commonalities generated a suspicion about the validity of the distinction between revealed religion and superstition. The deists, atheists, and materialists of the eighteenth century pointed to these parallels to prove that the distinction between Judaism and contemporary paganism was untenable.

It was this attack that subsequently made an anthropological discourse on Judaism impossible. Once it became clear that commonalities between the religion of ancient Jews and contemporary savages posed a problem for the unique and privileged status of Christianity, various strategies were devised to neutralize this powerful weapon of the Enlightenment. New schemes were developed to put such a chasm between ancient Judaism and savage religions that subsequent writers would no longer find it meaningful or relevant to draw attention to those similarities that had so intrigued earlier writers. In this way, the space that had momentarily cleared for a serious comparison of ancient Judaism and savage religions disappeared for another two centuries. It is to this attack and recovery that our attention now turns.

Judaism and Paganism in the Light of Reason

As reason emerged as a respected source of knowledge late in the seventeenth century and continued so throughout the eighteenth, nothing remained unchanged in the landscape of European discourse.[5] Facts that previously posed no problem to revealed religion now undermined it. Arguments marshaled in support of revelation now threatened its claim to divine origin. One such reversal involved the use of the observed similarities between ancient Judaism and contemporary and ancient paganism. Both the biblical story of creation and the overlapping religious stereotypes of Jews and savages had created an expectation that such commonalities would exist. But as reason vied with revelation for recognition as the ultimate source of all knowledge, these similarities became a potent weapon in the rationalist critique of revelation.

In the vocabulary of the Enlightenment, revelation referred to the religion of both the Old and New Testaments. For orthodox Christian thinkers, the revelation of the Old Testament verified the truth of the Christian revelation. The New Testament incessantly quoted from the Old to show how various incidents in the life of Christ were foreshadowed in the writings of the Hebrew prophets. The fact that Christ fulfilled the prophecies of the Old Testament provided the proof of his messiahship. The validity of the Christian revelation, therefore, required an affirmation that the Jewish testament was of divine origin. As the orthodox Christian of Thomas Morgan's *Moral Philoso-pher* (1738, 15) puts it, "What I mean by Christianity, strictly speaking, or reveal'd as distinguish'd from natural Religion, is the revealed Truths or Doctrines of Revelation as contained in the Books of the Old and New Testaments."

It is not surprising that in attacking the idea of revelation and traditional forms of Christianity, rationalists felt obliged to ridicule the religion of the Jews (Ettinger 1964, 183; Katz 1980, 29–30; Meyer 1963, 1176; Poliakov 1975, 120; Schwartz 1981, 24; Schwarzbach 1973, 361–74).[6] In launching this attack, deists in England, France, and Germany revived the strategies of ancient pagan philosophers who had attacked Christianity by heaping scorn on Jews and Judaism. Anthony Collins (1976 [1724], 26, 31) is representative of this impulse when he notes that if the proofs for Christianity drawn from the Old Testament

> are valid proofs then is Christianity strongly and invincibly established on its true foundations . . . because a proof drawn from an inspir'd book, is perfectly conclusive. . . . On the other side, if the proofs for Christianity from the Old Testament be not valid; if the arguments founded on those books be not conclusive; and the prophecies cited from thence be not fulfilled; then has Christianity no just foundation!

One powerful strategy in the emerging rationalist critique involved point-ing out the commonalities between revelation as embodied in the Old and New Testaments and contemporary heathenism. These commonalities gener-ated a series of embarrassing questions for the idea of revelation. If one be-lieved in a Devil, as some defenders of revelation did, how could one be sure that only the rites and beliefs of paganism were the work of the Devil? Perhaps those of Judaism and Christianity had a similar origin. Why should one be-lieve the miracles and prophecies of the Old and New Testaments but reject those claimed on behalf of contemporary savage religions? On what grounds could one confidently affirm the revelation to Moses yet deny revelations claimed by other peoples? Was there any fundamental difference between heathen sacrifices and the rites of sacrifice that God had commanded the Israelites to perform? Why should human sacrifices of savages be treated as abominations when God had sacrificed a son?

Questions such as these helped subvert the longstanding dichotomy be-tween revelation, on the one hand, and paganism, heathenism, or supersti-tion, on the other.[7] From the perspective of critical deists, these dichotomies were problematic because revelation did not have an exclusive claim to truth and because savages did not have a monopoly on superstition.[8] Savages had sometimes discovered the fundamental truths of reason, which rationalists called the Religion or Law of Nature. Revelation, for its part, contained countless practices and beliefs that were superstitious and antithetical to reason. For rationalists these facts confirmed their basic contention that reason makes revelation redundant and unnecessary. Everything that one needs to know can be derived by the exercise of reason alone. Otherwise principles of reason should not have been known to savages who had never been exposed to revelation. Revelation, then, was at best superfluous and at worst misleading. More moderate deists were gracious enough to grant revelation the right to exist, but only on the condition that revelation serve as reason's handmaid. In this subservient role, revelation would be allowed to provide knowledge on matters that were outside or "above" reason's purview. Revelation could also act as an external confirmation of what had already been shown by the internal light of reason. In what follows, we will see how deists used the commonalities between Judaism, Christianity, and heathenism to validate these larger claims.

Revelation Has No Monopoly on Truth, Heathenism Is Not the Only Superstition

Rationalists argued that the essential principles of religion could be known through the exercise of reason alone. By exercising that faculty, one could learn that God exists, that one has a duty to worship God, that virtue and piety are the best methods of worship, and that one should repent of one's sins.[9] Since these principles were accessible to all persons through the use of reason, revelation itself was unnecessary. There was no need for God to publish "externally" what could readily be known from the internal light of reason.

To demonstrate this point, some of reason's devotees, like Herbert of Cherbury, the seventeenth-century precursor of deism, suggested that the fundamental religious tenets of revelation were at least implicit in all forms of paganism, of both the modern and ancient variety (Hutcheson 1944). Even savages in the New World believed in and worshiped a superior deity who judged them for their sins in an afterlife. "These truths therefore that Flourish everywhere and always will flourish, are not confined by the limits of any one religion. For they are divinely inscribed on the Understanding itself, and are subject to no traditions written or unwritten" (Herbert 1944 [1645], 89). The five truths that Herbert believed flourish everywhere were: "1. that there is some supreme divinity 2. that this divinity ought to be worshipped 3. that virtue joined with piety is the best method of divine worship 4. that we should return to our right selves from sins 5. that reward or punishment is bestowed after this life is finished" (Herbert 1944 [1645], 126).

Deists such as Matthew Tindal and Thomas Chubb admitted that some peoples had not grasped these principles. Nonetheless, they argue that such truths are accessible to everyone in principle, if only reason be properly exercised (Tindal 1730, 77; Chubb 1978 [1731], 23).

> If we take a general view of those mischiefs mankind have at all times practis'd
> on a religious account, either upon themselves or others, we shall find them
> owning to their entertaining such notions of God, as are intirely inconsistent
> with his nature, and contrary to what their Reason, if attended to, wou'd inform
> them of the Design & End of the Laws of God. (Tindal 1730, 77)

The first prong of the deist attack involved the attempt to show that what
revelation defined as its own essence was already known or at least accessible
to savages. Without any revelation at all, humans in all times and all places
could discover those basic articles of religion if only they relied upon reason.
This Religion of Nature was, as Tindal puts it, "as old as creation." The basic
articles of the Jewish and Christian revelation simply represented a re-publica-
tion of principles already known to Adam.

But the similarities between revelation and superstition were formal as well
as substantive. Heathens legitimated their religions with precisely the same
kinds of "external" proofs used to validate Judaism and Christianity. Miracles, prophecies, revelations, and ancient traditions from the ancestors were
invoked by peoples the world over to defend their respective religions.

> Many faiths or religions, clearly, exist or once existed in various countries and
> ages, and certainly there is not one of them that the lawgivers have not pro-
> nounced to be as it were divinely ordained; so that the Wayfarer finds one in
> Europe, another in Africa, and in Asia, still another in the very Indies. (Herbert
> 1944 [1645], 87)

> Since those who, in every country, are hir'd to maintain them [i.e., the tradi-
> tional religions] will not fail to assert, they have all the external marks; such as
> uninterrupted tradition, incontested miracles, confession of adversaries, num-
> ber of proselites, and all those other external arguments, that the Papists &
> Mahometans set so high a value on. (Tindal 1730, 211).

These similarities, rationalists argued, forced defenders of revelation to
adopt a double standard. Their own external proofs were trustworthy; those
of other religions were false.

> As this is all the bulk of mankind, if they are not capable of judging from the
> Doctrines themselves of their truth, can say for their Religion, so they, in all
> places, make use of this argument, & with equal confidence aver, that, tho' all
> other traditionary Religions are full of gross falsehoods, & most absurd notions,
> which their Priests impudently impose on them as divine truths, yet our own
> Priests are such faithful representers of things. . . . (Tindal 1730, 210)

Revelation thus failed to see that what it named as superstition in other religions was also contained in itself. As Voltaire (1962 [1764], 476) succinctly
puts it, "It is therefore plain that what is fundamental to one sect's religion
passes for superstition with another sect." From the rationalist perspective,

the similarity between the claims of revelation and heathenism left defenders of revelation with but two options: if they continued to ridicule pagan claims to truth, they would have to criticize the identical kinds of claims made on behalf of revelation. Alternatively, if they continued to verify revelation in traditional ways, they would have to recognize the validity of those claims made by others. Either option signified revelation's demise. The first option would destroy revelation's foundation; the second would necessitate accepting the truth of religions in fundamental disagreement with it.

The superstitious nature of revelation, however, extended far beyond its formal claims. To Enlightenment thinkers, the doctrines and practices of revealed religions were as superstitious, absurd, and nonsensical as any found among the heathens. In fact, for rationalists the very idea of revelation contained an inherent contradiction and hence was irrational. If God were absolutely perfect and hence immutable, how could God have originally given humans one set of instructions (i.e., the Old Testament) and subsequently another (i.e., the New Testament)? For "if God is unchangeable, our duty to him must be too" (Tindal 1730, 56). The traditional idea of revelation implied that God was inconsistent. Nor could one argue that the second revelation supplemented the first revelation which had been incomplete. If that were so, God had given humanity an imperfect instruction and hence God would be imperfect.

In the light of reason, the doctrine of election also seemed absurd. According to this doctrine, God had made the divine will known to specific groups of people, first the Jews and subsequently the Gentiles. But numerous other peoples in the world had not been aware of these revelations. It followed that only the elect would know what to do in order to achieve future happiness. The idea of election thus presupposed an absurd notion of God.

> Superstitious men [i.e., defenders of revelation] are incapable of believing in a perfectly just and good God. They make him talk to all Mankind from corners . . . [and] to have favourite Nations and People, without any consideration of Merit. They make him put other Nations under Disadvantage without any Demerit. And so they are more properly to be stil'd Demonists than Theists. (Anthony Collins quoted in Gay 1968, 83)

> It is unreasonable, that God should make a species of creatures capable of future bliss or torment, and that he should pre-ordain a few of that species to a state of unspeakable and eternal happiness, and the rest of them to a state of extream and eternal misery. (Chubb 1978 [1731], 24)

Some deists considered the observance of the Sabbath to rest on an equally ridiculous conception of God. "What strange notions must the bulk of mankind . . . have of the Supreme Being, when he is said to have rested and been refreshed" (Tindal 1730, 227). The doctrines of transubstantiation and the trinity are other examples of absurdities rationalists found at the very heart of revelation. The Mohammedan in Lessing's *Vindication of Hieronymus Cardanus,* for example, emphasizes the polytheistic implications of the doctrine of the trinity and thus undermines attempts to use the dichotomy between monotheism and polytheism as a way to privilege Christianity (Allison 1966, 55).

In addition to such problematic doctrines, revealed religion contained numerous practices that were as contrary to reason as any found among the heathens. The ancient Jews, for example, practiced circumcision and animal sacrifice, customs as barbaric as the rites of mutilation and sacrifices found in other religions.

> Had such notions been adher'd to concerning the divine Goodness; as the Light of Nature dictates, the Egyptians, and some other Pagan Nations cou'd never have thought that cutting off the foreskin (not to be performed without great pain & hazard) cou'd have been esteem'd a religious duty acceptable to a good & gracious God, who makes nothing in vain, much less who requires the cutting off, even with extream danger as well as anguish. . . . The Heathen World must have very gross conceptions, not only of their inferior Gods, but of the Father of Gods and Men; when they imagined him of so cruel a nature, as to be delighted with the butchering of innocent animals; and that the stench of burnt flesh should be such a sweet smelling, of savour in his nostrils, as to atone for the wickedness of Men. (Tindal 1730, 79)

Although Tindal does not mention the religion of the Jews in this passage, it is clear that it is this religion which is the object of his scorn. Ancient Judaism is one of the "other Pagan nations" that cut off the foreskin. Moreover, it is the Old Testament that describes animal sacrifice as a sweet smell to God (Gen. 8:21; Exod. 29:18; Lev. 1:9, 13, 17).

Some of reason's most strident supporters went so far as to claim that human sacrifice, a practice so common among savages, was also condoned in the religion of the ancient Hebrews. The fact that Abraham responded to God's command to sacrifice Isaac (Gen. 22) and that Jephthah sacrificed his daughter in fulfillment of a vow (Judg. 11:29–40) indicates that the notion of human sacrifice was compatible with the religion of the ancient Jews (Morgan 1738, 131–33; Tindal 1730, 83; Voltaire 1962 [1764], 325). The idea of human sacrifice was also central to the Christian doctrine that God had sacrificed his own son.

While certain practices of revelation were considered particularly absurd, the deists considered all rites problematic. Any of the practices that had been instituted by revelation and that were not derived by reason (which included all of them) were simply superstitions. "They, who believe there are things merely positive in Religion, of which Reason affords no light how they are to be perform'd . . . must lye under endless doubts and fears, and according to the measure of their superstition, be wrought upon by designing Men to hate, damn, and persecute one another about such observances; as we see is actually done every where by different sects who are so absurd as to believe a God of infinite Wisdom & Goodness can give his creatures arbitrary commands" (Tindal 1730, 101).

The various rites and ceremonies contained in revelation were not different in essence from those savage practices reported by travelers. All rites and ceremonies owed their origin to the avarice of priests who introduced such practices under the guise of revelation and thereby made themselves indispensable. " 'Tis then no wonder the number of Gods multiply'd, since the more Gods, the more Sacrifices, and the Priests had better fare" (Tindal 1730, 81; see also Herbert quoted in Gay 1968, 35).

As is now obvious, rationalists sought to replace the old dichotomy between revelation and superstition with an alternative opposition, Natural Religion versus superstition.

> It is very well known, that there is, and always have been, two sorts or species of Religion in the world. The first is the Religion of Nature, which consisting in the eternal, immutable Rules and principles of moral Truth, Righteousness or Reason, has been always the same, and must for ever be alike apprehended, by the Understandings of all Mankind, as soon as it comes to be fairly proposed and considered. But beside this, there is another sort or Species of Religion, which has been commonly call'd positive, instituted, or revealed Religion, as distinguish'd from the former. And to avoid circumlocution, I shall call this the political Religion, or the Religion of Hierarchy. (Morgan 1738, 94)

This new way of slicing the pie completely subverted the old. In this new scheme, ancient Judaism, Christianity, and paganism met one another and mutually recognized their common nature and origin. Each had a share in Natural Religion and superstition:

> What reason has a Papist, for instance, to laugh at an Indian, who thinks it contributes to his future happiness to dye with a cow's tail in his hands, while he lays as great a stress on rubbing a dying Man with oil? Has not the Indian as much right to moralize this action of his, and shew its significancy, as the Papist any of his mystick rites, or Hocus Pocus tricks? which have as little foundation in the nature or reason of things. (Tindal 1730, 112)

According to reason there were simply no grounds for a radical distinction between Judaism and Christianity, on the one hand, and the religion of the heathens or savages, on the other.

In sum, rationalists capitalized on an opportunity made possible by revelation itself. Revelation predisposed travelers and missionaries to see resemblances between ancient Judaism and savage religions. Revelation taught that all peoples were descendants of one original human ancestor. That portrayal of human history led explorers and voyagers to the conclusion that religions in the New World had degenerated from religions of antiquity. Moreover, revelation had already generated a stereotype of ancient Judaism that was equally applicable to new heathen practices. In the sixteenth century, adherents to revelation did not yet anticipate the damaging implications of assimilating the religion of the Jews to that of the savages. But not long afterwards others did. The deists and other proponents of reason realized that such correspondences presented a serious problem for many of revelation's claims. In their judgment, the similarities between the revealed religions and ancient and modern varieties of paganism indicated that revelation was but another superstition, a fabrication of priests whose intent was self-aggrandizement. Defenders of revelation responded to these arguments immediately by suggesting other ways of understanding the similarities between revelation and heathenism. It is to these defensive strategies that our attention now turns.

2.

Reviving the Opposition

Christianity, Revelation, and
Religion in Their Own Defense

After the rationalist critique of revelation, it was no longer possible, as it had been for travelers and missionaries of the seventeenth century, to ponder the similarities between Judaism and savage religions without at the same time considering the status of revelation and the truth of Christianity. The Enlightenment, then, successfully forged a link between two kinds of concerns that had previously operated more or less independently of one another. It showed how the comparative study of Judaism posed a problem for revelation and the Christian religion. The linking of these concerns explains why a comparative perspective on Judaism has so often been suppressed or minimized in the discussions of religion subsequent to the Enlightenment. As long as Christianity claimed superiority to other religious traditions, it would have to deploy a variety of defensive strategies to deny or trivialize the presence of savage elements in Judaism.

At first such tactics were used to defend Christianity's status as revelation. But the debate between revelation and reason spawned unanticipated ways of privileging Christianity. New arguments emerged that defended Christianity's supremacy even as its status as revelation was denied. Some writers claimed that of all the religious traditions, Christianity alone represented the religion of reason. However, the presence of savage elements within Judaism created a difficulty for this position as well. How could the religion of reason be based on and emerge out of superstition? Consequently, methods of trivializing the savage elements in Judaism were adopted even in those discourses that did not treat Christianity as a supernatural revelation. The comparative study of Judaism remained a problem to any scheme that posited the superiority of Christianity. Ironically, the opposition between Judaism and primitive religions became so entrenched in European thought that it continued to survive even in the works of secular writers who envisioned the ultimate decline of Christianity itself. What began as a strategy to protect revelation and Christianity actually survived in discourses that aimed at Christianity's demise.

Four types of defensive strategies were deployed during and beyond the Enlightenment to cope with the savage presence in Judaism: denial, marginalization, excision, and temporization. The strategy of denial involved claiming that the similarities between the religions of Jews and heathens were superficial and the result of a misunderstanding. Such commonalities dissolved if one truly understood the character of Judaism. While the strategy of marginalization acknowledged the presence of savage elements in Judaism, it defused their potentially damaging implications by denying that those elements were part of Judaism's essence. Rather, such practices and beliefs were regarded as necessary evils that enabled true Judaism to survive in its pagan environment.

Excision and temporization were variations on the tactic of marginalization. Excision involved treating the offending practice as contaminations from some neighboring pagan culture. In its most radical form, excision involved severing the relationship between Judaism and Christianity entirely. Finally, the strategy of temporization trivialized the primitive aspects of Judaism by placing them within a developmental framework. According to this view, the savage elements within Judaism represented survivals of a primitive stage of religious development that by and large had been overcome. In general, those writers who defended Christianity's status as revelation commonly deployed the strategies of denial and marginalization. Those who privileged Christianity on other grounds typically relied on the tactics of excision and temporization.

The Strategy of Denial

In responding to the rationalist critique, defenders of revelation argued that the resemblances between Judaism and savage religions were superficial and consequently meaningless. According to this argument, the deists had committed "the fallacy of the panda's thumb." They had mistaken a similarity of form for an identity of substance. But formal similarities are often misleading. On the surface, a panda appears to have a thumb that performs some of the same functions as the human thumb. But investigation shows that in fact the panda's thumb derives from a completely different bone in the panda's paw and therefore is not anatomically speaking a finger (Gould 1982, 21–24). It may look like a thumb and serve some of the same functions, but it is not a true thumb at all. Rationalists had been similarly misled by formal similarities. To be sure, the appeals of heathen priests to ancient revelations, miracles, and prophecies appeared similar to Judeo-Christian claims. But in fact there was a fundamental difference. Only the miracles, revelation, and prophecies of Judaism and Christianity were from God. Those of other religions represented impostures of various kinds.

Substantive and formal differences made tenable the distinction between true religion and false imitations. To put it in Enlightenment vocabulary, Judaism and Christianity alone had the "internal" and "external" marks to establish them as truly revealed. "Internal" marks referred to the substantive content of revelation, while "external" marks referred to signs such as miracles and prophecies which verified the truth of the tradition.

Some defenders of revelation argued that the substantive content of the Old and New Testaments demonstrated their superiority to other traditions. Revelation "will indeed have this general internal mark to distinguish it from all false religions, that the wise and beneficent design of its author will plainly appear in the whole frame of it, and that even its peculiar principles will stand the test of reason" (Foster 1731, 168–69; see also Conybeare 1732, 432).

The substance of the Judeo-Christian revelation was sufficient to prove that the various miracles reported by the tradition were real miracles. Since miracles of other religions supported beliefs and practices that were not worthy of God, such miracles were lies and fabrications. "For it is a plain Distinction betwixt the miracles of Christ, and those pretended wonders of Imposters, that Christ's were to reestablish the Law of Reason . . . while those of Imposters are only to promote Doctrines and Superstitions either destructive of that End, or not at all availing to it" (Gildon 1976 [1705], 286; see also Foster 1731, 49). Other writers argued that true and false miracles can be distinguished without recourse to the substantive claims of religious traditions. By this view, certain formal criteria or external marks verify the historical truth of Judaism's and Christianity's miracles. Once the miracles are certified, they in turn confirm the divine origin of the tradition to which they are connected.

Charles Leslie in his *Short and Easy Method with the Deists* (1828 [1723], 7) argues that a miracle can be regarded as true if four criteria obtain: 1) the miracle involves matters of fact that people may judge by their senses of sight and hearing, 2) it was done publicly, 3) public monuments and observances were established in memory of the event, and 4) such monuments and observances were established immediately after the event in question. According to Leslie (1828 [1723], 5), "all these rules do meet in the matters of fact of Moses and of Christ and . . . they do not meet in the matters of fact of Mahomet, and the heathen deities, or can possibly meet in any imposture whatsoever." Consequently, the substantive claims of Moses must be true, "for his miracles, if true, do vouch the truth of what he delivered."

Other writers did not feel as confident in the human ability to distinguish true and false miracles. Sykes, for example, argues that a miracle can be certified as true only if accompanied by prophecies that are subsequently verified.

> So much Fiction has obtained in the world, partly through Superstition and Folly, and partly through pious Frauds, that it is very hard to produce evidence for real

Miracles, which will not be baffled and confounded by counter Evidence that may
be produced for fictitious ones. . . . [the] ten thousand [miracles] . . . at Home as
well as abroad are gravely and seriously related, and with such Circumstances,
that it will be very hard to distinguish betwixt the Evidence for Miracles really and
truly done, and those pretended to be done by these sanctified Cheats. However,
let it be hard as you please to distinguish, when nothing further is considered than
the bare miracle; yet when we take in the circumstance of prophecy, This alone
will easily distinguish the cases. (Sykes 1740, 204)

For this reason, Sykes (1740, 203) feels confident that the miracles performed
by Moses were real miracles and not impostures, since "the Events which he
foretold actually coming to pass, are a strong Evidence to us, that the Miracles which he is said to have performed are true."

The medium in which a tradition is preserved serves as another test of
its credibility. Written traditions by definition are more trustworthy than
oral ones.

Indeed, there is a great difference between oral tradition, and written. Things
which depend entirely on the former may be more easily corrupted, or lost; facts
may lose some of their most material circumstances, or be greatly exaggerated;
and 'tis hardly possible, that doctrines should be exactly remember'd, and
transmitted down as they were taught at first. (Foster 1731, 94; see also Sykes
1740, 208)

The difference between oral and written traditions thus becomes a sign of
the difference between truth and falsehood and between revelation and
superstition.

Many writers adopted a combination of formal and substantive arguments to differentiate revelation from its impostors. John Locke, for example, argues on substantive grounds that only Judaism, Christianity, and
Islam can be considered as candidates for true revelation. But of these three
only Judaism and Christianity have the formal requisites to establish them
as truth. These two religions, moreover, mutually confirm the truth of each
other.

Of such who have come in the name of the one only true God, professing to
bring a law from him, we have in history a clear account but of three, viz. Moses
Jesus and Mahomet. For what the Persees say of their Zoroaster, or the Indians
of their Brama . . . is so obscure, or so manifestly fabulous that no account can
be made of it. Now of the three before-mentioned, Mahomet having none to
produce, pretends to no miracles, for the vouching of his mission; so that the
only revelations that come attested by miracles, being only those of Moses and
Christ, and they confirming each other, the business of miracles, as it stands
really in matters of fact, has no manner of difficulty in it, and I think the most
scrupulous or sceptical cannot from miracles raise the least doubt against the
divine revelation of the gospel. (Locke 1967 [1706], 81)

As these quotations suggest, the devotees of revelation insisted that the difference between the Judeo-Christian tradition and other religions could and
should be coordinated with the opposition between religion and superstition, between morality and debauchery, and between historical reliability and
imaginative fabrication. All of these oppositions, moreover, are coordinated
with the one grand difference: divine truth and human error.

The linking of these various oppositions enabled believers in revelation to
deny the similarities between the "positive duties" of ancient Judaism and
savage religions. Some thinkers, for example, argued that the character of a
given practice is defined by the religious tradition in which it is embedded.
What constitutes a superstition in paganism is within the context of Judaism
a moral act. Consequently, even though a pagan and Jewish practice are out-
wardly identical, they are fundamentally different.

> The only charge, which remains against positive duties, is the charge of supersti-
> tion. Now in order to set this manner in a clear light, and shew that there is no
> foundation for such a charge, I would observe the following things . . . that
> what might justly be esteem'd superstition, if men were left to the direction of
> the light of nature only, will lose that character if God interposes, and by an
> express revelation enjoins the practice of it. . . . So that the manner of doing a
> thing, tho in itself absolutely indifferent, may be made a part of men's religious
> obligations by the great govenor of the world, consistently with his most perfect
> wisdom and goodness; which, if they themselves took upon them to fix it as a
> law binding conscience, would be weak and superstitious. If therefore we are
> convinced, that a command of this sort, which has been shewn to be worthy of
> God, is actually given by him; the yielding obedance to it is so far from being
> superstition, that it is a branch even of our moral duty. (Foster 1731, 289–90)

Similarities between ancient Judaism and other religions are not real commonalities at all. They appear as resemblances only from a mistaken point of
view. From the right perspective, ancient Judaism and savage religions are
categorically different.

Not all defenders of revelation, however, were satisfied with the attempt to
deny the commonalities between ancient Judaism and heathen religions. For
some, the similarities were simply too striking to dismiss out of hand. Moreover, the strategy of denial actually created a difficulty for the status of Christianity. Before the rationalist attack on revelation, the religion of Moses had
been treated as an outdated and primitive form of revelation which the Christian revelation had superseded. Christian thinkers had treated as primitive
precisely the traits in Judaism that it turned out to share with savage religions.
But if Judaism's practices were not primitive, as the defenders of revelation
now insisted, on what grounds could Christianity be treated as superior to
Judaism? Alternatively, if Judaism was inferior to Christianity because of its
many peculiar positive duties, on what grounds could Judaism be privileged
over primitive religions?

This tension is evident, for example, in Foster's reflections on the Mosaic ceremonial practices. Foster argues that Christianity is a superior religious form because of the minimal number of positive duties that it enjoins. In Foster's judgment, too many positive duties focus attention away from one's moral duties. But ·

> does not the observation which has been made reflect [negatively] on the Mosaic institution, in the same proportion as it does honour to the Christian? If it be a circumstance very much in favour of the latter, must it not be a great prejudice against the former, which was a law abounding in ceremonies, and ritual observances? I answer, that it undoubtedly proves the superiour excellence of the Christian religion; but, I apprehend, will not conclude what the adversaries of revelation would infer from it, viz, that the law of Moses was not of divine original. (Foster 1731, 304–5)

In other words, Christianity seemed to rest its own claim of superiority on the notion that Judaism was primitive, yet defend the idea of revelation by denying the primitive character of the Jewish religion. The defense of revelation in these terms thus either threatened the privileged position of Christianity or the revealed status of Judaism. For this reason, some defenders of revelation preferred the strategy of marginalization, which trivialized the primitive aspects of Judaism without undermining the status of Christianity.

The Strategy of Marginalization

Some admirers of revelation acknowledged the presence of primitive practices in ancient Judaism. But they did not conclude, as had the advocates of reason, that human cheats and impostors had introduced these rites and duties into the Mosaic legislation. Nor did the presence of such unreasonable elements in ancient Judaism undermine their confidence in the perfection of God's revelation. On the contrary, the presence of primitive practices actually testified to divine wisdom and foresight. God realized that without duties and rites of their own, the Jews would have been seduced by the heathen practices around them and would have forgotten the fundamental moral and theological principles contained in their revelation. Consequently, God gave the Jews their own innocuous practices so that they would remain a distinctive people and thereby preserve the essence of revelation, namely, the distinctive conception of the one God and the corresponding moral duties.

> There are circumstances supposeable, in which even a ceremonious religion may answer very valuable purposes. And this I take to have been the case with respect to the Jewish rites. And, I think, there will be no great difficulty in proving this, if we consider how the Jews were circumstanc'd. A people who had been strongly prejudic'd in favour of idolatrous and superstitious customs by

living in Egypt; in those early ages of the world the most famous seat and nur-
sery of superstition; who affected a religion of pomp and ceremony; were in-
compassed on all sides by idolaters; and appear to have been inclin'd, upon all
occasions, to fall in with the idolatry of the neighboring nations: a people, I say,
so situated and disposed, would probably have kept no order, if their national
weakness and prejudices had not been in some measure indulg'd. And the best
security against their joining in the idolatrous rites that prevail'd all around 'em
and renouncing the worship of the true God, was to divest them, by giving them
innocent ceremonies of their own. . . . In like manner those rites which were
design'd to hinder their free commerce with other nations, and imitating the
customs and usages among them especially, which had any relation to their superstition. (Foster 1731, 304–5, 300)

This argument marginalized the primitive practices of ancient Judaism by
treating them as a contingent means to a universal end. In this case, the similarity between a Jewish practice and a heathen one could be recognized by
treating it as outside of Judaism's (i.e., revelation's) essence. Whatever believers in revelation felt comfortable excluding from the core of Judaism could
potentially be assimilated to heathen practices. But what they could not exclude from the essence of Judaism, because it also appeared in Christianity or
served as a foundation for Christianity, would have to be opposed to paganism. The substantive content of the Jewish revelation thus diminished in pro-
portion to the increase in Judaism's savagery.

It is now possible to understand how the marginalization of offending
practices solved the difficulties generated by the strategy of denial. The writers who marginalized heathen aspects of Judaism had no difficulty explaining
why the Mosaic religion was inferior to Christianity yet superior to other religions. The essence of Judaism, namely, the emphasis on moral duties and a
correct understanding of the one God, made this religion better than paganism. But since God had to capitulate to the circumstances of the Jews by giving them ceremonies, this revelation still required improvement, a condition
realized only with the revelation of Christ.

Nonetheless, the strategy of marginalization generated its own distinctive
problems. Among other things, there was always the danger that the
marginalization of a given practice in Judaism would undermine the Christian revelation as well. The Hebrew practice of sacrifice is a case in point. On
the one hand, this practice certainly appears barbaric and crude and has parallels in the practices of savages. On the other hand, the Christian revelation is
itself premised on the idea that God sacrificed a son as expiation for the
world. If sacrifice is excluded from the core of the Jewish revelation, it seems
to follow that the idea of sacrifice will have to be treated as marginal in the
Christian revelation as well. The recognition of savagery on the margins of
Jewish revelation thus had ramifications for the conceptualization of Christianity. The more a defender of Christianity became convinced of the basic
parallel between ancient Judaism and paganism, the more problematic the

connection between Judaism and Christianity appeared. As a result, some writers felt compelled to rid Christianity of its "Judaical" elements.

The Strategy of Excision

The strategy of excision was a radical version of marginalization. The problem of Judaism's apparent barbarism was solved by completely severing the relationship between Judaism and Christianity. According to this view, the essence of Christianity had nothing in common with the religion of the Jews, which was no better (and may even have been worse) than other pagan religions of antiquity and the present. The recognition of commonalities between ancient Judaism and heathenism required a denial of any significant relationship between Judaism and Christianity.

If the strategies of denial and marginalization were used primarily by the defenders of revelation, the tactic of excision was developed and refined by the Christian deists. The Christian deists occupied an intermediate position between the secular deists discussed in the previous chapter and Christian defenders of revelation discussed above. Like the former, the Christian deists were skeptical about the possibility of and need for revelation. They believed that since reason could provide access to the Religion of Nature, revelation was superfluous. But the Christian deists did not follow their secular counterparts in concluding that Christianity was simply one more religion developed by priestly cheats and impostors. On the contrary, like the Christian defenders of revelation, they believed that Christianity was superior to all other religious forms. Indeed, they insisted that the religion established by Jesus was the Religion of Nature. Although other religions occasionally glimpsed aspects of this reasonable religion, Christianity alone was synonymous with it.

Thomas Morgan, for example, takes Christianity to be "that most complete and perfect scheme of moral Truth and Righteousness; which was first preach'd to the world by Christ, and his apostles, and from them convey'd down to us."[1] He also considers it "as certain, that every Doctrine which supposes the absolute necessity of moral Truth and Righteousness, and of nothing else in order to Happiness, is from God, and bears the stamp of divine authority. But any Doctrine which will not stand this Test, can be no part of True Religion, or real Christianity" (Morgan 1738, 95–96, 200).

From the standpoint of the century beyond the Enlightenment, the compromise achieved by the Christian deists was more important than either the position of the secular deists or the defenders of revelation. The Christian deists showed committed Christian thinkers that Christianity's supremacy could be maintained even as its status as revelation (traditionally conceived) was denied. In the nineteenth century, this sort of compromise would be made over and over again, especially in the works of Protestant thinkers. Ironically, then, rationalists both won and lost the debate with revelation's defenders. They won in that they created a discourse in which the traditional conception of revelation no longer played an important role. But they lost because that same discourse found other ways of privileging Christianity (Gay 1968, 10).

In identifying Christianity with the Religion of Nature, the Christian deists, like the defenders of revelation, had to account for the seemingly primitive side of the Jewish religion. How could the religion of reason be based on superstition? The strategy of excision solved this difficulty. By denying any significant relationship between Christianity and Judaism, these thinkers could discount the heathen aspects of the Mosaic religion. Morgan, for example, regards the law of Moses as "having neither truth nor goodness in it and as a wretched scheme of superstition, blindness, and slavery, contrary to all reason and common sense, set up under the specious popular pretence of a divine instruction and revelation from God" (quoted in Leland 1798, 186). The Jews, Morgan argues, absorbed many crude practices from Egypt, "the mother of superstition," and were "egyptianiz'd" during the period of slavery. In particular, the leaders of the Jews, such as Joseph and Moses, introduced many Egyptian practices into the Jewish religion. Indeed, Joseph had actually been an Egyptian priest (Morgan 1738, 247, 240–42).

In recognizing the commonalities between Judaism and heathenism, the Christian deists initially followed the secular deists. But they broke with their secular counterparts in treating such commonalities as evidence of Judaism's inferiority to Christianity rather than as weapons to undermine the Christian revelation. Moreover, by severing the connection between the essence of Christianity and the Jewish religion, Christian deists were also able to explain away the unreasonable elements within Christianity.

It was the Jews who were directly or indirectly responsible for the presence of irrational ceremonies in Christianity. Since Jesus brought his mission to a backward people, he had to package the religion of reason in such a way that this people would accept it. The eucharist and baptism, for example, were simply means to this end. Since the Jews customarily partook of biscuits and wine, Jesus gave this custom a symbolic interpretation. He told the Jewish proselytes that in the future this act should serve as a reminder of his mission. But "when the clergy had once got it into their Hands they soon made a Mystery, and afterward a Contradiction of it." Christ baptized Jewish proselytes because the Jews already understood this practice. But "Christ only intended [these ceremonies for] those who at first proselyted to Christianity not their descendants." Similarly, the idea of the crucifixion was based on a mistaken understanding of Christ's death. Christ simply died as a martyr for the religion of reason. But St. Paul told the Jews that Christ was sacrificed because they were committed to the doctrine of sacrifice. For this reason, Morgan took it as his task to "clear St. Paul from the Imputations of Judaism, and Christianity itself from the dead weight of that most gross and carnal Institution which has hitherto been laid upon it" (Morgan 1738, 107, 104–5,

163, 142). Those Christians who refused to de-judaize Christianity by rejecting baptism, the eucharist, and the idea of Christ's sacrifice, were therefore to
be regarded as "Jewish Christians" in contrast to proper Christians, who were
"deistical."

The strategy of excision was also employed by Kant in his *Religion within
the Limits of Reason Alone* (1794). Religion, Kant argues, must postulate a
deity who makes moral demands of human beings. Of all the historical faiths,
Christianity comes closest to achieving this ideal. But Judaism, in Kant's
view, does not qualify as a religion because its deity expects only outward
observance and makes no requirement upon the moral disposition of the individual. For this reason, Kant feels it necessary to sever all ties between Christianity and Judaism. "And first of all it is evident that the Jewish faith stands
in no essential connection whatever, i.e., in no unity of concepts, with this
ecclesiastical faith whose history we wish to consider, though the Jewish immediately preceded this (the Christian) church and provided the physical occasion for its establishment" (Kant 1960 [1794], 116). According to Kant,
earlier teachers emphasized the connection between Christianity and Judaism
to solve a practical problem. Their problem "was merely the discovery of the
most suitable means of introducing a purely moral religion in place of the old
worship, to which the people were all too well habituated, without directly
offending the people's prejudices" (Kant 1960 [1794], 118).

In its most radical formulation, the strategy of excision took the form of
making the history of religion irrelevant to Christianity. This position is
adopted, for example, by the mature Lessing. In his later writings, Lessing
suspects that in his haste as a young deist to reject the superstitious parts of
Christianity, he also rejected something of importance. "Still, it is not since
yesterday that I have been concerned that while discarding certain prejudices,
I might have thrown away a little too much, which I shall have to retrieve. It is
only the fear of dragging all the rubbish back into my house which has so far
hindered me from doing this" (Allison 1966, 81–82). The rejection of history
solves this problem for Lessing. Nothing the historian may discover about the
events in the first century or the character of Christianity at that time can
possibly affect the truth of Christianity.

> With me the Christian religion remains the same; it is only that I want to sepa-
> rate religion from the history of religion. It is only that I refuse to regard the
> historical knowledge of its origin and development, and a conviction of this
> knowledge; which positively no historical truth can yield, as indispensable. It is
> only that I consider objections against the history of religion irrelevant whether
> they can be answered or not. (Allison 1966, 119)

History is irrelevant because Christianity possesses an inner truth that is perceived by the believer, a truth that can be appreciated independently of any
historical claims that are made on behalf of religion. By making the historical

character of Christianity irrelevant to Christian truth, Lessing found a way to accommodate the radical deist critique of Christianity and Judaism without giving up his commitment to Christian truths (Allison 1966, 103). No matter how barbaric the historical forms of Judaism and early Christianity, one could continue to affirm the actual content of these religions.

These attempts to sever the essence of Christianity, first from Judaism and then from history itself, confirm one of the basic contentions of this archaeological investigation. As long as Judaism remains entangled in discourse on Christianity a comparative perspective on ancient Judaism is problematic. When the connection between these two religions is broken and the character of Judaism has no implications for the status of Christianity, the commonalities between Judaism and savage religions can be tolerated. Under these conditions, even the interpreter who remains committed to the positive evaluation of Christianity is able to acknowledge the savage elements within Judaism.

But for obvious reasons, most eighteenth- and nineteenth-century writers did not find the strategy of excision persuasive. If Christianity has no fundamental tie to Judaism then substantial parts of the New Testament have to be disregarded. After all, the New Testament incessantly cites the Old Testament to support various claims. Moreover, the attempt to dissociate the two religions requires a radical reconceptualization of Christianity itself. The Christianity that remains after all the "Judaical" elements are removed does not seem to be Christianity any more. As the "Jewish Christian" puts it in Thomas Morgan's *Moral Philosopher* (1738, 144), "When you have thrown the Jewish Legislator [Moses] out of your System, I doubt the Christian apostle will have no Reason to expect a much better fate." In the eyes of many Christian thinkers, the attempt to separate the two religions seemed to have disastrous consequences for Christianity itself. For better or worse, Christianity was stuck with Judaism.

When in the late eighteenth century Jewish writers were eventually permitted to join the European discussion of religion, they capitalized on the widely accepted connection between Judaism and Christianity. Moses Mendelssohn, for example, bluntly reminds one of his Christian critics that the fate of Judaism and Christianity are inextricably linked with one another. The critic in question had written an anonymous brochure claiming that Mendelssohn was acting inconsistently in remaining a Jew. If Mendelssohn wanted to embrace the religion of reason, as he claimed he did, should he not give up Judaism and convert to Christianity which had been "purified of the onerous statutes of the rabbis and augmented by new elements" (Altman 1983, 9)? Mendelssohn retorts:

[M]y dear sir, shall I take this step [of conversion to Christianity] without first deliberating whether it will indeed extricate me from the confusion in which you think I find myself? If it be true that the corner stones of my house are dislodged, and the structure threatens to collapse, do I act wisely if I remove my belongings from the lower to the upper floor for safety? Am I more secure there? Now Christianity, as you know, is built upon Judaism, and if the latter falls, it must necessarily collapse with it into one heap of reasons. You say that my conclusion undermines the foundation of Judaism, and you offer me the safety of your upper floor; must I not suppose that you mock me? Surely, the Christian who is in earnest about light and truth will not challenge the Jew to a fight when there seems to be a contradiction between truth and truth, between Scripture and reason. He will rather join him in an effort to discover the groundlessness of the contradiction. For this is their common concern. Whatever else they have to settle between themselves may be postponed to a later time. For the present, they must join forces to avert the danger. (Mendelssohn 1983 [1783], 87)

And join forces they did. Once Jewish writers began to produce discourse on religion they adopted the same sorts of strategies to privilege Judaism as Christian thinkers had adopted to protect Christianity. Combining the argument of the Christian deists with the classic conception of revelation, Mendelssohn argued that Judaism was both a religion of reason and a divinely revealed legislation that had never been abrogated (Altman 1983). But this defense of Judaism proved problematic almost immediately. It provided the basis for Kant's argument that Judaism did not qualify as a religion since its deity commanded outward observance, a conception of God that contradicted a religion of reason. Mendelssohn's disciples responded to Kant's criticism by endeavoring to show that the God of Judaism was purely an ethical God and that the outward observances were secondary accretions to the core (Graupe 1978, 113–22, 137–64; Schorsch 1975, 12–15). In this way, the strategies used to protect Christianity were appropriated by Jewish thinkers and remained an important way of explaining the primitive elements of Judaism among proponents of Jewish Reform and advocates of *Wissenschaft des Judentums* (Science of Judaism) throughout the nineteenth and into the twentieth century.

It was thus in the interest of both Christians and Jews to show that Judaism was not just one more form of paganism but had a share in the religion of reason. Christian and Jewish thinkers of course disagreed about how reasonable Judaism was. But they did come to an agreement that Judaism should be treated as more reasonable than most other religions. For this very reason, the Jewish contribution did little to change the tenor of the discussion. On the contrary, the emergent Jewish voice actually encouraged the Christian impulse to differentiate Judaism from other kinds of religions. For understandable political reasons, Jewish thinkers needed to privilege Judaism over other religions. But in mimicking their oppressors, Jewish thinkers inadvertently ended up collaborating with them. They confirmed the Christian view that Judaism was superior to other kinds of religious traditions and thus unwittingly contributed to the cause of committed Christians.

In sum, the strategy of excision solved the problem of the savage elements in Judaism. But it did so at a cost that was too great for most defenders of Christianity. Consequently, it did not become a widely accepted means of dealing with the savage side of Judaism. The most successful strategy for marginalizing the savage in Judaism appeared in the late eighteenth and early nineteenth centuries and dominated discourse on religion until well into the twentieth century. I am referring to the evolutionary perspective that placed religious phenomena along a temporal continuum. An evolutionary perspective solved all the problems that were inherent in the other strategies discussed above. As long as it dominated discourse, the savage aspects of Judaism posed no difficulty at all.

Temporization of Religion

The idea that religion developed gradually in a unilinear fashion from an immature to a mature form emerged late in the Enlightenment discussion of religion. Once articulated, however, this developmental perspective became the dominant framework for more than a century. From this perspective, the history of religions becomes a narrative of the development of an ideal form of religion. The known forms of religion reveal a progressive movement from primitive religion to a religion of reason. By most nineteenth-century accounts, Christianity defines the culmination of religious development and thus is identical with Absolute Religion. Ancient Judaism at best represents a distant runner-up and other religions fall somewhere nearer the other end of the spectrum. The evolutionary perspective thus converts the categorical difference between ancient Judaism and primitive religions into a temporal distance.

Although the evolutionary view of religions would eventually serve an apologetic purpose, its articulation was actually made possible by the rationalist attack on revelation. Until the traditional idea of revelation was abandoned, a developmental perspective on religion was inconceivable. In the traditional conception of revelation, truth was regarded as the result of a sudden intervention of God into human history. As long as truth came from outside history, the history of religions and the history of truth remained independent stories. Moreover, the evolutionary perspective reversed the scheme of religious development postulated by revelation. According to Scripture, the first human being was a monotheist, implying that the various superstitions that eventually developed were degenerated forms of original monotheism. Left to their own devices humans became progressively more immersed in polytheism and other superstitions.[2]

In rendering the traditional view of revelation problematic, the deists made possible the idea that religion had a "natural" history. But most deists, like the defenders of religion, thought that degeneration rather than evolution dominated the history of religions. The deists believed that the first human had access to all the insights of the Religion of Nature, which, as Tindal puts it, is "as old as creation." All historical forms of religion including Judaism and Christianity represented corrupted versions of this original and pure monotheism.

David Hume was one of the first to espouse a developmental perspective on religion.[3] In his *Natural History of Religion,* Hume challenges the traditional view that monotheism preceded polytheism.

> It appears to me, that, if we consider the improvement of human society, from rude beginnings to a state of greater perfection, polytheism or idolatry was, and necessarily must have been, the first and most ancient religion of mankind. . . . As far as writing or history reaches, mankind, in ancient times, appears universally to have been polytheists. Shall we assert, that, in more ancient times, before the knowledge of letters, or the discovery of any art of science, men entertained the principles of pure theism? That is, while they were ignorant and barbarous, they discovered truth: But fell into error, as soon as they acquired learning and politeness.
>
> But in this assertion you not only contradict all appearance of probability, but also our present experience concerning the principle and opinions of barbarous nations. The savage tribes of AMERICA, AFRICA, and ASIA are all idolaters. (Hume 1956 [1757], 23)

Hume goes on to suggest that polytheism represents the first human attempt to account for the vagaries of human existence.

> In short, the conduct of events, or what we call the plan of a particular providence, is so full of variety and uncertainty, that, if we suppose it immediately ordered by any intelligent being, we must acknowledge a contrariety in their designs and intentions, a constant combat of opposite powers. . . . We may conclude, therefore, that, in all nations which have embraced polytheism, the first idea of religion arose not from a contemplation of the works of nature, but from a concern with regard to the events of life, and from the incessant hopes and fears, which actuate the human mind. (1956 [1757], 27)

This account did more than reverse the longstanding assumption that monotheism preceded polytheism. It also challenged the rationalist belief that monotheism is the inevitable product of the mind's contemplation of the natural order. In Hume's view, the natural human response is to perceive disorder, which in turn generates polytheism, the belief that conflicting forces govern the world. Monotheism arose when one of the various gods that people recognized became the particular object of worship and respect. Modeling heaven on the organization of human society, people promoted this one god to the supreme position. As human fears became more urgent, people found greater and greater epithets of praise until they reached infinity itself. In this way, the one perfect God was born (Hume 1956 [1757], 42–43).

Hume's natural history of religion thus represented an attack on both the traditional Christian and the rationalist understanding of religion's develop-ment (Manuel 1959, 171). Monotheism was neither the gift of revelation nor the product of reason, but simply the result of a natural historical develop-ment in religious consciousness.

Hume could not possibly have realized that an evolutionary scheme was ideally suited to that new breed of thinker, the nonorthodox Christian apolo-gist, who would renounce the traditional conception of revelation but up-hold the superiority of Christianity. Yet in looking back on the evolutionary perspective over a century later, Ernst Troeltsch would conclude that "the evolutionary apologetic is closely related, in its motive and goal, to the apolo-getic of supernatural orthodox theology" (1971 [1901], 51). It is easy to see why so many committed Christians of the nineteenth century found tempo-ral schemes useful for organizing their discussion of religions. A three-tiered scheme naturally emerged whenever Christianity, Judaism, and primitive reli-gions were discussed together. Those thinkers who admired Christianity as-sumed that Christianity had superseded ancient Judaism. Yet these same interpreters were not willing to collapse Judaism and primitive religions into a single category because the validity of Christianity required a respectful stance toward the Old Testament. Consequently, Judaism had to be placed in a position superior to savage religions. An evolutionary perspective thus pro-vided a compelling way of justifying Judaism's inferiority to Christianity while simultaneously maintaining its superiority to other religions. A devel-opmental framework also explained away and trivialized the presence of bar-baric elements in ancient Judaism. Since Judaism had developed from a more primitive religious form, it had not entirely purged itself of its backward ele-ments. But the presence of such survivals in Judaism did not detract from the significant advance in religious consciousness that was evident in the Jewish religion.

These tendencies, which were already latent in Hume's evolutionary frame-work, became quite pronounced in the writings of major nineteenth-century Protestant thinkers. Consider, for example, the way that Judaism serves a me-diating role between primitive and Absolute Religion in Hegel's philosophi-cal-historical account of religion's development. According to Hegel, religions can be classified into three distinct categories which are temporally related: 1) religions of nature 2) religions of spiritual individuality, and 3) Absolute Religion. Hegel places Judaism at the second stage. The distinctive characteristic of this stage is the emergence of a separation between spirit and nature. God is a transcendent being who is beyond and outside the natural world. Nature and humanity are thus dependent on but separate from spirit.

Hegel argues that this level of religious development is superior to the reli-gion of nature, the prior stage of religious development. Since religions of nature recognize no distinction between God and some aspect of the material world, spirit and substance at this stage are inseparable. For this reason, the human individual as an independent consciousness does not exist. Hegel identifies this stage with African peoples, Mongols, and Chinese. Eventually, spirit is separated from the material world. But at first it is conceived of as simply a supreme power devoid of content or purpose. This religious form, which Hegel identifies with Oriental religions such as Hinduism and Buddhism, also lacks real spirituality because spirit itself has no consciousness.

Judaism, among other religions, represents a significant development beyond natural religion since it posits a spirit with a consciousness who acts with purpose and will. In taking this step, Judaism makes possible and celebrates the emergence of human freedom. Since spirit is conceived of as having a will, this aspect of the human being also assumes positive significance and individuals now have intrinsic significance of their own.

But Judaism is only one step beyond natural religion and as such does not actually achieve Absolute Religion. The liability inherent in Judaism is precisely its tendency to place God completely outside the natural order. Spirit is so sublime that the world, both human and natural, becomes insignificant. Moreover, the Jewish God is a being who demands compliance with the divine law and one who invokes fear and a permanent anxiety about sin. For these reasons, Judaism is inferior to other religious forms, most notably Christianity, which Hegel identifies with Absolute Religion.

Christianity deserves this status because it recognizes both universal spirit and the particular spirit, but at the same time realizes that they are inseparably joined. Consequently, Christianity represents the culmination of the development of religion. It incorporates the contribution of the Jews who gave spirit consciousness but it dialectically overcomes the chasm between the universal and individual spirit that was posited in the Jewish religion. Since Christianity alone represents the ideal of religion, it alone can be described as revealed (Reardon 1977, 38–76; Rotenstreich 1953).

This condensation of Hegel's philosophy of religions shows how the evolutionary perspective reconciled the primitive dimensions of ancient Judaism with Christianity's emergence out of that tradition. Although I have cited Hegel's work, similar approaches can be found in the leading Protestant thinkers of the nineteenth century (Reardon 1985; Tillich 1974; Welch 1972). Although each of these thinkers had a different conception of the ideal religion, each discovered that ideal in Christianity and found that Judaism represented a development toward the achievement of that form. Not surprisingly, nineteenth-century Jewish thinkers, such as the Reformers and proponents of *Wissenschaft des Judentums,* also found the evolutionary framework useful in conceptualizing Judaism (Graupe 1978, 137–65; Katz 1980, 63–64; Schorsch 1975, 12–15).

The temporization of religions had a number of advantages over the earlier strategies for dealing with the primitiveness of ancient Judaism. Those who adopted this perspective no longer had to deny the similarities between ancient Judaism and paganism as some defenders of revelation had done. These were now treated as survivals of a religious stage that Judaism had superseded. Nor did advocates of an evolutionary framework find themselves in the impossible situation of trying to deny the historical indebtedness of Christianity to its Jewish roots. On the contrary, they recognized Judaism as one of the necessary preconditions for the emergence of Christianity. This scheme thus enabled Christian thinkers to uphold the supremacy of Christianity while at the same time acknowledging the similarities between ancient Judaism and heathenism as well as Christianity's historical debt to the Jewish religion.

In this way, the evolutionary perspective finally neutralized one of the strongest weapons of the secular Enlightenment. Within this framework, Christianity was no longer embarrassed by similarities discovered between ancient Judaism and neighboring pagan religions. On the contrary, commonalities between the Jewish religion and other religions of antiquity were to be expected. Such similarities actually confirmed the basic assumption that religions underwent a process of evolution. Like all religions, Judaism retained traces of earlier stages in its development, which had since been transcended. In the very process of acknowledging these elements, therefore, the developmental perspective managed to trivialize and marginalize them as survivals from Judaism's past history. These primitive elements were less interesting and important than those aspects of Judaism that inaugurated a new stage of religious development.

The developmental theory of religion so captured the imagination of European thinkers that even those who envisioned the demise of religion posited an evolutionary sequence that treated Judaism as a mediation between primitive religions and Christianity, the pinnacle of religious development. Feuerbach's philosophy is a case in point.

For Feuerbach, religion is a fantasy, "a form of wishing—the expression of a lack or need and an attempt (in the imagination) to overcome that lack or need" (Kamenka 1970, 4). In other words, people seek in heaven what they cannot find on earth. "In every wish we find concealed a god; but in or behind every god there lies concealed nothing but a wish" (Kamenka 1970, 43). The problem with religion is that once human characteristics are deified, they are treated as if they have an independent existence and consequently are denied as human characteristics. In this way, religion alienates humanity from itself. The end of religion will be the discovery that everything that has been worshipped as divine is in fact human. When this happens, humanity will recognize that it is only the human species that it relies upon and values.

Given these views, Feuerbach considers monotheism superior to polytheism. In the polytheistic stage, people worship humanity only indirectly by making concrete objects of human needs into gods. But in monotheism, the human is worshiped directly in the form of a Divine Person. Christianity and Judaism, therefore, are developmentally superior to other religious forms. But Christianity comes closer than Judaism to achieving the ultimate goal of religion, which is the disclosure that religion is nothing more than the deification of the human species in general. The idea of the incarnation, the idea that God became human, is tantamount to the realization that God is human. Christianity is superior to Judaism because in the latter, "every tendency of man, however natural—even the impulse to cleanliness, is conceived by the Israelites as positive divine ordinance. . . . The Christian religion, on the other hand, in all these external things made man dependent on himself, i.e., placed in man what the Israelite placed out of himself in God" (Feuerbach 1959 [1841], 50, 31–32).

Although Feuerbach envisions a society without religion, he nonetheless accepts the evolutionary schema that treats Judaism as a mediation between primitive religions and Christianity. This was also the case of other secular thinkers of the nineteenth century who were less directly influenced by Hegel. For example, Comte, a precursor of the discipline of sociology, also accepts this developmental scheme uncritically. Comte imagines an evolutionary process that culminates in a religion of humanity. Christianity represents the apex of monotheistic development, a stage that is itself crucial for the development of positivism (Reardon 1985, 224).

As discussed in the Introduction, these evolutionary assumptions had a great deal to do with the emergence of anthropology as a distinctive discipline. The desire to understand the origin of religion and culture generated an interest in contemporary primitive societies, which were regarded as living fossils from the human past. Even after these evolutionary assumptions were repudiated, anthropology remained the disciplinary locus for the study of primitive religions. Judaism, for its part, fell outside the purview of anthropologists. As a higher religion, its study belonged to historians, philologists, and theologians. In this way, the antinomy between Judaism and primitive religions was institutionalized, thereby perpetuating this opposition even after the intellectual assumptions on which it originally had been based were called in question.

I have traced the emergence of the opposition between ancient Judaism and primitive religions from the seventeenth into the nineteenth century, the period when biblical studies and anthropology emerged as distinctive discourses. The need for such an opposition was the result of two converging factors, the perpetual entanglement of Judaism in the discourse on Christianity and the negative image of the savage. Similarities between ancient Judaism and primitive religions, however, entailed no difficulty for those interpreters who had no stake in protecting the status of ancient Judaism or early Christianity (e.g., the secular deists), or those who severed the connection between Christianity and the religion of the Jews (e.g., Morgan, Kant). As we shall now see, there is also a third kind of circumstance that encouraged interpreters to recognize commonalities between the religion of the ancient Jews and contemporary savages: a positive image of the savage.

3.

Romanticism, Relativism, and the Rehabilitation of the Savage

Had the savage not served as an anti-type in European imagination the opposition between Judaism and savage religions may never have arisen. At the very least, that opposition's history would have been different. As discussed previously, the negative image of the savage overlapped with the European stereotype of the Jew. These intersecting images helped generate the theory that the American Indians were descendants of the ancient Jews and thus enabled Christian travelers and missionaries to see the similarities between Judaism and the religions of American savages. Once recognized, however, these commonalities turned problematic. Rationalists reasoned that if Judaism and Christianity shared features with savage religions, they too fell into the category of superstition. Such arguments called forth the defensive strategies examined in the previous chapter, and so the opposition between Judaism and savage religions was born.

This opposition thus belongs to a tradition in which a negative image of the savage predominates. But alongside this tradition flowed another which evaluated primitive culture in an essentially positive way. This stream of thought recognized the virtue of the simple peoples in the New World and contrasted their dignity, pride, and bravery with the vices, depravity, and moral turpitude of contemporary society. In this tradition the savage also served as the anti-type of civilization. But now the valuation was reversed. The savage living close to nature enjoyed a simple innocence, a spontaneous and unadulterated form of life. Europeans, by contrast, lived under artificial, corrupt, and morally bankrupt conditions (Atkinson 1924; Chinard 1911, 1913; Bissell 1924; Fairchild 1961; Healy 1958). As might be expected, the positive evaluation of savage culture rendered unnecessary the need for an opposition between Judaism and primitive religions. It is this reversal and its effects that now draw our attention.

The Noble Savage and Romanticism

Already in 1580, Montaigne (1984 [1580], 108–9) had articulated the conception of the noble savage in his reflections "On Cannibals":

> I do not believe that, from what I have been told about this people, that there is anything barbarous or savage about them, except that we all call barbarous anything that is contrary to our own habits. Indeed we seem to have no other criterion of truth and reason than the type and kind of opinions and customs current in the land where we live. There we always see the perfect religion, the perfect political system, the perfect and most accomplished way of doing everything. These people are wild in the same way that fruits are wild, when nature has produced them by herself and in her ordinary way; whereas, in fact, it is those that we have artificially modified, and removed from the common order, that we ought to call wild. In the former, the true, most useful, and natural virtues and properties are alive and vigorous; in the latter we have bastardized them, and adapted them only to the gratification of our corrupt taste.

Montaigne goes on to describe in ethnographic style the manners and customs of the "cannibals," including their buildings, beds, eating habits, religious leaders, customs of warfare, and their cannibalistic practice of killing and eating their captives. But even this act does not make them more barbarous than Europeans. "I am not so anxious that we should note the horrible savagery of these acts as concerned that, whilst judging their faults so correctly, we should be so blind to our own" (1984, 113). For "under the cloak of piety and religion," Europeans sometimes "eat" a person alive through torture whereas the cannibals at least wait until after death before tearing out a person's flesh. "We are justified therefore in calling these people barbarians by reference to the laws of reason, but not in comparison with ourselves, who surpass them in every kind of barbarity" (1984, 114).

This tradition of "primitivism," with roots in antiquity (Lovejoy and Boas 1965), was nurtured and developed in the work of the Jesuit missionaries to the New World (Chinard 1911, 1913; Healy 1958).[1] In turn, the deists and *philosophes* capitalized on the noble savage tradition in their satirization of European society. In *L'Ingénu,* for example, Voltaire portrays the visit of a savage to civilization as a means of leveling a critique at European culture. By itself, however, the noble savage tradition did not disturb the opposition that had been posited between ancient Judaism and primitive religions. Rationalists like Voltaire would satirize Europeans by citing the virtues of the noble savage, yet turn around and criticize Christianity by comparing the Jewish revelation with the religion of savages. The savage was noble or depraved depending upon the critical needs of the moment.

Toward the end of the eighteenth century, a new cluster of ideas emerged that fundamentally changed the meaning of the noble savage tradition. This constellation of ideas, called Romanticism, redefined the conception of the savage and thereby made it possible for European discourse to overcome the antinomy between Judaism and savage religion. Within this tradition, the noble savage was reinterpreted in light of a conception of nature that differed from the one which dominated the Enlightenment. For the proponents of Enlightenment, nature was synonymous with reason. Consequently, when they pointed to the savage as exemplary of the natural state, they saw evidence of a rational being, one whose reason had not yet succumbed to authority, tradition, and priests. The noble savage of the Enlightenment, therefore, stood as an antithesis of religion.

In romantic writings, by contrast, nature is opposed to reason. Reason is abstract, governed by rules, and methodical, while nature is spontaneous, immediate, unconstrained, and instinctive. From this standpoint, the savage who lives in a state of nature is a being who is pure, innocent, spontaneous, and untainted by the corrupting and constraining influences of reason. This savage no longer represents an anti-type but is paradigmatic for religious life which is now regarded as the spontaneous, prereflective, creative, emotional, and imaginative tendencies of the human individual and the individual in community with others. The value of religion in this view is its ability to do what reason cannot: articulate the human sense of dependence, marshal the human impulses of imagination and creativity, and foster the sense of human community. For this reason, it was no longer necessary to equate Christianity with the religion of reason. Nor did the similarities between ancient Judaism and primitive religions present the same sort of dilemma they once had. Since ancient Judaism was assumed to be the religion of one of the first primitive peoples in the world, it represented a spontaneous, natural, innocent religion that was exemplary in some ways for religious life in general.

In addition to the new conception of nature, a second impulse in Romanticism helped interpreters appreciate comparisons between the religion of the Hebrews and savages: the celebration of cultural and religious diversity. This attitude marked a departure from the Enlightenment hostility toward human variation and difference. By the standards of reason, humans "should conform as nearly as possible to a standard conceived as universal, uncomplicated, immutable, uniform for every rational being" (Lovejoy and Boas 1965, 293). Consequently, rationalists despised diversity and sought a homogenous and universal culture of humankind. Romanticism, by contrast, celebrated the variety and multiplicity of cultural and religious forms. For the writers in this tradition, there is no absolute standard by which to judge all cultures and religions. Each people has its own independent standards of excellence. Multiplicity is necessary for the complete manifestation of religion, and God is revealed through the total array of cultural and religious forms of human life (Lovejoy 1936, 310; Reardon 1985). Each tradition is equally important in the development of "humanity," the term designating the full potential of the human species. The course of human history, therefore, does not progress toward some absolute, transcendent cultural or religious form, but is like a tree that branches out in all possible directions. In this tradition, variety is the essence of the human species.

This celebration of diversity produced a cultural relativism and an interest in history that was more or less absent from the Enlightenment. Not only were all forms of life potentially intelligible but there was a moral imperative to understand them. Romantic writers, therefore, appreciated primitive societies in an unprecedented way. They did not perceive a tension between human variety and the religious life. Indeed, it was only through an understanding of others that one appreciated the creation of the human species and thus the work of God.

The rehabilitation of the savage and the emergence of cultural relativism thus made palatable the savage character of ancient Judaism. This reversal is evident in the work of Herder, one of the originators of the German romantic movement (Gillies 1945, 115; see also Ergang 1966, 193).[2] In his writings, "the works of primitive peoples were looked upon . . . with something approximating to religious awe; for, having no barriers between themselves and the inexhaustible source of Creation, they were found to show its workings the more clearly" (Gillies 1945, 54). "The savage," writes Herder, "who loves himself, his wife and child with quiet joy and glows with limited activity for his tribe as for his own life is in my opinion a more real being than that cultivated shadow who is enraptured with the shadow of his whole species. . . . The former has room in his hut for every stranger . . . the inundated heart of the idle cosmopolite is a home for no one" (quoted in Ergang 1966, 97). Herder, then, categorically rejects the negative characterization of savages that was articulated by the Enlightenment. The entire second part of Herder's *Ideas for the Philosophy of History* is dedicated to proving the essential goodness and humanity of various primitive peoples, including the Eskimos, Cannibals, and Tierra del Fuego Indians (Clark 1955, 320).

In Herder's philosophy, savages exemplify the natural state in which individuals participate in an organic community which he calls a *Volk*. Such communities foster a more immediate, natural, and emotional experience of the world, an experience that the commitment to reason has destroyed. Herder thus categorizes contemporary savages with children and with peoples from "ages of ignorance." "In this feeling of natural beauty and sublimity the child often has the advantage of the man of gray hairs, and nations of the greatest simplicity have in their natural imagery and expression of natural feeling, the most elevated and touching poetry" (1980 [1782–83], 2:8).

For Herder "the ages of ignorance had great advantages over those, in which nature is studied, and becomes the object of knowledge. They had poetry—we have only description" (1980 [1782–83], 1:93). As a result, Herder admires "those times, when man's knowledge of nature was a living knowledge, when the eye was rendered discriminating by impassioned feeling, when analogies to what is human struck the view, and awakened feelings of astonishment" (1980 [1782–83], 1:93).

In particular, Herder admires folksong and poetry as instances of the highest expression of the national soul, and equates the creation of such poetry and song with revelation itself. Poetry and song possess a truth of a different sort from that expressed in scientific knowledge. "It will be observed that I use poetry and poetical invention, not in the sense of groundless fiction or falsehood; for in the sphere of the understanding, the import of a symbol poetically constructed is truth" (1980 [1782–83], 2:17). Such revelatory songs and poetry are typical of primitive peoples. "Among all nations whom we call savages and who are often more moral than we are, songs of this kind are often their entire treasury of life; doctrine and history, law and morals, ecstasy, joy and comfort, the hours of their heaven on earth are in them" (quoted in Clark 1955, 253). These songs and poetic expressions are powerful precisely because they are so concrete. Their concreteness has a way of tapping human emotion. "You know from nature-descriptions how forcefully and firmly savages always express themselves. They always visualize concretely, clearly and vividly the things they wish to express" (quoted in Schütze 1921, 127).

Primitive religions do not deserve the bad press they received during the Enlightenment. Early religion was not based on fear or stupidity as earlier writers had suggested, but was rather a noble, grand, and poetic reaction of the human to the natural world (1980 [1782–83], 1:51–52). Herder even ventures to describe polytheism as a poetical response to the world (1782, 1:56). Primitive myths, therefore, are not simple, unsophisticated attempts at explaining the unknown, but poetic statements about the particular experience of a given community in interaction with its geography, climate, and political experience. Herder also challenges the Enlightenment view that priests are self-serving and conniving. Priests too are "born and brought up in a tribal setting permeated by traditional beliefs" (1969 [1774], 301). Consequently, they do not create these ideas and practices as techniques to manipulate others, but serve as agents for the organic myths of the community. All in all, Herder treats the savage state as an ideal form of human existence, one from which Europeans have a great deal to learn.

This idealization of savages and "ages of ignorance" makes Herder willing to interpret the writings of the ancient Hebrews within the same categories. To point to Herder's work as exemplary in this respect is somewhat ironic. Herder's writings frequently exhibit precisely the kinds of impulses that are being criticized in this book. There are many statements in Herder's writings that privilege ancient Israel's religious writings over those of others. "Such images and ideas, as even the first chapters of Genesis have preserved for us, are impossible for a savage and uncultivated people" (1980 [1782–83], 2:28). Moreover, like other writers in the romantic tradition, Herder frequently suggests that all comparison is problematic. Since he believes that the culture of every group is ultimately unique, the task of the interpreter is to empathetically understand the individuality of each group. Similarities between different traditions are not important (Gillies 1945, 88–90). Finally, Herder is responsible for first treating the Jews as an "Oriental people," a categorization that undermines comparisons across time and place. In all of these respects, Herder's work is opposed to the comparative treatment of ancient Judaism and primitive religions.

But from the standpoint of this study what is extraordinary is Herder's willingness to entertain precisely the opposite possibility. He frequently makes explicit analogies between the religious writings of ancient Israel and the practices of savages. This tendency is readily evident, for example, in *The Spirit of Hebrew Poetry* (1782–83). The first half of this work is written as a dialogue that refutes the Enlightenment view of the Old Testament point by point. Euthyphron, a youth who speaks on behalf of Herder, convinces Alciphron, a representative of the Enlightenment, that the Hebrew Bible should not be judged by the standards of reason. It is not a book about scientific knowledge, but a natural and organic expression of the Jewish folk (Ergang 1966, 182), the first efforts of a gifted nation to express its own history and theology (Clark 1955, 325). Since Genesis is the oldest document of humankind, it comprises the first poetical expressions of the human species (Gillies 1945, 58). There are two different factors, then, that led Herder to compare the religious literature of the Hebrews with the poetical expressions of savages. As an expression of a natural community, this literature should share features with the song, music, and dance of other organic communities, including those of savages. Moreover, because of its antiquity, Genesis represents an early stage in the development of the human mind and sensibility:

> It was itself the first dawning of the illumination of the world, while our race was yet in its infancy. We see in it the earliest perceptions, the simplest forms, by which the human soul expressed its thought. . . . In it the earliest Logick of the Senses, the simplest analysis of ideas and the primary principles of morals, in short, the most ancient History of the human mind and heart, are brought before our eyes. Were it even the poetry of cannibals would you not think it worthy of attention for these purposes? (1980 [1782–83], 1:45–6)

Given this view of the Hebrew Bible, it is not surprising that Herder sees similarities between the language, myths, and songs of primitive peoples and the language, literature, and religious world view of the Hebrews. The Hebrew tongue itself is primitive in structure like the language of the Celtic poet Ossian. It appeals directly to the ear, the most immediate sense organ (Clark 1955, 296–97). Like the languages of other uncultivated peoples, action, imagery, passion, music, and rhythm are essential to the Hebrew language. It is not a good language for abstraction, but it is rich in sensuous representations (1980 [1782–83], 1:30).

The perplexing repetitiousness of Hebrew poetry can be accounted for in similar ways. Redundancy does not detract from it but lends it power. Like primitive dance, it reaches the emotions through repetition:

> A. [Alciphon] You are describing, I suppose, the celebrated parallelisms, in regard to which I shall hardly agree with you. Whoever has anything to say, let him say it at once, or carry his discourse regularly forward, but not repeat forever. . . .
> E. [Euthyphron] Have you ever witnessed a dance? . . . Suppose we compare the poetry of the Hebrew to the movements of the dance, or consider it as a shorter and simpler form of the choral ode.
> A. Add the systrum, the kettle-drums, and the symbals, and your dance of savages will be complete.
> E. Be it so. We are not to be frightened with names, while the thing itself is good. (1980 [1782–83], 1:39)

The Hebrew language and poetry share formal traits with the mythology and song of savages. It is these traits, moreover, that make it admirable.

In addition to formal similarities, Herder acknowledges that the Hebrew conceptions of the world resemble those of savages. When Alciphon (rationalist) asks Euthyphron (Herder) to speak about the primitive notions of the Hebrews, he responds as follows:

> With what else could I begin, than with the name of [the One], who in this ancient poetry animates and binds every thing together; whom it denominated the strong and the mighty; whose power was everywhere witnessed; whose unseen presence was felt with a shuddering of reverential fear; whom men honoured; whose name gave a sanction to the solemnities of an oath; whom they called by way of eminence, the Great Spirit, and whom all the wild and untaught nations of the earth still seek after, and feel and adore. Even among the most savage tribes, how elevated does poetry and sentiment become through the all-pervading feeling of this infinite invisible Spirit! (1980 [1782–83], 1:50)

Like the thought of savages, Hebrew language and poetry transfers the qualities of the human to the world. Herder celebrates this community with the natural world as the foundation of morality itself. The more one feels a resemblance to and sympathy for something, the more one will feel a moral duty toward it.

> The most ancient poetry, which exerted such a forming influence upon men in their savage state, made use of this foundation of overflowing sensibility to form and cherish in them the feelings of compassion and benevolence. In the blood

of Abel, his soul cries from the ground. So to Adam, surrounded by the brute creation, all seemed to be animated by his own feelings, and he sought among them all for a help-meet and companion. (1980 [1782–83], 2:12)

In this quotation, Herder explicitly identifies at least some parts of Genesis as the poetic production of the savage state.

The ancient Hebrews, like other ancient Oriental peoples, also enjoyed the spontaneity, innocence, and wonder of children and savages, uncorrupted by the guiles of reason:

It has been long remarked, that the human race in its successive ages and revolutions seems to follow the vicissitudes of our individual human life. . . . [children] look with child-like wonder and astonishment, before they learn to perceive with discrimination. Every thing appears to them in the dazzling splendour of novelty. . . . The tongue strives to express itself, and falls upon strong expressions, because its language is not become weak and facile from a multiplicity of empty sounds and stale metaphorical expressions. They often speak, too, as the Orientals, and as uncultivated savages speak, till at length with the progress of nature and art they learn to express themselves like polished or like fashionable men. Let them enjoy their years of childhood, and let those Orientals also in the infancy of the world form their poetical conceptions, speak, and rejoice with a child-like spirit. (1980 [1782–83], 2:9)

According to Herder, rationalists denigrated ancient Jewish literature because they forgot how to appreciate the kinds of experiences that gave rise to this sort of literary creation.

In general, Herder's relativistic perspective was overshadowed throughout the nineteenth century by the evolutionary perspective on religion discussed earlier. For example, although Herder's thought deeply influenced Hegel and Schleiermacher, both of these thinkers ultimately rejected the implications of Herder's relativism (Clark 1955, 329; Gillies 1945, 82). Hegel, as we have seen, adopted a developmental perspective on religion that placed Judaism in a position inferior to Christianity but superior to religions of nature. Hegel's commitment to a chronological sequence undercut the tendency in Herder's work to compare ancient Judaism and savage cultures (Manuel 1968, xiv). Schleiermacher, for his part, vacillated between these two positions (Welch 1972, 71). Like Herder, Schleiermacher believed that religion is manifested only in the infinite variety of religions. Each religion realizes in its own way the experience of dependence that is at the core of religion (Schleiermacher 1958 [1821], 74–75). But while Schleiermacher affirmed the validity and autonomy of all religious forms, he felt compelled to treat Christianity, both in his *Speeches* and in *The Christian Faith,* as the most excellent religion. Judaism, of course, qualifies as a higher religion, but a type inferior to Christianity:

On this highest plane, of Monotheism, history exhibits only three great communities—the Jewish, the Christian, and the Mohammedan; the first being almost in process of extinction, the other two still contending for the mastery of the human race. Judaism, by its limitation of the love of Jehovah to the race of Abraham betrays a lingering affinity with Fetichism. . . . And so, this comparison of Christianity with other similar religions is a sufficient warrant for saying that Christianity is in fact the most perfect of the most highly developed forms of religion. (1976 [1830], 8:4, 37–38)

While Schleiermacher shared many of Herder's assumptions, he did not draw the same relativist conclusions. Consequently, he ranked religions in a hierarchical system that posited a temporal, moral, and rational gulf between Judaism and primitive religions.

The Return of Relativism and the Death of the Savage: British Social Anthropology

If the nineteenth century represents an eclipse of a relativist perspective on religions, twentieth-century anthropology has in many ways rediscovered Herder's insights (Broce 1973). The reemergence of cultural relativism is one of the impulses that lies behind the recent interest among anthropologists in the religion of the ancient Jews. Mary Douglas and Edmund Leach, the first anthropologists since Frazer and Robertson Smith to make Israelite religion a central focus of their research, work out of anthropological traditions that call into question the categories of primitive religion and culture.[3]

The traditions in question are British social anthropology, which traces its line of descent back to Durkheim, and the structural anthropology of Lévi-Strauss, which is itself an offspring of the British tradition.[4] The writers in these traditions generally do not go as far as Herder in idealizing primitive life forms, although on occasion they do wax eloquent about the people they are studying. Nonetheless, the impulse toward cultural relativism leads these thinkers, as it did Herder, to rehabilitate the savage in a variety of important ways.[5] In what follows, I briefly highlight the development of these tendencies within social anthropology and show how they lie behind Douglas's and Leach's desire to subject Israelite religion to anthropological inquiry.

The development of British social anthropology was closely connected with the repudiation of the evolutionary assumptions of the nineteenth century. The functionalisms of Malinowski and Radcliffe-Brown and the growing emphasis on fieldwork as a research strategy had the intention and effect of undermining the longstanding portrayal of primitive culture and religion. Functionalism, the theory that religious beliefs and practices satisfied psychological or social needs, indicated that "primitive" religion was more than a mistaken understanding of the world, as Tylor and Frazer had suggested. Religion helped create and maintain social solidarity and enabled individuals to deal with their fears in a world they could not master. Myth was no longer a primitive attempt at science but a charter for society that "expresses, en-hances, and codifies belief," "enforces morality," "vouches for the efficacy of ritual and contains practical rules for the guidance of man. Myth is thus a vital ingredient of human civilization" (Malinowski 1954 [1925], 101).

The emerging emphasis on intensive fieldwork, an emphasis of both Mali-nowski and Radcliffe-Brown, also had the effect, if not the express purpose, of questioning the stereotype of primitive culture.

> Ethnology has introduced law and order into what seemed chaotic and freakish. It has transformed for us the sensational, wild and unaccountable world of 'sav-ages' into a number of well ordered communities, governed by law, behaving and thinking according to consistent principles. . . . It is a very far cry from the famous answer given long ago by a representative authority who, asked, what are the manners and customs of the natives, answered, "Customs none, man-ners beastly," to the position of the modern Ethnographer! (Malinowski 1961 [1922], 9–10)

Evans-Pritchard, a student of Malinowski and Radcliffe-Brown and a teacher of Mary Douglas, would subsequently describe the experience of fieldwork in romantic terms reminiscent of Herder. "I will only say that I learnt from African 'primitives' much more than they learnt from me, much that I was never taught at school, something more of courage, endurance, patience, res-ignation, and forebearance that I had no great understanding of before. Just to give one example: I would say that I learnt more about the nature of God and our human predicament from the Nuer than I ever learnt at home" (1976 [1937], 245). These sorts of views are obviously a long way from the evolu-tionary perspective that treated living savages as relics from the distant hu-man past.

Symptomatic of this changing viewpoint is a terminological shift. The perjoratives "savage" and "primitive" are placed in quotes if not discarded altogether in favor of more neutral terminology such as "natives," "tribal religions," "non-literate," "non-industrial," and "small face-to-face socie-ties." Radcliffe-Brown's dissatisfaction with the term "primitive" in 1931 be-came the standard view within British social anthropology.

> A word, the constant use of which has been a great obstacle to scientific think-ing in anthropology, is the word "primitive." It conveys the suggestion that any society to which we apply it represents for us something of the very beginnings of social life. Yet if culture had, as we may well assume, a single origin some hundreds of thousands of years ago, then any existing culture has just as long an history as any other. And although the rate of change may vary, every culture, just as every language, is constantly undergoing change. But, quite apart from this implication of the word as meaning in some sense "early," harm is done by the current application of it to the most diverse types of culture. The difference of culture between the Maori of New Zealand and the Aborigines of Australia is at least as great as that between ourselves and the Maori. Yet we group these two

cultures together as "primitive," and contrast them with our own as "not primitive." (1958 [1931], 80)

The only anthropologists who have persisted in using the term "savage" are those who, like Lévi-Strauss, intend to subvert the differences between "savages" and other kinds of peoples.

As the category of "savage" was called into question, the notion of primitive thought was likewise jeopardized. As I discussed in the Introduction, Malinowski challenged Lévy-Bruhl's theory that primitives have a different sort of mentality. Malinowski argued that if natives actually lived in a sea of mystical notions, as Lévy-Bruhl had suggested, the technological and material achievements of their cultures would have been inexplicable. The Coral Islanders know that magic alone does not make the gardens grow. They realize that they have to plant the seeds in the right kind of soil, in the proper season, and care for their growth in certain ways. Their practice thus reflects empirical knowledge which does not differ in essence from scientific knowledge.

This same impulse toward conceptual relativism is carried further by Evans-Pritchard. In his *Witchcraft, Oracles and Magic Among the Azande,* for example, Evans-Pritchard follows Malinowski in contesting certain well-established stereotypes about primitive thought. Among other things, he shows that the Azande belief in witches is empirical, experimental, attentive to principles of causation, and logically coherent. "Zande belief in witchcraft in no way contradicts empirical knowledge of cause and effect. The world known to the senses is just as real to them as it is to us" (1976 [1937], 25). The Zande mind "is logical and inquiring within the framework of its culture and insists on the coherence of its own idiom" (1976, 16). In support of such contentions, Evans-Pritchard discusses Azande statements that earlier interpreters would have taken as evidence of prelogical mentality or childlike reasoning. For example, when a granary collapses on people who are sitting under it for shade, the Zande blame the misfortune on witchcraft. But that does not mean, as Evans-Pritchard shows, that the Azande fail to realize that termites ate the supports and caused the granary to collapse. They too realize that the termites are the immediate causes of the tragedy. When they attribute the tragedy to witchcraft, they are answering a different question: "Why should these particular people have been sitting under this particular granary at the particular moment when it collapsed? That it should collapse is easily intelligible, but why should it have collapsed at the particular moment when these particular people were sitting beneath it?" (Evans-Pritchard 1976 [1937], 22)[6]

Beyond the Opposition: Anthropological Discourse on the Religion of the Jews

Clearly, a recurring feature of British social anthropology has been its predilection for undermining various distinctions between primitive and modern society. But as the category of the savage disappeared, anthropologists in this tradition were confronted with a dilemma. Anthropology had originally justified itself as the disciplinary locus for the study of primitive cultures. Since the category of "primitive" culture was no longer tenable, the original raison d'être of anthropology seemed to have vanished. Either anthropology no longer had a purpose and hence must disappear, or it must claim that insights afforded by the discipline transcended the study of "primitive" peoples. In the latter view, results from studying so-called primitive peoples turned out to be universally applicable because such peoples were simply instances of humanity in general. In principle, all forms of human culture and religion were potentially subject to anthropological inquiry. Since the opposition between primitive and nonprimitive religions or peoples no longer made sense, what anthropologists had discovered about so-called primitive religions could and should be generalized to the study of all religions. Already in 1931, Radcliffe-Brown was complaining that in "the present organization of anthropology the social anthropologist is supposed to confine himself to the study of the peoples without history, the so-called primitive or savage peoples who still survive outside Europe" (1958 [1931], 85). But the commitment to "primitive" societies was too strong for anthropology to overcome so readily in practice. Not until the work of Mary Douglas and Edmund Leach did British social anthropology carry its relativism to its logical conclusion.

The desire to collapse the distinction between primitive and other traditions is one of the principal factors that led Mary Douglas and Edmund Leach to scrutinize the religion of the Jews, a subject that previously fell outside the purview of anthropological inquiry.[7] Douglas's *Purity and Danger,* the volume in which she first applied a structuralist analysis to Israelite dietary laws, represents a sustained inquiry into the relation between pollution behavior, systems of cultural classification, and social structure. In developing her thesis that impurity restrictions and taboos frequently surround anomalous items, people, or situations, Douglas argues that there are fundamental similarities between primitive purification and prophylaxis and our own notions and behaviors toward dirt. Both sets of practices are concerned with order, with creating and maintaining a system of classification in an otherwise disorderly world. Douglas (1966, 32) strongly condemns "the opposite view—that primitive ritual has nothing whatever in common with our ideas of cleanness—this I deplore as equally harmful to the understanding of ritual. On this view, our washing, scrubbing, isolating and disinfecting has only superficial resemblance with ritual purifications. Our practices are solidly based on hygiene; theirs are symbolic: we kill germs, they ward off spirits." On this basis, Douglas refuses to posit an essential difference between the pollution behavior of Jews and "primitives."

> I was first interested in pollution behaviour by Professor Srinivas and the late Franz Steiner who each, as Brahmin and Jew, tried in their daily lives to handle

problems of ritual cleanness. I am grateful to them for making me sensitive to gestures of separation, classifying and cleansing. I next found myself doing fieldwork in a highly pollution-conscious culture in the Congo and discovered in myself a prejudice against piecemeal explanations. I count as piecemeal any explanations of ritual pollution which are limited to one kind of dirt or to one kind of context. (1966, vii)

In Douglas's view, an understanding of purity behavior leads inevitably to comparative religion.

Douglas's desire to treat all prophylactic practices within a single framework is part of her larger agenda which is to rethink the unfortunate oppositions that have characterized anthropological inquiry. The first chapter of *Purity and Danger* is a sustained attempt to criticize the sharp distinctions between primitive and nonprimitive religions bequeathed to twentieth-century interpreters from their nineteenth-century predecessors.[8] "The more intractable puzzles in comparative religion arise because human experience has been wrongly divided. In this book we try to re-unite some of the separated segments" (1966, 28). Among other things, she questions the distinction between magic and religion, particularly the attempt to associate the former with a mechanical understanding of the universe and the latter with an ethical one. Magic, on this view, is ritual which is automatically effective, while religious ritual depends on the actor's inner dispositions and hence on her or his relation to the deity. Douglas criticizes those nineteenth-century writers who assumed that primitive peoples practice magic, while more advanced peoples perform religious rites. "The European belief in primitive magic has led to a false distinction between primitive and modern cultures, and sadly inhibited comparative religion" (1966, 58). "Magical practice, in this sense of automatically effective ritual, is not a sign of primitiveness. Nor is a high ethical content the prerogative of evolved religions, as I hope to show" (1966, 19).

The concern to question the sharp differences between primitive and nonprimitive religions underlies Douglas's decision to examine the Israelite dietary laws, a system of prohibitions that are exemplary of a "higher" religion. Douglas sets out to debunk those rationalizations that seek to disguise the essential similarity of Israelite dietary rules and "primitive" taboos. The dietary restrictions are not based on hygienic considerations nor do they represent a polemic against the idolatry of Israel's neighbors. Rather, they are concerned with an imaginative order and they declare unfit all creatures that violate the categories through which reality is construed. The same principles and impulses are at work, therefore, in both the Israelite food prohibitions and in primitive myth and ritual.

Similar impulses underlie Edmund Leach's interest in the Hebrew Bible. Leach describes his project as an attempt to apply the structuralist assumptions of Lévi-Strauss to the religious narratives of ancient Israel. His intention, however, is not simply to apply a new method to the Hebrew Bible, although that motivation is also present. Leach believes that the subjection of biblical stories to structuralist analysis is necessary to dispel the idea that primitive myth and the biblical stories are somehow fundamentally different.

Ironically, Lévi-Strauss is at least partly responsible for this misunderstanding. From one point of view, Lévi-Strauss's work exhibits many of the same relativistic impulses present in the British tradition. In his *Structural Anthropology* (1963) and then again in *The Savage Mind* (1966), Lévi-Strauss argues that "primitive" thought is no different in principle from the Western or scientific mind:

> Prevalent attempts to explain alleged differences between the so-called primitive mind and scientific thought have resorted to qualitative differences between the working processes of the mind in both cases, while assuming that the entities which they were studying remained very much the same. If our interpretation is correct, we are led toward a completely different view—namely, that the kind of logic in mythical thought is as rigorous as that of modern science, and that the difference lies, not in the quality of the intellectual process, but in the nature of the things to which it is applied. . . . we may be able to show that the same logical processes operate in myth as in science, and that man has always been thinking equally well; the improvement lies, not in an alleged progress of man's mind, but in the discovery of new areas to which it may apply its unchanged and unchanging powers. (Lévi-Strauss 1963, 230)

The rehabilitation of the savage in Lévi-Strauss's work is, as in British social anthropology, linked to a romantic vision of primitive peoples.[9] Lévi-Strauss's *Tristes Tropiques* [The Melancholy Tropics] (1975), for example, is a book that Herder himself would have favorably reviewed. In this travelog, Lévi-Strauss weaves together reminiscences of various trips to South America and then into the interior of Brazil with critical reflections on the ills of civilization. The "virtuous savages," as he calls them in the title to one of his chapters, serve as a contrast to the barbarous Europeans and other "civilized" people whom he encounters on his voyages. Although Lévi-Strauss criticizes the naïve form of primitivism that views the natural state as an ideal, he uses the genre of the travelog to acquire a critical distance on contemporary society and its problems.

But for reasons that are not entirely clear, and perhaps having to do with his own Jewish background, Lévi-Strauss limited the application of the structuralist perspective to "primitive" myths and refused to apply the structuralist method to the literary productions of so-called "civilized" peoples such as the ancient Jews. By implication, his work suggested that the success of the structuralist perspective was itself tied to its peculiar object of study. Thus it seemed as if the structuralist perspective revealed something important about how primitive thought worked without, as Lévi-Strauss wanted to claim, revealing anything about the working of the human mind in general.

Seizing on this tension in Lévi-Strauss's work, Paul Ricoeur criticized Lévi-Strauss for attempting to generalize about human thought from the exceptional case of savage thought. Lévi-Strauss's insights were limited, Ricoeur argues, to exotic and ultimately not very important examples of humanity.

> For my part, I find it striking that all the examples were taken from the geographical area which was that of so-called totemic thought and never from Semitic, pre-Hellenic, or Indo-European thought; and I wonder what is implied in this initial limitation of the ethnographic and human material. Hasn't the author stacked the deck by relating the state of the savage mind to a cultural area—specifically, that of the "totemic illusion"—where the arrangements are more important than the contents? . . . Now, I wonder whether the mythical base from which we branch—with its Semitic (Egyptian, Babylonian, Aramaic, Hebrew), proto-Hellenic, and Indo-European cores—lends itself so easily to the same operation. . . . In the examples of *The Savage Mind,* the insignificance of the contents and the luxuriance of the arrangements seem to me to constitute an extreme example much more than a canonical form. It happens that a part of civilization, precisely the part from which our culture does not proceed, lends itself better than any other to the application of the structural method transposed from linguistics. But that does not prove that structural comprehension is just as enlightening elsewhere and, in particular, just as self-sufficient. I spoke above of the price to be paid: this price—the insignificance of the contents—is not a high price with the totemists, the counterpart being so great, that is, the great significance of the arrangements. Totemic thought, it seems to me, is precisely the one that has the greatest affinity to structuralism. I wonder whether its example is . . . exemplary or whether it is not exceptional. (1974, 41)

In attempting to distinguish totemic thought from the mythical thought of civilized peoples, Ricoeur invokes a distinction that sounds suspiciously like the one between primitive magic and religion, which Douglas criticizes. The former is empty and formal; the latter is content-saturated. To show that the narratives of the Hebrew Bible are actually different than totemic thought, Ricoeur appeals to von Rad's work:

> While I was reading *The Savage Mind* of Lévi-Strauss, I was also involved in Gerhard von Rad's remarkable book, *Theology of the Historical Traditions of Israel,* the first volume of his *Theology of the Old Testament.* . . . Here we find ourselves confronting a theological conception exactly the inverse of that of totemism and which, because it is the inverse, suggests an inverse relationship between diachrony and synchrony and raises more urgently the problem of the relationship between structural comprehension and hermeneutic comprehension. What is decisive in understanding the core of meaning of the Old Testament? Not nomenclatures or classifications, but founding events. If we limit ourselves to the theology of the Hexateuch, the signifying context is a kerygma, the sign of the action of Jahweh, constituted by a complex of events. It is a *Heilgeschichte.* (1974, 45)

There is an obvious irony in Ricoeur's reliance on von Rad to deny the similarity between the stories of ancient Israel and the myths of primitive peoples. Von Rad's own account of the Hebrew Bible stands in a theological tradition that already takes for granted precisely the dichotomy between the religion of savages and the ancient Jews that is here in question. Note, for example, that in Ricoeur's (= von Rad's) summation of the concerns of the Hebrew Bible, the whole book of Leviticus with its concern with "nomenclatures" and "classification" disappears. Appealing to von Rad's work to prove that primitive thought differs from Hebrew thought is like appealing to the Bible to disprove the theory of human evolution.

By applying the structuralist method to the narratives of the Hebrew Bible, Leach (1969, 25) intends to counter Ricoeur's argument and thus prevent the reassertion of the antinomy between primitive myth and the narratives of the ancient Jews. Leach notes, however, that Lévi-Strauss himself responded cautiously to Ricoeur's criticism. The founder of structural anthropology seems to confess that the structuralist perspective is inapplicable to the Hebrew Bible because the mythology of the ancient Jews has been "deformed" by an ongoing process of editorial revision. Moreover, Lévi-Strauss implies that the limited ethnographic knowledge of ancient Israel would create an obstacle for the application of the structuralist method to the narratives of the Hebrew Bible.

Leach, for his part, confesses his inability to understand Lévi-Strauss's reluctance to apply his insights to the Hebrew Bible. After all, Lévi-Strauss had previously applied a structuralist perspective to myths of peoples for whom we have little ethnographic information. Leach (1969, 26) is also of the opinion that an editorial process would not disfigure the structure of a system but only perpetuate it. One is thus left wondering whether Lévi-Strauss's reluctance has something to do with his identity as a Jew facing modernity (Cuddihy 1974).

The important point here is that Leach conceives of his own structuralist study of the Hebrew Bible as an attempt to overcome the dichotomy between primitive mythology and the narratives of the Hebrew Bible. Consequently, he describes Genesis as "myth" and denies that this kind of narrative differs from what has traditionally been conceived of as primitive myth. But even the presumably historical narratives such as are found in Samuel and Kings are simply myths of the same species as Lévi-Strauss studied. "We cannot know for certain just how the Palestinian Jews of the fourth century B.C. thought about their past, but their historiography is more likely to have resembled that of modern tribal societies than that of nineteenth century Europeans" (Leach 1969, 32).

Leach's desire to collapse the distinction between biblical stories and primitive myths springs from his more general concern to rid anthropology of its own prejudice against primitives—a consistent theme, as we have seen, among those trained in the British school of anthropology. This concern comes quite explicitly to the fore in Leach's "Virgin Birth" (1969, 85–109).[10] In this essay, Leach chides Melford Spiro for naïvely perpetuating the idea that primitives do not understand the facts of physiological paternity.[11] Spiro bases his conclusion on the fact that in some primitive societies pregnancy is attributed to a variety of events in a woman's experience, including the food she eats. Leach believes that people who make such statements nonetheless understand the relationship between copulation and pregnancy. These statements are rather ones of social concern that express how "the relationship between the woman's child and the clansmen of the woman's husband stems from public recognition of the bonds of marriage, rather than from the facts of cohabitation, which is a normal state of affairs" (Leach 1969, 87). After reviewing the evidence against the view of Spiro, Leach, with intentional irony, accuses Spiro of being ignorant of the facts and of refusing to recognize disconfirming evidence, accusations which anthropologists have often leveled at primitives. "I take note of the fact that the anthropologist's belief in the ignorance of his primitive contemporaries shows an astonishing resilience in the face of adverse evidence and I consider why anthropologists should be pre-disposed to think in this way" (Leach 1969, 85).

Leach concludes that this resistance testifies to the deep commitment of anthropologists to their prejudice against primitive peoples.

> Spiro's attitude is in fact typical. He is positively eager to believe that the aborigines were ignorant and he accepts their ignorance as a fact without investigating the evidence at all. . . . In anthropological writing, ignorance is a term of abuse. To say that a native is ignorant amounts to saying that he is childish, stupid, superstitious. Ignorance is the opposite of logical rationality; it is the quality which distinguishes the savage from the anthropologist. (1969, 92)

For Leach, therefore, it is not natives who are ignorant but those anthropologists who think of natives in that way.

In particular, Leach faults Spiro for resorting to an explanation for "primitive" practices that he would be unwilling to apply to our own. "If *we* believe such things [i.e., the myth of the Virgin Birth] we are devout; if *others* do so they are idiots" (1969, 93). Leach (1969, 97) admits that his "own prejudices go the other way: The data of ethnography are interesting to me because they so often seem directly relevant to my own allegedly civilized experiences. It is not only the differences between Europeans and Trobrianders which interest me, it is their similarities. This of course is a Malinowski precept, but let us try to put it into practice. Let us go back to the Christians" (1969, 97). Not surprisingly, Leach concludes his defense of so-called "primitive" understandings of conception by treating them within a framework that also explains the Christian idea of the Virgin Birth. He argues that this idea, like the primitive statements that deny the relevance of human male sexuality, responds to the problems created by positing a world of the Gods or God. The disjunction of the two worlds is overcome in the idea that men are descendants of Gods. The notion of a virgin birth and the irrelevance of male sexuality are related ideas. The biological father must be removed to make possible the fertilizing activity of God (1969, 109). Leach concludes his essay with this indictment of his cohorts:

If anthropologists are to justify their claim to be students of comparative religion, they need to be less polite. So far they have shown an extraordinary squeamishness about the analysis of Christianity and Judaism, religions in which they themselves or their close friends are deeply involved. Roth's Bulletin No. 5 on the North Queensland Aborigines was an ethnographic document of considerable interest; so is chapter 1 of the Gospel according to St. Matthew. Serious anthropologists should treat the two on a par; both are records of theological doctrine. (1969, 110)

Leach's interest in the Hebrew Bible, like Douglas's, makes sense as the logical culmination of the anthropological traditions within which both anthropologists worked. British social anthropology and Lévi-Strauss's structural anthropology each challenged the tendency within Western discourse to posit an opposition between primitive and nonprimitive peoples and religions. Informed by and drawing on those traditions, Leach and Douglas each conclude that anthropological discourse must inevitably lead to a scrutiny of ancient Judaism. In different ways, Douglas and Leach recommend the practice of the golden rule within anthropology. In Douglas's view, what we say about "primitives" we should also be willing to say about ourselves. Leach, for his part, insists that what we think is true about ourselves we should also be willing to consider true of "primitives." Douglas and Leach are crossing the same bridge in different directions—the bridge across that wide chasm that once divided the traditions of savagery from those of civilization.

Conclusion

The archaeological investigation carried out in this and the preceding chapters suggests that three different variables frequently influence whether a given discourse can tolerate comparisons between ancient Judaism and savage religions: (1) the evaluation of revelation and Christianity (2) the understanding of the connection between Christianity and Judaism, and (3) the image of the savage. Together these three variables may appear in eight distinct combinations as schematized in the table.

	I	II	III	IV	V	VI	VII	VIII
A. Positive view of Christianity or revelation	+	+	+	+	−	−	−	−
B. Strong connection between Judaism and Christianity	+	−	−	+	+	−	−	+
C. Positive image of the savage	−	−	+	+	−	−	+	+
D. Opposition between Judaism and savage religions	+	−	+	−	−	−	−	+

An opposition between ancient Judaism and savage religions invariably arises in discourses that seek to defend Christianity or revelation and that simultaneously posit a strong connection between Christianity and ancient Judaism and a negative image of the savage (I). This position, as we have seen, is typical of orthodox and nonorthodox defenders of revelation, Christianity, and Judaism. An antinomy is also generated when (VIII) a positive image of the savage is combined with a negative attitude toward Christianity and an assumption of a strong connection between the latter and Judaism. In this case, the opposition between ancient Judaism and primitive religions serves as a critique of Christianity and Judaism. Primitive religions, which are treated with respect, are contrasted with the religion of Jews and Christians. To some extent, we have seen this view represented in the literature of the deists, although in general these thinkers had a negative image of the savage. To cite a more recent example, this combination of variables is present in the writings of American neopagans. These writers consider natural religions and hence the religions of tribal societies to be morally superior and less alienating than the "Judeo-Christian tradition" (Adler 1986; Budapest 1986; Christ 1987; Starhawk 1979; 1982). Neopagans see a vast gulf between ancient Judaism and natural religions. By positing this gulf they intend to criticize Judaism and by extension Christianity (Eilberg-Schwartz 1989).

In all the other cases, comparisons between ancient Judaism and primitive religions can be tolerated *if there are independent motives for this sort of enterprise*. In four cases, such motives are present. In one of these, the purpose of the comparison is to cast Judaism in a positive light and by extension defend religion and Christianity as well. This positive motivation becomes apparent when a commitment to Christianity is combined with the assumption of a strong connection between Christianity and Judaism and a positive evaluation of the savage (IV). This tendency is evident to a certain extent in Herder's writings.

In two instances, a critical motivation operates behind the comparison. This occurs when a negative attitude toward Christianity interacts with the assumption of a strong connection between Christianity and Judaism and a negative image of the savage (V). In this case, exemplified by the deists, the comparison between Judaism and savage cultures constitutes an attack on Judaism and by extension a critique of Christianity, revelation, and religion.

A critical intent of a different sort can also generate an interest in comparing Judaism and primitive religions. Such comparisons can serve as a critique of Judaism and, by way of contrast, privilege the religion of Christ. This use of comparison emerges when a commitment to Christianity and a negative conception of the savage are combined with the assumption of a historical or conceptual rupture between Judaism and Christianity (II). We have seen this tendency represented in the work of Thomas Morgan and Kant, both of whom claimed that Christianity had nothing to do with Judaism and that Judaism was a primitive, barbaric religion, if a religion at all.

The other permutations are unattested in this investigation for reasons that are not difficult to imagine. Generally speaking the desire to sever the connection between Judaism and Christianity emerges only when there is a desire to privilege Christianity and deal with the problem of the savage character of Judaism. Consequently, when discourse posits a positive image of the savage, there is no reason to deny the connection between Judaism and Christianity (III, VII). Similarly, when there is no commitment to Christianity, a negative image of the savage does not necessitate severing the relationship between Judaism and Christianity (VI). One can imagine, however, types of people who could fall into these categories. A Christian pagan, for example, who had a positive view of tribal religions, might desire to deny any historical connection between Christianity and Judaism as a way to demonstrate the superiority of Christianity over Judaism (III). By the same token, a Jewish pagan might want to celebrate the relationship between ancient Judaism and primitive religions while denying the relationship between Christianity and Judaism (VII).

As useful as this investigation has been, it nonetheless remains incomplete. It does not do justice to another theoretical issue that is inextricably involved in the question of whether Judaism and "primitive" religions can and should be compared. I refer to the general problems of comparison. Is comparing religions a worthwhile endeavor and if so under what conditions and for what purposes? As has been clearly demonstrated, religious commitments do affect the way one answers these questions and may even be decisive. But there are also a variety of strictly theoretical issues at stake in the question of comparison. Are there commonalities among cultures that are not temporally or geographically connected? What are the nature of those commonalities and how may they be explained? Are there laws regulating human societies that may be generalized to all forms of social life, or is every culture unique and thus incomparable? Clearly, the view that comparison is problematic is often accompanied by a serious commitment to specific religious traditions. But reservations about comparative inquiry can be based on other concerns as well. In the next chapter, I return to the issue of comparison and attempt to provide a general justification for seeking insight into Judaism from the study of "primitive" religions.

4

Beyond Parallel-anoia

Comparative Inquiry and Cultural Interpretation

It seems to me that we are at a junction when biblical scholarship should recognize parallelomania for the disease that it is.

Sandmel 1962

"What kind of bird are you if you can't fly?" chirped the bird. "What kind of bird are you if you can't swim?" replied the duck.

Peter and the Wolf

Anthropologists—paladins of the comparative method *par excellence*—are fond of arguing that we do not understand any culture in and of itself, [but] only by comparison.

Fernandez 1986

Like other interpreters of Israelite religion and ancient Judaism, I was originally taught to be suspicious of "the comparative method," the enterprise of comparing cultures separated in time and place. I learned that the problems endemic to the comparative method were readily evident in the works of William Robertson Smith and James G. Frazer. Like other late nineteenth- and early twentieth-century proponents of the comparative method, these thinkers wrenched cultural items out of their larger cultural contexts and therefore misconstrued the meaning, function, and character of the practices, beliefs, or institutions in question. As a result, the "parallels" they discovered were not in fact comparable and consequently did not illuminate the elements under comparison.

In the course of my own intellectual development, I began to question this consensus. This change occurred slowly through my own exposure to anthropological theory and ethnographic literature, which was itself a consequence of my growing dissatisfactions with the paradigms currently governing discourse on Israelite religion and ancient Judaism (see below). Over a period of time, I came to the conclusion that comparative inquiry must be one crucial dimension in the larger enterprise of interpreting these religious cultures.[1] Indeed, as I shall argue, comparative inquiry actually enriches the other models of cultural interpretation in various ways. In this chapter, I explore the uses of comparison and then respond to some of the criticisms that have been leveled against comparative inquiry. I follow up these reflections in part 2 with specific studies that are informed by cross-cultural comparisons.

At the outset, it is important to note that there is no unanimity within anthropology about the value of comparative inquiry. Indeed, some anthropologists have many of the same reservations about cross-cultural comparisons as interpreters of Israelite religion and ancient Judaism. To anthropologists with such reservations, the following reflections are offered as a resident alien who thinks the native inhabitants have lost sight of a rich dimension of their own tradition. To interpreters of Israelite religion and ancient Judaism, they are offered in support of a small but growing trend to take comparative inquiry seriously.[2]

The Way Things Are

For some time now, discourse on Israelite religion and ancient Judaism has been dominated by two interpretive strategies, those of the contextualist and the diffusionist, both of which are hostile to comparisons between cultures separated in time and place. Although in practice these strategies may overlap, for analytical purposes they can be discussed separately.

The contextualist or integrationist paradigm assumes that cultures and religions have to be understood on their own terms, in their own context, with particular attention to the meanings that beliefs and practices have to actors. The interpreter seeks out relations between various parts of a religious and cultural system, with attention as well to the historical, political, economic, and social situation of the tradition under interpretation. This act of interpretation presupposes that there is a certain coherence and reasonableness in cultural and religious traditions; it is the task of the interpreter to sort out these interrelations.

This perspective is frequently justified in terms of a linguistic model of culture. The meaning of words in a language are determined within the set of relations that constitute that language. "Kind" means "to be nice" in English but "child" in German. The apparent similarity between these words is thus misleading. They are not "parallels," because when examined in the context of a system of relations their fundamental difference is evident. According to contextualists, cultural systems work in an analogous way. "Religious concepts or customs can have different meanings and purposes in two different religions, even when these religions are close neighbors geographically and historically" (Fohrer 1972, 25). It is thus a mistake to yank elements out of their systems of relations. The similarities one purports to find in this way disappear with a deeper understanding of how elements fit into larger cultural wholes. For this reason any sort of cross-cultural comparison is problematic, whether between cultures separated in time or space or between those that are geographically and temporally contiguous.

The diffusionist paradigm, by contrast, assumes that cultures that are geographically and temporally connected interact and influence one another in profound ways. No culture is an entirely closed system. Understanding a religious tradition like the religion of Israel must involve an attempt to see which of its elements are developments from other neighboring religions and cultures and how those foreign elements are reinterpreted or reconfigured within the larger system of beliefs and practices that define that tradition. In some cases, the diffusionist paradigm assumes that cultural patterns spread out from a center and dominate contiguous traditions. Diffusionists also appeal to information about neighboring cultures to round out the fragmentary picture of ancient Judaism. Thus, to discover that the Israelite conception of covenant resembles a treaty made between suzerain and vassal in the ancient Near East tells us something important about the conception of the relation between Israel and God in biblical literature.

That is not to say that the religion of ancient Jews was a sponge that soaked up everything around it. It both rejected and absorbed elements from neighboring traditions. Moreover, even when an element was absorbed it was often recast in distinctive ways. Familiarity with contiguous cultures thus supplies interpreters with knowledge of an element's meaning before its absorption in and transformation by the religious culture of Israelites and ancient Jews. The diffusionist perspective, therefore, attends to continuity and discontinuity. It attempts to understand how the traditions of Israelites and Jews are similar and different from those of neighboring peoples.

Clearly, the diffusionist perspective represents a kind of comparative method since it relies on comparisons between contiguous cultures. Although diffusionists are not in principle against comparative inquiry, they are skeptical of similarities between cultures that cannot be explained in terms of diffusion. "Comparison can be applied to societies which lie in the same 'historic stream' as biblical Israel. Comparisons on the 'grand scale' are better avoided" (Talmon 1977, 356). The comparative method of the diffusionist thus differs in practice and theoretical justification from the enterprise of comparing cultures separated in time and place, the type of inquiry I defend below. The former type of inquiry examines similarities between cultures in contact and hence can be called metonymic. The latter examines similarities between cultures separated temporally or geographically and is thus metaphoric. Both fall under the rubric of the comparative method, but different claims support and guide research in each case.

Beyond Parallel-anoia

The contextualist and diffusionist models of cultural interpretation were the ones through which I originally learned to think about Israelite religion and ancient Judaism. I found that by themselves they either did not provide answers to the kinds of questions I was interested in or the answers they offered were not particularly satisfying. For example, most interpreters seemed either uninterested in or ill equipped to deal with practices related to impurity, such as the menstrual taboo, the practice of circumcision, or the dietary restrictions, to mention but a few examples. In particular, I found that the theoretical categories used for thinking about such practices were impoverished. I was also disturbed by the lack of interest in how such practices related to similar ones in other religious traditions. Anthropology, I discovered, provided fresh ways of thinking about such issues. In turn, my exposure to anthropological theory and ethnographic literature fundamentally changed the ways in which I thought about what a religious culture was and how it should be interpreted. To cite one example from my own research, when I learned that in diverse traditions animals often serve as metaphors for human beings and that metaphors and rituals are often intertwined, I realized I had at hand a completely new way of understanding the dietary and other husbandry rules of ancient Israel (see chapter 5).

In retrospect, I view the changes in my own thinking as the result of the comparative thrust within anthropology. In this respect, the difference between anthropological and biblical studies is instructive. Because anthropology has traditionally focused on nonliterate peoples, the anthropologist produces the ethnographic text that is interpreted. By contrast, interpreters of Israelite religion and ancient Judaism rely on texts and material remains to which all interpreters have equal access. As Evans-Pritchard once put it,

> the historian is not faced here with the same difficulty [as the anthropologist]. He can select from the material at his disposal what is relevant to his theme and neglect the rest. What he leaves out of his books is not lost. The anthropologist, and to a large extent the archaeologist also, are in a very different position, for what they do not record may be, and often is, lost for ever. (Evans-Pritchard 1951, 88)

This difference has an important impact on the discourse that is generated. Strategically speaking, the ethnographer is in a very powerful position with regard to the interpretation that is produced, since she or he has a firsthand experience of the cultural tradition in question. Unless another ethnographer studies the same group (which occurs only rarely and often after a substantial time lapse), it is difficult to challenge the interpretation by pointing to other relevant facts that have been neglected or by pointing out misinterpretations of specific practices or institutions. For these reasons, the conversation between anthropologists who study different groups has tended to take place at a certain level of abstraction involving theoretical discussion about the nature of religion, culture, persons, social structure, ritual, symbols, myths, dietary restrictions, impurity, and so forth that transcends any specific tradition. The nature of anthropological discourse is thus closely tied to the fact that interpreters study different cultural traditions. A dimension of comparative inquiry is built into anthropological discourse and is responsible for generating second-order reflections on theoretical issues that are crucial to cultural analysis. To borrow insights from anthropological discourse is already to presuppose the results of comparative inquiry.

Imagine how anthropology would be different if all ethnographers studied the same cultural traditions. But this is precisely the situation among interpreters of Israelite religion and ancient Judaism. Since the culture in question is equally accessible or inaccessible to all, no single interpreter prima facie speaks more authoritatively than any other. All interpreters potentially have the same range of data at their disposal. As a result, discourse tends to operate on a less abstract level, focusing on the interpretation of specific practices, beliefs, and institutions. Interpreters of Israelite religion and ancient Judaism are much less likely than anthropologists to entertain theoretical questions that transcend the traditions under interpretation. While endless debates take place about the nature of the covenant or the nature of early Israelite social organization, little reflection occurs on the nature of a religious culture in general.

Comparative inquiry, therefore, generates second-order reflection that transforms the way in which interpreters think about and therefore analyze cultural traditions. This was one of the reasons I found anthropological discourse so helpful in my own research. I discovered a plethora of new models for thinking about Israelite practice and beliefs that had not been employed by interpreters of Israelite religion.

While initially I turned to anthropology for theoretical insights alone, over a period of time I became equally intrigued by the startling similarities in form and substance between Israelite practices and those in other traditions. These similarities disturbed me because the contextualist and diffusionist paradigms simply could not cope with them. If a practice is explained as the result of a process of diffusion or is viewed in its own context alone, the similarities between it and practices in other traditions disappear from view. But I was much more intrigued by how Israelites and ancient Jews were like other peoples than by how they were different. For these reasons, I was never entirely satisfied with the historically oriented explanations that worked only in the case of Israelites and ancient Jews. Consider the oft repeated argument that circumcision became important to Israelites during the Babylonian exile as a means of preserving national identity. This explanation obviously could not explain why circumcision was practiced in diverse cultural traditions. In thinking about that question, I came to a quite different understanding of why circumcision became important to Israelites (chapter 6).

There is yet a third way in which comparative inquiry influenced my thinking. Reading ethnographies convinced me that comparative inquiry was indispensable for interpreting cultures of the past. Since literary and material remains provide an incomplete picture of a tradition, historians by necessity engage in the process of reconstruction. It is ironic that the early advocates of the comparative method were condemned for their practice of "conjectural history." In hindsight, we can see that history is by definition conjectural. Their work was flawed, not because it was hypothetical, but because the presuppositions upon which their conjectures were based proved to be problematic.

Historians of Israelite religion and ancient Judaism are in the same predicament. The literature and material remains provide only a fragmentary picture of a lost whole. This insight only came home to me when I began reading ethnographies and constantly asked myself how Israelites might have answered that question or what might an ethnographer of ancient Judaism have found. Looking to comparative studies helped me to realize how little we actually know. The metaphor that captures this theory of cultural history is archaeology. Interpreters of Israelite religion and ancient Judaism are in the same position as the archaeologist who, on the basis of fragmentary remains, must attempt to reconstruct a larger cultural whole. The archaeology of culture involves the interpreter in the attempt to imagine how incomplete literary remains may reflect or distort a cultural reality of which they once formed a part. The cultural historian is by necessity engaged in an archaeology of culture.

Interpreters of Israelite religion and ancient Judaism have always been aware of this problem, but they avoided its logical implications. One implication is that Robertson Smith and Frazer were entirely right in attempting to envisage the larger picture by seeking analogies from other traditions. Unfortunately, their comparative inquiry was part of their attempt to reconstruct a historical sequence through which all cultures had passed. That sort of reconstruction was problematic. But historians of Israelite religion and ancient Judaism cannot escape the need of reconstruction, as they once thought they could. Hence the turn to comparative inquiry is essential.

To cite another example from my own research, I had always been intrigued by the fact that Leviticus 19:23 calls juvenile fruit trees "uncircumcised." But I never entirely understood the significance of that metaphor until I learned of the close connection between ritual and metaphor and until I discovered that in African circumcision rites the wood of fruit trees is used as fertility medicine. That led me to think more deeply about the assumptions that might underlie the metaphor of an uncircumcised fruit tree (see chapter 6).

As my own work began to incorporate a comparative dimension, I naturally began to reconsider the standard critique of the comparative method. I realized that the works of Robertson Smith and Frazer had themselves become symbols of the problems considered to be endemic to the comparative method. But as sometimes happens, the symbols in this case displaced the concepts they signified. Interpreters assumed that the abuses evident in Robertson Smith's and Frazer's works are intrinsic to the comparative method as such. But just as one should not reject the idea of diffusion because Elliot Smith abused the idea by assuming that all cultures are derivative of ancient Egyptian traditions, one also should not reject the comparative enterprise simply because its early adherents used the method problematically. A theoretical orientation must be judged by its most exemplary use. To reject comparative inquiry based on its application by Robertson Smith and Frazer is like deciding that Shakespeare is boring after watching a high school performance. As Marvin Harris put it, "the abuse of the comparative method must be dissociated from the general principle at issue" (1968, 134). That is not to deny that some serious challenges have been mounted against comparative inquiry. In what follows, I take up these criticisms and show how they are misleading in various ways.

Context and Comparability: When Is a Parallel a Parallel?

According to critics, contextualist and comparativist models of cultural interpretation are essentially incompatible. Comparative inquiry wrenches cultural elements out of context and thereby misconstrues their meaning, function, or character. As a result, the "parallels" that are discovered in this way are almost always misleading. When viewed in their larger context, the resemblances between the elements in question disappear. For example, twentieth-century interpreters of Israelite religion have argued that when seen in context the Israelite practice of circumcision differs fundamentally from circumcision practices in other religious traditions (see chapter 6). Without a doubt, late nineteenth- and early twentieth-century writers such as Frazer were insensitive to the larger cultural contexts in which elements were located. But the critical question is whether this problem is by definition intrinsic to comparative inquiry and if so, how one should respond to it.

To begin with, it is important to realize that when Robertson Smith and Frazer were writing, the whole enterprise of fieldwork had only begun to emerge. Since their time, however, there has been nearly a century of excellent ethnographies produced by researchers who reached a deep understanding of the cultures they interpreted. In theory, then, comparativists today are in a better position than their predecessors to take account of the larger cultural context in which elements are located.

But some theorists would argue that this problem is endemic to comparative inquiry, despite the rich ethnographic literature that has been produced in this century. They point out how notoriously difficult, if not impossible, it is to find comparable elements between cultures separated in time and place. For example, Franz Boas, the founder of American anthropology, pointed out that similar ethnological phenomena are not always due to the same causes. Boas (1940 [1896], 273, 275) demanded that "comparison be restricted to those phenomena which have been proved to be effects of the same causes. . . . In short, before extended comparisons are made, the comparability of the material must be proved." Similarly, Evans-Pritchard cautioned that it is "extremely problematic to say whether two cultural phenomena belong to the same class" (1965, 20).

While these objections are reasonable they are misleading in different sorts of ways. Take the issue of deciding what is comparable in different cultures. While it is always a difficult interpretive decision to say whether two elements are alike or not alike, this problem is not limited to the enterprise of comparing cultures separated temporally and geographically. It confronts the diffusionist as well. Consequently, it is ironic that Boas, along with many interpreters of Israelite religion and ancient Judaism, believed that he escaped the difficulty by turning to a paradigm of diffusion.

That the diffusionist may err by drawing false parallels has become particularly apparent in the study of Israelite religion and ancient Judaism. For example, H. Frankfort (1951) in "The Problem of Similarity in the Ancient Near Eastern Religions," which, incidentally, was delivered as a Frazer Lecture, acknowledged that this danger threatens the project of comparing contiguous cultures. He pointed to ways in which the proponents of the myth and ritual school were misled into thinking that Israelite religion replicated religious patterns of neighboring peoples. Since this essay, dozens of interpreters have pointed to the same danger (e.g., Anderson 1951, 285, 291; Sarna 1970, xxvii; Fohrer 1972, 25).

> What fully justifies our using the comparative method (i.e., comparisons between cultures in contact) is that it gives us a keen eye for the distinctive character of this or that religion. To apply the method correctly, however, is by no means a simple matter; and it has given occasion for so many *faux pas* that a lot of people will having nothing to do with it any more. The chief reason has been that in making the comparison it was usual to take as one's point of departure those features that are conspicuously akin and on that basis to declare the one religion straightway identical with, or deriving from, the other. Over and over again this turned out to be wrong. Religions may employ the same ideas and yet differ profoundly from one another in their essential nature. (Vriezen 1967, 23)

Diffusionists thus face the problem of deciding what is similar and what is different, and that decision is an interpretive one.

The same sort of worry led Samuel Sandmel to accuse scholars of Second Temple Judaism of "parallelomania," the disease of comparing incomparable elements within early Christianity and rabbinic Judaism. In particular, Sandmel notes how elements of rabbinic culture are frequently wrenched out of their larger context. "It seems to me," he writes, "that we are at a junction when biblical scholarship should recognize parallelomania for the disease

that it is" (Sandmel 1962, 13). Clearly, the diffusionist model of cultural interpretation does not escape the methodological conundrum of determining
what are comparable elements in different cultures. Since both comparative
methods (metonymic and metaphoric) must deal with the problem of comparability, this cannot be the basis for favoring one over the other.

Precisely for this reason, some interpreters conclude that the contextualist
and integrationist view of culture is superior since it avoids comparisons altogether. But while it is true that the contextualist paradigm escapes the problem of saying what is and is not a valid similarity, too often that advantage
leads to the more generalized assumption that there are no interpretive difficulties in the contextualist or integrationist paradigm. "Our danger lies in an
exclusive interest in similarities themselves; for it is—as always—the cultural
context which holds the secret of their significance" (Frankfort 1951, 23). In
fact, determining just what is "the context" is itself always an interpretive act.
Cultural wholes are complex and thus there are numerous ways in which the
interactions among cultural elements can be construed. Since it is impossible
to see everything as related to everything else, the interpreter is forced to
make a decision as to which elements in the system are related. In addition, it
is never entirely clear where "the context" begins and ends. Indeed, the difference between a contextualist and a diffusionist paradigm ultimately breaks
down. While from one perspective the diffusionist is comparing separate cultures, from another neighboring cultures are themselves part of the context
and the diffusionist is investigating the relations of elements in their context.

There has been a tendency in the twentieth century to assume that it is
easier to determine the context than to discover comparable practices, beliefs,
or institutions between cultures separated in time and place. To see that this
view is false, one simply has to look at debates among contextualists who
reject one another's positions because they disagree on the importance of or
connection among various parts of "the context." The twentieth-century refrain that cultural items have to be interpreted "in their context" hides more
than it reveals. The comparativist, then, can acknowledge the difficulty of
determining what elements are comparable without needing to feel overly
embarrassed. This is a problem that an advocate of comparative inquiry must
face. But it doesn't make this sort of approach any more hazardous than its
competitors.

Comparative Inquiry and the Native's Point of View

The realization that an interpretive operation is involved in the act of locat-
ing a belief or practice in context allows the comparativist to respond to a
second argument that privileges the contextual over the comparative model
of cultural interpretation. Developing the ideas of Wittgenstein, Peter Winch
has argued that cross-cultural comparisons are problematic because they ig-

nore the assumptions and categories that are indigenous to the cultures in question, thus discounting what has subsequently come to be called the "emic" or "native" point of view. In doing so, Winch claims, the interpreter is involved in a contradiction. The idea that something is a social rather than a natural phenomenon presupposes that it has meanings to actors. The comparativist assumes the element under interpretation is social but then proceeds to ignore precisely that which allows it to be seen as social in the first place. Winch writes:

> if the sociological investigator wants to regard them as *social* events . . . he has to take seriously the criteria which are applied for distinguishing 'different' kinds of actions and identifying the 'same' kinds of actions within the way of life he is studying. It is not open to him arbitrarily to impose his own standards from without. In so far as he does so, the events he is studying lose altogether their character as social events. (Winch 1959, 108)

Now this view seems to rule out comparison altogether. For comparing cultures automatically requires the interpreter to impose her or his own standards of what is alike and not alike. Comparative inquiry by definition adopts an "etic" perspective.

Consider the example Winch uses to illustrate his objection. Winch considers it problematic to compare Christian baptism with "pagan" practices of sprinkling water, because "a Christian would strenuously deny that the baptism rites of his faith were really the same in character as the acts of a pagan sprinkling lustral water or letting sacrificial blood" (Winch 1959, 108). In his view, if we deny what the Christian says, we are in effect falling into a self-contradiction because we are ignoring what makes baptism a social event, namely, the fact that it has certain meanings for Christians.

But this argument is mistaken for several reasons. First, when the interpreter asserts the comparability of baptism and pagan sprinkling, she or he does not deny *everything* that the actor says about the practice. The comparison is only suggested in the first place because Christians say baptism removes the taint of original sin and because "pagans" say that sprinkling water removes impurity. It is the actors' interpretations in their respective contexts that give rise to the hypothesis that these are comparable acts. True, it is the interpreter and not the actors who put these two social activities into the same category. The interpreter concludes that in both contexts there is a sense that the person is in a non-desirable state and that that state can be corrected by certain acts of purification that involve water. But this sort of comparative statement does not detract from the social character of the events, for it rests ultimately on the self-understandings of the actors.

Winch might respond to this objection by claiming that the interpreter has no right to say there is a similarity between removing the taint of original sin and removing impurity, because the concepts of original sin and impurity are fundamentally different. But that claim generates a variety of other problems. It means that Winch envisions a self-effacing interpreter who brackets entirely her or his own judgments about the traditions being studied. But if one takes this ideal seriously, the end result is regurgitation, not interpretation. To efface oneself means that one cannot say anything beyond what the actors or traditions under interpretation already say. If one took this stricture seriously, one could not even reorganize the material under analysis, since in doing so one imposes standards from without. It is even doubtful that an interpreter could justify asking questions that the people or traditions do not already themselves ask, since these questions come "from the outside." Indeed, as I argued above, a contextualist reading must rely on the interpreter's judgment of where the context begins and ends and how the elements within the confines of the context relate to one another. Since the interpreter's standards are always brought into play, comparative inquiry cannot be dismissed solely on the grounds that it involves the interpreter's own criteria of what is like and not alike.

That an interpreter must always invoke standards from the home culture is evident from Winch's own work. In a subsequent essay (1970, 78–111), Winch criticizes Evans-Pritchard and MacIntyre for comparing magic and science, which, in Winch's view, constitutes a category mistake. Instead, Winch suggests that we can begin to understand Azande magic when we think of it as analogous to Christian prayer (1970, 104–5)! Surely Christians would not be happy with that comparison and probably the Azande would not be either. What this shows is that Winch falls subject to his own critique. In interpreting an alien phenomenon, he invokes standards from his own frame of reference. But this is not because Winch is sloppy. It is because he is doing what all interpreters must do: invoking criteria from outside the tradition under interpretation.

But if an interpreter must necessarily employ ideas from outside the tradition under study, from where do they originate? As I suggested earlier, many of the theoretical concepts used in cultural analysis are part of a tradition of interpretation that has itself been practically tested against other traditions and are thus products of comparative inquiry. As we shall now see, this realization confounds the longstanding assumption that contextualist and comparative paradigms of cultural interpretation are incompatible. Indeed, contextualization and comparative inquiry presuppose one another.

Context, Comparison, and the Theory of Cultural Interpretation

There is a widespread perception that comparative inquiry is avoidable in the enterprise of cultural analysis. Contextualists are often convinced that the operation of seeing elements in their cultural contexts is fundamentally noncomparative. This view assumes that comparative inquiry is at best a secondary operation that occurs after contextualization has already taken place. The comparative enterprise is thus parasitic on the labor of ethnography or history. Generalizations are only possible on the basis of already existing studies that describe the development, meanings, and functions of a tradition in its own context.

These assumptions have some noteworthy advocates among anthropologists and interpreters of Israelite religion and ancient Judaism. For example, Boas argued that social laws could only be formulated once careful histories and ethnographies were carried out. In biblical studies, similar sentiments motivated Albright's emphasis on ancient Near Eastern cultures and archaeology. Israelite history, Albright argued, must be understood on its own terms first. Only subsequently could information about Israelite history be used for making generalizations about the development of religion in general. These sentiments continue to be echoed. "The interpretation of biblical features—whether of a socio-political, cultic, general-cultural, or literary nature—with the help of inner-biblical parallels *should always precede* the comparison with extra-biblical materials. In the evaluation of a societal phenomenon, attention should be paid to its function in the developing structure of the Israelite body politic *before one engages* in the comparison with parallel phenomena in other societies" (Talmon 1977, 356, emphasis supplied). "Systematic description must begin with the system to be described. Comparative description follows" (Neusner 1978, 179).

Upon scrutiny, the perception that comparison is a secondary operation proves to be a misapprehension. A pure ethnography or history that is uncontaminated by generalizations based on comparative inquiry is an ideal that cannot exist in practice. When ethnographers go out into the field, they are constantly refracting the traditions they encounter through the anthropological lens. That lens, constituted by the tradition of questions, assumptions, and concerns in which the ethnographer is trained, is part of the equipment that the ethnographer brings into the field. Indeed, the writing of the ethnography does not even take place at the scene but after the fact when the fieldworker returns to the home culture. To be accepted for publication, the ethnography must speak to concerns that already dominate discourse in the field. "The essential point to remember is that the anthropologist is working within a body of theoretical knowledge and that he makes his observations to solve problems which derive from it. . . . We tell our anthropological students to study problems and not peoples" (Evans-Pritchard 1951, 87).

What this means, of course, is that "thick" descriptions, those rich ethnographic interpretations favored by Geertz, always already presuppose comparative studies. When Geertz studied the Balinese cockfight, he had already spent years mastering the anthropological literature on totemism. So that article, as all of Geertz's pieces, was not written in a vacuum. Comparative analysis is simply unavoidable. If an interpreter repudiates it, it comes in the back door.

The same argument can be made in response to Boas's insistence that careful histories of individual societies precede generalizations. There are never unambiguous histories. There is always debate about what comes first and what follows, which items are causally related and which functionally, which are integrated and which are not. Historical accounts thus presuppose certain ideas about how parts of a cultural system fit together. These ideas are, at least in part, given to the historian by a tradition of interpretation, which has been practically tested against many individual cases. So history, like ethnography, always already presupposes comparative inquiry. Boas was aware of this to a certain extent. The study of discrete histories of individual societies "is not the ultimate aim of our science, because the general laws, although *implied in such a description,* cannot be clearly formulated nor their relative value appreciated without a thorough comparison to the manner in which they become manifest in different cultures" (Boas 1940 [1896], 279, emphasis supplied).

What this means is that there is no escaping the comparative enterprise. Even the most concrete, contextualist study presupposes certain notions about societies, cultures, and persons formulated to explain human behavior and experience in diverse contexts.

This conclusion has important implications for interpreters of Israelite religion and ancient Judaism. Whether acknowledged or not, any study of these religious cultures takes for granted notions about the mind, symbols, rituals, power, relations of economic, social, and political forces, and so forth. As long as cross-cultural comparison is denigrated, these concepts remain tacit and unexamined. But such concepts come in covertly because analysis of a religious culture must presuppose them.

Interpreters of Israelite religion and ancient Judaism absorb these ideas indirectly when they learn the traditions of scholarship in their field. The assumptions embedded in these traditions were themselves generalizations arrived at by earlier interpreters who had reflected on the nature of religion, culture, and society. Many of the ideas about what religion is and how it works were formulated initially in the late nineteenth and early twentieth century in a discourse that was strongly apologetic. Although biblical studies has transcended that apologetic, concepts from that original context continue to survive in current discourse. At the very least, the reemergence of a comparative discourse within the scholarship on Israelite religion and ancient Judaism will force these implicit assumptions up to the surface of inquiry. In many cases it will also provide fresh ways of conceptualizing the relations among the phenomena in question.

This is why I ultimately do not consider comparative inquiry intrinsically incompatible with the other paradigms that govern discourse on Israelite religion and ancient Judaism. Studying other cultures actually enriches my understanding of what a practice means in its Israelite and ancient Jewish context. Indeed, in many cases the interpretation reached by metaphoric comparisons can complement those that emerge out of a contextualist or diffusionist perspective. For example, diffusionists claim that the story of God instructing Abram to cut animals in half (Gen. 15) becomes comprehensible when one realizes that such acts were used to conclude treaties in the ancient Near East. But comparative inquiry suggests an alternative interpretation, namely, that cutting the animal in half represents an act whereby kinship relations are severed (see chapter 6). God instructs Abram to cut the animals to represent the disjuncture that is introduced into his father's genealogical line. Abram and his descendants are split off from other lines of descent. These two interpretations are not incompatible. The practice may simultaneously signify the conclusion of a covenant as well as the idea of a genealogical rupture. It is thus possible that in adopting a practice widely known in the ancient Near East, Israelites superimposed upon it a meaning that only becomes evident when comparisons are made to cultures geographically and temporally removed.

At other times, metaphoric comparisons will put a radically different interpretation on a given practice. For example, contextualists claim that circumcision has no associations with fertility in Israelite religion. This is why Israelites practiced circumcision on the eighth day after birth and not near puberty. But cross-cultural material can call this judgment into question (see chapter 6). When this conflict of interpretations occurs, the adherents of each paradigm will have to debate the respective merits and liabilities of each interpretation. This process of arguing between paradigms ultimately enriches and deepens our understanding of the traditions in question.

In fact, while these paradigms are separable analytically, they overlap in practice. When I develop comparisons between ancient Israelite religion and other traditions a great deal of my analysis relies on a contextualist reading of the Israelite material. But it is a contextualist reading that is shaped by my knowledge of other traditions. So while contextualist interpretations always presuppose comparative inquiry, the reverse is also the case: comparative inquiry always assumes some understanding of a practice in its context. That is not to say that all interpreters should read ethnographies or anthropological theory. But it does mean that the field will be enriched when those who want to operate within a more explicitly comparative framework are respected as participants in a common project.

Comparison, Social Laws, and Generalizations

This reconciliation of comparative inquiry and contextualization amounts to a reinterpretation of the role of comparison in cultural analysis. No longer is comparative inquiry justified as a method for uncovering universal social laws that operate cross-culturally. This understanding of the comparative enterprise, formulated by its early proponents, was linked to a positivist conception of the social sciences. Advocates desired a science of culture that would be as rigorous as the natural sciences. But this conception of the social sciences has proven naïve. Nowhere is this clearer than in the failure of the comparative method to discover social laws. Human phenomena are too complex to be captured in terms of simple formulae, rules, or laws. "One has only to find one negative instance which cannot be accounted for in terms of the formulation and it then must be either abandoned or reformulated; and one does not have to search long for such an instance" (Evans-Pritchard 1965, 29). Moreover, if one does find a "formula that no one can cite exceptions to, it has become so essentially logical, so remote from phenomena, that no one knows precisely what to do with it" (Kroeber 1935, 561).

The critical question is whether there is a role for cross-cultural comparisons once this scientific ideology is repudiated. Clearly, many interpreters do not think so. Geertz's repudiation of a scientific model of the cultural sciences is linked to an overt rejection of the comparative enterprise in favor of thick description, an understanding of how symbols shape and reflect human experience in discrete contexts.

In my judgment, there are several reasons why comparative work remains indispensable in the enterprise of cultural analysis. Although comparative studies have not produced laws, they have produced some valid generalizations. Cultures are indeed complex phenomena that have their own distinctive histories. But humans in different times and places struggle with similar sorts of issues, such as the meaning of existence, human sexuality, the difference between genders, the question of what happens at death, and so forth. To seek generalizations assumes that there are certain constraining influences on how cultures develop that emerge from the nature of our mind, our bodies, our environments, and from the fact that we are social beings. These constraints, though not determinative, are influential, and sometimes they lead different societies to solve similar problems in analogous ways.

Although comparative inquiry has not revealed any social law, it has produced some useful substantive and formal generalizations. By substantive generalizations I mean cases where similar themes, ideas, or issues are encountered in different contexts. Although I am not prepared to go as far as Lévi-Strauss in presupposing fundamental oppositions such as the raw and cooked that govern thought everywhere, I am convinced from his analysis and others that the mind in many contexts manipulates similar objects in similar ways. One thinks for example of the connection in many cultures between fruit, eating, and human sexuality. One finds that in many contexts the cooking pot is associated with intimate relationships. We know that virgin births are not limited to the Christian context. We know that flood stories are found in diverse cultural contexts. We know that many traditions equate women with nature and men with culture. These are some of the substantive ways in which different traditions converge.

Different cultural traditions also have formal similarities; that is, similar sorts of processes take place in different contexts. For example, in diverse societies descent plays a role in the organization of a community. Among such groups, one finds certain kinds of formal convergences in the religious world view (chapters 6, 8, and 9). One also finds that rites of initiation have certain common features in diverse contexts. As van Gennep (1960 [1908]) and then Turner (1969) showed, there is a process whereby the initiate undergoes a symbolic death before being born again into a new status or role. Or take the fact that metaphors play an important role in shaping human practice in diverse settings. Although different metaphors might govern in different contexts, there are important similarities in the process by which metaphor and practice interact. These and other insights are available because comparative work has been done in the past.

Although the comparative enterprise fails to uncover laws of human societies, it does presuppose a fundamental truth about human societies: that although different people have different histories and live in different contexts, cultures always have features that resemble those of others. The advocates of thick description, whether anthropologists or interpreters of ancient Jews, have no way of accounting for the similarities among cultures that are not in contact. When you ask them about such similarities they become inarticulate and either deny that such similarities exist or claim that they are uninteresting. Since such similarities do exist and since they are interesting, they should find a place in the larger picture we construct of humanity.

In conclusion, comparative inquiry is inescapable. Whether we perform comparisons consciously or not, our interpretations of cultures always presuppose ideas that derived from and can only be validated through comparison. In addition, comparative inquiry captures a truth about cultures: that despite their important differences there are certain interesting convergences that our account of human activity must try to comprehend. Finally, attending to more than one cultural tradition frees us to see the tradition under interpretation in new ways. Comparative inquiry, like other paradigms of interpretation, has its problems. But it also has its share of successes. Some of those successes are evident in the interpretations which follow.

The Jewish sow: an early German libel associated Jews with pig, which was forbidden by Jewish dietary restrictions. In this fifteenth-century woodcut, Jews are shown suckling the sow. Reprinted from *Encyclopedia Judaica* (Jerusalem: Keter Publishing House, 1971), p. 118, with permission of the Germanisches Nationalmuseum, Nürnberg.

Blood libel: the accusation that Jews murdered Christian children to obtain blood for the Passover ritual. This is a fifteenth-century woodcut showing Jews extracting blood from the body of Simon of Trent. The Jews are distinguished by a circular Jewish badge. Reprinted from Norman Cohn, *Warrant for Genocide* (New York: Harper & Row), p. **143**. Courtesy of Marburg/Art Resource, New York.

Sacrifice of captives by Aztecs, by Bernard Picart. Reprinted from J. F. Bernard, *Cérémonies et coutumes religieuses de tous les peuples du monde* (Amsterdam: 1752), vol. 1, 150–51. Courtesy of the Lilly Library, Bloomington, Indiana.

Cannibalism by Peruvians, by Bernard Picart. Reprinted from J. F. Bernard, *Cérémonies et coutumes religieuses de tous les peuples du monde* (Amsterdam: 1752), vol. 1, 98. Courtesy of the Lilly Library, Bloomington, Indiana.

An eighteenth-century woodcut depicting a sunken bathing place used by Jewesses in Fürth for ritual purification after menstruation. Reprinted from Hermann Heinrich Ploss, Max Bartels, and Paul Bartels, *Woman: An Historical, Gynaecological and Anthropological Compendium,* vol. 1, ed. Eric John Dingwall (St. Louis: The C. V. Mosby Co., 1938), p. 648.

Tent used among the "Indians" of North America for secluding women during menstruation. Reprinted from Hermann Heinrich Ploss, Max Bartels, and Paul Bartels, *Woman: An Historical, Gynaecological and Anthropological Compendium,* vol. 1, ed. Eric John Dingwall (St. Louis: The C. V. Mosby Co., 1938), p. 606.

Circumcision of infant by Portuguese Jews, by Bernard Picart. Reprinted from J. F. Bernard, *Cérémonies et coutumes religieuses de tous les peuples du monde* (Amsterdam: 1752), vol. 2, 1–3. Courtesy of the Lilly Library, Bloomington, Indiana.

Ceremonies of the Mexicans practiced on their infants, by Bernard Picart. Depicts infant circumcision by Aztecs. Reprinted from J. F. Bernard, *Cérémonies et costumes religieuses de tous les peuples du monde* (Amsterdam: 1752), vol. 1, 162–63. Courtesy of the Lilly Library, Bloomington, Indiana.

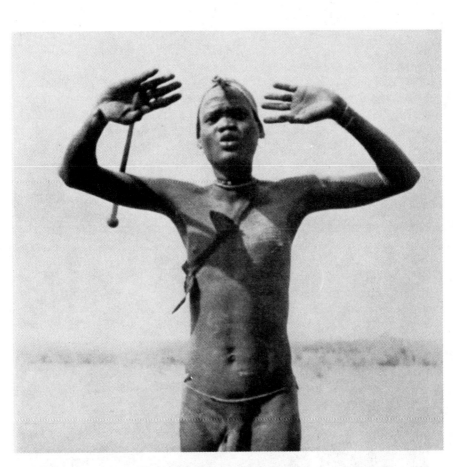

A Nuer youth singing in praise of his ox. His arms are raised in imitation of its horns. Reprinted from E. E. Evans-Pritchard, *Kinship and Marriage among the Nuer* (Oxford: Oxford University Press, 1951), with permission of the Pitt Rivers Museum, Oxford University.

Ox with spreading horns. Reprinted from E. E. Evans-Pritchard, *Kinship and Marriage among the Nuer* (Oxford: Oxford University Press, 1951), with permission of the Pitt Rivers Museum, Oxford University.

Part II

Cows, Blood, and Juvenile Fruit Trees

*Symbolic Language, Ritual,
and Social Structure in Israelite
Religion and Ancient Judaism*

5.

Israel in the
Mirror of Nature

Animal Metaphors in the
Rituals and Narratives
of Israelite Religion

What therefore is truth? A mobile army of metaphors, meton-
ymies, anthropomorphisms: in short a sum of human relations which become poetically and rhetorically intensified,
metamorphosed, adorned, and after long usage seem to a nation fixed, canonic and binding; truths are illusions of which
one has forgotten that they are illusions; worn-out metaphors
which have become powerless to affect the senses.

Nietzsche 1974

In 1880, William Robertson Smith published a small monograph entitled
"Animal Worship and Animal Tribes among the Arabs and in the Old Testament," in which he argued that the Semites had passed through a totemic
stage in their religious development. The inspiration for this hypothesis came
from J. F. McLennan's essay "The Worship of Plants and Animals" which
appeared in the *Fortnightly Review* of 1869 and 1870. In these essays, which at
the time stimulated a great deal of discussion among interpreters of religion,
McLennan argued that all religions had passed through a stage in which animals and plants were objects of worship, a stage McLennan referred to as
totemism. Totemism was defined as the form of religion in which people believed that they were actual descendants of a specific species of animal or
plant. Prohibitions generally forbade a person to hunt or eat the totem species, except on specific sacred occasions during which the descendants of a
given totem united to express their solidarity. McLennan believed this religious phenomenon was originally linked to a matrilineal form of kinship in
which the offspring inherited the totem of their mother's brother. Persons

who shared the same totem were frequently prohibited from marrying one another and sexual relations among persons of the same totem were considered incest. Since traces of totemism were visible in the historical record of civilized peoples and since totemism continued unabated among contemporary savages, McLennan concluded that all religions had developed from a totemic stage.

McLennan did not actually discuss the religion of the Semites. But Robertson Smith was convinced that McLennan's theory was applicable to Semitic religious history. "My results," wrote Robertson Smith (1880, 78) "are remarkably confirmatory of Mr. Maclennan's theory—a theory framed almost absolutely without reference to the Semitic races, but which nevertheless will be found to explain the true connection of a great number of facts which have hitherto remained unexplained and almost unobserved. It is not often that a historical speculation receives such notable experimental verification." Specifically, Robertson Smith argued that evidence of a totemic stage of religion was present in the earliest Semitic sources and that survivals of totemism were still evident in the Bible itself.

To support his contention, he pointed to, among other things, the frequent use in the Hebrew Bible of animal names to designate both individuals and groups of people who reckoned descent from a common ancestor. To cite but a few of the many examples: Eglon (calf) is a King of Moab and Nahash (serpent) is a King of the Ammonites. Numbered among David's ancestors is Nahshon (snake). Princes of Midian are called Oreb (raven) and Ze'eb (wolf). Animal names are given to five descendants of Seir the Horite (Gen. 36:20–21). His children include Shobal (young lion), Zibeon (hyena), Anah (wild ass), Dishon (antelope), and Dishan (antelope). Zibeon's sons in turn include Anah (wild ass) and Aiyah (kite). The Bible refers to a group called the Calebites, descendants of Caleb (dog). Descendants of Midian include Epher (fawn) (Gen. 25:4). The Shechemites call themselves sons of Hamor, the he-ass (Gen. 33:19). In a later work (1903 [1885], 254), Robertson Smith also pointed out that two of the matriarchs, Leah and Rachel, both have animal names. "Rachel" means "ewe" and "Leah" means "bovine antelope."[1] The use of so many animal names, Robertson Smith argued, indicated that Semitic tribes had once viewed themselves as descendants of various species of animals.

As Robertson Smith's contemporaries and successors pointed out, there were a variety of good reasons to reject this hypothetical reconstruction. Unfortunately, an important insight was lost when Robertson Smith's theory of Semitic totemism was repudiated. The fact that so many biblical characters have animal names is interesting and requires some sort of explanation. This lost insight can be recovered if we consider how the study of totemism developed within anthropology in the twentieth century. I suggest that were Robertson Smith alive today, his reading in ethnographic literature and anthropology would direct his attention to many of the same facts but he would see them in a different light. Specifically, the problems that nineteenth- and early twentieth-century thinkers treated under the rubric of totemism are now explicated with help from the concept of metaphor (Lévi-Strauss 1962; Geertz 1973, 412–54; Sapir and Crocker 1977; Urton 1985), which has recently emerged as a central tool in cultural analysis. The concept of metaphor makes it possible to see the significance of animal names in the Hebrew Bible. As I will suggest below, Israelite thought is saturated with metaphors drawn from domains of experience concerned with raising animals and growing crops. Fauna and agriculture supplied Israelites with images for thinking about human experience and social life and these metaphors shaped the practices and narratives of Israelite religion. Before spelling this out, it is first necessary to consider the place of metaphor in cultural analysis.

From Totemism to Metaphor

Metaphor is the activity of understanding or experiencing one thing in light of something else (e.g., he is a hotdog, she is a fox). Recent theoretical and ethnographic literature has shown that metaphor not only infuses thought but that language itself is metaphoric at its root (Lakoff and Johnson 1980). The concept of metaphor has had important repercussions in anthropology over the past thirty years and is itself linked to a shift in the metaphors that govern the practice of cultural analysis. As long as the social sciences were self-consciously modeled after the natural sciences, concepts like "structuralism," "functionalism," "biofeedback mechanisms," and "homeostasis" shaped and organized research agendas. The concept of metaphor became important in anthropological discourse as interpreters such as Lévi-Strauss, Turner, Geertz, and Fernandez began to think of culture as analogous to language and texts. Symptomatic of this change was the growing emphasis on concepts like "metaphor," "metonymy," and the "trope of cultures" which derived from linguistics and literary criticism.[2]

The concept of metaphor led to a reconceptualization of the entire question of totemism. Developing the insights of Radcliffe-Brown, Lévi-Strauss (1962) suggested that fauna and vegetation often serve as foundational metaphors among people who live close to nature. The metaphors that are used to reflect upon human life and social experience frequently revolve around animal life and agriculture. For example, since animals and plants serve as metaphorical human beings, differences between social groupings are metaphorically related to differences in species of animals. Moreover, a variety of existential dilemmas related to human existence, including the tension between life and death, sex and reproduction, differences between genders, between humans and gods, and between humans and animals, are explicated through the language of natural metaphors. When Lévi-Strauss says that animals are "good to think," he means that the human mind has exploited the differences among animals as a way of representing conceptual differences that enable the mind to reflect on the human condition.

More recently, the concept of metaphor has figured prominently in the analyses of Fernandez (1972; 1974; 1977), Geertz (1973, 412–54), Turner (1974), Sapir and Crocker (1977), and Urton (1985). In his famous analysis of Bali cockfighting, for example, Geertz argues that the cock is a metaphor for the virile, animalistic character of Balinese men. The cockfight, therefore, is something more than an activity of gambling. During the cockfight, a Balinese man metaphorically puts himself on the line. In this way, the cockfight constitutes a text through which the Balinese articulate and recognize their deeper, darker selves, the aggressive side of their culture, which is kept hidden beneath a veneer of restraint and politeness.

What emerges from the writings of these interpreters are two independent claims. First, animals and plants frequently serve as root metaphors in the thought of peoples who live close to nature. Second, the metaphors that dominate language and thought have an impact on shaping the structure and meaning of practice. Metaphor is not simply a way in which we think; social practice itself is related to and structured by the metaphors that dominate language and thought. Interpreting culture involves understanding not only how certain kinds of metaphors inform a body of thought but also how the metaphoric process is implicated in shaping cultural practices and organizing social life. If metaphors are "good to think," research has also shown that they are good to live by (Fernandez 1972; 1974; 1977; Lakoff and Johnson 1980).

It is difficult for us to grasp the importance of natural metaphors for people who live close to nature. In our own technological society, such metaphors have been displaced to a great extent by images drawn from production (Sahlins 1976; Martin 1987). Nonetheless, animal and plant metaphors still play an important role in our language and thought (e.g., "heard it through the grapevine," "horse around," "deflower," "hatch a plot," "sheepish," "sly as a fox," "she is a fox," "she's a peach," "follow the pack," "bring into the fold," "an idea takes root," "give him the bird," "she is cultivated," "tailend," "fruitful line of inquiry," and so forth). Natural metaphors also continue to structure some domains of experience in our culture, as evident in the names of American automobiles: Mustang, Lynx, Barracuda, Firebird, Sunbird, Cougar, Taurus, Colt, and so forth. These names point to the fast, flashy, and aggressive styles of driving that are both an ideal and reality in American culture. Imagine the experience of driving cars bearing the names "Sheep," "Pussy Cat," or "Elephant."

From Israelite Totemism to Natural Metaphors

The importance of metaphor in culture enables us to appreciate the importance of Robertson Smith's insight that so many biblical figures had animal names. This is one manifestation of how fauna and agriculture provided the metaphors through which Israelites came to understand who they were and what they wanted to be. Israelite religious thought, as expressed in prophetic genres, poetry, and narratives of the Hebrew Bible, relies self-consciously on a whole host of natural metaphors drawn from the domains of animal husbandry and agricultural life. As in many traditional societies, fauna and agriculture supplied a rich vocabulary for thinking about social and religious life (Douglas 1966; Fox 1971; Radcliffe-Brown 1965 [1952]; Tambiah 1969; Turner 1967). In the case of ancient Israel, these metaphors provided a language for conceptualizing the relationship of Israel to its neighbors and to God and for thinking about kinship and social relations. Nature, then, served as a foundational or root metaphor (Pepper 1942, 38–39) for ancient Israelite thought.[3]

The centrality of these natural metaphors in Israelite thought has important implications for understanding the large number of Israelite religious practices that revolve around animal husbandry and agriculture. One of the difficulties in interpreting such practices has been the reticence of biblical sources to provide any explicit account of their significance. But perhaps interpreters have been looking in the wrong place. It seems only natural to consider the relationship between the overt metaphors of Israelite thought and those religious practices and narratives that also involve fauna and agriculture. As I will argue below, these metaphors which are so common in Israelite thought gave rise to a number of religious practices and also provide an interpretive context in which a number of practices and narratives can be understood.

Before turning to my analysis, two methodological caveats are in order. First, in the discussion that follows I take for granted that Israelites would have found implausible the kinds of interpretations offered here. In fact, they probably would have considered such interpretations quite bizarre. I take as axiomatic that individuals are not aware of all the interconnections between their practices and the various strands of thought that exist in their culture. Consequently, the role of the interpreter is to disclose those connections that for one reason or another have remained unnoticed.

Second, I do not mean to imply that the interpretations I offer are the only ones possible. Turner, for example, has shown how symbols can be multivocal (Turner 1967). The same point can be made about religious practices. For example, a practice may be an instantiation of an ethical value articulated by the religious system and at the same time have a connection to foundational metaphors. Indeed, I would suggest that what often gives practices their power is precisely the fact that they make contact in diverse and numerous ways with other practices and with the thought of the religious system. In other words, people find religious rituals to be satisfying when they seem to fit together with many other parts of the religion in question.[4] Consequently, by accounting for various practices in terms of the metaphors governing Israelite thought, I by no means intend to rule out other interpretations of such practices.

Natural Metaphors in Israelite Thought

Fauna and agriculture serve as a source of metaphors throughout the Hebrew Bible, from the earliest to the latest sources. Such metaphors cut across genre, appearing in narratives, prophetic speech, and poetry. Moreover, with the help of natural imagery, the most important religious and national themes find articulation. Wildlife, for example, is used quite frequently to speak about the relations among the nations. Israel's neighbors are often pictured as wild beasts such as lions (Isa. 5:29; Jer. 2:15; 50:17; Joel 1:6; Pss. 7:2–3; 17:12), bees (Deut. 1:44), or vultures (Hab. 1:8) that attack and prey upon Israel. Egypt is described as the flesh of asses, the offspring of horses, and as fish (Ezek. 23:20; 29:4). Ammon and Edom are eagles (Jer. 49:16; Obad. 1:1–4), and Moab is likened to fugitive birds and doves (Isa. 16:2; Jer. 48:28). Israel is also compared to a wide range of animals, such as grasshoppers (Num. 13:33), he-goats (Jer. 50:8), a lion cub and lion (Ezek. 19:1–9), the choice of the flock (Ezek. 24:5), an ass (Hos. 8:9; Jer. 2:24), and a camel in heat (Jer. 2:23).

Similar images inform the theological vocabulary of Israelite writers. Ovine metaphors are particularly numerous. God is frequently described as the shepherd of Israel, the divine flock.[5] Generally, this image has positive connotations, expressing the conviction that God is the protector of Israel. "The sheep of My pasture are men, I will increase Israel with men as a flock" (Ezek. 34:31; 36:37).[6] But at times, God is the shepherd who brings the flock to slaughter (Jer. 12:3; Pss. 44:12, 23; 74:1). In the words of one psalmist, "Why, O God, do You reject us, do You fume in anger at the flock that You tend" (Ps. 74:1)? When Israel is deserving of punishment, God is sometimes described as a predatory animal, such as a lion that preys on the flock of Israel (Jer. 25:38). Israel's immoral behavior is also described in ovine imagery: Israel is like a flock that goes astray (Isa. 53:6).

Like the flock imagery, bovine metaphors are routinely invoked to express the positive and negative aspects of Israel's relation to God. Israel as God's faithful servant is like a heifer that God uses to plow and upon which God sets a yoke (Hos. 10:11). Those who fear God will gambol as calves in the stall (Mal. 3:20). But when people rebel against God, they are like a calf that has not been broken (Jer. 31:18) or a stubborn heifer (Hos. 4:16).

In addition to animal husbandry, agriculture also supplies numerous images for describing the relation between Israel and God. Israel is likened to an olive tree (Jer. 11:16), to a vine (Jer. 6:9; Ezek. 19:10; Ps. 80:9), to the first fruit of God's harvest (Jer. 2:3), to a watered garden (Jer. 31:12), to the growth of a field (Ezek. 16:7), to grapes in the wilderness (Hos. 9:10), and to first ripe figs (Isa. 28:4; Jer. 24:3–5; Hos. 9:10). Consequently, biblical writers describe Israel's security on its land in terms of taking root, sprouting, and blossoming (Isa. 27:6). When Israel deserves punishment, however, God will pull up that which was planted (Jer. 45:4), and Israel will cease to produce fruit (Hos. 9:16).

The relationship between God and individuals is also captured in husbandry and agricultural metaphors. A person who studies divine law is like a tree planted by a stream of water (Ps. 1:3). One whose soul longs for God is like a hart that pants after water (Ps. 42:2), and an individual who finds God is an olive tree in the house of God (Ps. 52:10). One who does not have wisdom is like a horse or mule (Ps. 32:9), while a person who finds protection in God is like a fledgling that finds shelter under its mother's wings (Ps. 91:4). Speakers of lies are like serpents with venom (Ps. 58:5).

Kinship and social relations are also couched in similar terminology. Children are described as the first fruit of their parents (Gen. 49:3; Deut. 21:17) or as olive saplings (Ps. 128:3). A man's wife is a fruitful vine (Ps. 128:3), a graceful mountain goat, and a loving doe whose breasts one is instructed to suckle (Prov. 5:19). A man who wanders from his place is like a bird that leaves a nest (Prov. 27:8). Various animals such as the bull, ram, lion, and he-goat are frequently used as metaphors for soldiers, leaders, princes, or nobles (Miller 1970). A male prostitute is called a dog (Deut. 23:19). There is also the interesting story in which Samson tells the Philistines a riddle. When Samson discovers that the Philistines had coaxed his wife to disclose the answer, he says to them, "Had you not plowed with my heifer, you would not have guessed my riddle" (Judg. 14:18) metaphorically equating his wife with livestock. Similarly, when Nathan the prophet tells King David a parable about a rich man who steals a poor man's ewe lamb to feed a guest, Nathan is metaphorically referring to David's affair with Bathsheba (2 Sam. 12).

This superficial overview only begins to show the extent to which faunal and agricultural imagery provides the vocabulary for expressing the theological, national, social, and moral conceptions of ancient Israel.[7] In the habits of animals, in their fighting and eating, mating and reproducing, Israel found a symbolic language for conceptualizing its own social life and its relations to its neighbors, and for comprehending the divine-human relationship. In short, animals, and to some extent the fields and their produce, were conceived of as a world parallel to Israelite society. This other world both reflected Israelite experience of life and served as a model for what Israelite communal and individual life should and could be.

The Said and the Unsaid in Israelite Religion

As is evident from the citations above, the prophetic writings, psalms, and proverbs, more than the genres of narrative and law, provide access to the symbolic language of Israelite religious culture. These genres do not impose the same constraints that are embedded in the narrative form. In Israelite narrative, attention is devoted to an unfolding sequence of events which moves inexorably toward a resolution of dramatic tension. Although such narratives presuppose a symbolic code, that code does not become the explicit subject of attention. But in poetry, oracles, and proverbs the constraints imposed by the logic of narrative are removed. Instead of a temporal sequence one finds a succession of metaphors and other tropes linked together by their appeal to a common theme or their use of a common image. Thus while the narratives describe the relationship between Israel and God in general by depicting a temporal sequence of events, prophetic writings and poetry portray the covenant by invoking an array of persuasive images (e.g., God is the shepherd and Israel the flock, or God is a farmer and Israel a vineyard or orchard). While these writings are more likely to make explicit the set of associations that constitute Israel's symbolic language, this language is, in fact, already presupposed in Israelite law and narrative, as we shall now see.

The Actualization of Metaphor in Israelite Ritual

Because metaphors organize thought, they also shape social practice. The importance of animal and agricultural metaphors in Israelite thought raises the possibility that such metaphors serve as a foundation in some sense for the religious rituals of ancient Israel. Specifically, a number of rituals can be interpreted as acting out or living out the implications of those metaphors that dominate Israelite thought. This process, which may be termed the actualization of metaphor, is most obvious in correspondences between rules regulating the social life of Israel and rules governing the treatment of livestock and agricultural activity. If the flocks, herds, and fields are metaphors for Israelites, it should not surprise us to find the Israelites enjoined to act toward the former as they ought to act toward one another.[8] For example:

1) Just as Israelites are commanded to cease their labors on the seventh day, so they are commanded to let their animals rest on the same day (Exod. 20:9; 23:12; Deut. 5:12–14). 2) Israelites who are sold into slavery work for six years but in the seventh year must be set free (Exod. 21:2; Deut. 15:12). By the same token, Israelites may work their fields for only six years; in the seventh the fields must lie fallow (Exod. 23:10–11; Lev. 25:1–7). 3) Firstborn male Israelites are consecrated to God and must be brought to the Temple. Similarly, the firstborn animals of the herds and flocks (Exod. 13:2; 22:28–9; 23:17; 34:19–20, 26; Num. 8:16; Deut. 15:19) as well as first fruits (Exod. 23:19; 34:26; Num. 18:13; Deut. 26:1–11; Neh. 10:36; Ezek. 44:30) belong to God and must be offered in the Temple. Moreover, as noted above, a man's firstborn offspring is in some places explicitly called his first fruits (Gen. 49:3; Deut. 21:17; Mic. 6:7). 4) Precisely the same kinds of blemishes that disqualify

priests from serving in the Temple disqualify animals from being used for sacrifices (Lev. 21:16–23; 22:19; Deut. 17:1; 23:2). 5) The circumcision of a male Israelite must take place on the eighth day after birth (Gen. 17:12; Lev. 12:3). The eighth day after birth is also the first day that a new born animal can be sacrificed (Exod. 22:29; Lev. 12:3; 22:27). Interestingly enough, trees are also described as "uncircumcised" (*'ărēlîm*) and having "foreskin" (*'orlātô*) until their fourth year of growth. Prior to that time, the fruit they produce cannot be consumed (Lev. 19:23–25). 6) Unpruned grapevines are called "nazirites" (Lev. 25:5), the same term that is applied to the Israelite who takes a religious vow to abstain from all grape products and to desist from cutting his hair (Num. 6). 7) The children of Israel are prohibited to eat an animal's thigh muscle because Israel's (= Jacob's) hip was injured in his fight with an angel (Gen. 32:32–33). 8) Just as murderers receive the death penalty (Exod. 21:12; Num. 35:16–20; Lev. 24:17), animals that kill human beings are also put to death (Exod. 21:28). 9) Israelites are commanded not to mix their seed with outsiders through marriage (Deut. 7:3; Ezra 10:2). This social rule finds its parallel in the prohibitions against planting a field with two different species of crops, wearing garments made of mixed weave, yoking an ox and an ass together to plow, and interbreeding two species of animals (Deut. 22:9; Lev. 19:19). 10) Leaven cannot be used in animal sacrifices or grain offerings (Exod. 23:18; 34:25; Lev. 2:11). By the same token, during the Passover season, Israelites are forbidden to eat leavening (Exod. 12:15, 18–19). 11) Both a human corpse and an animal carcass are considered sources of impurity (Num. 9:7; Lev. 11:24). 12) When a person is impaled for a capital offense, the corpse must be buried before morning (Deut. 21:22). A parallel rule applies to the thanksgiving offering which must be eaten the day it is sacrificed; none of it must remain unconsumed until morning (Lev. 22:29). 13) Just as Israelites are commanded to leave the corner (*pē'â*) of their fields unharvested (Lev. 19:9–10; 23:22; Deut. 24:19), so they are commanded to leave the "corners" (*pē'â*) of their faces unshaven (Lev. 19:27; 21:5).

As these rules make evident, a correspondence or parallelism is established between some of the rules that govern Israelite behavior and social relations and those that apply to animal husbandry and agriculture. At this point, one may want to follow Radcliffe-Brown (1965 [1952], 127), Douglas (1966, 1975), and Berger and Luckmann (1967) by giving such correspondences a functionalist interpretation. According to this view, the rules governing social relations are mirrored in nature in order to lend legitimacy and credibility to social rules. That is, societal rules are projected onto nature in order to deny their conventional character and to give individuals a sense that the rules they live by are part and parcel of the natural order. At the same time, this parallelism presumably strengthened the claim that the social order was of divine origin.

My viewpoint is somewhat different. As I see it, the correspondence of social rules and rules governing nature is the result of the metaphoric relation that Israelite religious thought establishes between Israelite society, on the one hand, and the flocks, herds, fields, and agricultural produce, on the other. The metaphor suggests that the animals and fields are in some sense like Israelites. It follows then that they should in some respects be treated like Israelites. And so they are. At the same time, the parallelism between the way Israelites treat one another and the way they treat livestock and fauna helps to sustain and strengthen the operative metaphors in the religious system. Rules of Israelite behavior constitute a kind of proof of the similarity between the people and their herds and flocks, for Israelites have similar obligations to both. Thus, there is a dialectical relation between the foundational metaphor and the practices to which it gives rise. As the latter emerge from the metaphor, they in turn reassert and strengthen it.

In the account I have given so far, I have been considering Israelite religion from a strictly synchronic perspective. I have taken for granted the existence of the Pentateuch as a redacted document and established that for Israelites who were familiar with this document as a whole, there existed a correspondence between the rules governing society and those governing the herds, flocks, and fields. The metaphoric relationship, therefore, was fully in place by the fifth to fourth centuries B.C.E. when the Pentateuchal sources were redacted. Of course the various sources that comprise the Pentateuch have a long history behind them. The question naturally arises as to whether this parallelism also exists when the sources are viewed from a diachronic perspective. If one takes into account the dating of the various sources, does one find that these corresponding rules derive from the same sources or do they appear in different strands of the literature and thus derive from different time periods? Since dating the sources is notoriously difficult, the following conclusions must be regarded as only tentative.

The rules about dedicating firstborn animals, male Israelites, and first fruits to God appear in precisely the same sources and go back to the earliest legal sources.[9] This is also true of the requirement of Israelites and their animals to rest on the Sabbath day and the rules that specify the death penalty for a person or animal that takes human life.[10] The rules in a second set of correspondences also appear together, but they are found only in later sources, such as Deuteronomy, the Holiness Code, and the Priestly Writings (7th–6th centuries). This category includes the rule that blemishes disqualify animals and priests from serving in the Temple, the prohibitions on forbidden mixtures, the idea that human corpses and animal carcasses are sources of impurity, the homologies between nazirites and unpruned grape vines, and the analogy between an uncircumcised male and a juvenile fruit tree.[11] Significantly, there may be one instance in which the rule concerning nature emerges prior to the corresponding rule for human beings, namely, in the case of circumcision. The rule that an animal cannot be sacrificed before the eighth day after its birth is found in one of the earliest sources (Exod. 22:29). But its corresponding social rule—that male Israelites are to be circumcised on the eighth day—is first given articulation in one of the later sources (P) (Gen. 17:12; 21:4; Lev. 12:3).[12]

At the very least, the diachronic perspective suggests that the homology between Israelite social rules and the rules governing the herds, flocks, and fields was at work in Israelite religion from its very inception and received its greatest articulation in the sources that were written between the seventh and fifth centuries. The sources also suggest, albeit tentatively, that once such a parallelism was established, it worked in two directions. If Israelite social relations provided a model for how to treat animals, in some cases the way they treated their animals also served as a paradigm for how they should treat each other.[13] Not only is nature a mirror of Israel, but Israel is also a mirror of nature.

Thus far I have argued that the correspondences between Israelite social rules and the rules governing the herds, flocks, and fields is a logical consequence of the root metaphors that dominate Israelite thought. It is reasonable now to ask whether the root metaphors are also at work in other biblical rules that have been recalcitrant to interpretation. For example, it seems plausible that there is a connection between the natural metaphors of Israelite thought and the biblical prohibition against eating any land animals that do not chew their cud and have cloven hooves (Lev. 11; Deut. 14). It is probably the case, as S. Driver (1895) and Mary Douglas (1966, 54) have suggested, that this rule is an a posteriori way of validating Israel's social life as pastoralists. Animals that chew the cud and have cloven hooves are the model of the proper kind of food for pastoralists. But given the centrality of bovine and ovine metaphors in Israelite thought, this interpretation misses another dimension of the prohibition. Significantly, cloven hooves and chewing the cud are precisely the traits that distinguish the kinds of animals that routinely serve as metaphors for Israelite society from those that generally do not. The flocks and herds which are the paradigmatic metaphors for Israelite society are also the model kind of food. Moreover, those animals that serve as metaphors for other nations, such as predatory animals, are defined as unclean. Thus the dietary restrictions carve up the animal world along the same lines as Israelite thought.[14] In a literal sense, therefore, the dietary restrictions specify what kinds of animals are "food for thought."

It is important to note that in this case the relationship between the foundational metaphor and religious practice is different from earlier examples. Previously I suggested that the root metaphors produced an expectation that Israelites should treat their animals in some respects the way they treat one another. The correspondences, therefore, were reasonable extensions of the metaphors. But here the metaphors are actualized differently. One might say that the dietary laws are a dramatization of the metaphors that govern Israelite thought. Israel identifies itself with the herds and flocks by eating them and dissociates itself from the animals that represent other nations by declar-

ing such animals inedible. In this case, then, religious practices enact the metaphorical structures that control Israelite thinking.

Asses and Neighbors

If the dietary restrictions capture the distinction between Israel and the
nations, the question also arises as to whether the animal world provides metaphoric representation of intermediate social categories such as the resident
alien and other friendly outsiders. The resident alien is a person who is not of
Israelite birth but who lives within the society. From the perspective of Israelite literature, the resident alien is one who more or less behaves like an Israelite but is not an Israelite by descent. Consequently, if the resident alien has a
metaphoric representation, it would have to be an animal that lives among
the flocks and herds but is unlike them.

The ass has everything necessary to serve as a metaphor for the resident
alien, for it stands in the same relation to the herds and flocks as the resident
alien stands in relation to Israelite society. Like the resident alien, the ass is a
loner, for it does not herd or flock with others of its kind but lives alongside
the herds and flocks. Moreover, the ass lacks the traits of chewing the cud and
cloven hooves, and consequently is not a true member of these communities.
For these reasons the ass can serve as an excellent metaphor for resident aliens
and other categories of persons who are neither complete insiders nor total
outsiders. It constitutes, then, what Fernandez (1972, 47) has called a structural metaphor, where the "translation between realms is based on some iso-
morphism of structure or similarity of relationship of parts." In this case, the
ass's position vis-à-vis the herds and flocks is parallel to the position of persons or groups who are neither Israelites nor hostile predators.[15]

There are two biblical narratives that may presuppose this sort of association.[16] In particular, this equation is evident in the account of Jacob's daughter Dinah being raped by a Canaanite named Shechem son of Hamor (Gen.
34). Now "Hamor" is the Hebrew word for ass.[17] It is no accident that Dinah
is raped by "the son of an ass," for one of the primary concerns of this story is
whether Israel, as represented by Jacob and his sons, should have social relations with non-Israelites alongside whom it dwells. It is also significant that
Dinah's brothers are out with the cattle when she is raped (Gen. 34:5), thus
expressing the opposition between the Canaanites and Jacob's sons in terms
of the difference between asses and cattle. As the story unfolds, Shechem's
father, Hamor (= the Ass), makes the following proposition to Jacob and his
sons: "Intermarry with us: give your daughters to us, and take our daughters
for yourselves. You will dwell among us, and the land will be open before you;
settle, move about, and acquire holdings in it" (Gen. 34:9–10). Jacob's sons
agree, with the stipulation that Hamor and his people undergo circumcision.
However, when the Canaanites are recovering from the surgical procedure

and are still incapacitated, Jacob's sons slaughter them. The story thus denies the possibility of social intercourse between "sons of an Ass" and "those of the herds and flocks."

By the same token, it is significant that the narrative of Balaam and the ass (Num. 22–25) is about an outsider who plans to curse Israel but who ends up singing Israel's praise. At the beginning of this narrative, Balak, king of Moab, is worried that Israel "will lick clean all that is about us as an ox licks up the grass of the field" (Num. 22:4). Consequently, Balak commissions Balaam to prophesy doom on Israel. But as Balaam is riding on an ass to join the Moabites, the ass sees an angel of God on the road and veers to avoid it. Eventually, Balaam too sees the angel, which suggests, in effect, that Balaam himself has become like the ass. Thus Balaam initially intends to prey on Israel but ends up being an ass that praises the dwelling places of Israel. Balaam, therefore, as portrayed in Num. 22–24, is the paradigmatic outsider who becomes a lover of Israel.

It may also be significant that in Zechariah's vision of the end of days the Messiah will appear riding on an ass (Zech. 9:9). I have no intention here of quarreling with the well-established view that riding an ass is a symbol of royalty in the ancient Near East (Sasson 1976). But it should be realized that this interpretation does not explain every use of asses in biblical narratives and law. It fails to explain, for example, why Balaam, the non-Israelite seer, and the Shunammite woman are riding asses (Num 22; 2 Kings 4:24). Moreover, as Sasson points out, it also does not explain why the firstborn male ass must be redeemed with an animal from the herd or flock (Exod. 12:46; 13:13; 34:20). An opening, therefore, emerges for an alternative interpretation. I suggest that given the association between asses and proximate outsiders, there may be an additional layer of meaning in Zechariah's idea that the Messiah will ride an ass. As Zechariah describes it, the messiah is to usher in the period of Israel's hegemony over her neighbors, when powerful nations shall become mere resident aliens. Thus Zechariah says that survivors of Philistia "shall belong to our God; They shall become like a clan in Judah, And Ekron shall be like the Jebusites" (= local Canaanites) (Zech. 9:7). In other words the notion that the Messiah rides an ass may also convey the idea that Israel will turn its predatory neighbors into asses, into neighbors with whom one can live. In this context, it is interesting that David and his sons Solomon and Absalom are described as riding on mules (2 Sam. 18:9; 1 Kings 1:33, 38, 45). Presumably, the narrative is alluding to the royal status of these characters. But it is curious that they each ride a mule *(pered)* while Saul (1 Sam. 9:3, 5; 10:14) and the Messiah are each described as riding on an ass *('ātôn)*. The mule, of course, differs from an ass in that it is a product of mixed seed. Is it possible that the narrative hints that David and his line are of mixed seed, since David is a grandson of a Moabite woman (Ruth 4:16–17)?[18]

As in the case of the metaphoric relationship between Israel and the herds and flocks, the metaphoric relationship between the ass and resident alien is actualized in practical correspondences. Thus the ass and local stranger are subject to parallel civil and religious laws. First, Israelite law explicitly says that the citizen and local stranger are to be treated alike (Deut. 10:19; 24:17). Israelites are commanded not to wrong or oppress a stranger (Exod. 22:20; 23:9; Lev. 19:33; 24:22) and consequently are expected to provide relief for local aliens (Deut. 24:19–22; Lev. 19:19; 23:22). By the same token, the ass is treated according to the same laws as the ox and sheep in the case of theft (Exod. 22:3, 9; 23:4–5; Deut. 22:4). Second, a resident alien is subject to some religious prohibitions such as the one against working on the Sabbath, a restriction that also applies to the ass (Deut. 5:13). In fact, in one formulation of this rule the resident alien is set parallel to the ass: "Six days you shall do your work, but on the seventh day you shall cease from labor, in order that your ox and your ass may rest, and that your bondman and the stranger may be refreshed" (Exod. 23:12). Third, the local stranger has other religious obligations, like not working on the Day of Atonement (Lev. 16:29) and having to observe certain laws of purity (Lev. 17:15). But at the same time, such a person is enough of a stranger to be excluded from participating in certain religious activities, such as eating the Passover offering (Exod. 12:46). The ass is in a similar no-man's-land. For example, while the firstborn male offspring of asses theoretically belong to God, an ass cannot be sacrificed. Instead, an animal from the flock or herd serves as a substitute for it (Exod. 12:46; 13:13; 34:20). So the ass is subject to some of the same obligations as the herds and flocks but excluded from others, just as the local stranger is liable to certain Israelite rules and not others. Finally, if the metaphoric equation of the ass and resident alien is operative, then the prohibition against plowing a field with an ass and an animal of the herd yoked together (Deut. 22:10) expresses in law the same idea as the story about Dinah being raped by Shechem, "the son of an ass." Both forbid close contact between an Israelite and the local outsider.

Incest and Husbandry

The correspondence between Israelite laws concerning animals and the rules governing social relations may also provide a way of understanding three rules whose interpretation has been much debated: the prohibitions (1) against boiling a kid-goat in its mother's milk (Exod. 23:19; 34:26; Deut. 14:21), (2) against taking both a mother bird and her fledglings from the same nest (Deut. 22:6), and (3) against sacrificing an animal from the herd or flock on the same day as its offspring (Lev. 22:28).

Haran (1979) treats these rules as deriving from a humanitarian concern to prevent cruelty to animals. But this view is difficult to reconcile with the Israelite practice of animal sacrifice. If cruelty to animals was so central an issue would not the sacrificing of animals qualify as inhumane? Moreover, in what sense is it less cruel to sacrifice an animal and its offspring on subsequent days rather than on the same day? More compelling is Milgrom's view (1981b; 1985) that these prohibitions demarcate a boundary between life and death. Following Philo, Milgrom (1981b, 7–8) argues that "milk is the symbol of life and the Bible prohibits using that which stands for life to bring death. The Torah is endemically opposed to the mixing of opposites. The commingling of holiness and impurity is forbidden on pain of death; so the commingling of life and death is equally disastrous." Milgrom (1981b, 7–8) offers a similar interpretation of the prohibition against slaughtering an animal and its young on the same day. "It is saying that the processes of life and death have to be kept separate. The same is true with the bird and her young; she is hatching her young. Let not that life-giving process be the occasion of her death." There is much to say for Milgrom's interpretation.[19] But to accept Milgrom's interpretation is not necessarily to rule out alternatives. Practices can encode more than one set of distinctions. As previously suggested, what gives rituals their power in a given community may be the diverse ways that they make contact with other elements of the cultural system.

Given the overall metaphoric relationship between Israelite society and the herds and flocks, and the number of correspondences noted earlier, it seems reasonable to ask whether these laws also have their social equivalents. Moreover, as noted above, other sexual prohibitions find their parallel in rules governing the animal world. The prohibition against intermarrying corresponds to the law against interbreeding two species of animals and to the rule against yoking an ox and ass together.

On my reading, the above rules correspond to Israelite incest prohibitions. I thus disagree with Douglas who argues that in biblical religion "we seek in vain a statement, however oblique, of a[n] . . . association between eating and sex" (1975, 262). According to my interpretation, the rule against boiling a kid-goat parallels the prohibition against a male child having intercourse with his mother (Deut. 27:20; Lev. 18:6). Just as an Israelite man may not be "stirred up" by his mother, it is forbidden to cook a kid-goat in its mother's juices. The other rules are somewhat different. They insist that a person may not perform a certain kind of act (either slaughtering or taking from the nest) on both an animal and its offspring. I will argue below that these rules correspond to the prohibitions against a man having intercourse with a woman and her mother (Deut. 27:23; Lev. 20:14) and with a woman and her daughter (Lev. 18:12).

Still the question arises as to why an incest rule should find its parallel in rules about cooking, hunting, or sacrificing. But let me turn the question around. What other kind of correspondence could be invented? From a strictly practical standpoint, it is impossible to forbid incestuous relations among animals; to do so would require creating a number of herds or flocks and separating animals at a very young age from others of the same lineage. Moreover, as Lévi-Strauss points out, domestication of animals requires interbreeding. Consequently, if the prohibitions of human incest are to find their parallels in rules governing animals they will have to take the form of some other cultural activity, whether it be eating, cooking, or slaughtering.

Indeed, ethnographies are full of cases in which a variety of cultural activities serve as metaphoric substitutes for intercourse. To cite a few examples, the Arapesh say, "Your own mother, your own sister, your own pigs, your own yams that you have piled up, you may not eat. Other people's mothers, other people's sisters, other people's pigs, other people's yams that they have piled up, you may eat" (Mead 1977 [1935], 83). Among the Ashanti, "eating of one's own blood" is the way to describe certain kinds of incest and "eating a man's wife" the way of describing adultery (Goody 1956, 290). The Rotinese describe the search for a marriageable girl as "to go for seed grain." Among the same group, the areca nut is a sign of a girl's sexuality and consequently, a girl publicly chews the nut to signify her readiness to marry (Fox 1971, 234, 236). In villages in Ceylon, the fact that a woman cooks food for a man is a public statement that they have a conjugal relationship (Tambiah 1969). Among the Masai, father-daughter incest is prohibited and a daughter also may not cook for her father or hand him a milk calabash (Llewelyn-Davies 1981, 337). Finally, Meigs in her study of the Hua of New Guinea points to a number of parallels between food and sexual prohibitions. She writes, for example, that among the Hua "eating has its incest rule too: a person may not eat food that he or she or his or her offspring have themselves produced" (Meigs 1984, 124). Again, Hua males claim never to touch a woman's vagina and they also do not eat snails whose secretion they claim is like the secretions of the vagina (Meigs 1984, 92).

The ethnographic evidence just cited lends a certain plausibility to the interpretation I have offered of the biblical laws cited above. It shows that food and eating often serve as metaphors for sexual activity and that such metaphors can and do structure human behavior. To be sure, the ethnographic literature in and of itself does not make a convincing case that a similar interpretation is valid for the Israelite practices. Therefore, let me now take up each of the Israelite rules individually and show how my reading is also plausible within the context of biblical literature.

In interpreting the prohibition against seething a kid-goat in its mother's milk I am developing the view of Jean Soler (1979, 29) who claims that this rule can be translated into the following statement, "You shall not put a mother and her son into the same pot, any more than into the same bed."[20] Milgrom (1981b, 1985, 51) has rejected this interpretation because the Hebrew term for kid, *"gĕdî,"* is asexual, meaning it refers to both female and male kids. According to Milgrom, therefore, the rule cannot be interpreted as a symbolic statement prohibiting a male Israelite from having intercourse with his mother. But Milgrom overlooks the fact that the word *gĕdî* is a masculine noun (BDB 1975 [1907], 152).[21] Moreover, an examination of the role of the kid-goat in Israelite narratives suggests that it sometimes serves as a symbolic substitute for a male child.

In the story of Jacob and Esau (Gen. 27), Jacob outfoxes his blind father by pretending to be Esau. This was quite a trick, for Esau was a hairy man and hunter while Jacob was smooth and a mama's boy. To effect the substitution, Jacob kills two kid-goats, which are used for a stew that tastes like freshly captured game. The hides of the kids are used to cover his arms, thus imitating the hairy arms of his brother. The substitution of kid-goats for wild game parallels the displacement of one kind of young man for another. Just as Isaac expects to eat a dish prepared from wild game but instead is served one made from a domesticated animal, so too he intends to bless Esau the hunter, but instead blesses Jacob the domestic.[22]

The kid-goat plays an analogous role in the story of Judah and Tamar (Gen. 38). At the beginning of the story, Tamar is married in succession to two of Judah's sons, each of whom subsequently dies. By Israelite law, Tamar should marry her dead husbands' brother, but in this case the only surviving brother is too young to marry. Judah promises that when his son matures he will carry out the levirate duties. But when the child grows up, it is clear that Judah has no intention of living up to his promise. Out of desperation, Tamar deceives Judah into thinking she is a harlot, so that she can produce a child of his seed. Significantly, when Judah asks to sleep with her, he promises to send her a kid from the flock as a fee. So while Judah actually owes Tamar his son, he tries to satisfy her by substituting a kid-goat. Once again, the kid-goat serves as a metaphoric equivalent to a male child. Just as Tamar never gets Judah's youngest son, she also never gets the kid-goat. The kid-goat also crops up in other stories where it may symbolize a young boy.[23]

The foregoing suggest that there is an association in Israelite thought between a kid-goat and an Israelite male. But what about the significance of boiling a kid-goat in its mother's milk? Lévi-Strauss (1968, 471–93) has argued that boiling is often associated with culture, as opposed to roasting which is often associated with nature. Boiling is linked to culture because to boil something one needs a cultural implement, a pot. The pot, moreover, is concave and has an inside and thus serves as a good symbol of being inside. Roasting, by contrast, does not require the use of a cultural implement since the food is cooked directly on the fire. Lévi-Strauss notes that these associations explain otherwise inexplicable practices. For example, in a number of cultures boiled food is reserved for insiders and roasted meat for strangers. Moreover, boiling is often considered women's work and pots are a symbol of women. The Ndembu, for example, say that "the mother is like a pot" (Turner 1967, 250). If men are permitted to cook at all, they often are prohibited from boiling food.

Is there any evidence to suggest that in Israelite culture boiling had these connotations? The stories of Jacob and Esau seem to presuppose similar associations. As noted above, Jacob and Esau are antithetical types. Esau, who is born with a hairy, red mantle, becomes a hunter. "Jacob" (= heel) is so named because he comes out of the womb clinging to the heel of his brother

(Gen. 25:21–26). Jacob turns into a mama's boy with smooth skin who does not venture far from home. It is significant then that Jacob is reported to have cooked a stew and as having presented his father with a stew cooked by his mother (Gen. 25:29, 27:9–15). Jacob, moreover, is one of the few biblical characters who marries matrilineally. His wives, Rachel and Leah, are the daughters of Laban, his mother's brother. Boiling in this context goes along with being unable to separate sufficiently from one's mother. Jacob only becomes a serious character when he flees Laban thus rejecting matrilocal marriage and matrilineal descent and returns to Canaan the home of his fathers. Along the way, he performs his first sacrifice to God during which he invokes his patrilineal ancestors (Gen. 31:54). Jacob's transformation from a mama's boy who marries matrilocally to a real man who can carry on the patrilineage is thus signified in his development from a boy who boils stew to one who sacrifices to God.[24] In this story at least, boiling is symptomatic of a dangerously close relationship between a boy and his mother.

This association is doubly emphasized in the prohibition against boiling a kid-goat in its mother's milk. Milk is often a natural symbol for the relationship between a woman and the offspring whom she suckles (Turner 1967, 19–47). All of these associations—kid-goat and male child, boiling and intimacy with mother, mother's milk and the mother-child relationship—provide grounds for arguing that the prohibition against cooking a goat in its mother's milk corresponds to the prohibition against incestuous relations between an Israelite man and his mother. In addition, it turns out that the narratives that equate a kid-goat and an Israelite male, on the one hand, and boiling and intimacy, on the other, derive from the J strand, which may also know of the prohibition against cooking a kid-goat in its mother's milk (Exod. 34:26).[25] Finally, one of the sources that defines relations with one's mother as incest (Deut. 27:20) also makes a point of mentioning the prohibition against cooking the kid-goat (Deut. 14:21).

Following a similar line of inquiry, we see that the prohibition against taking a mother bird and her fledglings from the nest (Deut. 22:6) also corresponds to an incest prohibition. This rule forbids capturing and eating both a mother and her offspring. When one takes the fledglings or eggs from the nest, one is commanded to send the mother away. There are a number of reasons to interpret this rule as paralleling the prohibition against incest. The exact expression "a mother with her young" (*ḥ'ēm ʿal habānîm*) is found only twice in biblical writings outside this context. In both cases it refers to certain disastrous consequences that might befall a human mother and her children (Gen. 32:12; Hos. 10:14). Moreover, we recall that the nest is sometimes a metaphor for the home (Hab. 2:9; Job 29:18; Ps. 84:4). "A man who wanders from his place is like a bird that leaves its nest" (Prov. 27:8). In addition, Israel's children are likened to birds that fly away (Hos. 9:11). It is also significant that a single term *(kānāp)* describes the wings of a bird and the corners of a man's garment. When the corners of a man's garment are cut off, his wings have been clipped (1 Sam. 24:6). Intercourse and espousal are described as spreading one's wings over a woman (Ezek. 16:8; Ruth 3:9). More to the point, incest with one's mother is described as displacing one's father's wings (Deut. 23:1; 27:20).

It is not an accident, then, that the prohibition against taking a mother bird and her offspring appears in the same source that proscribes sexual relations with one's mother-in-law (Deut. 27:23). In other words, the source that first articulates this sexual prohibition is also the only one to mention the law against taking a mother bird and her offspring. The parallel is nearly precise.[26] Deuteronomy commands Israelites "to take" the fledglings and send away the mother, just as it commands an Israelite not "to take" the mother of the woman he has already taken. It is also significant that when the same incest prohibition makes its appearance in another context (Lev. 20:14), its linguistic formulation is nearly identical to the rule about not taking the mother bird and fledglings. In Deuteronomy, the law is formulated as follows, "If you chance upon a bird's nest . . . do not *take* the mother together with her young." The incest prohibition as formulated in Leviticus states in similar language, "If a man *takes* a woman and her mother it is a depravity" (Lev. 20:14).

Thus far we have seen that the rules against boiling a kid-goat in the mother's milk and taking fledglings and their mother both appear in Deuteronomy and correspond to Deuteronomy's prohibitions on sexual relations between a man and his mother and between a man and his mother-in-law. As we leave Deuteronomy and turn to Leviticus, two interesting differences appear. First, Leviticus specifies a wider scope of incest prohibitions, and second, it does not mention the prohibition against taking a mother bird and her fledglings from the nest. Instead, it cites another prohibition which is structurally similar: the proscription not to sacrifice an animal and its offspring on the same day. This rule may also be viewed as paralleling a rule about social relationships, for it follows directly after the rule about not sacrificing an animal until the eighth day after birth which, as I suggested above, corresponds to the commandment that an Israelite male child must be circumcised on the eighth day. The parallel between a young animal and an Israelite child is already operative as one reads the law about sacrificing an animal and its offspring on the same day.

The differences between Deuteronomy and Leviticus, namely the different scope of incest prohibitions and the particular animal rules cited, may be interrelated. In following the subsequent argument, it may be helpful to make reference to the diagram provided below.

As I said earlier, the deuteronomic rule about birds corresponds to the deuteronomic incest prohibition against intercourse between a man and his mother-in-law. But this husbandry proscription does not cover the scope of the incest prohibitions found in Leviticus. In addition to prohibiting sexual relations between a man and his mother-in-law (Lev. 20:14), Leviticus also

Incest Prohibitions	Corresponding Animal Prohibitions
Deuteronomy:	
1. Intercourse between a man and his mother-in-law (Deut. 23:1; 27:33)	Taking mother bird and fledglings. Send away mother bird (Deut. 22:6).
Leviticus:	
1. Intercourse between a man and his mother-in-law (Lev. 20:14)	Slaughtering an animal and its offspring on the same day.
2. Intercourse between a man and his stepdaughter (Lev. 18:17).	Slaughter one or the other (Lev. 22:8).

forbids relations between a man and his wife's daughter by another marriage (Lev. 18:17), a prohibition not mentioned in Deuteronomy. In its deuteronomic formulation, the rule about birds does not parallel this levitical prohibition. To do so it would have to be reversed: instead of being commanded to take the fledglings and send off the mother, one would have to be instructed to take the mother bird and send away her fledglings. But even if the rule were reformulated in this way, there still would be a glaring discrepancy between the incest rule and the husbandry law. Although one can send a woman's daughter to live in another man's house, if one sends away fledglings they will surely die. The rule about birds, therefore, cannot be made to correspond to the levitical prohibition against intercourse with one's wife's daughter.[27]

By this account, it is not surprising that Leviticus substitutes for the rule about birds one that forbids sacrificing an animal and its offspring on the same day. This rule has the advantage, so to speak, of being able to cast a wider net. It corresponds both to the prohibition on relations with one's mother-in-law and with one's stepdaughter. This is because it does not specify which animal has to be sacrificed first. One can sacrifice the mother animal and leave the daughter for another day or one can take the mother and save the daughter for another occasion. But one cannot have both the mother and the daughter at the same time. For this reason, the law about sending away the mother bird has been displaced in Leviticus by the injunction against sacrificing an animal and its offspring on the same day. This displacement is emphasized by the fact that incest with one's mother is not described as uncovering what is under one's father's wings. In this context, the metaphoric relation of man and birds is not compelling.[28]

The Exploitation and Power of Metaphor

I have argued so far that the metaphoric relationship between Israel and the herds and flocks creates an expectation that Israelites treat one another the way they treat their animals. This expectation in turn generates a series of homologies between Israelite social practices and the rules governing the animal world. Expectations, however, are not always fulfilled. Sometimes they are exploited for other purposes. This appears to be the case in the Israelite sacrificial system. To begin with, the sacrificial institution capitalizes on the metaphoric relationship between Israelite society and the animal world. Despite objections to this view,[29] I would argue that the sacrificial system rests on the idea that an animal's life is a substitute for the life of the person who brings the animal to be slaughtered (Wenham 1979, 28). The sacrificial ritual itself suggests an identification of the sacrificial animal with the sacrificer or the person or persons who supply the animal. In some cases, for example, the hands of the person on whose behalf the animal is offered are placed on the animal before sacrificing it (Exod. 29:10, 15, 19; Lev. 3:2, 8, 13; 4:4, 15, 24), or the blood of the animal is sometimes sprinkled on the people on whose behalf it is offered (Exod. 24:8), or put on their ear lobes, right thumb, and right big-toe (Exod. 29:20; Lev. 14:14). Moreover, the earliest biblical laws recognize the idea that Israelites sacrifice the first-born males of their herds and flocks because God did not put to death their first-born male children in Egypt (Exod. 13:11–15). The dependence of the sacrificial system on the metaphoric relationship between Israelites and the herds and flocks explains why only animals from the herds and flocks can be used as offerings. Since these are the animals that normally serve as metaphors for Israel, only they can serve as sacrificial substitutes for Israelites.

While the sacrificial system takes for granted the metaphoric relationship between Israelites and the herds and flocks, it also exploits the expectations that those metaphors generate. As we have seen above, in a number of cases what Israelites do to their animals they also do to themselves. But the power of the sacrificial institution lies precisely in its deviation from this pattern. The very premise of the sacrificial system is that God will permit Israelites to sacrifice animals instead of sacrificing themselves and their children. In this case, one does to one's animals what one is *not* required to do to oneself. By violating the normal pattern of expectation, the sacrificial cult creates in participants the sense that something remains undone. This deviation may explain why the sacrificial rite is perceived to be so efficacious: it instills in actors the feeling that they should also be sacrificed. The fact that God does not require this of them reminds them of the divine capacity to forgive human failure (Exod. 34:7).

This understanding of sacrifice is at work in biblical narratives. Abraham, for example, is commanded to sacrifice his son Isaac (Gen. 22). Just as he is about to perform the act, God instructs him to offer up a ram which is caught in the thicket nearby. This story expresses the idea that although people theoretically owe their lives to God, God is sometimes willing to accept animals in their place. The story of Noah (Gen. 8) puts forward a similar idea. One of the important themes of this narrative is God's reconciliation to human imperfection and tendency to sin. At the beginning of the story, God brings the flood to wipe out human imperfection. But after the flood, God accepts humans for what they are and vows never to destroy the world again. It is significant that God's statement of reconciliation comes in response to Noah's sacrifice. Upon smelling the pleasing odor of Noah's sacrifice, God says, "Never again will I doom the world because of humanity, since the devisings of humans are evil from youth, nor will I ever again destroy every living being, as I have done" (Gen. 8:21). Thus the institutionalization of sacrifice occurs simultaneously with God's acceptance of humanity's imperfection. Although humans deserve to be destroyed, God accepts animal sacrifices in their place. It is important to note, however, that the substitution only appeases God for relatively minor sins, such as unwittingly violating a law (Lev. 4). For heinous crimes, such as murder, God demands that person's life. "You shall not accept a ransom for the life of a murderer who is guilty of a capital crime; he must be put to death" (Num. 35:31). Thus, the legitimacy of a given sacrifice depends on God's willingness to relinquish the divine right to put the person in question to death.[30]

This view of sacrifice sheds new light on the criticisms of the sacrificial cult that one finds in the prophetic writings. It is often said that the prophets viewed the sacrificial system as hypocritical. On the one hand, Israelites were committing numerous sins, such as oppressing the poor, yet on the other hand, they sacrificed to God as if the cultic activities in and of themselves would guarantee divine favor. The prophets argued, by contrast, that the cult without morality is meaningless (e.g., de Vaux 1965, 454–55). I would suggest, however, an additional reason for the prophets' criticism. As argued previously, a sacrifice is valid only when God is willing to overlook the commission of a sin. Extending this line of reasoning to the nation as a whole, the sacrificial institution will be legitimate only as long as God is willing to pardon Israel's collective sins. But when Israel's sins become too grievous, the substitution breaks down. In other words, when God decides to punish Israel directly, scapegoats are no longer acceptable.[31]

It is significant, therefore, that the prophets who criticize the institution of sacrifice are precisely the same ones who prophesy a devastating punishment for Israel, and frequently conceive of God as a lion that preys upon the flock of Israel. God will not accept animals in place of Israel, because Israel has become its own sacrificial victim. According to Isaiah, for example, God says "What need have I of all your sacrifices? . . . I am sated with burnt offerings of rams and suet of fatlings, and blood of bulls; And I have no delight in lambs and he-goats. . . . Bringing oblations is futile, incense is offensive to me" (Isa. 1:11). Isaiah also predicts God's vengeance against Israel. "As a lion—a great beast—growls over its prey and, when the shepherds gather in force against him, is not dismayed by their cries nor cowed by their noise—so the Lord of Hosts will descend to make war against the mount and hill of Zion" (Isa. 31:4). Similarly, Jeremiah criticizes the sacrificial cult (6:20; 7:21; 14:11) and speaks about God driving the flock of Israel to the slaughter (12:3). According to Hosea, God says, "I desire mercy and not sacrifice, knowledge of God rather than burnt-offerings" (Hos. 6:6, see also 8:13; 9:4). This is because Israel will be God's sacrificial victim: "I will be like a lion to Ephraim, like a great beast to the House of Judah, I, I will attack and stride away, carrying the prey that no one can rescue" (Hos. 5:14; see also 13:7–8). Amos also condemns sacrifice (4:4; 5:21) and foresees Israel's punishment (3:13; 5:16; 6:14; 7:17). There is no contradiction, therefore, when some of the prophets who criticize the institution of sacrifice nonetheless conceive of its existence in the end of days (Jer. 33:17; Mal. 3:4). At that time, the relationship between God and Israel will be restored. God will again be a protective shepherd and Israel the divine flock. Since Israel will not be subject to divine wrath, the substitution of animals for humans will again take place.

As is now evident, the bovine and ovine metaphors that inform Israelite thought are actualized in a variety of ways in Israelite religious practices. When metaphors provide a foundation for thought and practice as they do in Israelite religion, there is always a danger that such metaphors will be handled in inappropriate ways. At the same time that a religious system works to establish its metaphors it must simultaneously prevent them from getting out of hand. It is possible that one biblical narrative worries about this problem, namely, the story of the golden calf (Exod. 32). When Moses is up on the mountain receiving God's instruction, the people are at the foot of the mountain making a golden calf. They proclaim before this calf, "This is your God, O Israel, who brought you from the land of Egypt." Cross (1973, 74, 198) has argued that this story was originally a legend of the old sanctuary of Bethel that claimed Aaronic authority for its bull iconography. In its present formulation, Cross reasons, the story constitutes a polemic by another group of priests against the Aaronide priesthood and the bull iconography associated with it. Whether or not Cross's reconstruction is plausible, this narrative might convey other meanings, given the importance of bovine metaphors in Israelite thought and practice. In particular, the narrative of the golden calf can be seen to show concern about the process that Durkheim claimed was the essence of the religious life, namely, the tendency of societies to deify the symbols of their collective existence (Durkheim 1965 [1915]). In this case, the Israelites take their own metaphors so seriously that they mistake the calf for God. The story of the golden calf, therefore, recognizes the temptation for society to worship itself through its own symbols. Interestingly enough, Aaron as he is portrayed in this account realizes the power of metaphors to become uncontrollable. In response to Moses's accusation that he was responsible for the incident, Aaron says, "I said to them [the Israelites], 'Whoever has gold, take it off!' They gave it to me and I hurled it into the fire and out came this calf" (Exod. 32:24). This narrative suggests that the deification of one's metaphors can occur without one being aware of it. Moses's response to this incident is appropriate. He has to turn the calf from a deity back into a metaphor for Israelite society. He does this by grinding it into dust, mixing it

)

with water, and making the people drink it. In this way, Moses demotes the calf and re-establishes its identity with the people.

Conclusion: The Beginning and End of a Root Metaphor

By way of conclusion, it is worth considering why metaphors from the herds, flocks, and fields play such a prominent role in shaping Israelite religious practices. It is probably true that such images were readily available because animal husbandry and agriculture were important components of Israelite society. But pastoral metaphors are more important than agricultural ones in structuring Israelite practice. This is surprising since it appears that in the period during which the biblical texts were written, Israelite society was becoming less pastoral. And this development does not appear to have undermined the importance of animal metaphors in Israelite thought.

It is possible that animal metaphors won out over agricultural metaphors because, as Lévi-Strauss noted (1962; 1966), differences between animals are excellent for expressing various conceptual distinctions. Indeed, animals are better for representing social relations than plants because animals mate, eat, die, and are generally more like humans than plants are. It may be that the narrative about Cain and Abel (Gen. 4:1–16) is an allusion to the victory of herd and flock metaphors over agricultural ones. In that story Cain and Abel bring different kinds of offerings to God. Cain brings an agricultural gift while Abel brings an animal from his flock. God, however, looks more favorably on Abel's gift than Cain's. This story has sometimes been interpreted as reflecting the tension between the pastoral and agricultural forms of life (Speiser 1964, 31). But in light of the importance of pastoral metaphors in biblical thought, the story can be seen to reflect on the proper paradigm for Israelite thought. The fact that God looks more favorably on Abel's animal sacrifice than on Cain's agricultural gift intimates that animal metaphors will be more perspicacious than agricultural ones. One can only imagine how official Israelite religion might have developed had the dominant metaphors been drawn from the domain of agriculture.

There may have been other factors as well that contributed to the importance attached to animal metaphors. In official Israelite religion, the divine realm could not serve adequately as a source of metaphors as it often does in other religious traditions. In part, this is because Israel conceived of itself as having but one God. Moreover, biblical religion only attributed to God a limited number of human functions, including speech, jealousy, and anger. It did not ascribe to God the "lower" human functions such as hunger, thirst, and sexual activity. These theological ideas imposed certain kinds of limitations on what the divine realm could be used to represent, as is evident once one turns to the mythological systems of African and Australian religions, to name but two. In these systems, the gods not only eat and drink but fornicate and commit incest and adultery. Consequently, the whole range of cultural and social activities can be discussed in terms of the gods' activities. Israel's distinctive conception of God, therefore, foreclosed the possibility of the divine realm serving as either a model for or a model of Israelite society. When you have only one God and that God does not engage in very many human activities, it is difficult to represent social relationships in terms of theological statements. While God is described as the father and mother of Israel, God has no mother, sisters, or sisters-in-law with whom to commit incest.[32] By the same token, there are no wives available with whom to commit adultery. If these social relations are to be expressed, therefore, they must find their formulation in another set of terms. In the case of Israel, the herds and flocks obviously supplied the vocabulary that was used to reflect upon social life.

The herds and flocks remained unchallenged throughout the biblical period as the dominant source of metaphors for Israelite thought and practice. As suggested at the beginning of this chapter, revolutions in thought and practice are sometimes linked to the displacement of one root metaphor by another. According to this view, a change in operative metaphors may produce a new community. To some extent, the development of early Christianity out of Israelite religion is related to such an event. Given that the first Christians were urban (Meeks 1983), it is not surprising that they did not find bovine and ovine metaphors as compelling. Instead a new foundational metaphor emerged, namely, the body of Christ. In the letters of Paul, for example, the community of the faithful is described as the body of Christ and each member is a member of Christ's body (1 Cor. 6:15; 11:3, 7; 12:27). The equation of individual members with Christ's body generated the following proposition: just as Christ was crucified and resurrected, so the faithful figuratively underwent the same process. Moreover, since God can be imagined as having a human body, social relations can be expressed directly in theological propositions. Reference to Christ's body can explain the possibility that the community is unified despite its apparent diversity. "For as in one body, we have many members and all the members do not have the same function, so we, though many, are one body in Christ" (Rom. 12:4).[33] Sexual offenses also are couched in similar terms. "Do you not know that your bodies are members of Christ? Shall I therefore take the members of Christ and make them members of a prostitute? Never! Do you not know that he who joins himself to a prostitute becomes one body with her?" (1 Cor. 6:15–16). In Paul's writings, therefore, the body of Christ serves as the metaphor for making the kinds of statements that in Israelite thought found expression in husbandry metaphors.

When one root metaphor dislodges another, as in this case, several consequences naturally follow. First, new practices emerge to express and validate the importance of the new metaphoric system. In the early Christian communities, the eucharist embodied the new metaphor. By drinking the cup of wine and eating the bread, one consumed Christ's blood and flesh and literally became a member of Christ's body (1 Cor. 10:4; 11:23–24). Second, many ideas from the previous system of signification are reinterpreted in terms of the new body of metaphors. In this case, the new metaphoric system had the power to take over the notion of sacrifice from Israelite religion. The crucifixion of Christ was interpreted as the quintessential sacrificial act by God for humanity (Rom. 4:25). The death of Jesus thus saves humanity from God's wrath just as the sacrificial animal did in Israelite religion (Rom. 5:9). In a very real sense, then, the role of animals in Israelite religion was absorbed in early Christianity by the body of Christ. Indeed, according to Paul, Christ was the paschal lamb (1 Cor. 5:7). An interesting reversal, therefore, occurred as one root metaphor replaced another. In Israelite religion, the sacrifice of an animal was a substitute for the death of humans, while in early Christianity, the crucifixion of Christ was a substitute for sacrificing animals.

While a new metaphoric system can take over many aspects of a previous system, not everything can be accommodated. Consequently, as one root metaphor replaces another, those practices which cannot be assimilated will have to be repudiated. The displacement of husbandry metaphors by metaphors of Christ's body may explain in part why Paul rejected the requirement for gentiles to distinguish between clean and unclean animals (1 Cor. 10:25). To be sure, such rules had functioned as a way to keep Jews and gentiles apart, and consequently they were no longer necessary in the community envisioned by Paul. But it is also possible that the Israelite rules regarding animals lost their power once animal husbandry no longer served as the controlling metaphor. The difference between Israelite religion and early Christianity often has been mistakenly framed in terms of an opposition between ritualistic and nonritualistic systems. The fact is, early Christianity also instituted its own eating practices (such as the eucharist) that were governed by strict rules. "Whoever eats the bread or drinks the cup of the Lord in an unworthy manner will be guilty of profaning the body and blood of the Lord" (1 Cor. 11:27). The difference between the communities stemmed not from a different attitude toward ritual per se but from the kind of metaphors that governed their practices. Israelite practices based on animal metaphors were a stumbling block for Paul, who maintained that anything that was not founded on Christ was not a foundation at all. "For no other foundation can one lay than that which is laid, which is Jesus Christ" (1 Cor. 3:10). Thus the Gospel of Matthew was literally correct when it described Christ as the cornerstone that Israel had rejected. Israelite thought rejected the notion of God having a fully conceptualized or functioning body. This was the metaphor upon which early Christianity was founded. If the displacement of one root metaphor by another plays such a crucial role in creating a new community, it is evident why the transition from one religious system to the next is so often obscure. The next system is not created until the new metaphor has taken hold. But it does not take root until it has established itself in practice and crowded out practices founded on other metaphors. By that time, of course, everything is changed and people are already living in a different world.

6.

The Fruitful Cut

Circumcision and Israel's
Symbolic Language of Fertility,
Descent, and Gender

The origin and meaning of a custom so old and so widely
diffused cannot fail to be of absorbing interest to the anthropologist. Yet his conclusions will be of little interest to the
biblical scholar, except in so far as they help to point up the
remarkable transformation of the rite in Israel.

Sarna 1970

It is really regrettable that the Jews should have practiced [cir-
cumcision], for as a result Bible commentators have given it a
place apart which it in no ways deserves. If the Jews had
linked themselves with Yahweh by perforating the septum,
how much fewer would have been the errors in ethnographic
literature.

van Gennep 1960 (1908)

Surveying discussions of Israelite circumcision over the past several centuries,
one finds a diminishing interest in ethnographic data on circumcision. In the
seventeenth and eighteenth centuries, the discovery that savages in other
parts of the world practiced circumcision shocked writers and demanded
some sort of explanation. If circumcision was a sign of the covenant between
Abraham and God, why did so many other peoples practice the rite? Many
writers explained its distribution as reflecting the genealogy of peoples. People who practiced circumcision must have had contact with or descended
from the peoples who originally observed this rite. Ancient Israelites or Egyptians were often favored originators of this practice. Subsequent writers, who
were less naïve historically, realized that circumcision often developed independently among different peoples. But they did not deny the usefulness of
comparative data for understanding the Israelite practice. In their view, a

great deal about the Israelite practice could be inferred from the function and meaning of circumcision in other societies.[1]

In this century, however, the pendulum has swung in the other direction. Discussions of Israelite circumcision frequently ignore (e.g., Speiser 1964, 124–27; von Rad 1976, 197–203) or argue for the irrelevance of comparative data (e.g., Driver 1906, 190; Isaac 1964, 444–56; de Vaux 1965, 1:48; Hyatt 1976, 629–31; Plaut 1974, 157–64; Sarna 1970, 131–33).[2] These writers operate on the assumption that the Israelite practice of circumcision is distinctive and cannot be illuminated by ethnographic material. Their reasoning is twofold. Circumcision is a sign of the covenant between Abraham and God and hence is embedded in and takes its meaning from the distinctive theological conceptions of Israel. Moreover, at some point in the development of the Israelite practice, Israelites began to circumcise their male children on the eighth day after birth.[3] By this time, if not earlier, Israelite circumcision lost the sexual meanings and social functions it has among other peoples. Ethnographic literature, as we shall see, indicates that circumcision can be associated with a male's sexual and social maturation and, like other rites of passage, represents the change in an initiate's status as a symbolic death and rebirth. The close association between circumcision and birth in Israelite religion rules out similar interpretations of the Israelite practice.

Isaac (1964, 452) concludes that "the tenor of the biblical document is so 'anti-pagan' that the admission of circumcision as covenant symbol or token must mean that this is precisely what it was intended to be." De Vaux (1965, 1:47–48) admits that Israelite circumcision may originally have constituted an initiation rite into marriage and thus made a man fit for sexual life. But "this significance must have died out when the operation was performed soon after birth. Above all, religion gave the rite a more lofty significance." Vriezen (1967, 151) suggests that circumcision was originally a part of the Kenite initiation rites for males. But "once adopted by Yahwistic groups, circumcision became in effect a rite of religious initiation into the community of Yahweh; and then the demonic and sexual aspects of the original rites faded into the background."

Sarna (1970, 132) claims that "the Bible shifted its [circumcision's] performance from puberty to the eighth day of birth, a radical departure from well-nigh universal practice which not only marks the distinction in spiritual destiny between Isaac and Ishmael, but even more importantly establishes another essential differentiation of the biblical institution of circumcision from its contemporary pagan counterpart." Plaut (1974, 118) writes that "the command to Abraham shifts the practice away from young adulthood to the eighth day after birth and thereby from sexual to spiritual significance." In his article on circumcision in the *Interpreters Dictionary of the Bible Supplement,* Hyatt (1976, 630) reviews some possible "primitive" meanings that Israelite circumcision may have had in the distant past. He does not even mention fertility as one of the possible "early" meanings of Israelite circumcision. Instead, he concludes that "above all, it was an act of initiation into the covenant community. The rite served to indicate that a Hebrew was a son of the covenant." It is interesting to note that the same kind of view infiltrated twentieth-century ethnography. Writing about the Bathonga of Africa, Henry Junod (1962 [1912], 76), concludes that the Bathonga practice of removing the foreskin does "not have the high spiritual meaning of the Jewish circumcision."

These discussions of Israelite circumcision employ two of the strategies discussed in part 1. Some deny any deep similarities between the Israelite practice and its ethnographic parallels. Others make the similarities irrelevant by invoking a temporal framework in which the "primitive" aspects of the Israelite practice belong to the earliest phases of its development. In what follows, I argue that Israelite circumcision in fact carried many of the same meanings as circumcision rites practiced in other societies. I focus in particular on the understanding of circumcision among Israelite priests, who presided over the Temple cult in Jerusalem after the Babylonian exile in the fifth and fourth centuries. This circle is generally credited with the authorship of one important source in the Hebrew Bible, called simply "P," parts of which may date back to the seventh century B.C.E.[4] The literature produced by this group is the first to indicate that circumcision was practiced on the eighth day after birth and the first to explicitly describe circumcision as a sign of the covenant between Abraham and God (Gen. 17:12; 21:4; Lev. 12:3).[5] I focus on the priestly conception, because interpreters generally cite the priestly account of circumcision (Gen. 17) as evidence that the Israelite practice had been spiritualized and that it thus differed fundamentally from that of other peoples. I will show, however, that for the priestly community the practice of circumcision, despite its role in symbolizing the covenant and despite its performance just after birth, nonetheless symbolized the fertility of the initiate as well as his entrance into and ability to perpetuate a lineage of male descendants.[6] Circumcision among Israelites is thus comparable to circumcision ceremonies in other traditions that involve similar themes. After exploring such similarities, I take up the perplexing question of why the priests practiced a fertility rite so soon after birth.

I am aware, of course, of the charges frequently leveled at early advocates of the comparative enterprise. The meaning of circumcision in Africa, Australia, or New Guinea need not be its meaning in the distinctive cultural configuration of Israelite religion. For this reason, I ground my interpretation of the Israelite data in a symbolic exegesis of relevant biblical passages. Symbolic exegesis is the attempt to tease out implicit meanings that are embedded in the practice in question. My analysis assumes that a practice may have had a symbolic meaning that did not always find explicit articulation in Israelite literature. Since the historical anthropologist cannot question natives about the meaning of practices, she or he is in the position of doing cultural archaeology, a mode of interpretation which involves imagining what practices meant from incomplete cultural remains. Unstated meanings can often be detected from symbolic artifacts such as metaphors which point to larger complexes of meaning that never found explicit articulation. While ethnographic literature does not by itself determine the interpretation of an Israelite practice, it does suggest possible meanings and functions that the practice may have had. After teasing out the unstated meanings of Israelite circumcision, I show that the priest's conceptualization of circumcision fits into their overwhelming preoccupation with reproduction and intergenerational continuity between males, and how these themes ultimately spring from the form of their social relations.

Circumcision in Comparative Perspective

To limit the scope of this survey, the following comments are restricted to the practices of circumcision among traditional African peoples, since it is often such "savage" practices with which the Israelite rite is implicitly contrasted.[7] Ethnographic literature indicates that four interrelated themes are frequently embedded in African rites of circumcision: fertility, virility, maturity, and genealogy. Since circumcision frequently takes place at or near puberty (White 1953, 42; Spencer 1965, 215), it serves to initiate a boy into manhood. In these contexts, being a man generally involves the biological ability to reproduce, the responsibility of marrying, having children, and perpetuating the lineage, and competence in the knowledge and practices associated with adult life in a given community. This cluster of themes accompanies circumcision even when the practice takes place before puberty, leading van Gennep to describe such rites as initiation into "social puberty" rather than marking actual biological changes associated with puberty (van Gennep 1960 [1908], 46, 65–66; see also Gluckman 1949, 167). Like other religious practices (Turner 1967, 28), rites of circumcision have a fan of referents that can be grouped in terms of sensory and ideological dimensions. At the sensory level, these rites make graphic reference to the basic biological functions and processes including sexual maturation and the urge for sexual intercourse and reproduction, as well as the specific body fluids involved in these processes. At the ideological level, these practices allude to basic social values, including the novice's attainment of manhood, his social maturation, his place in the social organization, and his responsibilities to the ancestors.

One can see why circumcision serves as a "natural" symbol for these various themes. In exposing the male organ by removing the foreskin, circumcision is a graphic representation of a boy's emerging masculinity. Ndembu explicitly say that circumcision is making visible a boy's manhood (Turner 1962, 144). Removing the foreskin also gives the male member the appearance it has when erect, suggesting the emergent sexuality of the child and his reproductive responsibilities. As an operation on the male reproductive organ, circumcision symbolizes lines of descent. This is an especially powerful symbol in patrilineal societies, where descent is traced from father to son. But it also has such connotations among matrilineal societies where descent is traced from a woman's brother to her son (Turner 1962; 1967, 186–224). Since circumcision exposes a boy's sexual organ, it is also a natural symbol of his readiness for social intercourse. Sexual intercourse, after all, is one of the most powerful symbols of social intercourse (Collier and Rosaldo 1981, 314). When a person is outside or in transition between recognized social positions, sexual intercourse is prohibited. "Resumption of sexual relations is usually a ceremonial mark of return to society as a structure of statuses" (Turner 1969, 104). The penis, then, is what makes a boy a male, an adult, a father, and a continuator of his lineage. One might sum this up by saying that one must have a member to be a member.

In the argument that follows, I will flesh out these various meanings of circumcision seriatim, drawing first upon ethnographic literature, then considering their relevance within the Israelite context.

Circumcision and Fertility

There is a recurring connection between the theme of fertility and the practice of circumcision among numerous African peoples. For example, medicines that are used during Balovale and Ndembu circumcision rites include hardwood from fruit trees. The hardness of the wood makes the male's penis erect and hard. Since the wood derives from fruit trees, it also makes the novice fruitful (White 1953, 46; Turner 1962, 166). Commenting on the properties of Chikoli wood, a type of wood used by Ndembu in medicines for healing the initiate, one informant explains that "it stands upright like a strong penis" (Turner 1962, 166). Balovale novices urinate on sticks taken from fruit trees, an act which is conducive to having erections and being fertile (White 1953, 47–48). After circumcision, they tie special kinds of leaves around the penis, which are intended to enlarge the organ (White 1953, 49). Ndembu novices sit on trees symbolic of reproductive capacity (Turner 1962, 141). Among the Wiko, lodge ceremonies are intended to increase semen and fertility. Songs and rites refer constantly to copulation and sexual organs. During sexually provocative dances, men and women expose their genitals and imitate the genitals of the opposite sex (Gluckman 1949, 153, 156). Ndembu novices eat foods such as cassava mush and sweet potato porridge which symbolize semen, and the night before the circumcision rites, dancers mime copulation (Turner 1962, 148, 164). In order to make their penes grow hard and strong, Balovale novices play with the organs of the men supervising the lodge. If their supervisor has an erection, the boys make sucking noises with their lips and beckon with their hands to ensure that they acquire the ability to do likewise (1953, 49, 55). If a central purpose of circumcision is to ensure the fertility of the emerging man, the failure to comply with the rules produces the opposite result: it makes novices impotent and infertile (Gluckman 1949, 156; White 1953, 44, 47).

After the boys have healed from their operation, they are encouraged to engage in sexual intercourse. Circumcised Bajok initiates are assigned to a woman who teaches them techniques of sexual intercourse (Holdredge and Young 1927, 665). Each Wiko boy should have sexual intercourse with a woman or girl to remove the impurity of the lodge, lest he be infertile and never have sexual intercourse again (Gluckman 1949, 156). Toward the end of seclusion, each Ndembu novice is also given a small round cucumber or a fruit with a hole in it and is expected to feign intercourse with it. When initiation ends, novices mime copulation with a lodge official who dresses as a woman and is given a name which signifies "Woman" (Turner 1962, 159; 1967, 254). Balovale novices are expected to copulate with a woman in order to remove the impurity of circumcision. If the boy is too young to actually have intercourse, the supervisor carves a vagina from a cucumber or small pumpkin to let the boy practice. Such a cucumber is called "old woman" (White 1953, 52).

Circumcision and Fruitfulness in Ancient Israel

In turning to the meaning of Israelite circumcision, we must at least entertain the possibility, popularized by so many interpreters, that this rite served as a purely arbitrary sign of God's covenant with Abraham. On this view, there was in priestly ideology no intimate connection between circumcision and the particular substance of the covenant. Piercing the ear might have served equally well. "Circumcision is understood quite formally, i.e., without significant reference to the procedure itself, as a sign of the covenant, as an act of confession and as appropriation of the divine revealed will" (von Rad 1976, 201).

There are, however, a number of reasons to reject such a view. On pragmatic grounds alone, it is difficult to comprehend the arbitrary selection of such an invasive procedure. More importantly, circumcision is described as an *'ôt* of the covenant (Gen. 17:11). Examples of how the priests use this Hebrew word in other contexts indicate that it means "symbol," not "sign."[8] A symbol differs from a sign in that it has properties that make it appropriate for the content which it signifies.[9] For example, the priests say that the rainbow (Gen. 9:12, 17) is a symbol *('ôt)* of God's covenant with Noah. Since rainbows appear at the end of a storm, they serve as appropriate symbols of God's promise not to flood the world. The symbol has an intimate association with the content of the divine promise and thereby serves to remind God of the obligation undertaken to humankind (Gen. 9:15–16). The priestly writer also uses the term "symbol" *('ôt)* to describe the blood Israelites purportedly put on their doorposts before their departure from Egypt (Exod. **12:13**). This blood, which was taken from a slaughtered lamb or kid, indicated that God should pass over the home and slay only firstborn Egyptians. The blood of the animal serves as a symbol because it metaphorically parallels the blood of the Israelite child which God has chosen not to shed. Again, there is an intimate association between the symbol and its referent.

Since circumcision is described as a symbol of the covenant between Abraham and God, one is led to the conclusion that the practice has an intimate connection with the content of that covenant. The centerpiece of this covenant is God's promise that Abraham will have vast numbers of descendants. "I will establish My covenant between Me and you, and I will make you exceedingly numerous" (Gen. **17:2**). "As for Me, this is My covenant with you: You shall be the father of a multitude of nations. And you shall no longer be called Abram, but your name shall be Abraham, for I make you the father of a multitude of nations. I will make you exceedingly fertile, and make nations of you; and kings shall come forth from you" (Gen. **17:4–6**).

It should not be surprising that the priestly writer treats fertility as a central issue in the covenant between Abraham and God. This writer is preeminently concerned with human reproduction and its implications. In narrating world and Israelite history, this writer emphasizes in seven separate contexts the importance of human fertility. God once instructed Adam (Gen. **1:22**) and twice instructed Noah (Gen. **9:1, 7**) to be fruitful and multiply. When Isaac gives Jacob his final blessing, he prays that God "bless you, make you fertile and numerous, so that you become an assembly of peoples. May God grant the blessing of Abraham to you and your offspring, that you may possess the land where you are sojourning, which God gave to Abraham" (Gen. **28:3**). This blessing contrasts with the one that the Jahwist puts in Isaac's mouth, a blessing that does not include a petition for fertility (Gen. **27:28–29**). According to the priestly writer, God in fact blesses Jacob with fertility during his return to Canaan (Gen. **35:11**). When Jacob is about to die, he recalls the divine promise of fertility when adopting Joseph's sons into his patrilineage (Gen. **48:3**). Finally, this writer emphasizes that the children of Israel (= Jacob) were indeed fertile and prolific, as God had promised (Exod. **1:7**). In addition to these references, the priestly writer is preoccupied with the consequences of reproduction, a concern that manifests itself in the detailed genealogies this writer records (e.g., Gen. **5:1–28, 30–32; 10:1–7; 11:10–26; 25:12–18; 36:1–14; 46:6–27**).

For the priestly writer, then, the "blessing of Abraham" is the divine promise to multiply Abraham's descendants. But Abraham's fertility will be greater than either Adam's or Noah's, for God twice promises to multiply Abraham's descendents "exceedingly much" *(bimě'od mě'ōd)* (Gen. **17:2, 6**), an expression that does not appear in the blessings of Adam or Noah. Realizing that fertility is the central theme of the covenant, Abraham breaks down in laughter, "Can a child be born to a man a hundred years old, or can Sarah bear a child at ninety?" (Gen. 17:17). It is in this context that God commands Abraham to circumcise himself, all his male descendants, and all his slaves (Gen. 17:10–14).

Given this covenant's overwhelming emphasis on Abraham's fecundity, one can agree with Isaac (1964, 453) that "the cutting of a generative organ involved in Abraham's covenant is an appropriate symbol for a covenant made with the generations and dealing with offspring." It is an appropriate symbol because in this community the male organ is viewed as the primary vehicle by which reproduction and intergenerational continuity are ensured. This conclusion, moreover, makes sense of the fact that Abraham is said to have circumcised his son Ishmael (Gen. 17:23–25). God acquiesces to Abraham's wish that Ishmael be a progenitor of multitudes (Gen. 17:18–20). The circumcision of Ishmael is entirely in keeping with its symbolism of fertility. But Ishmael's circumcision would make no sense at all if circumcision was only a sign of the covenant, since the priests exclude Ishmael from the covenantal promise (Gen. 17:18–22).

It is also relevant to note the penalty that is prescribed for males who are not circumcised. Such a person "shall be cut off from his people" (Gen. 17:14). This may mean, as commentators suggest, that he is ostracized from his people or that God takes his life. But in light of ethnographic studies of circumcision, a new understanding is also possible. We have seen that failure to perform circumcision is sometimes equated with impotence and infertility. "Being cut off from one's people," therefore, might mean that the offender shall have no offspring and thus have no descendants to perpetuate his name in Israel, an interpretation suggested by medieval Jewish commentators.[10] One who is not circumcised becomes infertile.

The connection between circumcision and fertility explains why some commentators have been confused over whether circumcision is the covenant or simply a symbol of it (Skinner 1910, 294; Sarna 1970, 132). Circumcision is a symbol that God will make Abraham fruitful and multiply. At the same time, circumcision is also a fulfillment of that promise since the removal of the foreskin symbolically readies the organ for reproduction.

While these conclusions seem reasonable, it is important to realize that in Genesis 17 the priestly writer does not make the connection between circumcision and fruitfulness explicit. Nor is it at all obvious why cutting away the foreskin is a symbol of fertility. As we shall now see, however, other passages authored within and outside priestly circles make this connection more credible and provide a clue as to the basis for the association between the removal of excess skin from a male's penis and the idea of fruitfulness.

Uncircumcised Hearts, Ears, and Lips

The priestly writers, following the precedent of others before them, conceptualize other parts of the body as "uncircumcised." Jeremiah and the

Deuteronomist, for example, describe the person who lacks inner commitment to the covenant as a person with an uncircumcised heart (Jer. 9:25; Deut. 10:16). Such a person, according to Jeremiah, also has "uncircumcised" ears (Jer. 6:10). The priests, for their part, also make reference to an "uncircumcised heart" (Ezek. 44:7, 9; Lev. 26:41). In addition, they twice describe Moses's speech impediment as a problem of "uncircumcised lips" (Exod. 6:12, 30), preferring this expression to the alternative "heavy of lips," which is found in the narrative of the Jahwist (Exod. 3:10).

These expressions may represent a tendency to "spiritualize" the meaning of circumcision (Driver 1906, 191). But they also show that Israelite writers equated the lack of circumcision with the improper functioning of a human organ. Uncircumcised hearts, ears, and lips are organs that cannot do what God intended them to do. By extension, the removal of a man's foreskin symbolically enables the penis to more effectively discharge its divinely allotted task. That task, as suggested by the content of the covenant, is to impregnate women and produce offspring.

Uncircumcised Fruit Trees

The priests also extend the metaphor of circumcision in an unprecedented way. They conceptualize the fruit that grows on immature fruit trees as its "foreskin" and the tree itself as "uncircumcised." As suggested in chapter 5, the comparison of fruit trees and male organs is one example of how Israelites extended metaphors from the human and social domains to the domain of agriculture. In this case, the relevant passage deals with a divine proscription against eating the young fruit of any tree grown in the land of Israel. "When you enter the land and plant any tree for food, you shall regard its fruit as its foreskin.[11] Three years it shall be uncircumcised for you, not to be eaten. In the fourth year all its fruit shall be set aside for jubilation before the Lord; and only in the fifth year may you use its fruit—that its yield to you may be increased: I the Lord am your God" (Lev. 19:23–25). Most commentators understand the comparison between a male's foreskin and the fruit of young fruit trees to move in one direction only, from the domain of human circumcision to the domain of fruit trees. Consequently, they interpret this metaphor as a prohibition against using the fruit of juvenile trees (e.g., Onkelos ad loc.; Driver 1898, 89; Hoffman 1906, 2:51–54; Porter 1976, 156–57; Hertz 1961 [1935], 503; and Noth 1977, 143). "Anyone 'uncircumcised' was outside the holy community so produce not available to the community could be described this way" (Porter 1976, 157). "You shall regard its fruit as defective. The fruit tree in the first three years is to be regarded as a male infant during his first eight days, i.e., as unconsecrated" (Hertz, following Dillman, 1961 [1935], 503; Wenham 1979, 271). Based on this understanding, many translations simply substitute "forbidden" for "uncircumcised" (JPS 1962, 217; RSV 1971, 147; Hertz 1961 [1935], 503; Porter 1976, 156). But there is good reason to think that the metaphor between the male organ and fruit trees is grounded on other similarities as well. Of the dozens of other things that the priests declare forbidden, they apply the metaphors of "uncircumcised" and "foreskin" to none of them. Why then did they see a metaphoric relationship between this particular forbidden item and the male foreskin?

The answer emerges when one considers the physiology of fruit trees, and in particular the ones found in the land of Israel. During the early years of growth, fruit trees pass through a juvenile stage during which they generally do not flower and often produce little or no fruit. If the tree does bear a few fruit during this period, it is often defective. The juvenile period varies according to species. As a rule, however, the types of fruit trees growing in the land of Israel (e.g., dates, figs, olives, grapes, pomegranates, almonds; see Deut. 8:8; Num. 13:23; Judg. 9:10–13) do not bear fruit until the fourth year and beyond. Female date palms, for example, begin to bear dates at any age varying from four to twenty years, with an average of five from planting (Popenoe 1920, 212; Everett 1981, 3:1016; Horticultural Crops Group 1982, 35). Olives may bear a fair crop in the sixth year (Chandler 1950, 368). Fig seedlings growing from their own roots take five to seven years to come into full bearing (Janick and Moore 1975, 576; Condit 1947, 24). Pomegranates come into bearing in the fifth year and generally do not reach full maturity until the seventh (Simmons 1972, 284). Grape seedlings produce fruit in three to six years, and almond trees produce some flower buds in the fourth year and some fruit in the fifth (Janick and Moore 1975, 138, 396). Ancient sources confirm that ancient fruit trees produced fruit at approximately the same rates as those grown today. References in the Code of Hammurabi, for example, indicate that ancient Babylonians were able to rely on a respectable crop of dates in the fourth year (Popenoe 1973, 7; Wenham 1979, 271). The Tosefta (ca. 300 C.E.), defines a productive plantation as including vines that are five years old, fig trees six years old, and olive trees seven years old (T. Sheb 1:3).[12]

By equating a juvenile fruit tree with an uncircumcised Israelite male, this passage presupposes a symbolic association between circumcision and fertility. The infertile tree is "uncircumcised" just as a child, who is not yet rooted in the covenant, cannot bear fruit. Moreover, if a circumcised tree is one that yields a full harvest, the removal of a male's foreskin prepares him for a maximal yield. So the metaphor between fruit trees and the penis is not unidirectional. Fruit from juvenile fruit trees is proscribed like the male foreskin. By the same token, the uncircumcised male organ is like immature fruit trees in that it cannot produce fruit.

The extension of such metaphors to fruit trees might rest on another perceived similarity as well. Circumcising the male organ is analogous to pruning fruit trees. Both acts involve cutting away unwanted growth from a stem or trunk and the purpose of both cuttings is similar. Circumcision, as I have already argued, is a symbolic cut that ensures human fertility. Similarly, pruning a fruit tree is crucial for maximizing its yield either by developing a good framework or maximizing the surface area for fruit production.

Unfortunately, biblical literature provides little information about the horticultural practices of ancient Israel. Nonetheless, it does indicate that Israelites pruned their grapevines and regarded that practice as crucial for the success of the vineyard (Lev. 25:1–5; Isa. 5:6). Since biblical writers classified the grape vine as a kind of tree (Judg. 9:13; Joel 1:12; 2:22; Ezek. 15:2, 6), we know that Israelites regularly pruned at least one kind of fruit "tree" in order to maximize its yield.

There is no direct evidence that the priestly writer saw an analogy between circumcision and pruning. But the priestly work does make an explicit comparison between pruning and the act of cutting another part of the body, namely the hair. During the Sabbatical year, Israelites are instructed not to carry out any horticultural activity, including the pruning of grape vines. These untrimmed vines the priests call "your nazirites" *(nězîrekā)* or the "nazirites" of the fields *(nězirêhā)* (Lev. 25:5, 11). As noted in chapter 5, this use of the term "nazirite" is secondary. Its primary referent is an Israelite who has consecrated himself to God by vowing not to eat grape products or cut his hair (Num. 6). The extension of the term "nazirite" to untrimmed vines rests on a metaphoric association between an unpruned vineyard (which is being dedicated to God) and a man who has untrimmed hair (because he has consecrated himself to God). Here, then, is an incontrovertible instance where the priests recognize an analogy between not cutting part of the human body (i.e., the hair) and not pruning grape vines. The existence of this metaphor does not prove that the priests also saw an analogy between pruning and circumcision. But it does make that interpretation more plausible.

It may also be the case that the link between circumcision and pruning is presupposed in the notion that juvenile fruit trees are "uncircumcised" (Lev. 19:23). Now there is a certain ambiguity in this expression. Does it imply, as some commentators suggest, that the fruit is not cut during the first three years of the tree's growth? That the tree is "uncircumcised" because its fruit is not cut off like the foreskin of an uncircumcised male organ? By this reading, the tree's circumcision is its ceremonial stripping in the fourth year when the fruit harvest is dedicated to God (IB 1953, 2:98–99). There are, however, reasons to doubt this interpretation. To begin with, this passage only states that the fruit is the foreskin and that it cannot be eaten. It does not say that the fruit must remain on the tree. Furthermore, if the cutting of the fruit in the fourth year is the symbolic circumcision of the tree, then the foreskin of the tree is being offered to God. But in the priestly practice of human circumcision, the foreskin is not offered to God (see Gen. 17).

An alternative interpretation is thus called for. Calling the fruit "foreskin" might suggest that it should be cut off, just as the male foreskin is cut off. This interpretation would presuppose good horticultural practice, for pruning immature fruit trees is important for maximizing their yield in maturity. "For the first year or several years . . . fruit production is neither expected nor desired. The maturing of fruit and to a certain extent even the formation of fruit buds and potential fruiting wood might tax the energies of the plant so that increase in size would be checked seriously" (Gardner et al. 1952, 564). The greater the size of the tree the greater the surface area for the production of fruit. In the case of palms, "The grower must not let his young palms bear too many dates, particularly if he wants them to produce offshoots (for future fruiting) at the same time. In most cases, a palm may be allowed to bear its first two bunches of fruit in its fourth year, and 3 or 4 bunches in each of the next 2 years. If even a full grown palm is allowed to bear its limit in any year it is likely to bear less the following season" (Popenoe 1920, 211). Fig trees, for their part, require severe pruning as young trees in order to build up a good framework, which is crucial for maximizing subsequent yield (Simmons 1972, 127). By calling immature fruit "foreskin" and by forbidding the consumption of such fruit, the passage discourages farmers from attempting to maximize a tree's yield before it is sufficiently mature. Moreover, it may even encourage farmers to cut away the fruit of their young trees ("the foreskin"), just as they are expected to cut away the foreskin of their newborn son.

The expectation that farmers harvest their trees in the fourth year and beyond (Lev. 19:24–25) is consistent with the aim of increasing the yield. Allowing a tree to bear a full crop in these years does not tax its growth. That maximizing the yield is the central motivation behind these rules is confirmed by the exhortation that one should observe these rules "so that its yield to you may be increased" (Lev. 19:25). This probably means, as many commentators point out, that God will increase the yield when the divine laws concerning fruit trees are obeyed. But that theological meaning may well presuppose good horticultural practice. When a farmer discourages a tree's yield during its juvenile period, God will see to it that the tree bears a large number of fruit.

To summarize this line of argument, the symbolic equation of an uncircumcised male and a young fruit tree rests on two, and possibly three, associations. The fruit of a juvenile tree is proscribed like the foreskin of the male organ. Furthermore, a male who is uncircumcised and not part of the covenantal community is infertile like an immature fruit tree. Finally, this symbolic equation may draw part of its plausibility from an analogy between circumcision and pruning. Cutting away the foreskin is like pruning a fruit tree. Both acts of cutting remove unwanted excess and both increase the desired yield. One might say that when Israelites circumcise their male children, they are pruning the fruit trees of God.

As the above analysis indicates, the themes of procreation and fertility are central to the priestly conception of circumcision, even though priests circumcised their male children eight days after birth. This enables us to account for the otherwise "uncanny coincidence" that ancient Israelite priests and twentieth-century African tribes, separated in time and space, both make an association between circumcision and fruit trees. As we have seen, wood from fruit trees is frequently employed in African circumcision ceremonies to ensure the fertility of the novice and the strength of his organ.

The association between fruit trees and circumcision is based on two intersecting metaphors, each of which is found in diverse cultural contexts. The first is the metaphoric association between fruit, on the one hand, and human sexuality and genitalia, on the other. I have already given several examples of this association in the previous chapter. Here are additional ones: Ndembu openly compare a calabash with a phallus and use it to give training in sexual techniques at girls' puberty rituals (Turner 1969, 67). Describing how a novice's mother may not have sexual intercourse, one Ndembu man said, "A novice's mother is taboo, *nshindwa* fruit [a euphemism for the female genitalia] is forbidden" (Turner 1967, 205). At the end of mourning, Nyakyusa pass a flat basket of millet mixed with pumpkin seeds and lentils between the legs of the mourning woman, symbolizing that she may now engage in sexual intercourse (Wilson 1954, 231). Nyakyusa also treat plantain as a symbol of a man and the *iselya,* a sweet banana eaten ripe, as a metaphor for a woman (Wilson 1957, 2). "Nyakyusa women eat the plantain, a symbolic act representing intercourse" (Wilson 1957, 101). In Italy, the gesture "fico" (fig), the thumb inserted between the fore and middle fingers, is an insult analogous to the American "screw you" (Condit 1947, 5).

Trees, for their part, frequently serve as metaphors for the male organ. In Fang culture, women in women's society rituals insult men in songs by attributing impotence to them. "Worn out lance of a penis come bury yourself. I myself will cause to stand erect the rootless tree" (Fernandez 1982, 156). The roots that Nyakyusa put into female fertility medicines signify the impregnating activity of the male penis (Wilson 1957, 101). Finally, in a book advising advertisers about visual persuasion, Stephen Baker discusses the "sexing of objects" and suggests that trees (and wooden textures) reek of masculinity (quoted in Sahlins 1976, 218). Given the association in diverse cultures between fruit and human sexuality, on the one hand, and between trees and the male organ, on the other, it is not surprising that fruit trees become symbolically connected with circumcision rites in contexts that are geographically and temporally remote from one another. Nor are the Israelite priests alone in drawing an analogy between a circumcised penis and a circumcised tree. The Ndembu see a resemblance between the act of removing the foreskin and the act of planting a *muyombu* tree to the ancestors. When the tree is planted for this purpose, "the bark and some of the wood is removed at the top leaving a peg of bright white wood, which is compared to a circumcised penis." Ndembu explain that removing the bark in this way makes it sprout better (Turner 1967, 154; 1962, 144). Significantly, Ndembu novices are carried over a transplanted *muyombu* tree during circumcision ceremonies. Van Gennep, himself an interpreter of religion, found the cutting of wood a helpful analogy for circumcision and other practices of mutilation. Reflecting on the wide distribution of such practices, he comments that "it becomes apparent that the human body has been treated like a simple piece of wood which each has cut and trimmed to suit him" (van Gennep 1960 [1908], 72).

The Israelite priests are also not unique in justifying a food restriction by appealing to the uncircumcised character of the food in question. Ndembu forbid novices to eat the elephant shrew, which has a long trunk and appears to the Ndembu like a boy with a foreskin (Turner 1967, 222).

Other Readers, Similar Conclusions

Since my analysis of Israelite circumcision has relied heavily on ethnographic literature, it is worthwhile pointing out that my interpretations dovetail in some interesting ways with the insights of ancient interpreters: Philo, a first-century Egyptian Jew, who attempted to reconcile Platonism and biblical religion, and the early rabbis (200–600), an elite group of Jewish interpreters who undertook an extensive reinterpretation of the faith and practices of ancient Israel.

Philo cites several justifications for circumcision, including its medical benefits, its role as a purification rite, and its effects on fertility. Explaining the latter justification, Philo concludes that semen is often caught in the folds of the foreskin and hence is scattered unfruitfully. But when the foreskin is removed there is a greater chance of its reaching its destination. "For this reason such nations as practise circumcision increase greatly in population" (Philo 3:48; 1971, 244).

Although the foreskin does not in fact inhibit procreation as Philo believed, Philo was led to this conclusion because he sensed the centrality of procreation in God's covenant with Abraham (Gen. 17). He was also aware that Egyptians circumcised their children in proximity to puberty and that the ritual was associated with sexual maturation (Philo 3:48; 1971, 244). More significantly, Philo drew attention to the similarity between pruning and circumcision:

> Why does one circumcise (both) the home-born and the purchased (child) . . . as for the deeper meaning, the home-born characters are those which are moved by nature, while the purchased ones are those who are able to improve through reason and teaching. There is need for both of these to be purified and trimmed like plants, both those which are natural and genuine, and those which are able to bear fruit constantly; for well-grown (plants) produce many superfluous (fruits) because of their fertility, which it is useful to cut off. But those who are taught by teachers shave off their ignorance. (Philo 3:50; 1971, 251)

Philo's understanding of circumcision as signifying the shaving off of ignorance finds no support in Israelite writings. However, for our purposes it is significant that Philo saw an analogy between pruning fruit trees and circumcising the male organ. Both acts remove unnecessary excess.

Like Philo, the rabbis also saw circumcision as fundamentally linked to issues of procreation. This connection becomes evident when the rabbis consider how Abraham knew he was supposed to circumcise the penis and not some other organ. After all, God instructs Abraham to circumcise "the flesh of his foreskin." How did Abraham know that God intended him to circumcise the sexual organ and not the foreskin of his heart or ears? "Rav Huna said in Bar Kappara's name: Abraham made the following analogy (*gezerah shavah*). Scripture uses the word 'foreskin' in reference to a tree (Lev. 19:23) and in reference to man (Gen. 17:11). Just as foreskin of trees refers to the place where it yields fruit, foreskin of man must refer to the place where he produces fruit (GR 46:4; see also LR 25:6, and B. Shab. 108a). Another sage disagrees and suggests that the covenantal language itself signalled that God had in mind the foreskin of the penis. " 'And I will make My covenant between Me and thee, and will multiply thee exceedingly' (Gen. 17:2). This means 'I will put my covenant between me and you, in the place that is fruitful and multiplies' " (LR 25:6). Like Philo, the rabbis also saw an analogy between circumcision and horticultural practices. Explaining the significance of Abraham's circumcision occurring at a "ripe" old age, "R. Simeon b. Lakish said, '[God said], I will set up a cinnamon tree in the world: just as the cinnamon tree yields fruit as long as you manure and hoe [around] it, so too in the case of Abraham, [he will be fruitful] even when his blood runs sluggishly and his passions and desire has ceased' " (GR 46:2). The rabbis do not equate pruning and circumcision. But they do see an analogy between the work required to maximize the yield of a cinnamon tree and circumcision which enables Abraham to produce fruit at a very old age.

These interpretations do not have the status of "native exegesis" when it comes to understanding what circumcision meant to priests who lived at least five centuries earlier. They derive from the distinctive points of view of their authors. These same authors, moreover, offer other interpretations of circumcision that find no substantiation in Israelite literature. Nonetheless, these interpretations show that the symbolic exegesis performed above is not simply an idiosyncratic reading possible only from the vantage point of symbolic anthropology. Other readers, reading from other points of view, arrived at similar conclusions. These interpretations also show that the connection between circumcision and horticultural practices made sense to those who lived in cultures in which agriculture played a central role. The rabbis were alive to this understanding of circumcision because they also relied on agricultural metaphors to conceptualize human sexuality. To provide one example among many, the rabbis compare the stages in a girl's sexual maturation to the ripening of a fig. During childhood, she is like an unripe fig; during puberty, she is like a ripening fig; when she becomes a woman, she is like a fully ripened fig (M. Nid. 5:7).[13]

Israel, the Orchard and Vineyard of God

My claim that fruit trees serve as metaphors for male organs in the priestly writings gains further plausibility when one realizes that this association represents an elaboration of other metaphors already operative in Israelite thought. Before the priestly source was produced, the analogy between fruit trees and Israel as a religious community was already deeply engrained in the religious imagination of Israel. Time and again, Israelite writers depict God's relation to Israel in terms of metaphors related to the cultivation of orchards and vineyards. It would take dozens of pages to reproduce all the passages in which such metaphors appear. As the following representative examples make clear, such metaphors cut across the entire tradition, whether surveyed by genre or chronologically. They appear in early and late prophetic literature, in writings of the Deuteronomist, and in wisdom literature. Such metaphors provide the basis for several chapter-long parables in prophetic literature (Isa. 5; Jer. 24; Ezek. 17; 31), Psalms (80:9–16), and the deuteronomic narratives (Judg. 9:10ff). They appear in sources composed before and after the rise and fall of the Assyrian empire as well as in literature composed before, during, and immediately following the Babylonian exile.

If such metaphors are not limited to a particular genre or historical period, they are concentrated in passages that deal with a limited repertoire of themes. These themes typically involve the various stages in the unfolding relationship between Israel, as a collective entity, and God. For example, writers compare the early phase of this developing relationship, which is frequently conceived of as idyllic, to a farmer who lovingly plants an orchard or vineyard (e.g., Jer. 2:21; 11:16; Ps. 44:3; 80:9–12). "Let me sing," writes Isaiah, "for my beloved. A song of my lover about his vineyard. My beloved [i.e., God] had a vineyard [i.e., Israel] on a fruitful hill. He broke the ground, cleared it of stones, and planted it with choice vine. He built a watchtower inside it. He even hewed a wine press in it, for he hoped it would yield grapes" (Isa. 5:1–2). According to Hosea, God experienced the first encounter with Israel as pleasing as "grapes in the wilderness," and considered the patriarchs "as first figs to ripen on a fig tree" (Hos. 9:10).

The relationship, however, did not bear fruit in the way that God anticipated. God hoped the vineyard "would yield grapes. Instead, it yielded wild grapes" (Isa. 5:2) and turned into an alien vine (Jer. 2:21). Consequently, God withheld the care formerly lavished on Israel. "Now I am going to tell you what I will do to My vineyard: I will remove its hedge. I will break down its wall, that it may be trampled. And I will make it a desolation; it shall not be pruned or hoed" (Isa. 5:5–6). By breaching the wall, God enabled every passerby to eat the fruit of the vineyard (Ps. 80:9–16), and out of anger, God even set fire to the vineyard (Ezek. 15:16; Ps. 80:17). When God's punishment is completed, Israel will be desolate like the olive tree when the vintage is over (Isa. 24:13) or an olive tree to which God has set fire (Jer. 11:15). After Israel's punishment "only the gleanings shall be left . . . as when one beats an olive tree. Two berries or three on the topmost branch, four or five on the boughs of the crown" (Isa. 17:6). God will "uproot" Israel from the land (Jer. 1:10; 18:19; 31:28; 44:4) and discard Israel like a farmer discards bad figs (Jer. 24).

Although God makes Israel undergo terrible sufferings in the form of military defeats and exile, there still remains hope that the relationship between God and Israel will be restored to its former vitality. At that time God will plant Israel once again firmly on its soil. "I will restore my people Israel. They shall plant vineyards and drink their wine. They shall till their gardens and eat their fruits. And I will plant them on their soil, nevermore to be uprooted from the soil I have given them" (Amos 9:15).

At this time, God will be to Israel like the dew, and Israel will blossom like the vine and be as beautiful as the olive tree (Hos. 14:6–8). "See a time is coming when I will sow the house of Israel and the house of Judah with seed of men and seed of cattle, and just as I was watchful over them to uproot and to pull down . . . so I will be watchful over them to build and to plant" (Jer. 31, 27–28). "And your people, all of them righteous, shall possess the land for all time. They are the shoot that I planted" (Isa. 60:21; see also 61:3; Ezek. 24:26).

The restoration is sometimes compared to the way that a tree destroyed by fire or storm has the capacity to regenerate itself. "And the survivors of the house of Judah that have escaped shall renew its trunk below and produce fruit above" (Isa. 37; 31). A shoot will grow out of the stump of Jesse (Isa. 11:1; Zech. 6:12–13) and God will raise up a branch of David's line (Jer. 23:5; 33:15). Alternatively, Israel is like a shoot cut from a tree which is replanted (Isa. 60:21).

From these examples, it is easy to see why orchards and vineyards served as popular metaphors for describing the relationship between God and Israel. Israelite writers saw an analogy between Israel dwelling securely on its land and fruit trees growing productively under the care of the farmer. Israel's insecurity is compared to an orchard or vineyard that is either unprotected or destroyed by its planter.

Israelite writers also draw on the domain of horticulture to conceptualize the relationship between God and individual Israelites. These metaphors are concentrated in but not limited to the Psalms. For example, one who studies the teaching of the Lord "is like a tree planted beside streams of water that yields its fruit in season whose foliage never fades and whatever it produces thrives" (Ps. 1:3). In contrast to the wicked, "I am a thriving olive tree in God's house. I trust in the faithfulness of God forever and ever" (Ps. 52:10). "The righteous bloom like a date-palm. They thrive like the cedar in Lebanon, planted in the house of the Lord. They flourish in the courts of our God, in old age they still produce fruit" (Ps. 92:13).

According to Jeremiah, a person who places trust in the Lord is like "a tree planted by waters, sending forth its roots by a stream. . . . It has not a care in a year of drought, it does not cease to yield fruit" (Jer. 17:8). When Jeremiah's enemies plot his downfall, the prophet conceptualizes their scheme as an attempt to uproot him. "I did not realize it was against me they fashioned their plots. 'Let us destroy the tree in full sap, let us cut him off from the land of the living' " (Jer. 11:19).[14] Exasperated by the flourishing of the wicked, Jeremiah accuses God of injustice: "Why are the workers of treachery at ease? You have planted them, and they have taken root. They spread, they even bear fruit" (Jer. 12:1–2). By contrast, Eliphaz, one of Job's interlocutors, believes that a wicked man "will wither before his time, his boughs never having flourished. He will drop his unripe grapes like a vine. He will shed his blossoms like an olive tree . . . their womb has produced deceit" (Job. 15:32–33).

Fruit trees also serve as metaphors for the domestic unit. "Our sons are like saplings well tended in their youth; Our daughters are like corner stones trimmed to give shape to a palace" (Ps. 144:12). "Your wife shall be like a fruitful vine within your house; your sons like olive saplings around your table" (Ps. 128:3).

Human Fruitfulness

Given the frequent comparison between the prosperity of Israel and the thriving of an orchard or vineyard, it is not surprising that some Israelite writers associate the harvest of fruit trees with human progeny. Just as a farmer who cares for an orchard sees its fruit ripen and enjoys its harvest, so Israelites who are securely rooted on their land will produce children and see them grow to maturity. The symbolic connection between agricultural and human yields is given linguistic and literary expression in Israelite writings. In Hebrew, as in English, a single term *(zeraʾ)* is applied to agricultural and human "seed." The Hebrew stem that means "be fruitful" *(pĕrû)* derives from the same stem as the word for "fruit" *(pĕrî)*. Firstborn children are referred to as a person's first yield (Ps. 105:35; Deut. 18:4; 21:7). The E writer refers to children as "fruit of the womb" (Gen. 30:2). In addition, we have seen how the terms "twig," "shoot," "stump," and "branch" are used in reference to descendants from the house of David (Isa. 11:1; Jer. 23:5; 33:15; Zech. 6:12–13). One writer even applies the term "son" *(bēn)* to describe the stem of the tree, Israel, that God metaphorically plants on the land (Ps. 80:16). The domains of human reproduction and horticultural yield are each structured to a significant extent in terms drawn from the corresponding domain.[15]

Numerous biblical passages treat the fate of Israelite fruit trees and children as parallel themes. According to Jeremiah, God said to the exiled community in Babylonia, "Build houses and live in them, plant gardens and eat their fruit, take wives and beget sons and daughters . . . multiply there do not decrease" (Jer. 29:5). The Psalmist declares that the faithful "plant vineyards that yield a fruitful harvest. God blesses them and they increase greatly" (Ps. 107:37). The postexilic writer of Isaiah 65 extends the metaphor still further, drawing an analogy between enjoying the fruit of one's harvest and experiencing the joy of seeing one's children grow to maturity. At the time of restoration, Israelites "shall plant vineyards and enjoy their fruit. They shall not build for others to dwell in, or plant for others to enjoy. For the days of My people shall be as long as the days of a tree. . . . They shall not bear children in vain.[16] But they shall be a people blessed by the Lord and their offspring shall remain with them" (Isa. 65:21).

The association between a plentiful yield from fruit trees and the thriving of human children was more than just metaphoric. War, one of the conditions that undermined the productivity of orchards and vineyards, also threatened families. War took men from the home and from the farm, and consequently, neither Israelite women nor fruit trees would receive the attention required to bear fruit. The Deuteronomist thus instructs army officials to make the following declaration before an army departs for war: "Is there anyone who has planted a vineyard but has never harvested it? Let him go back to his home, lest he die in battle and another initiate it. Is there anyone who has paid the brideprice for a wife, but who has not yet taken her? Let him go back to his home, lest he die in battle and another man take her" (Deut. 20:6). In addition to taking men away from the home, invading armies extirpated Israel's orchards and children. During times of war, people would see neither the fruit of their trees nor the fruit of their wombs reach maturity. "They will devour your harvest and food, they will devour your sons and daughters, herds and flocks, vines and fig trees" (Jer. 5:17).

> Though you plant vineyards and till them, you shall have no wine to drink or store, for the worm shall devour them. Although you have olive trees throughout your territory, you shall have no oil for anointment, for your olives shall drop off. Though you beget sons and daughters, they shall not remain with you, for they shall go into captivity. The cricket shall take over all the trees and produce of your land. (Deut. 28:40)

In the above passages, the themes of harvesting a fruit tree and the ripening of fruit are treated as analogous to the harvesting of a woman and the maturing of one's children. That is why these themes are so often set in parallel.

Other passages make the connection between the fertility of fruit trees and humans still more explicit. One psalmist, we recall, likens a "good wife" to a fruitful vine that produces much fruit (Ps. 128:3). A postexilic writer invokes the image of a withered tree to describe an infertile man. "Let not the eunuch say, 'I am a withered tree,' for thus said the Lord, 'As regards eunuchs who keep My sabbaths, who have chosen what I desire and hold fast to My covenant, I will give them . . . a monument and a name better than sons or daughters' " (Isa. 56:3–6). In concluding the argument of this section, it is perhaps interesting to note that the analogy between fruit and children continues to capture the imagination of those living in the land of Israel. The authors of *The Fruits of the Holy Land* (Goor and Nurock 1968) dedicate the book "in humble thankfulness and overwhelming pride to the heroic fighters of Israel's Eternal City, June 1967; For are they not the finest fruit of Israel?"

As the preceeding discussion makes evident, the association between fruit and fruit trees, on the one hand, and human sexuality and fertility, on the other, was widely familiar in ancient Israel. If Israel repudiated the fertility cults of its neighbors as histories of Israelite religion so often suggest, it did not do so because the theme of human fertility represented an abomination. Human fecundity constituted a central preoccupation in Israel's understanding of God's covenantal obligations. Like other peoples, Israelites regarded fruit and fruit trees as appropriate symbols of that theme. In turn, fruit and fruit trees became connected to the idea of covenant.

There are several grounds for assuming that the priests who wrote during or shortly after the exile were familiar with the metaphoric equation of Israel and fruit trees. The large number of such comparisons in diverse sources suggests that this theme was not limited to any particular religious circle. More specifically, the extensive use of such metaphors by the prophet Ezekiel, who was also a priest, shows that such metaphors were considered persuasive in priestly circles (Ezek. 15:6; 17:1–24; 33:3; 34:26ff; 37:16–19). Finally, since the metaphoric association between Israelites and fruit trees was popular among writers describing the exile and restoration, it is reasonable to assume that the priests, who may also have written during the same period of time, were conversant with it.

We now see that the priestly analogy between a juvenile fruit tree and an uncircumcised male member builds directly on those metaphors already circulating in Israelite religious culture. Before the priests gave literary expression to their conception of circumcision, Israelite writers had already invoked the images of fruitful orchards and vineyards to express the covenantal promise. If Israel trusted in God, God would plant Israel on the land. The act of planting trees already symbolized God's covenant with Israel. "I will restore my people Israel. . . . And I will plant them on their soil, nevermore to be uprooted from the soil I have given them" (Amos 9:15). "I will make an everlasting covenant with them that I will not turn away from them and that I will treat them graciously . . . I will delight in treating them graciously, and I will plant them in this land faithfully, with all My heart and soul" (Jer. 32:41). "I will grant them a covenant of friendship. . . . The trees of the field shall yield their fruit and the land shall yield its produce. [My people] shall continue secure on its own soil . . . I shall establish for them a planting of renown" (Ezek. 34:25–29). Since the priests also considered circumcision a sign of the covenant, it is not surprising that they saw an analogy between the male organ and fruit trees. After all, both served as symbols of Israel's faithfulness to God and God's reciprocal promise to multiply the seed of Abraham. If the postexilic Isaiah adopted the image of a withered tree as a metaphor for a eunuch, is it surprising that the priests regarded juvenile fruit trees as a symbol of an uncircumcised boy, a child who was not yet rooted in the covenant and hence could not yet produce fruit?

From Explicit Metaphors to Unconscious Associations

In chapter 5, I noted how the symbolic language of Israelite religion often found its most explicit articulation in psalms, proverbs, and prophetic writings, those genres which were not tied to the logic of narrative. I also argued that the symbolic associations that find their expression in those contexts are often presupposed in the narratives and laws. The present analysis has confirmed that description. In this case, the association of fruit trees, fertility, and covenant, themes intertwined throughout Israelite literature, is taken for granted in the priestly proscription on juvenile fruit trees.

Given the recurrence of this symbolic complex, one must also probe the significance of what might otherwise appear to be trivial and incidental elements of Israelite narratives. Turning to the narratives themselves, one does indeed find instances where an association between fruit, trees, and fertility seems to be presupposed. These associations need not have been conscious. As I argued in the Introduction, writers often have the feeling that the addition or subtraction of an element to a story makes the narrative "work," even if they are not always able to explain this sense of fit. But the sense that one element works better in the narrative than another may be rooted in a set of cultural associations of which the author is not aware. This is all the more true of Israelite narratives, which probably underwent a period of oral transmission.

The association between human fertility and agricultural produce, for example, seems to underlie the Jahwist's story about Adam and Eve. According to the Jahwist, the first humans became aware of their nakedness only after eating from the fruit of a tree in the garden. In response to that awareness they sewed together fig leaves to cover their loins (Gen. 3:6–7). The first mention of sexual intercourse comes after Adam and Eve have eaten fruit. According to the Jahwist, moreover, God metes out parallel punishments for disobeying the divine command against eating fruit from the Tree of Knowledge. Women will have severe pain during childbirth and men will bring forth agricultural yield with the greatest of toil. The male labor in harvesting the crop, therefore, is set parallel to the female labor of bearing children (Gen. 3:16–19). The Jahwist is also the one who gives the name Tamar (date palm) to Judah's daughter-in-law. Like a date palm, Tamar turns out to be fertile and thus produces twins (Gen. 38:27). The Tamar of the deuteronomic narrative does not seem to have any associations with fertility (2 Sam. 13). The Jahwist is also responsible for the story about Rachel using mandrakes to open her womb (Gen. 30:14–16). Finally, this is the writer who describes Jacob's method of ensuring the fertility of the speckled and spotted goats and the dark colored sheep of Laban's flock. Jacob peels white stripes in poplar and almond shoots and sets these up in the watering troughs of the goats, particularly when the sturdier animals were mating (Gen. 30:31–43). Here, the tree branch is supposed to influence the reproductive behavior of animals. This narrative intersects in suggestive ways with the priestly association between fruit trees and pruning on the one hand and the male organ and circumcision on the other. Given these associations in the Jahwist strand between fruit, fruit trees, and human sexuality, one may even be tempted to see a parallelism between this writer's idea that Eve was created from Adam's rib and the method of propagating fruit trees by taking a cutting. If this seems improbable, recall the many instances cited above in which Israelite writers poetically compared the birth of human progeny with the planting of shoots taken from a mature tree. These observations can be offered only tentatively. But given the recurring use of fruit and fruit trees as metaphor for various aspects of the human experience, they do have some measure of plausibility.

The discussion of fruit and fruit trees as Israelite symbolic language was necessitated by the desire to understand how Israelite priests understood circumcision and why they conceived of fruit trees as being uncircumcised. The meaning of circumcision, however, is not exhausted by this constellation of themes. Like all rituals, circumcision is polysemous. As we shall now see, it inscribes more than the themes of fertility and reproduction on the male body.

Circumcision as Symbol of Kinship

In addition to readying a male for his reproductive responsibilities, circumcision is often a mechanism for making visible and solidifying kinship bonds. There is an obvious connection between the themes of procreation and kinship since it is only by reproducing that one ensures the continuity of one's lineage. In many contexts, circumcision ceremonies develop solidarity among male cohorts and solidify individual commitment to lines of descent. The experience of undergoing the ordeal of circumcision and having their blood spilled together provides each generation of males with strong feelings of connectedness to their cohorts. Circumcision is thus a kind of blood brotherhood (Gluckman 1949). The Balovale, for example, prohibit novices from washing during and after their seclusion. The novices, as Balovale express it, have "eaten each other's uncleanness" (White 1953, 43, 49). Circumcision also provides a blood brotherhood across generations. The initiation of youths reminds the participating men of the experience they have all undergone. Among the Luimbi, for example, the intergenerational connection is symbolized by blood which the adult circumciser draws from the subincision of his own penis and smears on the novices (Tucker 1949, 313).

For this reason, circumcision rites frequently display and solidify lines of male descent. This is important since kinship ties between a father and his offspring are always more precarious than the relationship between a child and his or her biological mother. Maternal identity is always self-evident; paternal identity is never as obvious (see, however, Delaney 1986). The problem of paternal identity is a widespread concern among numerous peoples (Jay 1985). Ndembu, for example, say that they trace descent through the mother because the mother is self-evident and manifest, whereas one can never be sure who is the begetter (Turner 1967, 6, 154). For the same reason, people of San Blas in southeastern Spain are hesitant to say a newborn looks like the mother, because this indirectly raises the question of paternal identity (Brandes 1981, 228). The issue of doubtful paternity presents a serious problem to societies structured by patrilineal descent. Various rituals overcome this problem by enabling men to assert intergenerational ties to their male descendants. One way of doing this is through rites of sacrifice. Sacrificing together is an assertion of kinship ties (Jay 1985; 1988). Another way is by sharing the same medicines (Wilson 1957, 101, 104).

The practice of circumcision can also make tangible the links among generations of men. The connection between circumcision and male kinship is evident in a variety of ways. Wiko men, for example, say that "women want to grab children [during the rite of circumcision] but we prevent them" (Gluckman 1949, 158). Men thus associate circumcision with the desire to deny the connection between mother and son and emphasize that between father and son. Fathers anxiously watch the circumcision of their son and claim they are ready to kill the circumciser if he should do damage to his son. Damage to the child's organ, of course, would jeopardize the perpetuation of the father's line. In Bwiti, men of the boy's patrilineage speak words of encouragement to him during the operation (Fernandez 1982, 200). During circumcision rites, frequent reference is also made to patrilineal ancestors. "Since the ceremonies are to make the novices fertile, the ancestor's interest in the continuity of the tribe and of their own lines through the production of many people is manifested" (Gluckman 1949, 164). The Wiko also claim that the blood of circumcision is dangerous to female reproduction. If a woman walks over the spot where the blood has been buried she will bleed continuously and thus be unable to reproduce (Gluckman 1949, 155). Circumcision blood is treated as dangerous to female reproduction because it is the vehicle by which males attempt to build their own kinship ties and minimize those between mother and son.

Israelite Circumcision as a Symbol of Kinship and Descent

Numerous interpreters of Israelite circumcision have suggested that the practice represented a tribal initiation into the community of Yahweh and thus served as a way of distinguishing Israelites from their neighbors (Josephus 1978, 190–194; Wellhausen 1973 [1878], 116; Driver 1906, 190; Skinner 1910, 294; Oesterly and Robinson 1937, 245; Vriezen 1967, 150; Fohrer 1972, 312). There is also a general consensus that circumcision increased in importance during the Babylonian exile (587–533 B.C.E.) as one way to prevent assimilation with Babylonians who were uncircumcised. This is why circumcision becomes central in the priestly writings which may have been composed during and shortly after the exile (Wellhausen 1973 [1878], 116; Oesterly and Robinson 1937, 245; Fohrer 1972, 312). According to this interpretation, the priestly understanding of circumcision is essentially continuous with its meaning in earlier writings, where circumcision serves as a mark that distinguishes Israelites from uncircumcised neighbors (e.g., Gen. 34:14=J; 1 Sam. 17:26; 18:25; 2 Sam. 3:14).

I do not wish to contest this understanding as much as supplement and deepen it in various ways. This understanding focuses on the connection between circumcision and the external circumstances of the Israelite people. What is missing is any attempt to understand the practice of circumcision in terms of the internal politics of Israel. In what ways did circumcision address problems that arose directly from the nature of the priestly community? Moreover, the above understanding of circumcision does not incorporate the connection between circumcision and fertility that has been disclosed above. In what follows, then, I explore the way that circumcision spoke to concerns arising out of the social organization of the priestly community. Specifically, the importance of descent in determining membership in the priestly community played an important role in making circumcision a central symbol of the covenant and in defining the meanings of that practice within priestly circles. This sort of account has two important advantages over the historical interpretation. First, it makes sense of the importance and meaning of circumcision in the priestly community even if the priestly writings are pre-exilic, as some scholars have suggested. Thus this interpretation is not dependent on knowing the precise dating of the priestly writings. Moreover, since it focuses on the concerns arising from the structure of the priestly community, it enables us to account for the similarities between the conception of circumcision among the priests and other peoples who are not geographically or temporally contiguous with ancient Israel but whose social structure gives rise to similar issues.

The Function and Structure of the Priestly Community

The priests were the group of men designated as officiants of the Israelite sacrificial cult. Before the centralization of the cult in Jerusalem (ca. 622 B.C.E.), each cultic center was supervised by priests to whom Israelites would bring their sacrifices (Amos 7:10; 1 Sam. 1–3). In addition to overseeing the sacrificial cult, the priests' duties included using lots *(urim* and *tumim)* (Deut. 33:8; 1 Sam. 24:41–42) to deliver oracles (Judg. 18:5–6) and teaching norms (*torot*) to Israel (Mic. 3:11; Jer. 18:18; Deut. 33:10; de Vaux 1965, 354). After the various cultic centers were closed down and the cult centralized in Jerusalem, the priests formed a community that oversaw the sacrificial service in the Temple and guarded the purity of the Temple precincts. They continued their role of presiding over the sacrifices and teaching norms to Israel. But their role in delivering oracles seems to have ceased. At the time the cult was centralized, if not earlier (cf. 1 Sam. 2:12–17), the priests received remuneration for their work in the Temple. They ate the meat from several of the animal and agricultural offerings (Lev. 2:3; 6:9; 6:19, 22; 7:6), received the firstborn of all animals, and a redemption price for all firstborn Israelite children (Num. 18:7).

The priests thus served as mediators between other Israelites and God. But in contrast to prophets and sages whose piety, charisma, or wisdom determined their sacred status, the priestly office was transmitted patrilineally from father to son. Descent defined the boundaries of the priestly community. Anyone serving as a priest could allegedly trace his genealogy back through the generations, showing that all of his male forebears had been priests before him. Precisely when the priesthood became an inherited office is difficult to determine. Information about the early priesthood comes from later sources, such as the deuteronomic history (late seventh century) and writings produced in priestly circles (Ezekiel, the P document, Ezra, Nehemiah, and Chronicles) during the exile and beyond (sixth and fifth centuries). Each of these sources has its bias and can only be used with caution to reconstruct the nature of the priesthood in earlier periods. However, by the time circumcision became the priest's symbol of the covenant with God (sixth to fifth century at the latest), descent clearly played a crucial role in defining the boundaries of the priestly community. We know this because from the late seventh century on, Israelite writers assume that the early priesthood was hereditary. To be sure, these writers do not agree on which lineage in particular carried the priestly prerogatives. The Deuteronomist, for example, assumes that "sons of Sadoq" dominated the priesthood during the monarchy. For the priestly writer, by contrast, "sons of Aaron" are the legitimate inheritors of the priestly office. Moreover, Ezekiel, Deuteronomy, and the priestly writings all seem to presuppose a distinction between groups of Levites, some of whom have an inferior status and are called simply Levites, and others who are privileged to serve in the Temple cult in Jerusalem and are called either "priests" or "levitical priests." There are various historical reconstructions that attempt to account for the development of these various terminologies (see Wellhausen 1973 [1878], 121–67; de Vaux 1965 2:289–405; and Cross 1973, 195–215).

For the present purposes, however, the important point is that by the time of the exile, genealogy served as an important idiom in the self-definition of the priestly community. The priests' claim to authority and power derived from their alleged genealogical connection to some important descendant of

Levi. Individual priests did not claim, as did prophets, to have been selected directly by God for their office. Their privileges were inherited from some specified ancestor whom God had selected as the originator of the priestly lineage. Genealogy also provided the means of differentiating among groups of priests with higher and lower status. God had selected one Levite lineage as the central players in the Temple cult; other Levite lineages had only a secondary role.

The importance of descent in the self-understanding and self-presentation of the priestly community helps account for the prominence of genealogy and related matters in the priestly source. The attention to genealogy is not to be explained simply in terms of the need for continuity in an age of discontinuity, but also as a means of legitimating priestly power in the postexilic community (Blenkinsopp 1983, 105). The priests' claim to power rested on the assertion that each individual priest could trace his male ancestors in an uninterrupted line back to Sadoq, Aaron, Moses, or Levi. That claim would only have been plausible to the priests themselves and to those outside their community if genealogical records could be produced that traced unambiguous lines of descent back into the distant historical past. The books of Ezra and Nehemiah, for example, record a list of priests who purportedly returned to Jerusalem and Judah following the Babylonian exile. Among "the sons of the priests, the sons of Habaiah, the sons of Hakkoz, the sons of Barzillai who had married a daughter of Barzillai and had taken his name—these searched for their genealogical records, but they could not be found, so they were disqualified from the priesthood. The Tirshatha [a Persian title] ordered them not to eat of the most holy things until a priest with Urim and Thummim should appear [who could determine through divination whether they were of priestly descent]" (Ezra 2:61–63; Neh. 7:64). Thus, to claim in the seventh, sixth, or fifth centuries that one descended from Levi, Sadoq, Aaron, or Moses, one would have to produce clear records of these men's descendants. It is not at all surprising, therefore, that the priestly writer felt it necessary to add detailed genealogies to the narratives of Israelite history.

But the priestly interest in genealogy is not simply a vehicle of communal justification. The priests could have justified their credentials without worrying about the lines of descent before Abraham or about other lineages beside that of Levi. Although these genealogies do nothing to further the priests' claim to power, the priestly writer is careful to record them (e.g., Gen. 5:1–28; 30–32; 10:1–7; 11:10–26; Num. 1). The interest in descent is not entirely motivated by concerns of legitimation. Rather, the communal self-definition of this group shaped what its members considered interesting and relevant. To priests, the story of human history was incomplete without a detailed account of human genealogy, and knowing a man's character meant finding out his pedigree.

In addition to the problem of tracing lines of descent, the priests were urgently concerned about human sexuality and reproduction, matters that are intimately related to the problem of developing and perpetuating a lineage. Thus one of the priestly writer's favorite themes is human fertility (Gen. 1:22; 9:1, 7; 17:2, 3, 10; 28:3–4; 35:11–12; 48:4; Exod. 1:7). The priests were concerned further with possible contamination of lines of descent by incest or marrying foreign women. These concerns constantly work their way into the priestly narration of human and Israelite history and underlie many of the laws in the priestly code. In what follows I will focus on the connection between descent and circumcision. In subsequent chapters I will discuss the impact of descent on other parts of the priestly religious system.

Circumcision, Procreation, and Descent

Given the importance of a descent idiom for the self-definition of the priestly community, one can see why circumcision seemed like a natural symbol for the covenant between God and Abraham. Circumcision solved several vexing problems that, from the priests' perspective, would face anyone founding a new lineage. As the progenitor of a new lineage, Abraham had to be distinguished from all humans who had come before. But he also had to be connected to all his descendants. Circumcision solved both of these problems simultaneously.

In order for a man to found a new lineage upon which his former male kin have no claim, there must be a sharp break between himself and his predecessors. Without such a division in the lineage, it is not clear that this man, rather than his father or grandfather, founded the new line. For people to recognize themselves as "sons of Abraham" and not "sons of Terah," there would have to be some clear-cut distinction between Abraham and his forebears. By distinguishing Abraham from his fathers, uncles, brothers, and nephews, circumcision introduced a disjunction into this genealogy. This break is also emphasized by the change in Abraham's name, which signifies his rebirth. Terah's son's name was Abram, but the founder of the new lineage was Abraham. The other descendants of Terah, therefore, could never lay claim to Abraham's inheritance, since their brother had been someone with a different name. Circumcision thus solved the problem that had not arisen in the case of either Noah or Adam, both of whom were progenitors of lineages. Since Adam was the original human being there was no need to separate him from those who came before. As for Noah, the flood separated him from all his ancestors and marked a new beginning for humankind.

The priestly author was not the first Israelite writer to worry about the demarcation of lineages. The same impulse is evident in the Jahwist story of how Jacob wrestles with the angel and is renamed "Israel" (Gen. 32:23–33). From that point forward, Jacob's descendants are no longer children of Abraham or Isaac but "children of Israel." They "do not eat the thigh muscle that is on the socket of the hip, inasmuch as Jacob's hip socket was wrenched at the thigh

muscle" (Gen. 32:33). The children of Israel can now be identified as a distinctive line within the larger lineage emanating from Abraham. It is important to
note that this genealogical distinction is not altogether different from circumcision. The thigh is often a metaphor for the male organ in the J narrative (Gen.
24:2; 47:29) and children are said to issue from the thigh (Gen. 46:27=P; Exod.
1:5=P; Judg. 8:30 [Sarna 1970, 171, 179]). In not eating the sciatic muscle,
Jacob's descendants dramatize their connection to Jacob's thigh.

    The same sort of concern underlies the Jahwist's selection of a covenantal
symbol as well. According to the Jahwist, God instructed Abraham to cut in
half a three-year-old heifer, a she-goat, and a ram as a symbol of the divine
promise that Abraham would have an heir and would inherit the land. After
Abraham did so, a smoking oven and flaming torch passed between the pieces
(Gen. 15:1–2, 6–12, 17–20).[17] Numerous interpreters have noted that in the
ancient Near East cutting an animal in half was the act by which a covenant or
treaty was ratified.[18] But this explanation is not satisfactory by itself. It does not
explain why Israelite writers invoked the image of cutting an animal in particular covenantal scenes and not others. In this case, the division of the animals
alludes directly to the substance of the divine promise. God promises that
Abraham, not his father, brothers, or their descendants, would inherit the land.
Cutting the animals in two (presumably longitudinally through the genitals)
symbolizes the split that initiated this genealogical division. Significantly, in
the Jahwist narrative, this symbolic act follows directly upon the dispute over
land between the herdsmen of Abraham and Lot, Abraham's patrilineal
cousin. The quarrel ends with Abraham and Lot agreeing to live in different
parts of the land. But the quarrel is symptomatic of the potential for Lot and
his descendants to lay claim to Abraham's inheritance. Immediately after this
incident, the Jahwist inserts the covenant between Abraham and God and the
act of cutting the animals in half. It should be noted that my interpretation
builds directly on the argument of the previous chapter, where I showed that
animals of the herds and flocks are frequently metaphoric Israelites.[19]

    The idea of introducing a division between kin by cutting an object is not
unique to ancient Israel. Among the Nuer, for example, the relationship between fraternal clans is considered to be very distant because the ancestor of
the clans is believed to have cut an ox longitudinally to permit intermarriage
between the descendants of his sons. When a Nuer man is going to marry a
woman to whom he has some ambiguous kinship tie, a gourd is split in half to
end the kinship relation. They say "we split kinship," "it is split with a
gourd." In addition, for severe violations of incest a goat, sheep, or ox must
be cut vertically in two (through the gonads). Similarly before a man fulfills
the duty of levirate marriage and marries his brother's widow, he first breaks
the relationship between his spouse-to-be and her former husband by sacrificing a sheep. Nuer say "he divides them with a sheep," or "the brother is removed" (Evans-Pritchard 1951, 30–32, 38, 42).[20]

    If cutting an animal in two represents the introduction of a genealogical

break, why did the priestly community replace this symbolic act with the practice of circumcision, which served the same function? From the priest's standpoint, circumcision had an important advantage over the symbolic act of
cutting an animal in two. In addition to symbolizing a genealogical division,
it had associations with the idea of fertility. Given the centrality of descent in
the self-definition of the priestly community, it was only natural for the
priestly writer to adopt a symbol of fertility to represent the covenant between God, Abraham, and Abraham's male descendants. Indeed, from the
perspective of the priests, the only real symbol that would have strengthened
Abraham's faith in the covenant would allude to his and his children's fertility. After all, according to tradition, God had promised Abraham that a new
lineage would descend from a son who had not yet been born. Any man
might be skeptical of such a promise, let alone an old man. The priests, therefore, wanted a symbol that would manifest the substance of the covenant to
Abraham. But the act of cutting an animal in two did not have the necessary
substantive connection with the promise of Abraham's genealogical success.
Instead, the priests chose circumcision, which both marked a division in the
genealogical line and symbolized the fecundity of Abraham and his
descendants.[21]

It is evident why the priests considered the male generative organ to be
such an appropriate spot for the symbol of the covenant. Its connection with
fertility, its role in marking off Abraham's genealogy, and its metonymic connection with descendants made the male organ a natural spot to place a cut.
But there is another reason as well. The male organ is itself a symbol of kinship in general and patrilineal descent in particular.

This association is already operative in two different contexts in the narratives of the Jahwist. Just before he dies, Abraham asks Eliezer to put his hand
under his "thigh" and take an oath that he will find a wife for Abraham's son
Isaac from the place of Abraham's birth (Gen. 24:2). Similarly, on his death-
bed Jacob asks that Joseph put his hand under Jacob's thigh and promise to
bury him in the land of Canaan with his fathers (Gen. 47:29–30). Von Rad
(1976, 254) suggests that swearing by the genital organ is a very ancient custom. "It presupposes a special sanctity of this part of the body, which was no
longer alive in the Israelite period." Sarna (1970, 170–71) is closer to the
meaning when he notes that the thigh in biblical usage is symbolic of the
reproductive organs, and offspring are described as "those who issue from the
thigh." "The placing of the hand on the thigh when taking an oath in connection with the last wishes of a superior symbolizes, therefore, an involvement
of the posterity in the faithful implementation of the instructions and gives
added weight to the solemnity and inviolability of the obligation incurred."
But in the first case, Abraham's posterity is not involved in the implementation of his instructions. Abraham makes the request of Eliezer, who is the
servant and overseer of his house, not his biological offspring. In both of
these contexts, however, the substance of the request has to do with the patri-

lineage. Abraham makes Eliezer swear that he will find a wife for Isaac from among the women in Abraham's place of origin. As the narrative unfolds, it becomes clear that Eliezer will bring back Rebekah, Isaac's patrilineal relative (i.e., the daughter of his father's brother's son). Abraham also makes Eliezer swear that he will not allow Isaac to marry matrilocally, that is, to live with his wife's family, which would endanger the autonomy of Abraham's lineage. Similarly, Jacob makes his son Joseph swear to bury Jacob with his patrilineal ancestors, Abraham, Isaac, and their wives, in the land that had been inherited patrilineally from the time of Abraham. In each case, the act of swearing by the male genital organ involves a request related to the concerns of the patrilineage.

Like the Jahwist narratives, the priestly writings also presuppose an association between the male organ and the idea of kinship. Several laws in the priestly code treat the male organ as an instrument that creates kinship ties. For example, priests are only permitted to bury their next of kin, since a dead body is a source of impurity and will contaminate a priest. The category "next of kin" includes the priest's parents, brothers, offspring, and virgin sisters. But priests cannot bury a sister who is already married (Lev. 21:2–4). By virtue of having had intercourse with some man, she is no longer considered a priest's next of kin; she is now the other man's relative. By the same token, when a daughter of a priest marries a man who is not a priest, she can no longer eat priestly rations, for she has entered a nonpriestly lineage. Only if she is widowed or divorced and has no offspring can she be reabsorbed into her father's line and eat priestly rations again (Lev. 22:13–14).

The idea that the male organ is the instrument that establishes kinship is given linguistic expression in the priestly writings in two different ways. Literature emanating from priestly circles uses the word "flesh" (*bāśār*) as both a metaphor for kinship and as a euphemism for "penis." The priests are not the first to use the term "flesh" as a metaphor for kinship. According to the Jahwist, when Eve is first brought to Adam, he proclaims, "This one at last is bone of my bones and flesh of my flesh" (Gen. 2:23). The Jahwist adds the comment, "hence a man leaves his father and mother and clings to his wife, so that they become one flesh" (Gen. 2:24). According to the same writer, Laban says to Jacob "you are truly my bone and flesh" (Gen. 29:14), and Judah pleads that his brothers not kill Joseph, for "he is our brother, our own flesh" (Gen. 37:27). In these contexts, "one flesh" is a way of saying that the people have some sort of kinship tie, whether genealogical or through marriage. But the Jahwist never uses the term "flesh" to refer to the penis. Priestly authors, by contrast, use the term "flesh" both as a metaphor for kinship (Lev. 18:6) as well as a euphemism for the male organ (Ezek. 16:26; 23:20; 44:7; Lev. 17:13; 15:2–3). This linguistic connection is not fortuitous but reflects the conceptual association between the penis and relations of kinship.

The priestly code also refers to a kinship tie through marriage as "exposing the nakedness" of some male relative (Lev. 18:7–8, 14, 16). For example, in the list of forbidden relations, sex with one's father's wife is referred to as "exposing the nakedness of one's father." This curious expression means that when one has relations with this woman, one is trespassing upon the spot where the nakedness of one's father has already been exposed.[22] Similarly, when incest occurs with a father's brother's wife or a brother's wife, the nakedness of these men is exposed. For the priestly writer a kinship tie through marriage is metaphorically "a man's nakedness." It is the nakedness of a male relative that has made these women kin. The same conceptual connection is sometimes found in other societies in which patrilineal descent plays a prominent role in social organization. The Sambia, to cite one example, use the term *moyu* to refer to the male genitals and patrilineality (Herdt 1987, 83). Not surprisingly milk sometimes becomes the symbol of descent in matrilineal societies (Turner 1962, 134).

The association between the male organ and the idea of kinship made the penis doubly appropriate as the spot for the symbol of God's covenant. God had promised to make Abraham fertile and provide him with a successful progeny. As we have seen, the removal of the foreskin symbolizes the fertility of the organ. But the cut also suggests that this lineage, represented by the penis, is set apart from all others. In this way, circumcision symbolizes and helps create intergenerational continuity between men. It graphically represents patrilineal descent by giving men of this line a distinctive mark that binds them together.

Since circumcision binds together men within and across generations, it also establishes an opposition between men and women. Women cannot bear the symbol of the covenant. Only the bodies of men can commemorate the promise of God to Abraham. The rabbis were alert to this meaning of circumcision in their commentary on Gen. 17:14: "any uncircumcised male who fails to circumcise the flesh of his foreskin" shall be cut off from his people. Since, as the rabbis assumed, there was no such thing as an uncircumcised female, why did Scripture bother to specify "uncircumcised *male?*" According to the commentary, the superfluous reference to "male" indicates that one circumcises the part of the body that one examines to distinguish males and females (LR 25:6).

The fact that circumcision sets up an opposition between men and women makes sense in terms of what we know about the priests' conception of genealogy. As Jay (1985; 1988) has pointed out, the priestly writers suppress the names of women in their genealogies. Their genealogies generally list only the names of men, as if women played no role at all in the continuation of the generations. Circumcision is one of the rituals that justifies this fiction. It provides physical evidence for the kinship ties between men. Moreover, we shall see that the blood of the male infant is spilled precisely at the moment when he leaves the state of severe impurity caused during childbirth by the blood of his mother. In creating an opposition between male and female, the priestly symbol of the covenant brings to the surface a latent association in the Hebrew language between masculinity and commemoration. In biblical Hebrew, the stem for "commemorate" or "remember" *(zkr)* is etymologically related to the word for male *(zkr)*. Both derive from the same proto-Semitic root (BDB 1975 [1907], 270–71). In Arabic, one of Hebrew's cognate languages, the word for male also means "male organ" and "call upon in worship." The priestly symbol of the covenant ties together these themes, for only a male's body can bear the symbol of the covenant. To put it another way, in the priestly community, remembering the covenant requires having the appropriate member.

The association in the priestly source between the male organ and patrilineal descent suggests an additional reason for the linkage between the penis and fruit trees discussed earlier. That association, we recall, is based on an analogy between human progeny and agricultural yield. But trees are also symbols of lineage. The prophets, as we have seen, use fruit trees metaphorically to refer to Israelites and their descendants. Similarly, the lineage of David is described as a shoot or branch from his stock (Isa. 11:1; Zech. 6:12–13). Trees have a similar meaning for the priestly writer. According to the priestly author, when the Israelites question the special status of Aaron's lineage, God tells Moses to take one staff for each ancestral line and inscribe the chieftain's name on each. After God declares that "the staff of the man whom I choose shall sprout," Aaron's staff blossoms and produces almonds (Num. 17:16–24), symbolizing that God had chosen Aaron's line over all others. The priestly analogy between fruit trees and the male organ, therefore, may also rest on their mutual signification of Israelite lineage.

The above analysis shows that the most common explanation for the importance of circumcision among the priests is too simplistic. The experience in the exile may have made circumcision more important, as other interpreters suggest. But the symbol of circumcision also spoke to the interests of a group in which descent figured as an important factor in the organization and self-definition of the community. Similar symbolic processes are evident among other groups for whom the idiom of descent plays an important role in shaping their self-understanding and in organizing social relations. Among the Nuer, for example, a man's spear represents his lineage and a boy receives a spear during initiation. Each genealogical line has its own spear name and during ritual performances a male struts around brandishing his spear and calling out the name of his ancestor's spear (Evans-Pritchard 1956, 231–47). For the Ndembu, the "milk tree" which produces white sap symbolizes matrilineal descent. Girls are initiated under it to represent, among other things, their incorporation into their maternal lines (Turner 1967, 19–47). The importance of descent in the communal self-understanding of the priests thus explains why many of the meanings of circumcision for the priests overlap with the meanings of circumcision in communities at other times and places. The ethnographic studies of circumcision cited earlier all involve peoples among whom descent plays a crucial role in their self-definition. For them, as for the priests, reproductive success and intergenerational continuity among males is crucial. For them, as for the priests, circumcision symbolizes these crucial themes. As is now evident, it is a mistake to assume that Israelite circumcision is fundamentally distinctive either because it took place on the eighth day after birth or because it symbolized the covenant between God and Israel. The themes of fertility, procreation, and intergenerational continuity between males are central to this Israelite practice.

Why, then, is circumcision a rite of passage associated with birth? Indeed, given the connection with fertility it would seem more appropriate for circumcision to serve as a rite of passage into manhood. In African contexts, in fact, circumcision is usually a rite of passage associated with social maturation. After surveying this evidence, I consider why Israelite circumcision differed in this respect from African rites.

Circumcision, Masculinity, and Social Maturity

In addition to ensuring a boy's fertility, African circumcision ceremonies are frequently believed to be important for the cultivation of a boy's virility. Virility and fertility are deeply connected in many cultures as in our own. The English word "virility" means both "masculinity" and the "ability to procreate." Before circumcision rites, the initiate is a mama's boy who may eat with the women and sleep in his mother's hut (Tucker 1949, 59; Gluckman 1949, 151; White 1953, 42). After the ceremonies, however, he cannot sleep in his mother's hut and his mother may no longer see his penis (Gluckman 1949, 151; Turner 1967, 265–66). The development of a boy's masculinity is spatially represented in the separation of boys from their mothers before and during the circumcision ceremonies. During the seclusion only the fathers and brothers may visit (Turner 1962, 155–56). In some cases, the foreskin is compared to a woman's labia and its removal signifies the removal of a boy's feminine attributes (Turner 1962, 161; 1967, 265–74). Indeed, part of the filth of infancy is the boy's close tie to his mother (Turner 1962, 171). Since such rites denigrate womanhood, novices spit when anyone mentions the word "vagina" (White 1953, 55). In addition to a rite of separation from women, circumcision is frequently thought of as an ordeal which tests the character of the emerging man (Spencer 1965, 255).

Not surprisingly, the transition from boy to man is at the same time a transition from childhood to social maturity. The birth of virility, in other words, is the sign that a male has become ready to participate in the affairs that define the life of the adult male community, including full participation in religious, political, and jural activities and discussions (Gluckman 1949, 151).

Since circumcision is a rite of passage in these various senses, it is frequently accompanied by symbols of death and rebirth. The place of circumcision is often called the place of dying, and the symbolic actions that constitute the rite sometimes signify the death and rebirth of the initiate (Gluckman 1949, 148; Hambly 1935, 37; Tucker 1949, 58; Turner 1962, 128–30; White 1953, 42). The transformation of a boy into a man and a child into an adult is frequently represented in the acquisition of a new name (Hambly 1935, 37; Holdredge and Young 1927, 668; Tucker 1949, 58). Using the old name would be tantamount to calling the man a baby (Holdredge and Young 1927, 665).

Israelite Circumcision as a Ritual of Birth

The Israelite practice of circumcising males on the eighth day of life raises two separate but related questions. First, why does circumcision occur so close to birth and second, why does it occur on the eighth day in particular? The latter question is easier to answer than the former. As Skinner (1910, 294) has noted, after the birth of a male child a woman is in a state of impurity as severe as when she has her menstrual period (Lev. 12:1–2). During her menstrual period, she contaminates anyone who touches her and anything she sits on. If a man has intercourse with her during this period, he is unclean seven days and contaminates any bedding upon which he lies (Lev. 15:19–24). After seven days have elapsed from the birth of a son, a mother enters a lesser state of impurity. At this time, she contaminates consecrated things and the Temple sanctuary, but she does not contaminate other people or household objects (Lev. 12:4).

One can infer from these rules that during the seven days following birth, a male infant is also unclean and would contaminate any man who performed the circumcision. Circumcision, therefore, is delayed until the eighth day, when the son enters a lesser state of impurity and does not contaminate the circumciser. That is why the author of Leviticus interrupts the discussion of a woman's impurity at childbirth to mention circumcision. "When a woman at childbirth bears a male, she shall be unclean seven days; she shall be unclean as at the time of her menstrual infirmity. On the eighth day the flesh of his foreskin shall be circumcised. She shall remain in a state of blood purification for thirty-three days" (Lev. 12:1–4). Circumcision is mentioned here because its timing is coordinated with the diminishing of the mother's impurity. We see that here as in other cultural contexts, circumcision is a postpartum ritual associated with the separation of a male child from the impurity of his mother. When the child has recovered from the impurity of his mother's blood, he is brought into the covenant when his own male blood is spilled. His blood is clean, unifying, and symbolic of God's covenant. His mother's is filthy, socially disruptive, and contaminating. Indeed, as we shall see in the next chapter, women's blood is symbolically associated with death. Circumcision thus removes the male from the realm of death through the shedding of his own blood, just as the sacrifice of an animal eventually removes the boy's mother from the impurity caused by the birth process (Lev. 12:6–7). Although Israelite circumcision is not a rite of passage into manhood, it is a rite that marks the passage from the impurity of being born of woman to the purity of life in a community of men. That passage, like rites of adult initiation, is connected, however obliquely, with a passage from death to life.[23]

In the previous chapter, I noted that the occurrence of circumcision on the eighth day after birth corresponds to the ruling that an animal cannot be sacrificed before the eighth day after birth (Exod. 22:28–29; Lev. 22:27). In that context, I argued that this homology is part of a more general metaphoric relation between Israelites and the herds and flocks. Having now analyzed the rite of circumcision, we can see further reasons for the correspondence between circumcision and sacrifice. Jay (1985; 1988) has persuasively argued that Israelite sacrifice itself is a way of creating and demonstrating patrilineal kinship ties among men. Circumcision and sacrifice thus have overlapping functions. This correspondence might be one of the reasons that circumcision was held on the eighth day after birth. An early code (Exod. 22:28–29) had already ruled that an animal could not be sacrificed prior to the eighth day after birth. Since one of circumcision's functions overlapped with that of sacrifice, the time frame of the latter was imposed on the former.

But there were also other, independent factors that led the priests to treat circumcision as a rite associated with birth. These factors emerge when we once again consider the importance of descent for the priestly community. Since the priesthood was not a calling but an inherited office, one could only serve as a priest if one claimed to be fathered by a man who was himself a priest. In the priests' official self-understanding, one had no control over who one was. One's self-definition was determined at birth by factors outside one's own control. Membership in the priestly community was not something that could be earned; it was a privilege of birth. This idiom and social experience shaped the understanding of the covenant within the priestly community. For the priests, the salient dimension of the covenant was the fact that a male was born into it. Entrance into the covenant was a not a mature, reflective decision of adult life. It is for this reason that circumcision is performed as close to birth as possible. Entrance into the covenantal community was a privilege of being part of the genealogy of Abraham.

Circumcision on the eighth day represents the fact that the child has no choice about being a member of the covenantal community. Philo sensed this meaning of circumcision when reflecting on the difference between the Israelite practice and the practice of Egyptians, which took place near puberty. According to Philo, circumcising on the eighth day reflects the wisdom of the Legislator. "It is very much better and more far-sighted of us to prescribe circumcision for infants, for perhaps one who is full-grown would hesitate through fear to carry out this ordinance of his own free will" (Philo 3:48; 1971, 244).

As a ceremony of birth, Israelite circumcision did not incorporate themes of virility and social maturity. But it did symbolize the initiate's fertility. As the priests saw it, a boy's procreative powers were granted by God as a privilege for having been born into Abraham's line. They were granted in fulfillment of the divine promise that Abraham and his descendants would be fruitful, multiply, and inherit the land. A male's ability to reproduce was not simply the outcome of his maturation but also a privilege of having a certain genealogy. Circumcision was thus a rite which simultaneously conferred and confirmed one's pedigree.

At this point, one might reasonably object that the above explanation seems to be contradicted by the fact that descent is often important in other societies where circumcision ceremonies are rites of passage into social manhood. Why, then, in the priestly community did descent have such a definitive effect on the practice of circumcision?

There is one important difference between the priestly community and the African societies discussed above. In the latter, all members of the social system are defined genealogically. There are many different lineages, but all persons trace themselves back to some ancestor. The priests, however, competed with Israelites for whom descent played little or no role in their own self-understanding and in their consequent conception of the covenant. Several of the prophets and the Deuteronomist, for example, emphasized the importance of making a mature, adult commitment to the covenant. Jeremiah speaks of God as the one who "probes the heart and searches the mind" (Jer. 17:10) and the children of Israel as being "uncircumcised of the heart" (Jer. 9:25). The Deuteronomist insists that one must love God with all one's heart (Deut. 6:5–6; 11:13; 30:2, 6), that one must cut away the thickening about one's heart (Deut. 10:16), and impress God's teaching on one's heart, hand, and forehead (Deut. 6:8; 11:18), for God looks into the heart (Deut. 8:2; 13:4). For this reason, the Deuteronomist describes the covenant as a choice, a choice between life and death. "Choose life . . . by loving the Lord your God, heeding the divine commands and holding fast to God. For thereby you shall have life and shall long endure upon the soil that the Lord your God swore to Abraham, Isaac, and Jacob to give to them" (Deut. 30:20).

As is evident from these quotations, the priests struggled against definitions of the covenantal community that differed radically from their own. For them, a community was a group of men who had descended from the same ancestor. Belonging to that community meant having a place in a lineage and having the obligations that go along with perpetuating the line and keeping it genealogically pure. To make these points, to themselves and those beyond their community, the priests adopted circumcision as a sign of the covenant. Circumcision had previously been a sign of belonging to God's people. But in absorbing this practice into their own system, the priests interpreted it in a way that gave articulation to their own preoccupations and concerns, which sprang from the self-definition and organization of their community.

7.

Menstrual Blood, Semen, and Discharge
The Fluid Symbolism of the Human Body

> However men may analyse their experiences within any domain, they inevitably know and understand them best by referring them to other domains for elucidation. It is in that metaphoric cross-referencing of domains, perhaps, that culture is integrated, providing us with the sensation of wholeness.
>
> Fernandez 1986

The body is one of the places in which social concerns are symbolically enacted. This enactment is evident in a variety of ways in the preceding analysis of circumcision. The cutting of the male organ not only marked a male's entrance into a covenanted brotherhood, it also expressed the corresponding privileges and responsibilities that such membership entailed. Most importantly, this rite symbolized the fertility of the boy, a theme that anticipates his responsibility in reproducing and perpetuating the genealogy of Israel. The male member was a natural place to display such themes because it is a powerful symbol of lineage, kinship, and procreation.

This analysis of circumcision thus confirms Mary Douglas's insight that the human body serves as a mirror for society. Working out of the Durkheimian tradition, Douglas (1966, 115) argues that

> the body is a model which can stand for any bounded system. Its boundaries can represent any boundaries which are threatened and precarious. The body is a complex structure. The functions of its different parts and their relation afford a source of symbols for other complex structures. We cannot possibly interpret rituals concerning excreta, breast milk, saliva and the rest unless we are prepared to see in the body a symbol of society, and to see the powers and dangers credited to social structure reproduced in small on the human body.

But the analysis of circumcision also shows that Douglas's understanding does not exhaust the body's cultural function. In addition to reflecting the powers and dangers of the social structure, the body serves as a space for a whole range of social representations. In this sense, the body is a prime locus for the articulation of larger complexes of meaning which constitute a cultural system. The regulations of the body tie together abstract themes of social concern with the concrete practices of everyday life and in this way give ideas a practical reality that affects the individual's own relationship with her or his body. The body, then, is one of the places in which culture and psychology meet. In this chapter, I explore the relevance of these insights to understanding the prohibitions on the menstruating woman in Israelite religion.

Menstrual Blood in Israelite Religion

The Israelite rules concerning the menstruating woman are first set out in the writings of the priests (Leviticus 15:19–33). A menstruating woman is considered impure for seven days and contaminates anything upon which she sits or lies during that period. Anyone who has contact with her or with something she has contaminated must bathe in water and is considered impure until evening. According to one source, intercourse with a menstruating woman makes a man unclean for seven days (Lev. 15:24) while other sources forbid such intercourse altogether on the penalty of excommunication (Lev. 18:19; 20:18; Ezek. 18:6; 22:10).[1] Similar sorts of proscriptions apply to a woman who discharges blood at any point in the middle of her cycle. To end her state of impurity in any of these cases, a woman must wait seven clean days and then offer two turtledoves and two pigeons to God. When a woman gives birth she is also "unclean as at the time of her menstrual infirmity" (Lev. 12:2). However, the length of her contamination depends on whether a son or daughter is born. When the baby is male, the mother is in a state of severe impurity for seven days. During this time, she observes the same restrictions as the menstruous woman. For the next thirty-three days, she enters a period of light impurity, during which she can contaminate sacred objects or places but not profane objects (Noth 1977, 98). When a daughter is born, the severe restrictions are in force for fourteen days; the milder restrictions extend for sixty-six days. These various rules of purity are directed to Israelite priests who officiate in the sacred precincts of the Temple and who eat priestly rations (Lev. 15:31). They may in addition have been intended for the wider segments of Israelite society (Wenham 1979, 221).

Mary Douglas has argued that proscriptions on menstrual blood make sense when the body is understood as a symbol of society. Since threats to society are reproduced symbolically in conceptions of the human body, "we should expect the orifices of the body to symbolize its specially vulnerable points." Since Israelites were always a hard-pressed minority, they believed that discharges from the body were polluting. "The threatened boundaries of their body politic would be well mirrored in their care for the integrity, unity, and purity of the physical body" (1966, 121, 124). While Douglas's line of analysis is suggestive, its application to the Israelite case is problematic, at least as it now stands. If concerns about the threatened borders of society were mirrored in worries about the loss of bodily fluids then we might expect the loss of all fluids, including urine, saliva, tears, and mucus to be polluting. But in Israelite religion and ancient Judaism these fluids are not contaminating. Douglas's analysis thus fails to explain why certain fluids contaminate a person while others do not. As we shall see, the differences between contaminating and noncontaminating fluids signify and sustain other symbolic meanings that constitute the religious culture of Israel. The fluids of the body turn out to be a kind of language in which various religious themes find their voice. These themes do speak to concerns generated by the social structure. But they are concerns that come from within that body rather than from without. Moreover, these themes do not simply reflect the tensions of the social structure as much as articulate prejudices, hopes, and ideals that are in part generated by the organization and self-understanding of the priestly community.

Fluid Symbolism in Israelite Religion

In isolation, the menstrual prohibitions might be regarded as stemming from a "horror of blood" or from the belief that blood contains a person's life force (Freud 1974, 74). Indeed, there is warrant for arguing that the latter view in fact explains the menstrual taboo in Israelite religion, since Scripture states unequivocally that blood carries the essence of life (Gen. 9:4; Lev. 17:11–14; Deut. 12:23 [Feldman 1977, 37; Patai 1959, 152]). But the contrast between menstrual blood, which is contaminating, and the blood of circumcision or sacrifice, which is positively marked, indicates that only some kinds of blood are contaminating. The prohibitions on the menstruous woman have nothing to do with an inherent quality of blood. Freud himself warned interpreters "not to exaggerate the influence of a fact such as the horror of blood. After all, the latter does not suffice to suppress customs like circumcision of boys . . . which are practised to some extent by the same races, nor to abolish the prevalence of other ceremonies at which blood is shed" (Freud 1974, 74). Blood has different meanings depending upon how it originates and from whom it comes. Significantly, the familiar Israelite idea that "life is in the blood" appears only in contexts related to the slaughter of animals or murder, that is, acts in which a living being dies. Some blood is symbolic of life; other kinds of blood are not.

If the contrast between menstrual and circumcision blood is taken as a clue to the meaning of fluid symbolism, then the menstrual prohibitions may be the sign par excellence of "the difference of woman from man, . . . her eternally inexplicable, mysterious and strange nature, which thus seems hostile" (Freud 1974, 76).[2] In the previous chapter, I already suggested that gender differences are represented in the contrast between female and male blood. Circumcision coincides with the end of a boy's impurity caused by the mother's blood at birth. The entrance of a male into the covenant thus occurs with his transition from female blood to male blood. The contrast between circumcision and the blood of birthing not only reflects differences between genders but it interprets them. Women's blood is contaminating; men's blood has the power to create covenant.[3]

That female blood has the opposite valence of male blood is evident in a number of other ways in Israelite literature in general and priestly writings in particular. The priestly narrative in which God tells Abraham that circumcision is a sign of the covenant is prefaced with God's command to "walk in my ways and be blameless" (or whole) *(tāmîm)* (Gen. 17:1). Circumcision is implicitly associated with wholeness and purity. By contrast, blood discharged during birthing makes the woman "unclean as at the time of her menstrual infirmity" (Lev. 12:2). A similar attitude is reflected in Ezekiel's description of how God rescued Israel from the blood of birth.

> Thus said the Lord God to Jerusalem: By origin and birth you are from the land of the Canaanites—your father was an Amorite and your mother a Hittite. As for your birth, when you were born your navel cord was not cut, and you were not bathed in water to smoothe you; you were not rubbed with salt, nor were you swaddled. No one pitied you enough to do any of these things for you out of compassion for you; on the day you were born, you were left lying, rejected, in the open field. When I passed by you and saw you wallowing in your blood, I said to you, "Live in spite of your blood." (Ezek. 16:3–7)

As a priest, Ezekiel speaks out of the same religious culture as the author of Leviticus. It is significant that in his account God redeems Israel from the blood of birth, which is contrasted with life. This national act of redemption parallels the movement that a male child undergoes as he passes from the blood of birth to circumcision.[4]

Like blood discharged during the birthing process, menstrual blood also has negative associations.[5] To begin with, the proscription on sexual relations with a menstruating woman is included in a list of heinous sexual offenses including various forms of incest, homosexuality, and bestiality (Lev. 18:19–23; 20:10–21). A woman who is menstruating is also described as "unwell" or "ill" *(dāwāh)* (Lev. 20:18) (BDB 1975 [1907], 188). Negative associations are also presupposed in the metaphorical extension of menstruation to other domains. The term used to describe a menstruous woman *(niddātâh)* is also used to describe the "depravity" that is committed when a man commits incest with his sister-in-law (Lev. 20:21). When Jerusalem is destroyed for the sins of "her" inhabitants, "she" is likened to a menstruating woman whose uncleanness clings to her skirts (Lam. 1:8, 17). By the same token, when the land of Israel is unclean by virtue of its foreign inhabitants, "she" is compared to a menstruating woman (Ezra 9:11). According to Ezekiel, God proclaimed that "when the House of Israel dwelt on their own soil, they defiled it with their ways and their deeds; their ways were in My sight like the uncleanness of a menstruous woman. So I poured out My wrath on them *for the blood which they shed upon their land,* and for the fetishes with which they defiled it" (Ezek. 36:17–18). In this case menstruation is a metaphor for murder. Women's bleeding is symbolic of violent bloodshed and God's revulsion over such acts is equated with Israelite's purported reaction to menstrual blood. In theory, circumcision or sacrificial blood could have served equally well as metaphors in this context since they also involve the spilling of blood. Had those images not already had positive connotations, perhaps Ezekiel might have heard God say that "their ways were in My sight like a boy after circumcision or like the altar after a sacrifice." Nor is it surprising that Israelite religion never makes what could have been a positive metaphoric association between menstrual bleeding and the flow of blood from a sacrifice.[6] Had such an association occurred, perhaps Israelites would have sprinkled menstrual blood on the altar.

The gender of blood may also be a symbol of different kinds of social relationships. As argued in the previous chapter, circumcision and by extension blood from the male organ, is symbolic of patrilineal descent. By contrast, the term used to describe menstruation is also used as a pejorative adjective to describe incest (Lev. 20:21). So while circumcision is a symbol of a man's belonging to Israelite lineage, menstrual blood is associated with the violation of kinship laws.

Clearly, the gender of blood signifies other kinds of differences, such as the opposition between covenant, righteousness, and wholeness on the one hand, and sin, indecency, and death on the other. One might summarize this by saying that menstruation is everything that circumcision is not. It is through the contrast of women's and men's genital bleeding that a larger set of distinctions are encoded. Gender and fluid symbolism work together to articulate larger cultural themes.

These correspondences, however, disappear when menstrual blood is placed in the wider context of fluid symbolism. In this system of relations, the gender of fluids ceases to determine their meanings. This is for the simple reason that the male body also produces fluids that are contaminating. When a male produces semen he is unclean until evening. Anything semen touches must be washed and remains unclean for the same amount of time. Thus even licit sexual intercourse makes the husband and wife unclean until evening (Lev. 15:16–18). A nonseminal discharge from the penis is nearly as contaminating as menstrual blood. A man who has such a discharge contaminates anything he touches or sits on, including a saddle, bedding, and clothes, as well as other people. He also contaminates anyone who comes in contact with his saliva. Like the menstruous woman, he remains unclean for seven days beyond his discharge. At the end of that time, he must bathe and sacrifice two turtledoves or pigeons to God (Lev. 15:2–13).

When placed in this wider context of fluid symbolism, the contrast between purity and impurity no longer corresponds to gender differences since men's bodies also produce contamination. Impurity thus appears as a state which both genders generate and occupy. It belongs to neither gender exclusively. The signification of women's bleeding thus depends upon the context in which it is viewed. When contrasted with the blood of circumcision, a contrast suggested by the proximity of circumcision to the bleeding associated with birth, female blood is a symbol of women's exclusion from the covenant. But this contrast disappears when menstrual blood is treated among other body emissions.

The significance of bodily liquids is thus fluid and depends upon the cultural scene in which they are enacted. The shifting significance of bodily fluids is only problematic when culture is conceptualized as totally systematic. But if culture is constituted by various domains of significance which interpenetrate, then the meanings of a given substance need not be the same in all of them. I have already had occasion to emphasize how practices can encode numerous meanings. We saw, for example, that the prohibition on cooking a kid-goat in its mother's milk could represent a distinction between life and death yet simultaneously parallel the prohibition on incest between a son and his mother. Women's bleeding also carries different valences depending upon the system of relations that defines it. When placed in the wider symbolism of bodily fluids, menstrual blood signifies meanings that are not as straightforwardly connected to differences in gender. It is to these other meanings that our attention now turns.

Demarcating Life and Death

Leviticus designates the following bodily emissions as polluting: menstrual blood and other bloody discharges from the vagina, nonseminal discharges from the penis, and semen (Lev. 15). Other bodily fluids such as saliva, mucus, sweat, breast milk, and pus are not sources of impurity. What underlying distinctions are presupposed when these fluids are viewed as a system of relations? To begin with, there is no simple coordination between the topography of the body and the themes of purity and impurity, as occurs in some traditions (Douglas 1966, 123; Bakhtin 1984, 18–25). While it is true that none of the fluids from the "upper" regions of the body are contaminating, there are fluids such as urine that emanate from the "lower" regions of the body without causing contamination. In this domain, the upper and lower regions of the body are not symbolic of cultural values. The symbolism, therefore, has to be sought in the contrasts contained within the bodily fluids themselves.

Several interpreters have already suggested that the fluids that pollute the body symbolize or allude to death; those which do not have this connotation are not contaminating. According to this interpretation, the loss of menstrual blood by a woman or semen by a man represents a missed opportunity for creating life anew (Adler 1973; Feldman 1977, 35–37; Wenham 1979, 188). This interpretation is also able to make sense of the negative assessment of masturbation, which represents an unnecessary wasting of seed (Gen. 38:10=J).[7]

Pushing this insight further, I suggest that a related symbolism accounts for the prohibition on sexual relations with a menstruous woman. Since a menstruating woman cannot conceive, sexual relations with her are unproductive. Powers (1980, 62–63) has noted how this sort of motivation lies behind prohibitions on menstruating women among many native American tribes. Since semen is perceived as being finite the prescriptions about sexual relations with menstruating women ensure that semen will not be "wasted" on a woman at a time when she cannot conceive.

There is no explicit evidence that this kind of motivation lies behind the priestly prohibition on intercourse with a menstruating woman. Nonetheless, there are several hints that this might be the case. To begin with, we have already seen how important procreation is in the priestly writings (chapter 6) and how menstruation is used as a metaphor for death. Moreover, the prohibition on sexual intercourse with a menstruous woman is not listed where we might expect it, namely, with the other rules regarding the impurity of menstruation (Lev. 15). Instead it appears in two lists of heinous crimes, including incest, adultery, bestiality, and homosexuality (Lev. 18:19; 20:18). On the surface, these lists seem to deal with grave sins of the flesh. But closer inspection shows that not all of these sins are associated with sexual deviance. Both lists include the prohibition against offering one's offspring to the foreign God Molech (Lev. 18:21; 20:2–6). What justifies the inclusion of this law along with incest, adultery, homosexuality, bestiality, and the prohibition against menstruous intercourse? From the standpoint of reproductive politics (Paige and Paige 1981), all of these acts pose a threat to the integrity of Israelite lineage. Incest violations and adultery pervert and obscure lines of descent. By the same token, homosexuality, bestiality performed by a man, and offering one's children to Molech waste Israelite seed (Lev. 18:21–23). The same is true of sexual relations with a menstruating woman. Intercourse with a woman during her period is no better than sex with a cow. It is true that when a woman has intercourse with an animal, Israelite seed is not wasted. But since this sexual act cannot result in conception, it too is considered a "perversion."

There is another indirect piece of evidence that menstruation is considered antithetical to fertility. As noted above, the term used to describe menstruation is also used to describe the "depravity" of incest between a man and his sister-in-law (Lev. 20:21). But of all the incest prohibitions, what is it about this incest relationship in particular that evokes the association to menstrual depravity? This turns out to be one of the two sexual violations for which the penalty of childlessness is explicitly prescribed (Lev. 20:20–21). Thus it may be significant that this incest prohibition and not others is associated with menstruation. It is as if menstrual blood is the symbolic inversion of circumcision. While circumcision is a symbol of fertility, the type of incest which results in childlessness is deemed a "bloody" act.

If this line of analysis is valid, we are in a position to account for the asymmetrical treatment of men and women during their respective periods of contamination. Since a man's impurity does not interfere with procreation, there is no prohibition on sexual relations when he is unclean. But since a woman's uncleanness is a symbol of her inability to procreate, intercourse with her is proscribed.

It is less readily apparent why nonmenstrual or nonseminal discharges are considered unclean, since the nature of these discharges is not at all clear (Wenham 1979, 218). It may be that these fluids are signs of venereal disease and hence associated with death (Snaith 1967, 106; Wenham 1977, 218). If so, then as a total system the rules governing bodily emissions draw a sharp distinction between the themes of life and death.

The preceding analysis which treats body emissions as symbolic of life and death has a great deal to recommend it. In addition to making sense of the distinctions among bodily fluids, it shows how that system links up with a still wider system of pollution. The association between death and impurity, for example, is evident in the fact that the human corpse is the most powerful source of contamination. When a person dies, the body contaminates nearly everything inside the home including persons who enter (Num. 19; 31:14–15, 19–24). A person who is contaminated by a corpse must undergo an elaborate ritual of purification that involves being sprinkled with a mixture made from the ashes of a red cow, cedar wood, hyssop, and crimson. One who fails to remove corpse impurity "shall be cut off from Israel" (Num. 19:13). Animal carcasses are also sources of contamination (Lev. 11:32). The association between death and impurity may also be presupposed in the rules regarding various skin diseases (Feldman 1977, 38; Lewis 1987, 593–612). When Miriam is afflicted with one of these diseases, Aaron prays that she "not be as one dead, who emerges from the womb with half the flesh eaten away" (Num. 12:12). Significantly, the process of cleansing a person from the contamination of skin disease involves creating a mixture from "living" water (Lev. 14:5).

Nor is the theme of separating life and death limited to the laws of purity. Milgrom, we recall, sees a similar symbolism at work in the prohibitions against boiling a kid-goat in its mother's milk, against taking a mother bird and her fledglings from the nest at the same time, and against killing an animal and its offspring on the same day (see chapter 5). These themes, which are at work in the "lower" order of Israelite religious culture, are also evident in the realm of theology. As Feldman has pointed out, God and life are nearly synonymous in Israelite theology. In Israelite literature

> *ḥayim* [life] is almost synonymous with God. The goodness of God can only be witnessed in the *erez ha-ḥayim* [the land of the living] (Pss. 27:13; 116:9; Isa. 38:11); one walks before Him in the *'or ha-ḥayim*, "the light of life" (Ps. 56:14); fear of Him is the source of *ḥayim* (Prov. 14:27); those who find him find *ḥayim* (Prov. 8:35); those who do justice walk in his statute of *ḥayim* (Ezek. 33:15). (Feldman 1977, 25)

God is also described as the "living God" on thirteen occasions. Since God is symbolic of life, "death is the utmost desacralization and in the biblical/ rabbinic scheme, defilement represents estrangement from God." "Death removes the Israelite, not only from the realm of life, but from God, who wishes to work within the context of life" (Feldman 1977, xix, 18).

For all of these reasons, it seems sensible to see an association in the priestly imagination between menstrual blood, on the one hand, and death and loss of potential life, on the other. Nor are these associations limited to the Israelite context (Delaney 1988, 75–80; Freidl 1979, 29; Buckley and Gottlieb 1988, 38–39). To be sure, menstrual blood does not have such negative connotations in all traditions. Among the Beng of the Ivory Coast, for example, menstrual blood is symbolic of fertility since it is connected with a woman's reproductive powers. The Beng example serves as an illuminating contrast for the present discussion. Since Beng treat menstrual blood as a symbol of life, rather than death, their practices regarding menstruation are the inverse of those found in the levitical system. For example, Beng women are forbidden to touch a corpse when they are menstruating but they are permitted to have intercourse with their husbands (Gottlieb 1988, 57–74), whereas in the levitical system menstruating women are impure like a corpse and may not have sexual intercourse. Moreover, the Beng associate menstrual blood with fruit trees, an image that Israelite priests identify with the male organ and circumcision (chapter 6).[8]

Thus far I have suggested that the priestly rules governing bodily emissions constitute a subsystem of a larger set of prohibitions that express a distinction between life and death. This interpretation goes a long way in making sense of what otherwise appear to be arbitrary distinctions in the practices governing bodily emissions. However, there are some anomalies that stubbornly resist this symbolic interpretation. These anomalies point to another latent symbolism that has achieved a partial articulation in the language of bodily fluids.

It is not clear, for example, why the ejaculation of semen should be a less severe source of impurity than nonseminal discharge or menstrual blood. Semen contaminates a person only until evening, while these other fluids contaminate a person for seven days and have a variety of secondary effects that semen does not generate (Lev. 15). If the ejaculation of semen represents a missed opportunity for reproduction, why should it be any less polluting than nonseminal fluid which has no connection with reproduction at all? And if menstrual blood and semen are both missed opportunities for reproduction, then why should menstrual blood be the more polluting of the two? Particularly problematic for the above interpretation is the fact that semen is contaminating even during intercourse, the very act of procreation. Furthermore, the priests do not proscribe sexual relations during pregnancy even though there is no chance of conception. And if life and death symbolism totally controls the distinctions among the body fluids, why is the blood of birth impure, when it could be a sign par excellence of reproductive success?[9]

It may also be significant that the priests never say that excrement is a source of impurity, a pollutant mentioned explicitly in Deuteronomy (23:10–15). If death symbolism was the only factor governing these distinctions in the priestly writings, one might expect excrement, a kind of human waste, to be contaminating as well.[10] The claim that skin disease is symbolically associated with death also encounters an anomaly. One sign that skin disease is polluting is the appearance of "living" (i.e., raw) flesh (Lev. 13:10, 14). Finally, if bodily emissions are contaminating because they represent death, why is it that the end of the contamination is marked by the sacrificial death of an animal? Why should the killing of an animal be involved in the symbolic passage of a person from the death of impurity to life?

These anomalies, though significant, do not undermine the previous interpretation. They simply show that a single symbolism is not in total control of the religious system. Culture is an order constructed out of many symbolic domains that play off and struggle against one another. In any given domain, evidence of this struggle may be evident.

Some of the anomalies mentioned above may reflect the domination of gender concerns over the symbolism of life and death. Rather than draw attention to the possible association between birth blood and reproductive success, the levitical system links women's blood and death, an association that helps underscore the contrasting association of circumcision and male fecundity. The difference between semen and menstrual blood might also be part of the symbolic domination of women. Although the loss of both fluids represents a missed opportunity for procreation, menstrual blood is more contaminating simply because of its gender. But as I shall now suggest, there is another way of explaining these and some of the other anomalies. They point to still a third symbolism latent in the rules governing bodily emissions.

Impurity and Uncontrollability

A clue to this third symbolism is contained in the different treatment of semen, on the one hand, and nonseminal discharge and menstrual blood on the other. As noted above, semen contaminates a person only until evening, while the other fluids contaminate for seven days and have numerous other secondary effects which semen does not produce. The principal difference between seminal and nonseminal fluids and between semen and menstrual blood is in the way they leave the body. Since semen is ejaculated from the body through orgasm, its loss is symbolically associated with direct action and conscious thought. Nonseminal discharge and menstrual blood, on the other hand, are passively released from the body. Priestly terminology describes such emissions as "discharges" *(zāb),* the same term used to describe the land "flowing" with milk and honey (e.g., Exod. 3:8, 17; 13:5; 33:3). The Hebrew phrase for "semen," by contrast, is literally "a laying of seed" *(šikĕbat-zāraʿ)* Lev. 15:18 [BDB 1975 (1907), 1012]). In addition, the priestly literature describes insemination as "putting seed" (Lev. 18:20; 20:15). The difference between the ejaculation of semen and the release of nonseminal fluids or menstrual blood is the difference between a controlled, conscious act and a passive, involuntary occurrence.[11] There thus seems to be an association between controllability and power to contaminate. Nonseminal and menstrual discharges which are less controllable than semen are also more polluting. This analysis also accounts for urine, which falls at the opposite end of the spectrum. It is a fluid over which men and women can and indeed are expected to exercise a great deal of control. The fluids which are released from the genitals thus comprise a system which expresses various degrees of human control. Urine, at the one end, being the most controllable, can never contaminate the body. Sperm which is ejaculated, and thus subject to human control on certain occasions, makes the body impure only until evening. Menstrual blood, non-menstrual blood, and non-seminal discharge are completely uncontrollable, and consequently make the body impure for seven days. In other words, there is a direct relation between the controllability of a bodily fluid and its power to contaminate the body.

The association of menstrual blood, pollution, and uncontrollability are found in other cultural traditions as well. In Samoa, for example, "blood is referred to as *palapala* (literally 'mud') or *ʾeleʾele* ('dirt'), *but only when it flows uncontrolled from the body.* Thus, blood flowing from a wound accidentally contracted or menstrual blood may be called 'dirt' in respectful address" (Shore 1981, 198, emphasis in original).

In the Israelite system, however, the symbolism of control is not limited to menstrual blood or genital fluids. This is why fluids from the upper regions of the body do not contaminate. Tears, saliva, mucus, milk, and ear wax are similar to urine in that a person can exercise a certain amount of control over them. One holds back tears, spits saliva, expresses milk, and blows one's nose. Since these fluids are controllable they do not contaminate the body.

The distinction between control and lack of control is also implied in the contrast between circumcision (male blood) and sacrifice, on the one hand, and blood of birth on the other. In circumcision and sacrifice, blood is intentionally spilled, whereas a woman's blood flows uncontrollably during and after the birthing process. This "bloody" contrast is thus the place where several symbolic complexes converge. The relationship of circumcision (male blood) to blood of birth corresponds to the oppositions between men and women as well as to the opposition between control and lack of control. Through a kind of ritual transitivity, the contrast in bloods generates an association between gender and control. Males are disciplined and orderly, females disorderly and out of control. The association between gender and control is also evidenced elsewhere in Israelite literature. Loose sexual behavior is often a metaphor for Israel's relations with "her" neighbors (e.g., Hos. 3; Ezek. 16).

The importance of control in this system also suggests a way of understanding the otherwise paradoxical fact that one sacrifices animals as part of the process of cleansing oneself from the "death" of impurity.[12] Lévi-Strauss (1978, 332–39) has suggested that rituals often correct a situation by symbolically reversing it. For example, symbolically cooking a person is sometimes the ritual remedy when that person is undergoing an intense physiological experience. Thus, a woman who gives birth is sometimes warmed under a fire. Here cooking, which is a symbol of culture, remedies the woman's overabundance of nature, which is associated with childbirth. A similar phenomenon might be occurring in the levitical system. Sacrifice is the controllable spilling of blood; contamination is the result of some uncontrollable incident. Sacrifice remedies contamination because it reverses the process by which contamination occurred. Similarly, circumcision "remedies" birth from woman by a symbolic reversal. The boy is contaminated by the blood that flows uncontrollably from his mother's genitals. To correct the situation, blood is intentionally spilled from his genitals. Finally, a person is cleansed of corpse impurity when sprinkled with a mixture from the ashes of a red heifer (Num. 19). The hide, flesh, blood, and even the dung of the animal shall be burned, along with cedar wood, hyssop, and crimson material (Num. 19). This mixture is called "waters of *niddah*," the same term used to describe a menstruous woman. The connection with "menstrual blood" is also suggested in the abundance of red symbolism (red heifer, cedar wood which is red, and crimson). In addition, the animal involved must be female. To make the analogy with menstruation complete, men are contaminated in the process of producing this red fluid. But while women's menstrual blood, which flows uncontrollably, contaminates all sorts of other things, men's "menstrual fluid," which is intentionally produced, has the power to reverse the contamination of death, the worst form of impurity. Moreover, in contrast to women's menstrual blood, which is associated with death, men's "menstrual fluid" is made from "living" water (Num. 19:17).

If controllability is as symbolically important as this analysis suggests, it may explain some other characteristics of the priestly system. For example, it is tempting to see the issue of control behind the ruling that priests cannot marry divorced women or those degraded by harlotry (Lev. 21:7). These are women whose hymens have been broken by other men. It may be that a priest is expected to marry a woman who has never had intercourse so that he can be the one responsible for bringing forth her blood. The association between impurity and uncontrollability may also explain why the Israelite priests do not list excrement as a source of contamination. Since excrement is a controllable product they may not have regarded it as polluting. Finally, it is interesting that the priestly writer neglected to explicitly proscribe masturbation, a rather surprising omission for a writer so obsessed with crimes of the flesh. This act would have different valences given the particular symbolism that controlled it. In terms of the life/death symbolism, masturbation would be reprehensible because it would represent a waste of seed. But if the issue of control is paramount, masturbation would not be quite as reprehensible since it represents a conscious, willful ejaculation of bodily fluid.

To summarize my argument thus far, the levitical rules regarding bodily fluids represent a kind of palimpsest, in which symbolisms are superimposed on the same raw data. The distinctions among the bodily fluids simultaneously make allusion to the oppositions men/women, life/death, and control/lack of control. These various symbolisms exploit many of the same distinctions (e.g., menstrual blood vs. semen = death/life, lack of control/control, female/male), which is not surprising since each of these contrasts interacts with the others, each one struggling for control. Nowhere is this struggle of symbolisms more evident than in the case of blood discharged during the birthing process. As noted above, this blood is devalued because it is the blood of woman and uncontrollable. Completely suppressed is the potential association between this blood and life.

At this point, it is reasonable to ask about the social significance of these body symbolisms. Can these be construed as reflecting the dangers and powers of the social structure as Douglas suggested, and if so, what dangers and powers are being represented?

Fluid Symbolism and Social Structure

The discrimination between male and female blood obviously reflects the social differentiation of men and women generally. Here Douglas is right: body symbolism reflects the structure of Israelite society. But it is not, as Douglas suggests, the relations between Israelite and non-Israelite societies that are being represented, but relations internal to Israelite society, a possibility Douglas considers in other cases but not in the case of Israel (1966, 129–39).

But there is a more fundamental difficulty with Douglas's theory. While from one point of view these rules seem to *symbolize* gender differences, from another point of view they can be seen as partly *constitutive* of those differ-

ences. That is, the discrimination between men's and women's blood is part
of what it means to be men and women in the priestly community. Without
practical rules such as these there would be no gender differences. In this
view, the rules in question are part and parcel of the social structure. They are
not simply its reflections but its very building blocks.

What about the symbolic distinction between life and death? The relation
of these themes to social structure is not as readily apparent. Interpreters who
have discussed this symbolism sometimes treat it as a consequence of Israelite
theology, which values life over death (Feldman 1977; Milgrom 1981a;
1981b; 1985). But a theme that cuts across Israelite literature may not have
the same associations for all Israelite communities. Since the rules governing
the human body are found in the priestly writings, it is important to consider
whether life and death symbolism has any distinctive significance in priestly
circles.

In the previous chapter, I discussed how the issue of procreation was central to the priestly writings and how the theme sprung from the importance of
descent in the self-definition and organization of the priestly community.
The emphasis on genealogy expressed itself in the symbolism of circumcision, which was connected with fertility and the ability to perpetuate the lineage of Israel. Given that the theme of procreation is so deeply connected to
the priests' conception of the covenant, it is not surprising to find that death
is regarded as an antithesis. While reproduction replenishes Israel's genealogy, death diminishes it. As Durkheim once put it, "When someone dies, the
family group to which he belongs feels itself lessened" (Durkheim 1965
[1915], 445). Reproduction and death are thus opposing forces. Since the
covenant promises reproductive and genealogical success, death is inevitably
in tension with the covenantal promise.

The biblical refrain that "one who observes the commandments shall live
through them" (Lev. 18:5; Ezek. 20:11, 13, 21; 18:19, 21; 33:13) may have had
connotations for the priests that it did not have for other Israelites. In addition to suggesting that God would preserve the life of a righteous person, an
idea found throughout Israelite literature, it alludes to the connection between covenantal obligations and God's reciprocal promise to multiply the
seed of Abraham. That the priests interpreted life and death symbolism in
light of their concerns about lineage and kinship is suggested by the preface to
the levitical rules concerning forbidden sexual relations. "You shall keep My
laws and My rules, by the pursuit of which man shall live: I am the Lord"
(18:5). Why is this particular preface chosen to introduce laws concerning
forbidden sexual relations, when other kinds of justifications are given for
other levitical laws? For example, Israel is frequently enjoined to observe the
laws in order to be holy since God is holy (e.g., Lev. 11:44; 20:8). Thus the
theme of life and the concern about the purity of Israelite lineage are closely
connected in the priestly imagination.

But it was not just reproduction in general that the priests valued. Since it was a patrilineal community, it was the birth of males that was considered particularly valuable. This helps account for the asymmetrical rules regarding the birth of a boy and a girl (Lev. 12). As we have noted, a mother passes through a period of severe and mild contamination following the birth of a boy (seven days, thirty-three days). The length of each stage of her impurity is doubled in the case of a girl. These rules treat the birth of a boy as a mitigating circumstance. Given "the product," a son who can perpetuate the patrilineage of Israel, the woman's blood is shed for a good cause.

In sum, it would be misleading to treat the distinction between life and death, which is embedded in the rules governing bodily fluids, as simply an embodiment of an abstract theme of Israelite theology. This symbolism also springs from and speaks to the practical concern of how to expand the genealogy of Israel. Concern that the social body be perpetuated was inscribed in worries over losses to the human body.

Having disclosed a connection between the symbolism of life and death and the importance of descent in the organization and self-understanding of the priestly community, we now turn to the symbolism of control, the third theme implicit in rules governing bodily emissions. We recall that the more uncontrollable a bodily emission, the more it generates impurity. In what ways might this symbolism have spoken to the concerns of the body politic?

Control and Domination

Following Foucault (1979), I suggest that the association between impurity and lack of control is a technique of cultural domination. By cultural domination, I have in mind two related yet separate processes. Cultural domination refers to the ways in which one group dominates another through symbolic means. The priestly regulations governing bodily emissions clearly exploit associations of masculinity, fertility, and control and contrast these with femininity, death, and disorder, in a way that symbolically suppresses women. But cultural domination also refers to the way in which a religious culture controls the members of its own community. Religious cultures are powerful to the extent to which they intrude into the affairs of daily life. Control over the body is one of the ways in which the abstract ideals of social life are turned into practical realities.

Since in this case the rules governing bodily emissions are applicable to priests and their families, these rules are a vehicle by which the priestly religious culture entered into the most private aspects of a priest's affairs. The practical association between impurity, death, and lack of control embodied the abstract and familiar idea in Israelite religion that a person must exercise self-control in order to fulfill his or her covenantal obligations and thus be closer to God.

The cycle of contamination and purification was a periodic reminder of what might happen as a result of a willful infraction of covenantal rules. For brief periods of time, the priest had no commerce with the sacred and hence was cut off from God. Contamination was a kind of flirtation with excommunication, the punishment for flagrant violation of covenantal norms. The purity rules thus symbolically enacted a much more serious drama. This was only a symbolic enactment because contamination was not considered a sin. But temporary isolation from the cult provided a taste of the more permanent exile that would follow serious offenses. In this sense, the symbolism of control reflected the "powers and dangers" credited to the social structure (Douglas 1966).

There is another way as well in which this symbolism of control may be linked to the organization of the priestly community. As I shall argue in more detail in chapter 8, this sort of symbolism is particularly plausible to a community such as the priests in which descent figures prominently in the communal self-understanding and social organization. As discussed previously, the priesthood was an office inherited patrilineally. Consequently, a priest had no control over his own status; a priest was what one was, not what one became. In a community such as this, where status is ascribed rather than achieved, individuals find plausible a purity system in which one's status with respect to impurity is essentially outside control. The system of purity thus works the same way as the social system itself. In both cases, status is tied in crucial ways to factors that are beyond human control. This argument is developed in much greater detail in the chapter that follows.

People of the Body

As is now evident, rules governing the bodies of Israelite men and women did reflect the dangers and powers credited to the social structure. But that by no means exhausted their social function. In addition, they were fertile grounds for the representation of other themes related to the abstract ideals and practical hopes of the priestly religious culture. Although fluid symbolism contributed to the symbolic domination of women, that was not its only role. In addition, it further emphasized the importance of procreation, a central theme in priestly reproductive politics. Finally, these rules equated uncontrollability and impurity, symbolically suggesting that persons who violate the social order are as good as dead. None of these symbolisms controlled all the distinctions among the bodily fluids, and neither was any entirely independent of the others. Nonetheless, in the play of these relations upon the human body, abstract ideals of Israelite religion were turned into practical realities, realities that intruded into the daily affairs of men and women and controlled their relations with themselves and one another.

The analysis of fluid symbolism in Israelite religion as well as the study of circumcision in the previous chapter shows how important the human body was in Israelite religion as a scene for cultural representations and a place for the display of power. While the body has these functions cross-culturally, it is important to realize that there may have been reasons internal to the religious conceptions of Israel that engendered this preoccupation with the body. In Israelite theology, God has no-body—neither others with whom to interact, nor a completely conceptualized or fully functioning body with which to do it. But according to the religious convictions of the Israelite priests, humans are made in the likeness and image of God (Gen. 1:26–27). Herein lie a number of fundamental contradictions. Since Israel conceived of itself as having only one God, God had no one with whom to interact. As discussed in chapter 5, this meant that various sorts of human relationships and activities, such as marriage and sexuality, could not find adequate representation in the divine realm. Thus while Israelites married, procreated, and had children, their God did not.[13] Consequently, the more Israel's religious conceptions tended toward a strict monotheism, the less these sorts of human relationships and activities had divine models. Thus being Godlike and being human were incompatible in certain fundamental ways.

Similar conflicts are inevitable given the various limitations Israelite thought placed on the representation of God. Israelite literature acknowledges that certain religious virtuosi see God and that God has human features and form (Exod. 24:9–11; 33:17–23; Amos 9:1; Isa. 6:1; Ezek. 1:26–28). Nonetheless, there is a general reluctance about describing the divine body (Barr 1959). According to one passage, God is careful that Moses only sees the divine back, because "you cannot see My face, for no person may see Me and live" (Exod. 33:17–23), although other passages claim Moses spoke to God "face to face" (Exod. 33:11; Num. 12:8). Only Ezekiel's vision provides some detail of God's appearance. Ezekiel sees the "semblance of a throne," on top of which "there was the semblance of a human form. From what appeared as his loins up, I saw a gleam as of amber . . . and from what appeared as his loins down, I saw what looked like fire. There was a radiance all about him. . . . That was the appearance of the semblance of the Presence of the Lord" (Ezek. 1:26–28). But even this description does not indicate whether God has a full body. It is not clear, for example, whether God's "nether" regions are human in form. This hesitation about describing God's appearance is carried over into the religious proscription against depicting the divine form in plastic art (Exod. 20:4; 20:23; 34:17; Lev. 19:4; Deut. 5:8; 27:15), adherence to which is confirmed by archaeological evidence (Hendel 1988). In Israelite art, no deity appears on the divine throne when it is depicted. This contrasts with the plastic art of other ancient Near Eastern cultures that represented deities on the throne. In the official conceptions of Israelite religion, therefore, God's body was incompletely represented. This circumspection about God's body—about describing and representing it—is also expressed in Israelite literature by the avoidance of certain kinds of anthropomorphisms. While God does a variety of humanlike things, including speaking, walking, and laughing, God does not perform "baser" human functions, such as eating, digesting, procreating, urinating, or defecating.

All of these limitations on the divine body would not pose a problem for the human body if it were agreed that Adam was made from the dust of the earth (Gen. 2:7=J). As an earthly substance, humans clearly would have functions and needs that God does not. But when humans are believed to be created in the likeness and image of God, as the priests suggest (Gen. 1:26–27), the difference between the divine and human bodies becomes a problem. Being like God would thus seem to entail the renunciation of the body, at least certain of its processes such as sex and eating. How, for example, can the idea of being made in the divine image be reconciled with the division of the sexes?[14] Does God have genitals and if so for what purpose? Whichever way this question is answered shows that humans are not completely made in the likeness of God. If God has no genitals, then it is only part of the human body that is made in the image and likeness of God. Alternatively, suppose God does have genitals. Since God is normally described as a man and in male metaphors, one must assume that God has a male organ. But if this God does in fact have a penis, what, to put matters bluntly, does He do with it? After all, the monotheism of official Israelite religion precludes the possibility of a female god with whom this God can have intercourse and procreate.

We now understand why the body and its processes preoccupy the Israelite priests more than other writers of ancient Israel. The priests' conviction that humans are made in the divine image generates a number of inescapable cultural conflicts—a kind of cultural neurosis. The injunction that Israelites be holy because God is holy (Lev. 11:45) would seem to require a renunciation of their bodies, which are a continual source of contamination and which remove them from the sacred and divine service. Yet in the priests' view, Israelites cannot renounce their bodies because the covenant requires them to be fruitful and multiply. Sexual intercourse, the very act of discharging covenantal obligations, involves Israelite men in the creation of impurity, which is antithetical to everything that the sacrificial cult represents. While the penis is the symbol of fertility and the covenant, it is also the source of semen, which is polluting. From the priests' perspective, Israelites are damned if they do and damned if they don't. There is no escaping the cultural conflict that surrounds sexuality. The fact that the body is the place where conflicting representations meet and clash helps explain why it plays such an important role in the symbolic system of the Israelite priests.

8.

The Status of Impurity
Descent, Social Experience, and Plausibility

The first logical categories were social categories; the first classes of things were classes of men, into which these things were integrated.

Durkheim and Mauss 1963 (1903)

Most theorists seem to agree that religious statements are believed to be true because religious actors have had social experiences which, corresponding to those beliefs, provide them with face validity.

Spiro 1966

For the Israelite priests, contamination originated in events and processes over which a person exercised little or no control. Death, skin disease, and uncontrollable emissions from the body all introduced pollution into the human domain. On the surface, the connection between pollution and lack of control might not appear all that difficult to understand. If dirt is simply matter out of place (Douglas 1966, 35), then uncontrollable events are by definition a threat to order. But to frame matters this way is misleading. It hides the perplexing fact that the connection between contamination and uncontrollability was not self-evident, at least in the same ways, to groups of Jews who lived after the priests. Indeed, as the priestly system of impurity is appropriated it is precisely the link between contamination and uncontrollability that is rethought and challenged. In differing degrees, the community at the Dead Sea, the early rabbis, and Christians each make contamination more dependent on factors that are within human control. This process of linking contamination to controllability represents a symbolic reversal of the priestly system. This historical transformation, which is the subject of the present chapter, raises a fundamental question: What enabled this symbolism to speak to priests in a way that it could not to the other groups that followed?

To anticipate the historical argument made below, the link between lack of control and impurity is particularly plausible to the priests as a community in which genealogy played a fundamental role in ideology and social relations. The emphasis on descent is precisely what differentiated the priestly community from those that came afterwards. As descent lost its importance in defining the boundaries of a community and as an idiom for communal self-understanding, the connection between contamination and lack of control weakened. Increasingly for the groups that followed, contamination could be controlled by human action and will.

The idea that a symbolic transformation may be linked to fundamental changes in the nature of religious communities derives from Durkheim's and Mauss's *Primitive Classification* (1963 [1903]) and Durkheim's subsequent *Elementary Forms of the Religious Life* (1965 [1915]). Durkheim and Mauss argued that the form or organization of a community shapes the religious symbolism through which that community sees the world. Societies divided into two subgroups tend to think of the entire world as divided into two opposing classes which are conceived as antitheses. If the sun is in one class, the moon and the stars would be in the other. Moreover, all the items in the same category would be interrelated. In the same category as the sun, one might find all light colored animals and animals that are active during the daylight hours, while nocturnal animals or those of a dark color would fall in the opposing side of the dichotomy. If the two subgroups of a tribe are further subdivided into clans, then corresponding subdivisions will be found in the classification scheme.

For a variety of reasons, this theory about the relationship between religious symbolism and social structure has recently fallen out of favor. In part this is the consequence of other studies which have shown that there is no one-to-one correspondence between the form of a group's classification scheme and its organization.[1] Some societies use a bipartite scheme of classification even though the social organization is more complex.[2] But the fact that religious symbolism does not correspond to social relations in the manner Durkheim and Mauss suggested does not necessarily mean there is no connection at all between them. The relationship may simply be of a different kind than they thought.

There is, I suggest, a probative connection between the way in which status is assigned to individuals in a social system and the symbolic distinctions that govern the system of impurity. Specifically, I have in mind the distinction between ascribed and achieved status, first suggested by Linton (1936), and elaborated upon by Parsons (1951, 57, 84) and Parsons and Shils (1951, 63–64). Ascription means assignment of status or prestige on the basis of qualities or attributes such as sex, age, certain physical characteristics, or kinship ties. By contrast, when status is based on achievement, it is determined by an actor's performance, by her or his effectiveness or success in achieving certain specified goals. In the latter case status depends on treating the individual according to what she or he does as opposed to what she or he is.

The way status is determined in a given community may play a crucial role in determining the kind of symbolism that a community considers compelling. But to push beyond this Durkheimian formulation, it is crucial to specify the mechanism by which a given symbolism is rendered plausible or implausible. What is the process by which a change in social relations gets translated into a change in symbolism?

Status assignation has a critical impact on shaping individuals' experiences of social life, and those experiences are expressed in symbolic processes. The more ascription plays a role in defining status, the less control individuals have in determining who they ultimately are or will be. A variety of things about their lives are determined independently of their own decisions, including their occupation, whom they can marry, whether they can own land, what kinds of foods they can eat, and so forth. In such communities, individuals feel that they have relatively little power to alter who they are.

By contrast, when achievement or performance is weighted more heavily, individuals have much more control over their lives. Through the choices they make, hard work, and a general commitment to pursuing certain goals, they have, at least in theory, the power to alter their status and thus determine their lifestyle. In such communities, individuals are not so much affected by factors outside human control. Such people experience the world differently from their counterparts in communities where ascription is of great importance. They feel as if their own personal decisions, choices, and efforts make a difference and have an impact on their world. The two kinds of experience described here are implicit in Parson's and Shil's terminology. When status is ascribed, they speak of individuals as "objects," signaling the essentially passive way in which they are treated. When performance is involved, individuals are referred to as "actors" (1951, 64).[3]

The social experiences linked to the forms of status determination can be particularly powerful in shaping the symbolism of impurity. When status depends primarily upon ascription, the idea of contamination takes a corresponding form in the religious system. Just as an ascribed status is something over which one has little or no say and which is experienced as imposed from the outside, impurity is something which is "out there," an intrinsic property of objects. In this sense, impurity is a thing, since the "most important characteristic of a 'thing' is the impossibility of its modification by a simple effort of the will" (Durkheim 1968 [1895], 28). If the body is a source of contamination, pollution is associated with body functions that are largely uncontrollable, such as the discharge of bodily fluids from the genitals and the appearance of skin disease. Individuals are thus powerless to avoid impurity, and becoming contaminated is an inevitable consequence of living. In short, impurity has the same "objective" quality that status does. It is beyond a person's power to control and therefore experienced as coming from the outside. Furthermore, an individual's actions or intentions will have virtually no impact on the functioning of the system.

This system of contamination remains intact as long as ascription is critical in the determination of status. But as individual performance increases in importance, this understanding of contamination loses its plausibility. A system that treats impurity as an objective, physical, and uncontrollable aspect of life makes little sense to individuals whose statuses are to some extent determined by their choices. The power of the individual to shape the world may express itself in the understanding of contamination in a variety of ways.

First, human action becomes a source of contamination. Contamination is a consequence of what one does, rather than a result of what happens to one's body or the kinds of objects with which one accidentally comes in contact. Consequently, one can avoid contamination simply by deciding not to execute certain kinds of actions. Furthermore, the more that contamination is understood as the consequence of one's actions, the less the external world is treated as a source of pollution. Impurity is no longer an intrinsic property of objects but is localized inside the human body, in the mind, heart, or kidneys depending on the particular religious system. The internal organs of the body are treated as sources of impurity because the ability to exercise control is often linked to the interior of the human body. The more contamination is understood as being subject to human control, the more likely its source will be inside the body.

In communities where ascription and achievement are weighted more evenly, the theory of contamination displays a similar ambivalence. While objects and uncontrollable bodily processes are sources of impurity, human action and intention also become catalysts in the system. Just as an individual's status is partially controllable, so impurity is partially subject to human control.

It is now time to ground these generalizations in specific historical arguments. The connection between status, social experience, and the symbolism of impurity emerges from an analysis of the literature produced by four communities of Jews in antiquity: the Israelite priests, the Qumran community at the Dead Sea, the early rabbis, and the early Christians. In the previous chapter, I have already looked in some detail at the conception of contamination among the Israelite priests (ca. 7th–5th centuries B.C.E.). Since the priestly writings were incorporated into Scripture, all subsequent groups of Jews had to contend with the priests' theory of contamination. Each group, as we shall see, disrupted the priests' symbolism in different ways and to different degrees. The Qumran community (ca. 170 B.C.E.–70 C.E.), which is known from the Dead Sea Scrolls, regarded the priesthood that was officiating in the Temple during its time as illegitimate. As a result, this group established a sectarian community along the Dead Sea that regarded itself as a symbolic replacement for the Temple and cult. Many of the priestly rules regarding contamination were transferred to this sectarian fellowship. However, this community also introduced new restrictions that indicated a different conception of impurity. In contrast to the Dead Sea community, early rabbinic circles widened the priestly rules of contamination to include all of Israelite society. According to the early rabbis, all Israelites were expected to cook and eat their food according to rules of cultic purity. As we shall see from the Mishnah, the first document to be produced by the rabbis (ca. 200 C.E.), the sages reverse the symbolism of the priestly system as much as possible without actually repudiating it. The early Christians, at least those influenced by the letters of the apostle Paul (ca. 51–59 C.E.), and those who stand behind the Gospels, go further than either of the other groups by repudiating the central premises of the priestly understanding of impurity.

The priestly and the early Christian communities would line up at either end of a spectrum depicting methods of status assignation. Ascription plays a fundamental role in the priestly community but is self-consciously challenged as a basis for assigning status in the early Christian communities. There is a similar antagonism between the conceptions of purity in these two communities. The other two groups, the early rabbis and the Qumran community at the Dead Sea, fall somewhere between the two poles of the spectrum. Both recognize ascription and achievement as factors in determining social status, although the Dead Sea community gives preference to ascription. Although these communities adopt aspects of the priestly theory of contamination, each introduces significant modifications into that scheme. I will suggest that these revisions correspond to the increased importance of performance in the determination of status. Neither community, however, goes so far as the early Christians in reshaping the priestly symbolism of purity.

Status and Purity in Priestly and Early Christian Communities

One of the most important differences between the priestly and early Christian communities was their membership criteria. As we have seen, descent was the single most important factor in determining membership in the priestly community. To be a priest, one not only had to be of Israelite origin, but also descended from the genealogical line of Levi or one of his descendants.[4] According to the priests, God had appointed members of this genealogical line to serve as Temple functionaries who would perform sacrifices for their fellow Israelites and oversee the proper functioning of the cult. Entrance into this community was not a matter of choice but was determined at birth. In chapters 6 and 7 I discussed various symbolic interests that sprang from this concern with descent, including the interest in procreation and detailed genealogies. In this context, I simply wish to add that the priestly writer never justified the privileged status of priests vis-à-vis other Israelites in terms of performance. In fact, in a narrative that specifically deals with challenges to priestly authority (Num. 16), the priestly writer offers no explanation as to why God preferred this genealogical line over others.

In addition to descent, the priests recognized another form of ascription.

Physical deformities or blemishes that were the result of either congenital defects or injury excluded priests from serving in the Temple cult (Lev. 21:16–23). Birth defects are obviously not subject to a person's control and physical injuries during one's lifetime are often unavoidable and unforeseeable. Here, then, is another example of how a priest's characteristics rather than his performance determined his status.

A sharply contrasting picture emerges from the literary sources of early Christianity. From the letters of Paul and to some extent from the Gospels as well, it is clear that certain forms of ascription were losing their importance in the early Christian community. Paul denied, for example, the relevance of descent in determining membership or social standing in the new community (Rom. 1:16; 2:9). In his view, God showed no partiality for one people over another (Rom. 2:11; 10:12). Being born a Jew, gentile, or Greek was neither an advantage nor a liability, for one's genealogy would not guarantee salvation. According to Paul, only those who had faith in Christ would be saved (Rom. 10:9–12). Just as the priests' preoccupation with genealogy was reflected in their narration of Israel's story, Paul's antagonism toward descent was evident in his reinterpretation of human history. Paul was careful, for example, to deny the importance of descent in determining membership in the covenant that, according to Scripture, God had made with Abraham and his descendants (Gen. 12). With exegetical finesse, Paul argued that this passage does not refer to Abraham's physical descendants but to those who emulate Abraham's faith in God. "So you see that it is men of faith who are the sons of Abraham" (Gal. 3:7), and "if you are Christ's, then you are Abraham's offspring, heirs according to the promise" (Gal. 3:29). If people who are not actual descendants of Abraham can be his "offspring," persons who do spring from this genealogical line may not qualify as his descendants: "For not . . . all are children of Abraham because they are his descendants; but 'Through Isaac shall your descendants be named.' This means that it is not the children of the flesh who are the children of God, but the children of the promise are reckoned as descendants" (Rom. 9:6).

Not only did Paul dismiss descent as a relevant criterion for defining the community, he went so far as to claim that one's genealogical background is actually obliterated upon entrance into the new community. According to Paul, baptism constitutes a kind of rebirth and has the effect of severing all prior genealogical relations. In Christ, the distinctions between people cease to be meaningful, for the Jew and gentile are both baptised into one body (1 Cor. 12:12). By the same token, one's kinship ties are rendered meaningless, because membership in the community supplies a new set of relationships that replaces those based on descent (Meeks 1983, 88). In Paul's letters, therefore, kinship terminology is applied to other members of the early Christian community (Meeks 1983, 86–88). Paul refers to the members of the church as his children and brethren (Gal. 4:19; 1 Cor. 4:14; 2 Cor. 6:13; 12:14). The contrast with the priestly community cannot be more striking. For the priests, kinship relations defined the boundaries of the priestly community, while for Paul it was the community that determined the nature of kinship. Within this community, one had kinship relations with those who shared common commitments and a similar lifestyle, not simply with those who shared the same parents or ancestors.

The devaluation of descent and kinship that runs through Paul's letters is also evident in the portrayal of Jesus in the synoptic Gospels. Jesus is reported to have said that "whoever does the will of God is my brother, and sister, and mother" (Mark 3:34) and "my mother and my brothers are those who hear the word of God and do it" (Luke 8:21). Indeed, when his own mother and brother come asking to speak to him, Jesus responds by saying " 'Who is my mother, and who are my brothers?' And stretching out his hand toward his disciples, he said, 'Here are my mother and my brothers' " (Matt. 12:46–48). Moreover, the Gospels, like Paul's letters, understand membership in the Christian community to involve a renunciation of actual kinship ties. "He who loves father or mother more than me is not worthy of me; and he who loves son or daughter more than me is not worthy of me" (Matt. 10:37). In the Gospel of Luke, Jesus says "if any one comes to me and does not hate his own father and mother and wife and children and brothers and sisters, yes, and even his own life, he cannot be my disciple" (Luke 14:26). But the same book claims that the loss of actual kinship ties would be more than adequately compensated by the new brothers and sisters one would acquire (Luke 18:29). This disruption in genealogical forms is also evident in what Jewish readers must have experienced as a jarring introduction to the Gospel of Matthew, which is described as "the book of the genealogy of Jesus Christ, the son of David, the son of Abraham." The Gospel begins by reviewing the line of descent from Abraham through David to Joseph, the husband of Jesus's mother. The reader expects the point of this genealogy to be how Jesus's pedigree extends back to David and Abraham. But the virgin birth disrupts this physical descent and thus highlights Jesus's true pedigree as the son of God. Jesus is only symbolically a descendant of Abraham.

What defined one's membership in the community, at least in Paul's view, was a commitment to the set of beliefs and pattern of behavior that the community espoused. Paul's rhetoric stresses the fact that membership in the community of Christ was open to anyone who oriented him or herself in the right way.

> The word is near you, on your lips and in your heart . . . because if you confess with your lips that Jesus is Lord and believe in your heart that God raised him from the dead, you will be saved. For man believes with his heart and so is justified and he confesses with his lips and so is saved. . . . For there is no distinction between Jew and Greek; the same Lord is Lord of all and bestows his riches upon all who call upon him. For "every one who calls upon the name of the Lord will be saved." (Rom. 10:8–13).

Membership in this community was a privilege that depended on one's performance, not on factors beyond one's control. Paul's negative evaluation of ascription is also evident from his discussions of how prestige should be established within the community. Of particular interest is Paul's first letter to the Christians in Corinth, which considers the value of spiritual gifts. Apparently some members of the community claimed that individuals who possessed certain gifts, such as the capacity to speak in tongues, were entitled to more prestige than others. As the community understood it, speaking in tongues was a gift from God. Therefore, if status were assigned on the basis of such a gift, this would constitute a form of ascription, for status would be based on a trait that was not subject to human control. Significantly, Paul denies that speaking in tongues is more prestigious than the ability to interpret in a normal state. "In church I would rather speak five words with my mind, in order to instruct others, than ten thousand words in tongue" (1 Cor. 14:19). Moreover, in order to downplay ascription, Paul widens the category of "spiritual gifts" to include qualities such as assistance and leadership, which are performative. In Paul's view, the best gifts are those qualities that a person has the power to shape and develop (Meeks 1983, 123).

In addition to the dissatisfaction with descent, the early Christian community also repudiated the second form of ascription operative in the priestly community. The synoptic Gospels frequently portray Jesus as ministering to persons with congenital defects, such as blindness, deafness, lameness, and a variety of other physical injuries (e.g., Mark 2:5–6; 7:32; 8:22; 10:26; Matt. 9:27; 15:30; 20:29; Luke 18:29; also Acts 3:1). There is also the story of a woman who suffered a bloody discharge for twelve years and who is instantly cured when she touches Jesus's garment (Mark 5:25–34). When Jesus becomes aware of her action, he is not worried about contamination. Instead he says "Daughter, your faith has made you well; go in peace, and be healed of your disease" (Mark 5:34). One point of such stories clearly is to indicate Jesus's power as magician and miracle worker who can cure even the most intractable physical problems. But at the same time, the Gospels are polemicizing against the priestly view that treats congenital defects and physical injuries as criteria for defining status. According to the Gospels, membership in the community has nothing to do with a person's physical characteristics, but with the strength of one's faith in Christ. These stories suggest that faith in Christ can overcome any congenital liabilities. Disfigured persons who have faith in Christ are more fit for the community than those persons who have no blemishes but who lack faith.

It would be misleading to suggest that status in either the priestly community or early Christian communities was entirely ascribed or achieved. Presumably performance did play a role within priestly circles by determining, for example, who would be high priest as well as the general pecking order within the priestly hierarchy. By the same token, certain forms of ascription did play a role in the early Christian community. As we noted above, certain spiritual gifts did give individuals some amount of prestige, Paul's reservations not withstanding. Gender differences, too, were made the basis for differences in religious authority and religious practice (1 Cor. 14:33–36). Nonetheless, it is clear that the overwhelming tendency within the two communities was to rely on different methods of assigning status.

This difference, I have suggested, would have given individuals in the two communities divergent experiences of community life. In the priestly community, individuals would have felt that factors beyond human control played a considerable role in establishing their identity and lifestyle. After all, one has no control over who one's parents are or whether one is born with a birth defect. Yet these are precisely the kinds of factors that determined the priest's status. By the same token, a priest would have felt that a variety of decisions had been taken away from him at birth. Being the male offspring of a priest meant that one's occupation was effectively determined, that certain kinds of marriages were forbidden (Lev. 21:7–8, 13–15), and that one would have to observe a higher standard of purity than other Israelites (Lev. 21:1–4, 10–12). Whether or not these restrictions were experienced as a privilege or a burden is really beside the point. The fact is that a great many decisions were made for the priests rather than by them. In short, being a priest was not something one chose to do but something that one was.

For the early Christian, the experience would have been quite different. He or she decided to join the community out of a commitment to its ways and vision. Consequently, characteristics of the self that were outside human control were declared irrelevant to attaining membership. In fact, one could overcome any such liabilities simply by opting to become a member of the community and adhering to its ways. This is why Paul describes entrance into the Christian community as providing a person with a new body (Meeks 1977). In this community, a person experienced the possibility of remaking him or herself, even to the extent of determining who counted as brothers and sisters. If the priests experienced status as imposed from the outside, for the early Christians status was much more a consequence of an autonomous choice and personal decision.

Insofar as purity rules constitute a symbolic vocabulary that expresses people's experiences of communal life, the differences outlined above should shape the conception of purity articulated by these groups. There is in fact a striking correspondence between the conceptions of purity and methods of assigning status in both of these communities. The sources of impurity in each system have a number of important features in common with sources of status in each group.

Recall the range of things that contaminate a person according to the priests: a corpse, certain types of dead animals, skin disease, bloody discharge from the vagina, the birth of a child, semen, and nonseminal discharge from the penis (Lev. 11–16). There are two notable characteristics of this list. First, impurity is treated here as an intrinsic property of certain kinds of objects (such as dead animals and corpses). Consequently, impurity is not simply a status that is imposed on things. It is an actual property of the external world, no different than an odor that may originate from a rotting substance.

Second, when impurity originates in the body it is generally associated with a bodily function or process that is unavoidable and uncontrollable (chapter 7). Indeed, I have suggested that there is a direct relationship between the power of a bodily fluid to contaminate a person and the degree to which it flows uncontrollably. The less subject it is to control, the more powerfully it contaminates the body.

The priestly conception of impurity offers an appropriate vocabulary for articulating the experience individuals would have in a community in which status is ascribed. The status of priest was experienced as imposed from the outside, entirely a consequence of factors beyond a person's control. By the same token, impurity was viewed as "out there" in the world, an intrinsic property of certain objects. Furthermore, the sources of contamination were no more controllable than the factors that decided the priest's status. A priest's will, desires, and actions neither altered who he was nor affected the production of pollution.

There is only one important exception to be noted. In the priestly writings, a person becomes contaminated by sexual intercourse (Lev. 15:17). Sexual intercourse represents the only source of impurity in the priestly system whose occurrence was the result of human intention. But it was also the paradigmatic act by which status was determined in the priestly community. The choice of sexual partners determined a priest's own status and that of his offspring. Various forms of sexual deviation were punishable by death, childlessness, or excommunication (Lev. 18:29; 20:10–21). If a high priest married a woman of his own kin who was not a virgin, his offspring were profaned (Lev. 21:14–15). Sexual intercourse was thus an exception that proves the rule. Since intercourse was the one voluntary act that contributed to the determination of status, it was the one willful act that produced contamination.

In turning to the early Christian writings, one discovers a conception of purity that articulates the experience of individuals in a community where status was primarily achieved. Since in the early Christian community status was not associated with inherent traits of individuals, it would not have been experienced as imposed from the outside. Instead, individuals would have perceived their status as resulting from their life decisions and actions. It is significant, therefore, that one of the central points in the letters of Paul and the Gospels is that objects are not intrinsically impure. "Do not, for the sake of food, destroy the work of God. Everything is indeed clean" (Rom. 14:20). "Food will not commend to God. We are no worse off if we do not eat and no better off if we do" (1 Cor. 8:7). "Eat whatever is sold in the meat market without raising any question on the ground of conscience. . . . If one of the unbelievers invites you to dinner and you are disposed to go, eat whatever is set before you without raising any question on the ground of conscience" (1 Cor. 10:25).

Since impurity no longer originates in objects, it is not considered in any sense "out there" in the world. For similar reasons, uncontrollable body processes are no longer considered sources of contamination. As noted above, the Gospels have no compunction about portraying Jesus as touching persons afflicted with skin diseases and menstrual discharges.

This does not mean that Paul altogether rejects the concept of purity. On the contrary, the community is still expected to maintain certain standards of purity (Newton 1985, 52–110). But the sources of contamination are now a person's actions or conscience. "But some, though being hitherto accustomed to idols, eat food as really offered to an idol; and their conscience, being weak, is defiled" (1 Cor. 8:7). "Whoever eats the bread and drinks the cup of the Lord in an unworthy manner will be guilty of profaning the body and blood. . . . For anyone who eats and drinks without discerning the body eats and drinks judgment on himself" (1 Cor. 11:27).

It is precisely this shift in the origin of impurity from objects to the human will that is so significant. "I know and am persuaded in the Lord Jesus that nothing is unclean in itself; but it is unclean for anyone who thinks it unclean" (Rom. 14:14). Just as the individual in the community is told that the source of his or her own status is inside, within human control, the sources of impurity are also located within the human body. "There is nothing outside a man which by going into him can defile him; but the things which come out of a man are what defile him" (Mark 7:15; Matt. 15:10–11).

To contrast the priestly and Christian theories of impurity in terms of the inside and the outside of the body is actually misleading. The priests also considered the inside of the body to be a source of impurity. After all, they viewed various discharges that emanate from inside the body as sources of pollution. The early Christians, for their part, did not consider all kinds of things that came out of the body as polluting. They did not, for example, regard the discharge of blood from the vagina as polluting (Mark 5:25–34). The contrast between inside and outside the body was thus a symbolic way of describing the differences between what is and is not controllable. "Do you not see that whatever goes in the mouth passes into the stomach and so passes on? But what comes out of the mouth proceeds from the heart and this defiles a man. For out of the heart comes evil thoughts, murder, adultery, fornication, theft, false witness, slander. These are what defile a man; but to eat with unwashed hands does not defile a man" (Matt. 15:17–20).

Since this community considered the human will to be the origin of contamination, purity rules that related to objects made no sense without reinterpretation. Consequently, there is a tendency within the early Christian writings to turn those rules that are concerned with the purity of objects into statements about the purity of the human will and the self: "Woe to you scribes and Pharisees, hypocrites! for you cleanse the outside of the cup and the plate but inside they are full of extortion and rapacity. You blind Pharisees first cleanse the inside of the cup and of the plate that the outside also may be clean" (Matt. 23:25). "And the Lord said to him, 'Now you Pharisees cleanse the outside of the cup and of the dish, but inside you are full of extortion and wickedness. You fools! Did not he who made the outside make the inside also?' " (Luke 11:39). In these passages, rules about the purity or impurity of dishes are treated as metaphorical statements about the purity of the human body. These statements illustrate the larger processes at work in the Christian reformulation of the concept of purity, namely, the desire to make contamination a consequence of human actions and intentions and not a property of objects.

To summarize, then, the symbolism of impurity in the writings of the priests and early Christians differs fundamentally. These differences can be accounted for in terms of the divergent experiences each community provided its members. Whereas the priests experienced their world as given, to a great extent determined at birth by factors beyond human control, early Christians had the power to transform themselves by acquiring a "new body" and a new set of kin relations. Who he or she was depended on who he or she wanted to be. The conception of contamination in each community in turn reflected these experiences: the priests treated impurity as an intrinsic property of objects and as an inescapable aspect of life. By contrast, the early Christians viewed impurity as a consequence of one's actions and decisions and therefore subject to human control. In turning now to the writings of the community at the Dead Sea and the early rabbis, we examine two communities in which ascription and achievement are more evenly weighted. Significantly, the conception of purity in each of these communities combines characteristics of both the priestly and Christian conceptions.

Purity and Status in the Dead Sea and Early Rabbinic Communities

At Qumran and in the early rabbinic communities, ascription and achievement played competing roles in defining status, although one method or the other predominated. The literature discovered at the Dead Sea, for example, testifies to a group that placed a great deal of emphasis on pedigree. Like the priests, and in contrast to the early Christians, this community recognized descent as relevant to determining membership in the community as well as to defining a person's place in its internal hierarchy. Israelite birth, for example, was a prerequisite for membership in the community and priestly descent provided additional prestige that entitled a person to important privileges and duties. A priest, for example, was required to be in attendance at every gathering of ten or more people, whether for debate, study, or prayer (CD 14:3; 1QS 6; Vermes 1975, 81). Priests sat and spoke first during communal gatherings, and were the first to say blessings before meals (1QS 6; Vermes

1975, 81). It also appears that the highest office of the community, the Guardian, was a priest (Vermes 1977, 90). Moreover, like the priests, the Qumran community treated congenital defects and certain other physical deformities as an indication of status. Anyone with certain kinds of blemishes, such as blindness or lameness, was excluded from the monastic community at the Dead Sea, although such persons may have been allowed to participate in the satellite communities in the towns (1QM 7:4–5; 11Q Temple 45:12–14; Yadin 1977, 2:218, 224–25).

Nonetheless, in certain crucial ways performance begins to compete with ascription as a relevant criterion. Although Israelite descent was a prerequisite for membership, not all Israelites were admitted to the community. By the same token, although priestly descent entitled members to a special status, it too did not guarantee acceptance in the community. All new members, whatever their pedigree, had to prove through a lengthy process of testing that they were worthy of becoming insiders. Potential members were observed and examined for a period of two years and admitted only if they performed successfully during that period of time. Even children born into the community had to take vows committing themselves to the group's ways and understanding of God's will once they reached the age of twenty. Joining the community was a personal adult decision (1QS 1; 5; Vermes 1977, 72, 79, 80, 81).

The importance of one's performance did not end with admittance to the community. Rank within the community was closely linked to achievement as defined by knowledge of the community's distinctive interpretation of God's will as well as a commitment to the community's rules. Violation of those rules resulted in demotion or even loss of membership.

Given the dual emphasis on ascription and performance in this community, it is not surprising that at times the two methods of assigning status came into conflict with one another. The Damascus Document, for example, considers what would happen if the available priest was not actually an expert in the matters at hand:

> And where there are ten [people], there shall never be lacking a Priest learned in the Book of Meditation; they shall all be ruled by him. But should he not be experienced in these matters, whereas one of the Levites is experienced in them, then it shall be determined that all the members of the camp shall go and come according to the latter's word. But should there be a case of applying the law of leprosy to a man, then the Priest [who is not an expert] shall come and shall stand in the camp and the Guardian shall instruct him in the exact interpretation of the law. Even if the Priest is a simpleton, it is he who shall lock [up the leper] for theirs is the judgment (CD 13:3; Vermes 1975, 115).

This passage explores the potential conflict between ascription and performance. In some matters, a priest had to relinquish his privileges if he was not properly trained. What is striking, however, is that his power was not turned over to the person with the most expertise on the matter in question, but to a Levite, a person from the genealogical line of the next highest status. Moreover, in matters pertaining to leprosy, it had to be a priest who made the judicial decisions, even if he was a "simpleton." Although expertise was important, pedigree still had the upper hand.

The tension between ascription and achievement is reflected in the community's ideology as well. It viewed the world in terms of a dualism between forces of light and darkness and characterized its own members as "sons of light" and those who did not subscribe to its vision and way of life as "sons of darkness." The writings at Qumran are equivocal as to how one becomes a son of light (Vermes 1977, 171; Ringgren 1963, 74, 110–11). One strand of the literature articulates a theory of predestination (Ringgren 1963, 68–80, 108–9; Allegro 1956, 126; Licht 1958). According to this view, God decided to which camp or "lot" a person would belong before birth (1QS 4:23–26).

> I know that the inclination of every spirit [is in Thy hand]; Thou didst establish [all] its [ways] before ever creating it, and how can any man change Thy words? Thou alone didst [create] the just and establish him from the womb for the time of goodwill. . . . But the wicked Thou didst create for [the time] of Thy [wrath], Thou didst vow them from the womb to the Day of Massacre. (1QH 15:13–20; Vermes 1975, 195)

The idea of predestination is the ideological counterpart to ascription. Predestination asserts that the individual has no choice about who he or she is, whether a child of light or darkness. "God did not choose you because of your deeds but because of the covenant with your fathers" (CD 8:26).

But there is another theory that competes with the ideology of predestination. This theory suggests that individuals have the power to shape their destiny, to determine whether they are sons of light or of darkness. A number of statements stress the voluntary nature of the individual's decision to join the community (Vermes 1977, 171; Ringgren 1963, 74). One joins with a free will (1QS 1:7) and one is a volunteer for God's truth (1QS 1:11–12; CD 16:4). This stream of thought is in tension with the idea of predestination in precisely the way that performance competes with ascription as a method of determining social status. To summarize, then, while the Qumran community gave ascription a dominant role, it by no means ignored performance. If the priestly and Christian communities define the two poles of a spectrum, the Qumran community falls near the middle, although on the side closer to the priests.

From the evidence of the Mishnah, the first document produced by the rabbis, the early rabbinic community also falls somewhere between the two poles of the spectrum. But in contrast to the Qumran group, it belongs somewhat closer to the pole defined by early Christianity. This placement of the rabbinic community is evident from its attitude toward genealogy. According to the rabbis, Israelite birth automatically guaranteed a person admittance to the larger Israelite community. But membership was not limited to those of Israelite origin. Conversion served as a mechanism that allowed non-Israelites to become part of the community. In this respect, the nature of the rabbinic community obviously differed from the priestly and Dead Sea communities which made Israelite descent a prerequisite for membership. In conceiving of membership as being possible for non-Israelites, the rabbinic community more closely approximates that of the early Christians.

Still there is an important difference between these groups as well. In the rabbis' view, Israelite kinship ties were constitutive of the basic community to which others could be admitted. But conversion did not entail being inscribed in the Israelite kinship system. By joining the community, one did not become an "offspring of Abraham." Thus in reciting prayers, converts were not permitted to say "O God of our fathers." Instead, they had to say "O God of your fathers" (M. Bik. 1:4). Paul, of course, was a great deal more radical in allowing kinship to be established by membership itself. For Paul, the descendants of Abraham were those persons who became brothers and sisters "in Christ."

The early rabbinic community also recognized pedigree as a factor determining status within the community. The sages, for example, gave the priests the same privileges and duties that the priests had claimed for themselves: they were entitled to priestly dues, and had certain marriage restrictions and cultic obligations. In addition, the sages recognized that certain blessings could be said only by priests (M. Ber. 5:4) and that a priest had the honor of reading from Scripture before other Israelites (M. Git. 5:8). But apart from these perquisites, the Mishnah does not give the priests any privileges or honors that are not already specified in the priestly writings. In fact, there are a number of indications that the sages were ambivalent about the priests' status altogether. For example, the sages claimed that the priestly privilege of reading from Scripture before other Israelites was simply decided "in the interest of peace" (M. Git. 5:8). By implication this statement suggests that the priests were not really entitled to this honor more than other Israelites. Their privilege was simply the result of a practical decision to prevent fighting within the community.[5]

The decreasing interest in genealogy is matched in the Mishnah by an increasing emphasis on performance. The early rabbis viewed mastery of Scripture and its interpretive tradition as the central criterion in defining authority and status of a sage. "These are things whose fruits a man enjoys in this world while the capital is laid up for him in the world to come: honoring one's father and mother, deeds of loving-kindness, making peace between two people, but the study of Torah is equal to them all" (M. Peah 1:1). Consequently, the most important skill one could teach one's son was how to study Torah (M. Qid. 4:14). Mastery of Scripture, as previously discussed, was important in the Dead Sea community as well. But the early rabbinic community went further. As far as the sages were concerned, knowledge of Scripture contributed more to status than genealogy.

> [In all matters of prestige] a priest takes precedence over a Levite, a Levite over an Israelite, an Israelite over a child of a forbidden union. . . . When does this ruling apply? When they are all equal [with respect to their knowledge of Scripture and its interpretive tradition]. But if the bastard is a sage's disciple and the high priest is unknowledgeable—the bastard who is a disciple takes precedence over the high priest who is unknowledgeable. (M. Hor. 3:8)

The rabbis did not indicate the specific situations in which they regarded training as more important to a person's standing than genealogical background. But it is clear that in at least some cases performance effectively competed with descent in the determination of prestige. Consequently, a person who mastered Scripture had more honor than a priest who was inadequately trained in Torah study.

Equally dramatic is the way in which kinship ties were superseded by relations of choice. Thus Torah-ties, relations developed through discipleship to a sage, had a stronger claim on an individual than the obligations to biological relations.

> If one finds the lost property of one's father and one's teacher—[the obligation to restore the lost property of] one's teacher takes precedence, for one's father brought one into this world but one's teacher from whom one acquired wisdom brings one to the life of the world to come. But if one's father is a sage, [the obligation to restore his lost property] takes precedence over [the lost property of] one's teacher.
>
> If one's father and one's teacher are both carrying loads, one should provide relief for one's teacher before assisting one's father. If one's father and teacher were in captivity, one should first ransom one's teacher before one's father. But if one's father is a sage, he should ransom his father and then his teacher. (M. B.M. 2:11; see also M. Ker. 6:9)

Like the previous passage, this one shows how mastery of Scripture and commitment to Torah were more important as an index of honor and prestige than any of a person's innate characteristics. While the relationship between parent and child remained important, it ultimately was displaced by the relationship between teacher and student (see chapter 9). In making the study of Scripture the central act of religious piety, the rabbinic community enabled males to play an important role in shaping the kind of persons they would ultimately become. No matter what a man's pedigree may have been, he could become a sage and thus earn the highest status in the community.

In sum, neither the early rabbinic community nor the community of Qumran repudiated descent as a factor in determining status. But both supplemented it with an emphasis on performance. As we shall now see, the conception of contamination that both of these groups articulated is similarly ambivalent. It is striking that neither of these communities rejected outright any of the priestly ideas about what constitute sources of impurity. The range of objects and the kinds of bodily processes that the priests treated as sources of impurity are reiterated without substantial alteration in the writings at Qumran and in the early rabbinic literature. Both recognized genital discharges, skin diseases, corpses, and certain kinds of dead animals as sources of pollution. For these communities, contamination was an intrinsic property of objects and to some extent beyond human control, just as status was to some extent based on those human characteristics that were not governed by human will. It was only when descent was repudiated altogether, as in Paul's writings, that impurity ceased to have its origins in objects and in uncontrollable bodily functions.

Nonetheless, the developing emphasis on performance in the Dead Sea and rabbinic communities did find corresponding innovations in these groups' conceptions of pollution. In both cases, the innovations in question involved giving human actions and intentions a more powerful role in producing and controlling the spread of contamination. As status came to depend on human performance, the human will became a force to contend with in the system of impurity. Or to state this transition in reverse terms, as intrinsic human characteristics ceased to be the only factors on which a person's status depended, so the intrinsic properties of objects were only one of several sources of impurity.

The Qumran community, for example, considered the deeds of the wicked as sources of defilement (1QS 5; Vermes 1975, 80). Violation of communal norms contaminated an individual and prevented him from participating in the pure meals of the community (Neusner 1973, 54; Schiffman 1983, 164–65; Newton 1985, 40–49). Among other things, a person was defiled by lying deliberately about matters concerning property, by speaking in anger against one of the priests, and by deliberately insulting one's companion (1QS 7; Vermes 1975, 83). In addition, the intent of an action played an important role in determining its religious significance. The act of bathing, for example, did not purify a person unless accompanied by a humble submission of the soul (1QS 3; Vermes 1975, 75). In sum, the Qumran writings identify two quite different sources of impurity. On the one hand, contamination is said to originate from certain kinds of objects and uncontrollable bodily processes. On the other hand, it is also a consequence of performing certain kinds of actions. The latter conception would eventually find its greatest expression in early Christianity. But in the writings of the Dead Sea community, this understanding of impurity did not yet have the strength to overturn the symbolism in the earlier priestly writings. The two conceptions existed side by side, just as the two methods of assigning status operated simultaneously.

In the early rabbinic community, the violation of norms was not treated as a source of impurity. That development occurred in later rabbinic circles (Neusner 1973, 72–107). Nonetheless, the early rabbis introduced numerous innovations that made the symbolic association between contamination and control much more visible. To be sure, the rabbis did not go so far as the early Christians, dissociating contamination entirely from objects or uncontrollable body processes. Like the priests, they believed that various objects were sources of and susceptible to contamination. But they did de-emphasize the importance of physical characteristics. In their interpretations, human interaction with an object partly determined its status.

The sages frequently discussed the kinds of objects that are susceptible to impurity. While the priestly sources disposed of this issue in but a few sentences (Lev. 11:31–36), whole tractates of the Mishnah are devoted to it. Consequently, it is here that one discovers one of the rabbis' important contributions to the idea of contamination. In case after case, the Mishnah insists that the capacity to become contaminated is not an object's intrinsic characteristic. According to the sages, susceptibility to impurity was a function of how an individual uses or conceives of a given object (Neusner 1981, 270–80; Eilberg-Schwartz 1986, 95–141).

For example, the rabbis followed the priests in thinking that "food" is susceptible to contamination. But the priests apparently felt that the definition of food was self-evident for they did not specify the range of things that constitute food (Lev. 11:34). For the early rabbis, however, determining whether something was "food" was exceedingly problematic since people do not always treat the same range of substances as food. The sages rejected edibility— an inherent property of substances—as the sole criterion for determining whether something falls into the category of food. In their view, something is food only if an individual intends to eat it or people normally eat that type of substance. The sages, therefore, arrived at the conclusion that identical substances may have a different status with respect to impurity if they are in two different locations (Eilberg-Schwartz 1986, 120–22, 130–37).

Consider the case of a bird that has been improperly slaughtered. Can such a bird become contaminated? The answer depends on whether it falls under the rubric of food. According to mishnaic law, an Israelite may not eat any animal that has not been slaughtered according to the prescribed procedure. Nonetheless, such a bird is "food" if an Israelite intends to sell it to a gentile, who is permitted to eat such substances. To determine the likelihood of the bird being sold to a gentile, the sages take account of the bird's location. If the fowl is in the marketplace, it automatically falls into the category of food since it is probable that the Israelite will sell it. But if the fowl is in the village, which is some distance from the marketplace, it is by no means self-evident that the Israelite will take the trouble of finding a gentile buyer. In this case, the status of the bird is determined by what the Israelite decides to do with it. If the owner decides to take it to the marketplace, it immediately enters the category of food and can become contaminated. But if the Israelite decides to throw it away, it falls into the category of waste and cannot become impure (M. Uqs. 3:1–3; Eilberg-Schwartz, 1986, 132–36).

Precisely the same tendency is evident in the Mishnah's treatment of household objects. Again following the priests, the rabbis claim that "useful" objects can become contaminated. But the priests did not specify the criteria for usefulness (Lev. 11:31–36). In the rabbis' view, the usefulness of the object is primarily determined by the intentions and actions of the owner (Eilberg-Schwartz 1986, 115–20, 123–30). As in the case of edible substances, it is possible that identical objects can have different statuses when owned by different people. For example, an untanned leather hide in the possession of an Israelite householder may or may not be subject to contamination, depending on whether the householder has formed an intention to use it. But an untanned hide belonging to a tanner is automatically defined as useless on the presumption that tanners generally do not consider unfinished hides to be useful things (M. Kel. 26:8; Eilberg-Schwartz 1986, 123–24).

Clearly, susceptibility to impurity is not an inherent property of objects. If it were, an object's ability to become contaminated would remain the same regardless of location or owner. But it does not. Susceptibility to impurity is a status or quality that is imposed on an object as a result of human decisions and actions. In this respect, the rabbis seriously modify the objective nature of contamination as defined by the priests. This development, I have argued, is connected with the emergence of performance as a significant criterion in the determination of status. When status depends on what individuals do, members of a community feel as though they play a role in making their worlds. This experience is reflected in the belief that the important characteristics of objects are also defined by human actions and intentions.

Despite the emphasis on having control over the world, the sages do not claim that the status of an object is completely determined by human will. Intrinsic properties of objects do affect their statuses, just as inherited characteristics of people affect theirs. The status of an object is the product of an interplay between human actions and intentions and the object's physical characteristics. Nowhere is this more evident than in the way the sages determine whether a hole in the wall will permit impurity to flow outside a house.

Suppose that a person dies in a house that has a fissure in one wall. According to mishnaic law, a corpse contaminates everything in the house. In some cases, corpse pollution can also pass through an opening in the wall and contaminate things outside the house. The size of the hole plays an important role in determining whether it permits impurity to pass beyond the wall. If a hole is bigger than a fist, it automatically permits contamination to flow outside. But if it is smaller than a drill hole, it prevents the leakage of contamination. When a hole falls between these sizes, the perceptions and judgments of the householder become decisive. If the householder intends to use the hole to admit light to the house, it need only be the size of a drill-hole to permit the passage of impurity. But if the householder decides to use it as a niche for storing household vessels, the hole must reach the size of at least a hand-breadth before it allows impurity to pass outside (M. Oh. 13:1; Eilberg-Schwartz 1986, 128).

The capacity of a hole to transmit impurity is not solely a function of its size. The size determines whether or not the hole qualifies as one that can potentially transmit impurity. But it is the householder's intention that decides whether the hole in question in fact permits contamination to pass through the wall. Consequently, a hole in one house may permit impurity to go through the wall, whereas a hole of the same size in another house may not permit the flow of contamination because that householder regarded it differently. What this example shows is how individuals exercise a great deal of power over the flow of contamination. But this power is by no means absolute. It is constrained by certain physical characteristics of objects.

The interplay between physical characteristics of objects and human perceptions and judgments about those objects parallels the interaction between ascription and performance in determining social status. In the early rabbinic community, a man's intrinsic characteristics, such as his genealogy, did play a role in defining social status. But such factors were not as important as they had been for either the priests or the community at Qumran. In the rabbinic community, a man's achievement also had a tremendous impact on his standing in the community. By committing himself to mastery of Scripture and its interpretive tradition, a man could significantly increase his prestige within the group. Indeed, even if he was a product of an incestuous union, he could overcome that status by training with a sage and demonstrating his proficiency in Scripture. In this community, the methods of assigning status to objects and persons were virtually identical: intrinsic characteristics, whether of objects or people, were de-emphasized in favor of factors that were subject to human control.

A similar symbolic transformation is evident in the way the rabbinic authors of the Mishnah modified the priestly rules governing emissions from the body. The sages followed the priests in treating menstrual blood, nonmenstrual bleeding, semen, and nonseminal discharges as sources of contamination. But they also discussed a variety of other bodily emissions that were completely ignored by the priests, including urine, tears, saliva, phlegm, mucus, ear wax, milk, pus, blood from a medicinal bloodletting, and sweat. By taking up these emissions, the rabbis were able to subtly reverse the symbolism of the priestly system in significant ways. Without actually repudiating the priestly rules, the sages nonetheless forged a link between control and contamination in this domain as well.

Since urine, tears, saliva, phlegm, mucus, ear wax, and milk are subject to a great deal of control, they were simply inert in the priestly system. This is not the case in the laws of the Mishnah. These emissions not only come under rabbinic scrutiny but become catalysts in the rabbinic conception of contamination. According to the sages' theory, these emissions are capable of making food susceptible to contamination (M. Mahk. 6:4, 5, 8). This notion springs from the ruling in Leviticus that "any food that might be eaten, it shall become unclean if it came in contact with water [and subsequently made contact with the carcass of an animal]. . . . If such a carcass falls upon seed grain that is to be sown it is clean; but if water has fallen on the seed and any part of a carcass falls upon it, it shall be unclean for you" (Lev. 11:34). Clearly, there is no direct warrant in the priestly rules for the assumption that bodily emissions can make food susceptible to impurity. Why then did the rabbis of the Mishnah claim that urine, saliva, tears, ear wax, phlegm and breast milk do have this power? In doing so, they linked controllability and contamination. Fluids that are subject to human control now had an important role in determining whether food becomes susceptible to impurity. Thus the same symbolic innovation is evident here as in the rabbinic rules governing the impurity of objects. Without actually repudiating the priestly rules, the rabbis found ways to make contamination more obviously connected to human control.

The sages also discussed another group of emissions never discussed by the priests: blood from a medicinal blood-letting, sweat, pus, the blood accompanying sweat or pus, and excrement. According to the rabbis, these products neither make food susceptible to contamination nor contaminate the body (M. Makh. 2:1; 6:7). What these fluids have in common and what distinguishes them from other bodily fluids is their point of origin. The body fluids previously discussed all leave the body through an orifice, while these fluids do not.[6] Why did the rabbis treat as inert those fluids that did not leave the body through an orifice? Body orifices apparently fulfilled a symbolic function. They are generally muscular and are good symbols for the ability to control. Fluids that leave the body through an orifice and which are theoretically subject to human control are catalysts in the mishnaic system, that is, they have some sort of consequence. Other fluids are not invested with powers. They are treated as uninteresting.

When taken as a system by themselves, the rabbinic innovations reverse the priestly symbolism of bodily emissions. Bodily fluids that do not leave the body through an orifice, a symbol of control, are inert; they have no relevance in the system of contamination. Fluids that do leave via orifices and which are theoretically controllable are the very fluids that make food susceptible to impurity.

Conclusion

The connection between contamination and lack of control was disrupted to differing degrees by the communities that followed the priests. As this analysis suggests, the intensity of that disruption corresponded to the degree to which descent was rejected as a criterion for assigning social status. The more status depended on a person's actions and commitments, the more implausible the priestly conception of pollution became.

It is possible to give this symbolic transformation a functionalist interpretation. On this view, the theory of contamination validates the way that social status is assigned in a given community. The purity system provides legitimation, reinforced by divine sanction, for the methods by which each community assigns social status. By reflecting on the rules of purity, members of each group come to believe that the way society operates is in fact part of the natural order. The status of individuals is determined in precisely the same way as any other type of object. To the members of society it would appear that the same rules that govern the natural order also govern the social order (Radcliffe-Brown 1965 [1952], 117–52; Douglas 1966; Berger and Luckmann 1966).

While a functionalist interpretation makes sense of the data, individual experience disappears completely from analysis. This is why I have emphasized the category of experience. In doing so, I hope to focus attention on the way that individuals might have been affected by various forms of communal life. On my view, purity systems are a language that expresses individuals' experiences of social life, which are in turn shaped by social factors such as the means by which status is determined. In other words, purity rules are treated here as analogous to religious poetry or prayer that expresses individuals' collective experience of life in a religious community.

The more that status depends on factors beyond human control, the more an individual experiences her or his own status as imposed from the outside and independent of human control. This experience is reflected in the notions of what constitute sources of impurity. In such a case, impurity is an intrinsic property of objects in the same way that status is based on the inherent characteristics of individuals. Impurity has an "objective" quality to it, because it is out there in the world and largely beyond human control. In addition, the sources of impurity may be uncontrollable, as is the case of bodily processes that contaminate a person. Conversely, in communities in which achievement is relevant to the determination of status, individuals feel as though they exercise more control over who they are and want to be. This experience in turn is reflected in the tendency to treat human actions and intentions as sources of pollution.

9.

Creation, Classification, and the Genealogy of Knowledge

> Any human act . . . acquires effectiveness to the extent to which it exactly repeats an act performed at the beginning of time by a god, a hero, or an ancestor.
>
> Eliade 1954

According to the Israelite priests, humans were made in the image of God (Gen. 1:26–27). This familiar idea actually hides as much as it discloses. As discussed previously, the upper realm was in fact incapable of representing a variety of social concerns of Israelite religion. The fact that God had "nobody"—neither others with whom to interact nor a fully conceptualized or functioning body with which to do it—meant that critical sorts of social issues could not be represented in theological reflection. While worship of foreign gods was compared to adultery and whoredom, there was little possibility of using theological conceptions to think about incest, murder, polygyny and a variety of other human actions or institutions that concerned Israelites. Israelite writers were very cautious about representing God's form. Even sources that suggest that God appeared in human form hesitate to ascribe to God the necessary body parts for lower functions such as digestion, urination, defecation, and sexual intercourse. In crucial aspects of their embodiment, then, humans were not made in the image of God and human activity does not replicate divine activity. Thus while God created the world by speaking, humans procreate by joining their bodies, an act that creates contamination. Thus the divine realm served as much as an anti-image for the human realm as a mirror of it.[1]

But God's activity of creation was paradigmatic for Israelites in other sorts of ways. In what follows, I explore some of the ways in which the story of creation was exemplary for two groups of ancient Jews, the Israelite priests and the early rabbis. As I will suggest, some of the fundamental ontological

differences that divided these groups (see chapter 8) are reflected in their respective conceptions of creation and procreation.

Creation and Classification

Mircea Eliade (1954; 1963) deserves credit for elucidating the way that ontology recapitulates cosmogony.[2] Ontology is a term that refers to a branch of
metaphysics dealing with being. But it is sometimes used in a less technical
sense to refer to a set of presuppositions about the nature of the world and the
character of reality.[3] In this sense, most religious systems articulate some ontology. They posit a description of the world and make assumptions about
what makes it the way it is. Cosmogony is the story or theory of the world's
creation. In many religious systems, ontology and cosmogony go hand in
hand. Ideas about creation shape and express conceptions of reality and vice
versa.

A notable example of the interaction between ontology and cosmogony is
evident in Mary Douglas's (1966, 41–57) analysis of Israelite dietary rules.[4]
Douglas does not acknowledge Eliade's work.[5] Yet her analysis of Israelite
food taboos is essentially a variation on the same theory. Douglas argues that
the creation myth (Genesis 1:1–2:4) provides a conceptual model for understanding the universe. In this account of creation reality is demarcated and
defined. Anything that violates the classifications established in this story is
treated as a flaw in creation and hence is considered abnormal and unclean.
What conforms to the cherished classifications is holy.

The creation story divides the world into three distinct realms (sky, earth,
and water), each of which has a form of locomotion that is proper to it. Flying
is the specified mode of movement in the sky. Walking, hopping, or jumping
are appropriate forms of movement on the earth, and swimming the correct
way of moving about in the water. The animals deemed unclean are those
which are not equipped for the appropriate form of locomotion. Since swimming things normally have fins and scales, anything without these is deemed
to be unclean. Since the paradigmatic type of flying animals have only two
feet, four-footed flying things are considered unclean. Land animals typically
walk, hop, or jump. Those that crawl or swarm are impure.[6]

Although Douglas's analysis has been favorably received,[7] some important
challenges have been raised. Robert Alter (1979, 49), for example, has noted
that Douglas's theory cannot explain why certain birds such as the chicken
and duck are considered clean. Both of these birds are anomalous. The
chicken has wings but does not fly. The duck has wings and can fly but spends
most of its time in the water. Despite their anomalous character, these birds
are not considered impure. This objection, I think, is a weighty one. Nonetheless, with some modification, Douglas's analysis remains convincing.

In her analysis, Douglas argues that the dietary laws derive from the conceptual distinctions set out in Genesis 1. To begin with, it is important to note that the dietary rules appear in two different versions in the Israelite literature (Deuteronomy 14:3–20 and Leviticus 11:2–47). Close inspection of these passages shows that it is Leviticus 11, and not Deuteronomy 14, which corresponds significantly with the story of creation in Genesis 1. This is not accidental. Taking my lead from Fishbane's (1985) recent work on intrabiblical exegesis, I suggest that Leviticus 11 reworks Deuteronomy 14 in such a way as to bring it into closer correspondence to the creation story.[8] While Leviticus follows Deuteronomy pretty much word for word, those places where Leviticus deviates from the language of Deuteronomy can be explained as attempts to link the dietary laws to the creation story in Genesis 1. This is evident in a number of ways.

First, Deuteronomy knows of only one type of land animal, while Leviticus is careful to distinguish three classes (domesticated animals, wild animals, and creeping things), paralleling the account in Genesis 1.[9] Second, Leviticus introduces the notion of things that swarm in the water (Lev. 11:10), a category mentioned in Genesis 1:20 but absent altogether in Deuteronomy. Third, while Deuteronomy uses the term *ṣipôr* (Deut. 14:11) for bird, Leviticus substitutes the word *ʿôp* (Lev. 11:13), the same word used in Genesis 1. Fourth, when Deuteronomy fails to mention the domain in which the animals live (Deut. 14:4), Leviticus is careful to spell this out (11:2), thereby emphasizing that the animals are divided into three distinct realms, an important concern of the creation story. Finally, Leviticus supplements Deuteronomy in such a way that the discussion of the wildlife appears to follow the order in which they were created in Genesis 1.[10]

On this reading, the creation story did not give rise to the dietary laws as Douglas seems to suggest. Rather, the priestly authors of Leviticus, in incorporating the dietary laws into their own system, attempted to link them to their creation account. This interpretation, incidentally, disposes of Alter's objection. Since the creation story did not actually give rise to the dietary laws, there will be animals that cannot be adequately explained in terms of the creation story. It is merely that the framers of Leviticus 11 interpreted the received rules in light of their understanding of creation.

This modification of Douglas's theory obviously fits well with the consensus among biblical scholars that the priestly author was responsible for both Genesis 1:1–2:4 and Leviticus. Douglas has unwittingly shown how one group's creation story supports and makes tenable one aspect of its larger religious world view. To be more specific, Douglas has discovered a close connection between the priests' understanding of creation and their theory of classification. Even a superficial reading of Leviticus shows that the priests conceive of classification as being an integral part of the religious life. Carrying out the divine will involves keeping things in their proper categories.

The importance of classification in Leviticus becomes understandable in light of the priestly creation story. According to that account, one important aspect of creation was the classification of the natural world (Snaith 1967, 89; Porter 1976, 93; Otzen et al. 1980, 27–28). God distinguished the light from darkness, the water below (the oceans) from the waters above (the sky), and the land from the waters. What we have here is a classic example of *imitatio Dei*. Just as God classified the world at creation, so God's holy people is expected to classify its world.

More specifically, Israel is expected to reaffirm and uphold the distinctions God implanted in the world at creation. This is expressed in a number of ways in Israelite law. Israelites must not (1) mate two kinds of cattle, (2) plant two species of grain in a single field, or (3) weave a garment of two kinds of material (Lev. 19:19), for in creating any of these mixtures, Israelites undermine the distinctions that God embedded in creation. By the same token, Leviticus conceives of certain sexual acts as unnatural because they threaten the order established at creation. Bestiality violates the separation God made between humans and animals (Lev. 18:23; Gen. 1:27–28). Homosexuality is unnatural because God created man and woman for each other (Lev. 18:22; Gen. 1:27). In observing the Sabbath, Israelites affirm a basic distinction between sacred and profane time, a distinction God also established at creation (Gen. 2:1–4). In the priestly writings, then, creation and classification go hand in hand. The creation story supplies a rationale both for the preoccupation with taxonomy in general and for many of the specific distinctions proposed in Leviticus (Douglas 1966; Soler 1979).

But there is an even deeper way in which creation and classification are linked in the priestly system. The two distinctive traits of the priests' taxonomy are themselves authorized by the priests' creation story. First, the general tendency of Leviticus is to categorize objects on the basis of their physical traits or characteristics. For example, the distinction between clean and unclean animals depends on the presence or absence of two features: whether the animal chews the cud and has split hooves (Lev. 11:2–8, 24). Only those animals which have both of these characteristics are considered clean and may be eaten. By the same token, aquatic life is deemed clean or unclean on the basis of whether it has fins and scales (Lev. 11:9–12). Again, a ready-made physical attribute of the animal is the sole criterion for classification. Blemishes on the body determine whether a priest can serve in the Temple and whether animals can be used for offerings (Lev. 21:16–23; 22:20–24). Finally, skin and hair color and the emission of bodily fluids determine whether a person's own body is unclean (Lev. 12–15).

The fact that the physical attributes of objects often serve as criteria for classification generates the second distinctive feature of the priestly taxonomy, namely, the fixed and unalterable character of its categories. By this I mean that all objects which share a specified set of physical traits fall into the same classification. It is inconceiveable that objects with identical characteristics could fall into opposing categories. Moreover, it is impossible for a given object to belong to different categories at different points in time, unless basic physical traits of the object undergo alteration. Thus an animal that chews its cud and has split hooves is by definition a clean animal.

The two characteristics of the priestly taxonomy are precisely those that one might expect to find in a system that links its classification scheme to God's activity at creation. In creating the world, God implanted distinct physical traits in objects so that Israel would be able to discriminate between them in the way that God wished. The physical characteristics are important, therefore, because they are concrete manifestations of divine will. In addition, the link between classification and creation may also explain the rigidity of the priestly scheme. Since the criteria of classification are fixed by God, no one has the power or right to tamper with them.

Given the close correspondence between creation and classification in the writings of the priests, we might expect any modification in taxonomic theory to involve a corresponding change in cosmogony. In other words, any group that finds the priests' classificatory system problematic will probably also distance itself from the priestly story of creation.

Such a symbolic disruption is at work in the writings of the early rabbis. In chapter 8, I discussed how the early rabbis, among other groups of Jews, introduced some major innovations into the priests' classificatory scheme. I now elaborate more fully on the differences between the priestly and rabbinic theories of classification and show how they entail a reconceptualization of creation as well.

Norms, Actions, and Intention: Rabbinic Criteria of Classification

The rabbinic dissatisfactions with the priestly method of classification are already evident in the Mishnah, the founding document of the rabbinic canon, written by sages living in the land of Israel ca. 200 C.E. In essence, the Mishnah is a handbook of rules which claims to present a systematic account of what it means to live a life in accordance with the divine will. The Mishnah's rules are elaborations and interpretations of scriptural laws, which provide the underpinnings for the system as a whole. In particular, the Mishnah is indebted in fundamental respects to the priestly writings of Scripture, taking up and elaborating on almost all of the topics that preoccupied the writers of Leviticus (Neusner 1981; 1983). In fact, the Mishnah devotes two of its six divisions to elaborating the laws of the Temple cult and laws of purity, both topics critical to Leviticus. In addition, the sages of the Mishnah absorb into their system the same preoccupation with classification that characterizes the writings of the priests.

Despite the Mishnah's substantial dependence on the writings of the priests, the method of classifying things differs in the two systems. While the Mishnah works with the same basic dichotomies that are found in the priestly writings (such as sacred and profane, clean and unclean), the Mishnah tends to categorize objects in its own distinctive way. As previously discussed (chapter 8), the physical traits of objects, though taken into consideration, recede into the background. Of far greater importance in the Mishnah's taxonomy are human activity and thought.[11] The Mishnah specifies three ways in which humans can affect the classification of things: through their actions (what individuals do with objects), through their intentions (what they intend to do with objects), and through the norms which are spontaneously generated by the community (what Israelites typically do with a given kind of object) (Eilberg-Schwartz 1986, 115–43).

Since the Mishnah makes the classification of objects dependent on human activity and thought, its taxonomy is more flexible and mobile than the priestly scheme of classification. The mishnaic scheme permits objects with the same physical traits to fall into different, even opposing categories, as may happen when two individuals intend to use identical objects for different purposes. The mishnaic and the priestly taxonomies, therefore, are in some respects mirror images of one another. The priestly scheme emphasizes the physical traits of objects and downplays and even ignores the role of humans in the classification scheme. The Mishnah reverses these criteria, making human activity and thought more decisive than an object's physical characteristics.

The distinction I am describing between the two taxonomies is not absolute. Examples are found in Leviticus that leave open the *possibility* that human activity and thought play a role in the classification scheme. Nonetheless, these statements are neither in the majority nor are they as fully conceptualized as they are in the Mishnah. By the same token, we find cases in the Mishnah in which an object's physical attributes play a more important role than human activity and thought. But this is principally due to the fact that the Mishnah accepted Leviticus as authoritative, and thus appropriated the criteria of classification that Leviticus proposed. Consequently, when Leviticus is clear about the criteria it considers important, the Mishnah adopts the same criteria.

The difference between the two taxonomies emerges precisely when the Mishnah is given room to maneuver as, for example, when the language of Leviticus is ambiguous or terse. In such cases, the Mishnah pushes in directions that are not only unpredictable from the priestly writings but are in tension in fundamental ways with the priestly point of view.

A striking example of this tendency is evident from the laws dealing with the types of objects that can become contaminated by impurity. The Mishnah follows Leviticus in making a categorical distinction between food and waste and between useful and useless things. The first item in each of these dichotomies (i.e., food and useful things) can become impure if it comes in contact with a source of impurity such as a dead, creeping thing. The other item in each pair (waste and useless objects), however, cannot be contaminated, even if it is brought in contact with a source of impurity. Leviticus formulates the rule this way: "And anything on which one [of the swarming things] falls when dead shall be unclean: be it any article of wood, or a cloth, or a skin, or a sack—any such article that can be put to use. . . . As to any food that may be eaten, it shall become unclean if it comes in contact with water [and then comes in contact with a swarming thing which has died]" (Lev. 11:32–34).

This is an example in which Leviticus does not spell out its criteria for classification. It does not explain what it means by "any article that may be put to use" or by "any food that may be eaten." Presumably, the authors of Leviticus conceive of these categories as self-evident and unproblematic.[12]

The Mishnah, however, seizes upon the reticence of the priestly text to advocate its own conception of taxonomy. According to the Mishnah, one determines whether an object is useful or useless, or whether a given substance is food or waste, by considering how individual Israelites use or intend to use a given object, and how the Israelite community as a whole tends to use such things (Eilberg-Schwartz 1986, 95–143).

The following rule illustrates how the Mishnah actually invokes these criteria in categorizing a specific object. In this passage, the sages consider whether an untanned leather hide falls under the rubric of a useful or a useless thing.

A. [Concerning untanned] hides belonging to a householder—the householder's intention to use them [places them into the category of useful things and hence] makes them susceptible to impurity.

B. But [concerning] the untanned hides belonging to a tanner—the tanner's intention to use them does not [place them into the category of useful things and hence does not] make them susceptible to impurity. (M. Kel 26:8)

This rule illustrates how an object's physical attributes are relatively unimportant in the Mishnah's taxonomy. Items with identical characteristics may potentially fall into opposing classes. An untanned hide in one context may be considered useful (i.e., when it belongs to a householder), whereas in another context it may be considered useless (i.e., if it belongs to a tanner). This is because the Mishnah shifts the criteria of classification from the traits of the object to human action and thought.

The classification of the hide differs when in the possession of tanners and householders because the Mishnah appeals to norms presumed to exist among persons of these occupations. The sages take for granted that tanners generally use leather of a superior quality, and hence do not put untanned hides to use. Consequently, while in the possession of a tanner, an unfinished hide is automatically defined as useless (B).[13] There is, however, an ambiguity in the classification of a hide in the possession of a householder. Some householders use unfinished hides, others do not. Since there are conflicting practices among householders, the sages make the object's classification dependent on the intention of the householder who owns the leather in question. If he intends to use it, it falls under the rubric of useful things, while the intention to discard it places it into the category of useless things.

The tendency of the Mishnah to rely on social norms and human intentions signals an important departure from the taxonomy of the priests. To be sure, one might argue that the Mishnah is merely elaborating on what Leviticus means when it says that "anything that may be used" is susceptible to impurity. It is true that the Mishnah is providing a plausible interpretation of these words. Yet given the overall thrust of the levitical taxonomy—with its emphasis on the physical traits of objects—it seems doubtful that the priests would have been comfortable with the Mishnah's attempt to subordinate the physical characteristics of objects to human action and thought.

Moreover, in stressing the importance of humans in the classification scheme, the Mishnah comes into conflict with the priests' desire to link their taxonomy to God's activity at creation. According to the priestly conception, humans merely uphold distinctions God had already implanted in the world and have no independent role in determining the makeup of each category. In the Mishnah, by contrast, humans have a degree of autonomy and power in determining the categories into which various objects fall. In effect, the Mishnah severs or at the very least weakens the link between the classification scheme and God's activity at creation.

The following passage illustrates this tendency within the mishnaic system. The case concerns an Israelite who ritually slaughters a pregnant cow and finds a placenta inside the carcass. Here the sages discuss whether the placenta is food and hence susceptible to impurity, or whether it is waste and immune to contamination. But the sages recognize two competing definitions of food: a divine conception of food and a human one. Significantly, it is the human definition, not God's, that determines whether the placenta in question is susceptible to impurity!

A. [Concerning an Israelite] who slaughters an animal [according to the correct procedure] and finds a placenta within it—
B. a person with a strong stomach may eat it.
C. [Nonetheless, it falls into the category of waste, with the result that it] cannot absorb food impurity.
D. If [however, the slaughterer] intended [to eat] it [before carrying out the slaughter—the placenta falls into the category of food with the result that it] is susceptible to impurity. (M. Hul. 4:7)

According to this rule, Israelites may eat a placenta found in the carcass of a properly slaughtered animal if they wish to do so (A–B). In saying this, the sages indicate their view that God considers a placenta to be legitimate food for Israelites. Otherwise, the sages would certainly prohibit Israelites from eating such a substance. But God's classification of a placenta does not necessarily determine its taxonomic status. This is evident from the fact that the

Mishnah does not consider it to be susceptible to impurity (C). In fact, unless the slaughterer actually intends to eat the placenta, it falls under the rubric of waste. The sages base the classification of the placenta on the normal behavior of Israelites. They know that Israelites typically consider a placenta to be a repulsive substance and thus do not usually eat it. In defining a placenta as waste, therefore, the Mishnah is in effect claiming that human definitions of food are more important than God's in determining whether something is susceptible to impurity. Although God considers a placenta to be food, its classification is ultimately dependent on what the Israelite community actually does.

This case illustrates how far the Mishnah has pushed beyond the priestly conceptions. In making human activity and thought decisive criteria for classification, the Mishnah claims that God's own categorizations are sometimes irrelevant. This is a long way from the priestly view that the classifications of reality hearken back to creation itself.

Having shown that the Mishnah revises the conception of classification in Leviticus, we might expect to find reverberations of this change in the Mishnah's understanding of creation. After all, as Douglas has shown, the priests' theory of classification was justified by and rooted in their own particular conception of creation. Once the classification scheme is fundamentally altered, the priestly story of creation may also be problematic. A story about God implanting distinctions in the world at creation does not mesh with a theory of classification that gives humans an important role in shaping the categories. In what follows, I will try to show that the sages of the Mishnah did in fact distance themselves from the priests' understanding of creation.

Creation and Classification in the Mishnah

Unlike the priests, the sages of the Mishnah did not write their own creation story but accepted as authoritative what Scripture said about creation. The priestly story of creation, however, is not the only account of the creation recorded in the Bible. Scripture contains another story of creation (Genesis 2:4b–24) which has a different focus and point of view. The sages of the Mishnah, therefore, had before them two stories of creation which were, at least in theory, equally authoritative. In reading these two stories together, the sages in effect produced a new understanding of creation that corresponded to their own distinctive conception of classification.

Since the sages do not explicitly spell out their cosmogony, we can only infer it indirectly by showing how the biblical stories of creation shaped mishnaic thought and language. It is readily apparent that the priestly story of creation exerted an influence on the sages of the Mishnah. The Mishnah cites this story a number of times to justify certain rulings and to support certain theological propositions.[14]

More importantly, there is evidence that the priestly cosmogony directly
influenced the conception of taxonomy which underlies the Mishnah's
system of purity. There are, for example, striking conceptual similarities between the priests' story of creation and the mishnaic ideas about
classification:

> When God began to create the heaven and the earth. . . . God said, "Let there
> be light;" and there was light. God saw that the light was good, and God sepa-
> rated the light from the darkness. God called the light Day, and the darkness
> God called Night. God made the expanse, and separated the water which was
> below the expanse from the water which was above the expanse. And it was so.
> God called the expanse Sky. . . . God said "Let the water below the sky be gath-
> ered into one area that the dry land may appear." And it was so. God called the
> dry land Earth, and the gathering of waters Seas (Genesis 1:1–9).

This story conceives of the act of classifying as being instrumental in determining the character of the world. According to the priests, God separated
light from darkness, the heavens above from the waters below, and dry land
from the seas. The divine act of classification, therefore, is what gives the
world its texture. This creation myth anticipates the mishnaic idea that classification plays a fundamental role in determining the character of objects. As
we have seen, the Mishnah claims that when the classification of an object is
altered, one of its most basic properties changes as well, namely, its ability to
withstand or absorb contamination. According to the Mishnah, a change in
an object's classification has important practical ramifications. Once the object enters the category of food and can be contaminated, people must go out
of their way to keep it from coming in contact with sources of impurity. In
both the priestly story of creation and the Mishnah, classification plays a fundamental role in shaping reality.

To be sure, conceptual similarities by themselves do not prove that the
priestly story of creation was actually paradigmatic for the classification
scheme which underlies the mishnaic laws of purity. However, in two passages the Mishnah explicitly links its system of impurity to God's activity at
creation. In the first, the Mishnah cites a dispute between two sages over
whether the sea can serve as an immersion pool for the purposes of cleansing a
person from impurity (M. Miq. 5:4; M. Par. 8:8). In rabbinic Hebrew, an
immersion pool is called a *miqěwēh*. One sage cites Genesis 1:10 as proof that
the sea can serve such a purpose. In that passage, God calls "the gathering"
(*miqěwēh*) of water "seas." According to this sage, since God classified the
seas as a *miqěwēh*, they can serve as an immersion pool (*miqěwēh*) for the purposes of ritual purification. This source thus claims that God's act of naming
at creation is linked to the distinctions which govern the sages' own system of
purity.

The Mishnah also claims that the materials which are susceptible to impurity were created on alternate days of creation:

On the first day [of creation] something was created which is susceptible to impurity [when made into a vessel], but on the second day of creation [nothing was created] which is susceptible to impurity. On the third day [of creation], something was created which is susceptible to impurity, but on the fourth and fifth days, nothing [was created] that is susceptible to impurity. . . . Everything that was created on the sixth day of creation is susceptible to impurity. (M. Kel. 17:14)

In seeking to link the type of material which is susceptible to impurity to the creation story, the Mishnah in effect claims that God's act of ordering the world is directly related to the classifications which govern the Mishnah's system of impurity. By distinguishing things which can and cannot absorb impurity, Israelites carry forward a basic distinction that God implanted in the world at creation. These two passages, therefore, demonstrate a direct connection between the priestly story of creation and the mishnaic understanding of classification.

Nonetheless, one aspect of the Mishnah's theory finds no justification in the priestly cosmogony: the idea that human activity and thought serve as criteria for classifying things. By implication, the Mishnah equates the human capacity to classify with the divine work of creation. Human acts of categorization, like God's, have the power to change basic properties of objects. This perspective is by no means implied by the priestly conception of creation. On the contrary, the priests believed that God established the membership of the various categories and humans merely reaffirm the distinctions which God had made. The sages of the Mishnah, however, found ample warrant for their view in the other biblical story of creation, which is attributed to the Yahwist (Genesis 2:4b–24). "And the Lord God formed out of the earth all the wild beasts and all the birds of the sky, and brought them to the man to see what he would call them; and whatever the man called each living creature, that would be its name. And the man gave names to all the cattle and to the birds of the sky and to all the wild beasts" (Gen. 2:19–20).

The similarities between this story and the Mishnah's theory of classification are self-evident. This passage conceives of Adam as acting like God by bringing order out of chaos (von Rad 1976, 82–83; Cassuto 1969, 86; Otzen et al. 1980, 41, 44; Westermann 1984, 228–29). By giving names to the animals, Adam completes the work of creation, labeling and thereby distinguishing one type of animal from another. Adam, of course, is the prototype for humanity. Like the Mishnah, this story conceives of the human capacity to classify as being analogous to the divine power to create the world through an exercise of divine will.

This story anticipates the Mishnah in a second important respect: the Israelite idea of naming is conceptually similar to the Mishnah's understanding of classification. In Israelite thought, a name is intimately connected to and perhaps even determinative of the character of the thing named (von Rad

1976, 53, 83; Cassuto 1969, 15; Westermann 1984, 87). This is why Israelite writers represent a change in a person's character by changing his or her name. The priestly writers, for example, suggest that God changed Abram's and Sarai's names to Abraham and Sarah to reflect the fact that a covenant had been made with them, and thus to signal a basic alteration in their character. Since a name is intimately connected to the character of the thing to which it refers, knowing the name of something represents understanding it and thus having control over it. For this reason, in several biblical stories an angel refuses to reveal its name to a human being, signifying that the angel has not relinquished control or power to the person in question (Gen. 32:30; Judg. 13:17–18). That God asks Adam to name the animals implies that God confers on humanity the power to define the character of wildlife and thus master it. This is precisely the kind of claim that the Mishnah makes about human acts of classification. By designating an object for one use rather than another, a person in effect determines that object's character.

The Mishnah does not explicitly cite the Jahwist's story of creation in any of its laws. However, the Mishnah's debt to this story is evident in the terminology that the Mishnah uses in articulating its classification scheme. The Mishnah frequently refers to classifying objects as "calling them a name" (*lqrt šm*) (M. Dem. 4:3; 4:4; 7:6; M. Ter. 3:5; 5:1; M. M.S. 4:4; 5:9; M. Pes. 3:3). This is precisely the same expression that is used in the biblical passage about Adam's naming of the animals. According to Genesis 2, God brought the animals to Adam "to see what he would call them; and whatever the man called each living creature, that would be its name. And the man gave [lit., called] names (*wayyiqěrā' šēmôt*) to all the cattle and the birds of the sky and to all the wild beasts." The Mishnah also uses the biblical word "name" (*šēm*) to mean "category." For example, when two objects do not belong to the same category, the Mishnah says that they do not derive from the [same] name (*'enô min hašēm*) (M. Ker. 3:4; M. Mak. 3:9). The fact that the Mishnah appropriates language from Genesis 2 supports the claim that this creation myth provides part of the conceptual underpinnings for the Mishnah's understanding of taxonomy.

The Mishnah's revision of the priestly theory of classification thus involves the emergence of a broader conception of creation. By itself the priestly story of creation cannot provide a legitimation of the new theory of classification which the Mishnah articulates. Indeed, Genesis 1 threatens to undermine the Mishnah's claims by portraying the constituent categories of the world as being set in place by God at creation. But Scripture supplies a second story of creation which claims that God commissioned Adam to complete the work of creation by categorizing the world into its constituent categories. In this story of creation, the Mishnah finds ample warrant for its view that humans play a role in classifying the world and thus in shaping their own reality.

In the previous chapter, I argued that the differences between the priestly and rabbinic theories of classification were homologous to the ways those communities determined the status of individuals. Clearly, this same line of analysis is equally applicable to the differences in their conceptions of creation. In the priests' ontology, everything has a clearly defined place that God determined at creation itself. This notion is analogous to the priests' conception of the priesthood as a hereditary office passed on to all of Aaron's descendants. Just as the status of objects is fixed by God at creation, so a priest's status is determined by procreation. For the sages, by contrast, the title of "rabbi" was not conferred by birth but was the result of discipleship to a sage. Since their own status was not fixed, they did not find plausible the idea that God had established all classifications for all times at the creation of the world. The shifts in taxonomy and cosmogony are both linked to the decreasing importance of descent as an element in the self-understanding and organization of the rabbinic community.

From Procreation to the Genealogy and Reproduction of Knowledge

There is one final symbolism that we might expect to have been disrupted when the priestly system was appropriated by the early rabbis, namely, the themes of procreation and genealogy. As previously argued, these themes were central to the self-understanding of the priestly community. When descent ceased to dominate the cultural system, as occurred in the early rabbinic community, these themes became a kind of symbolic surplus. Hence, they were available to be appropriated for other purposes.

That is not to say that the sages did not share the priests' concern for procreation and genealogy. They repeat, for example, the priestly injunction that people must multiply and procreate (M. Yeb. 6:6). But far more interesting is the way in which these symbolic concerns are transferred to Torah study and Torah knowledge.[15]

Torah literally means "instruction" and refers in rabbinic sources to Scripture and the accompanying traditions of interpretation received and produced in the rabbinic community. As Torah study emerged as the paradigmatic religious act for early rabbis, it absorbed the symbolic capital which the priests had invested in human procreation. In other words, concerns about reproduction and transmission are shifted from the human body to Torah knowledge itself. Safrai (1987, 69), who is writing with other issues in mind, inadvertently makes this point for me. As he puts it, the aspiration of the sage was "to disseminate Torah and raise many disciples, to inspire every person to realize his right and duty 'to make Torah increase,' and to encourage the asking of questions." For the rabbis, the reproduction of Torah knowledge and clear lines of Torah dissemination are of paramount concern. This symbolism is to some extent evident in the Mishnah and even clearer in Avot, the first sustained rabbinic work on the meaning of Torah study (third century C.E.). It becomes even clearer in some later rabbinic sources.

Already in the earliest rabbinic sources there is a recognized analogy between teacher-disciple and father-son relationships. Consequently, obligations are generalized from the biological to the educational relationship. I already cited an example of this transference in the previous chapter. The Mishnah rules that a man's obligation to his teacher supersedes his obligation to his father. If his father and teacher are both in captivity, he must redeem his teacher before his father. If he finds the lost property of both his father and teacher, or if his father and teacher are both struggling with a load, the obligations to the teacher take precedence. This is because his father brought him into this world, while his teacher brings him into the world to come (M. B.M. 2:11; Ker. 6:9). In later rabbinic writings, the analogy becomes still more explicit. Sages sometime refer to a disciple as "my son." Scriptural references to "your children" are interpreted as references to "your disciples" (Aberbach 1976, 202). It is possible, although by no means possible to prove, that the term "rabbi" (rabbî) (my teacher/my master) was connected in the sages' imagination with the term for "my father" ('abî). Such attentiveness to the phonetic interconnections among Hebrew words was common in later rabbinic culture (Eilberg-Schwartz 1987a) and is a widely exploited cultural phenomenon.

In any case, the analogy between disciples and sons is what enabled the symbolism of reproduction and genealogy to be extended from kinship to Torah-ties. Just as a son must perpetuate his father's lineage, a disciple must preserve his rabbi's teaching and transmit it without contamination to posterity. The genealogy of Torah knowledge is thus reminiscent and perhaps imitative of the priestly genealogies. "Moses received the Torah from Sinai and transmitted it to Joshua, and Joshua to the elders, and the elders to the Prophets, and the Prophets transmitted it to the men of the Great Assembly" (Avot 1:1). "The chain of tradition is direct, specific, and, in context, genealogical. Just as the priests validate their standing through their family records, so Patriarchs and sages validate their standing—their Torah tradition—through the record of who received, and who handed on, that Torah tradition" (Neusner 1986b, 55). This concern with Torah genealogy manifests itself in the rabbinic concern with attributions. Nearly every passage of the Mishnah contains an attribution of some statement to some sage. Moreover, we already find incipient in the Mishnah an interest in more elaborate genealogies: "Said Rabbi Joshua, 'I received [the preceding tradition] from Rabban Yohanan ben Zakkai, who heard it from his teacher, and his teacher from his teacher, a norm from Moses on Sinai' " (M. Eduy. 8:7; M. Yad. 4:3). In postmishnaic works, this reckoning of Torah genealogy develops more fully. Typical is the expression "Said Rabbi so-and-so in (bĕ) [the name of] Rabbi so-and-so." It is interesting that the word "the name of" (bĕšēm) often drops out of this expression. When it does, the Hebrew is reminiscent of the expression "Rabbi so-and-so *son* of (bēn) so-and-so," as if to suggest an affinity between the disciple-sage and father-son relationships.

Just as the priests were concerned that their sons keep their lines genealogically pure, the sages expected their disciples to preserve the purity of the Torah transmission. "Be wary of your words lest you incur exile and are exiled to a place of evil waters and the students who follow you drink and die, and the Name of Heaven be profaned" (Avot 1:11). This commitment to adequate transmission means that outdated terminology is sometimes preserved because "a man must use the language of his teacher" (M. Eduy. 1:3). The sages' obsessive concern about the loss of Torah knowledge is reminiscent of the priests' worries about the waste of semen. One who forgets a single matter of what he has learned or one who interrupts his memorization of Torah to admire a blossoming tree is compared to a person who has committed a capital offense (Avot 3:7, 8). One sage is praised for never losing a drop of Torah (Avot 2:8). It is hard to miss the association between "a drop" of Torah and "a drop" of semen, which is referred to by the same document several passages later (Avot 3:1).

The emphasis on biological reproduction, a central concern of the priests, is appropriated in two different ways in the rabbinic community. To begin with, sages are expected to produce numerous disciples. The men of the great assembly are reported to have advised men to "be deliberate in judgment, raise up many disciples, and make a fence around the Torah" (Avot 1:1). The Tosefta, a work that may postdate the Mishnah, suggests that the title of "sage" is itself predicated on one's disciples being remembered. "If a scholar has disciples and disciples of disciples, he is quoted as Rabbi; if his direct disciples are forgotten, he is quoted as Rabban; if both are forgotten, he is quoted by his name" (T. Eduy. 3:4). It is as if the title "rabbi" is authorized by the production of a genealogy. Just as a man who has not produced children cannot be a "father," so a man who does not have memorable disciples cannot be a "rabbi."

In addition to this form of reproduction, the sages were also expected to multiply and increase Torah knowledge. The Tractate Avot makes explicit this reproductive obligation. "One who does not increase [Torah knowledge] decreases it. One who does not learn is worthy of death" (Avot 1:13). It is important to note that the word for increasing Torah (*marĕbeh*) derives from the stem *rbh*, the same stem that is used in the priestly formulation of the requirement that humans be fruitful and multiply (*rĕbu*) (Gen 1:28). The term for "rabbi" also derives from this same stem. It is difficult to believe that the sages might have missed these connections, given their attentiveness to this sort of linguistic association (Eilberg-Schwartz 1987a, 765–88) and given the repetitiveness with which tractate Avot uses the words "rabbi" and "increase." The responsibility of increasing Torah is thus implied by the very title "rabbi," linguistically indicating that the task of reproducing Torah is at the center of what it means to be a rabbi.[16]

Torah production, then, is the symbolic and spiritual equivalent of biological reproduction. The sages seem to have been conscious of this analogy as is evident in the earlier citation concerning a man's obligations to his teacher. Those obligations supersede the obligations to a father because, as the sages put it, "one's father brought one into this world, but a sage brings one into the world to come" (M. B.M. 2:11). In addition to the analogy between birth and rebirth, which is explicit here, there is an implicit comparison between procreation and Torah study. One's biological father brought one into this world through sexual intercourse, but one's teacher brings one into the next world through Torah study. Sexual relations are to birth as Torah study is to rebirth. Whereas for the priests perpetuity was ensured by reproduction, for the sages Torah study served that function. "The more Torah the more life. . . . One who acquires words of Torah acquires life in the world to come" (Avot 2:7).

This symbolic equation of Torah study with reproduction becomes even more explicit in later rabbinic sources. A tale is told of R. Jonathan who was accompanied by an ass-driver on his pilgrimage to Jerusalem (GR 32:10). Along the way, Jonathan was accosted by a Samaritan who challenged him to explain why Jonathan should pray at Jerusalem rather than at Mount Gerizim, the sacred Samaritan mountain. When Jonathan forgot the appropriate answer, his ass-driver interceded and properly answered the Samaritan. This event enabled Jonathan to grasp the significance of God's promise that "there shall not be male or female barren among you, or among your cattle" (Deut. 7:14). In this verse, Jonathan concluded, cattle is a metaphor for cattle drivers. What is interesting about this story for the present discussion is the way that a biblical reference to "barrenness" is understood metaphorically as a lack of knowledge. The ass-driver's ability to answer the Samaritan's question indicated that he was not barren but fertile with divine wisdom. Torah knowledge is for the rabbis the really significant kind of fertility.

The idea that Torah study serves as a kind of symbolic act of reproduction suggests why Torah study may have been in tension with sexuality. In the passage cited earlier, for example, the observation that "the more Torah the more life" is contrasted with the observation that "the more flesh the more worms" (Avot 2:7). This tension is possible precisely because the rabbis have distanced themselves from the priestly preoccupation with biological reproduction. For the priests, the flesh was at the core of the covenant: God had promised that Abraham's descendants would increase and multiply. Sexual intercourse was thus the means by which Israelites could fulfill their end of the covenantal bargain. This is why the priests stressed circumcision as the sign of the covenant, when other Israelite writers had never made that connection explicit. As noted above, the rabbis do not entirely repudiate these concerns. But in shifting the symbolism of genealogy and procreation to the Torah community, the flesh ceased to be the sole instrument of propagation. The rabbis, in other words, created a form of reproduction that could dispense with the flesh.

It was also a form of reproduction that could do without women. Women, we recall, had presented a particular problem to the priests. On the one hand, the priests' desire to emphasize patrilineal descent led them to stress the connection of males to one another and to devalue and minimize women's roles in reproduction; hence the negative evaluation of blood shed during the birthing process. On the other hand, women were obviously needed to reproduce, which was one of the central concerns in the priestly religious system. The priests, therefore, could not live with women and they could not live without them. But in the rabbinic form of reproduction women were altogether dispensable. Males could now reproduce homosexually. If husbands inseminated women, sages disseminated Torah to their male students. As noted above, a good disciple is one who never loses "a drop" (Avot 2:8). The relationship between sage and disciple thus competes with that between husband and wife. Women become the very antithesis of Torah and Torah study. "Do not talk overly much with a woman. The sages made the preceding statement in reference to a man's wife. All the more so with respect to another man's wife. On this basis the sages ruled, 'Whenever a man talks overly much with a woman, he causes evil to himself, he neglects Torah study, and will inherit Gehenna [hell]' " (Avot 1:5). To be sure, the sages continue to recognize the sexual urge of both men and women. Indeed, the rabbis believe that scriptural law guarantees men and women sexual satisfaction in marriage (Exod. 21:10 [M. Ket. 5:6–7]). But this biological urge actually disrupts the more important reproductive enterprise of Torah learning. Sages, along with other kinds of workers, are given special dispensations relieving them of the obligation to have intercourse (M. Ket. 5:6).

Given the transference of reproductive and genealogical symbolism from the body to the community of learning, it is not surprising that trees and especially fruit trees become symbols of Torah. We recall that for the priests and other Israelite writers fruit trees had symbolized human fecundity. This is one of the reasons the priests had seen a connection between the male organ and fruit trees (chapter 6). But already in Israelite wisdom literature, the tree had become a symbol of wisdom. "Happy is the man who finds wisdom, the man who attains understanding. . . . She is a tree of life to those who grasp her, and whoever holds on to her is happy" (Prov. 3:13, 18). "Happy is the man who has not followed the counsel of the wicked . . . the teaching of the Lord is his delight and he studies that teaching day and night. He is like a tree planted beside streams of water, that yields its fruit in season, whose foliage never fades, and whatever it produces thrives" (Ps. 1:1–3). This symbolic association continues in rabbinic literature. In the story of the ass-driver cited above, Jonathan compares the wise ass-driver to a pomegranate split open. A man with wisdom is like a pomegranate full of seeds. "Just as a plant bears fruit and multiplies, so the words of Torah bear fruit and multiply" (T. Sot. 7:11; P. Sot. 3; P. Hag. 1; B. Sot. 3a). A later source considers why "the words of the Torah are likened to the fig tree. The more one searches in it, the more figs he finds. Thus are the words of the Torah, the more one studies them, the more wisdom one finds" (B. Erub. 54a).

In sum, a number of symbolic differences between the priestly and rabbinic communities are linked to the decreasing preoccupation with reproduction and the increasing interest in Torah propagation. While the priests understood themselves as descendants of Aaron, the rabbis stressed that they were "students of Aaron" (Avot 1:12; 5:19). Thus the priestly office was given by birth, but the "knowledge of Torah is not yours by inheritance" (Avot 2:12). In contrast to the priests who projected the obligation to procreate back into the story of creation (Gen. 1:28), the rabbis claimed that one who studies a great deal of Torah should "not claim any merit, for you were created for this purpose" (Avot 2:8). Torah study and knowledge thus performed for the rabbis the function that reproduction fulfilled in the priestly community. As this substitution took place, the concern with a lineage of male descendants was displaced by the preoccupation with the reproduction and genealogy of knowledge.

CONCLUSION

❧

Savaging Judaism

Anthropology of Judaism as Cultural Critique

> The anthropologist is the less able to ignore his own civiliza-
> tion and to dissociate himself from its faults in that his very
> existence is incomprehensible except as an attempt at re-
> demption: he is the symbol of atonement.
>
> Lévi-Strauss 1975

In a profound essay on the nature of anthropology, Lévi-Strauss (1975, 383–93) ponders the contradictions involved in being a critic at home and a conformist abroad. In particular, he points to the paradox that the anthropologist feels obliged to respect those characteristics of other societies that she or he would find intolerable at home. "While often inclined to subversion among his own people and in revolt against traditional behaviour, the anthropologist appears respectful to the point of conservatism as soon as he is dealing with a society different from his own" (1975, 383). This apparent contradiction, Lévi-Strauss suggests, can be justified as a kind of moral imperative. "However, by getting to know them better, we are enabled to detach ourselves from our own society. Not that our own society is peculiarly or absolutely bad. But it is the only one from which we have a duty to free ourselves" (1975, 392).

This understanding of anthropology is misleading in a revealing sort of way. If anthropological inquiry is a means of turning the critical gaze home-ward, then why have anthropologists been so noticeably reluctant to treat Judaism as a legitimate subject of anthropological inquiry? This blind spot points to a basic contradiction within anthropology itself: in the very process of dismantling the opposition between savage religions and others, the disci-pline of anthropology has inadvertently helped to perpetuate it.

Anthropology, we recall, was born in the late nineteenth century as a discipline dedicated to the study of primitive religion and culture. In the twentieth century anthropologists have successfully challenged the very assumptions that gave rise to the primitive as a distinctive object of inquiry. But the effects of that dichotomy had already found institutional support. Anthropologists continued to study "small face-to-face societies" while interpreters of Judaism and other "world" religions generally ignored anthropology. As long as anthropological inquiry was reserved only for others, the very difference that anthropology was purportedly calling into question was itself preserved. The anthropological study of Judaism is thus the logical culmination of a relativist critique which has been so reluctant to turn its critical gaze on traditions at home.

Turning the anthropological gaze on Israelite religion and ancient Judaism is therefore a political act. It represents an attempt to do away once and for all with the effects of the old dichotomy between savage religions and Judaism. No longer is it tolerable that different kinds of discourses be reserved for different religious traditions. The allocation of some traditions to anthropology and others to history or religious studies is simply a survival of earlier prejudices that once sorted traditions into the categories of savagery and civilization.

The insistence on subjecting Judaism to an inquiry historically developed to understand "savages" thus denies the claim that there is an unbridgeable gap between Judaism and "savage" religions. Equally important, the Judaism that is seen under the anthropological lens is a Judaism different from the one so often popularized in modern discourses on religion. What formerly were construed as traits of savage traditions are now discovered at the heart of Judaism. Totemism, for example, is no longer just a phenomenon of primitive religions. Israelite religion had its own form of totemism (chapter 5). As in "primitive" societies, animals provided the foundational metaphors through which Israelites articulated their understanding of who they were and what they wanted to be. These metaphors, which provided an idiom for theological, national, and social reflections, fundamentally shaped the practices of Israelite religion. Fertility, procreation, and reproduction are other themes that have frequently been associated with primitive religions. Consequently, these themes are typically ignored or downplayed by interpreters of ancient Israel, even though they were critical to the conception of the covenant between Israel and God and were embodied in a number of practices including circumcision (chapter 6), the rules governing bodily emissions (chapter 7), and Torah study (chapter 9).

The anthropological gaze has another related effect on the perception of Israelite religion and ancient Judaism. Because of its historical association with primitive and hence "low" traditions, anthropological inquiry has developed a special gift for dealing with "low" culture.[1] Low culture refers to the symbolic processes surrounding activities closely connected with the body (e.g., eating, sexual relations, and digestive and excretory functions). Such activities are often devalued because of this connection. But Douglas (1966; 1975; 1979) has shown how metaphysical ideas are often encoded in subtle distinctions governing mundane practices such as eating. Lévi-Strauss (1969; 1973; 1978) has drawn attention to the deep connections between different symbolic orders including eating, sex, and cooking. Turner (1967) has pointed out how ritual often unites the abstract themes of social life with the sensory and physiological processes of the human body. Anthropology, in other words, has an elaborate theoretical apparatus for dealing with these concerns of the "nether" world.

Yet it is precisely this attention to low culture that interpreters of Israelite religion and ancient Judaism have so often ignored. Discussions of Judaism tend to deal with the soaring and abstract matters of theology and pay little attention to how those themes are embodied in practice or symbolized in metaphor, let alone pay attention to more mundane themes themselves. Whether this is because Christianity has always been the implicit other to which Judaism is compared, or because higher religions are not expected to have lower cultures, is not entirely clear. Perhaps interpreters have been misled by the tradition they are studying: if humans are made in God's image and God has "no-body"—neither others with whom to interact nor a fully conceptualized or functioning body with which to do it—then the functions of copulation, reproduction, digestion, and excretion are irrelevant. But when Judaism is passed under the anthropological lens these lower orders become accessible and interesting. The parallel between prohibitions on cooking and incest (chapter 5) represents the kind of discovery that becomes possible. Similarly, the associations between the male member and membership in Israel, the connection between circumcision and the pruning of fruit trees (chapter 6), and the symbolic distinctions encoded in body fluids (chapter 7) are all insights made available when practices related to the body are attended to and understood as symbolically constituted. The anthropological study of Judaism treats Judaism not just as theology but as culture: as a complex set of intersecting symbolic domains that deal with the full range of human experience. Israelites and Jews had bodies: they ate, excreted, copulated, and reproduced and their experiences of their bodies were part and parcel of their religious cultures.

The notion of a religious culture as a multiplicity of symbolic domains also turns attention to the implicit meanings generated when these various domains interact and compete. The meanings of one order are always constituted through metaphorical borrowings from another. God is a shepherd; Israel the flock. Juvenile fruit trees are uncircumcised. Israel is a menstruous woman. Such meanings, which are produced as various domains interpenetrate, are not necessarily consciously grasped by members of a given culture. When religion is understood as culture, and not simply as theology or history, these unverbalized and sometimes unconscious meanings become the prime focus of attention.

When the conception of Judaism as religious culture takes hold, the old approaches will cease to be satisfying. Comparative inquiry will become much more central in the attempts to reconstruct the religious culture of ancient Jews. Historical anthropology of this sort is a reconstructive art. It is an attempt, on the basis of certain ideas about what religious cultures are and how they work, to imagine what the religious culture of a specific people might have been like. But since in studying Israelites and ancient Jews we cannot question the natives, we must imagine those larger wholes from the fragmentary remains that are left behind. The only controls over the flight of imagination are sensitive readings of ancient texts, attention to archaeological evidence, and a familiarity with religious cultures in other times and other places.

It is this last requirement that has been so frequently ignored or denigrated. Indeed, the negative attitude toward comparative inquiry among interpreters of Israelite religion and ancient Judaism is itself a product of that same dichotomy that is being called into question by this project. The desire to deny the similarities between ancient Judaism and primitive religions encouraged interpreters to denounce the comparative method as a problematic interpretive tool. That attitude toward comparative inquiry became an unquestioned axiom, accepted by subsequent interpreters who might not have agreed with its political implications had they thought about them. To put it simply, one who is against comparison is in favor of preserving the dichotomy between Judaism and savage religions. No matter what the reasons might be for rejecting cross-cultural comparisons, the effect of that rejection is to reproduce this pernicious opposition that has been perpetuated in modern discourse. Those who are against this opposition have no choice but to encourage an anthropology of Judaism, an inquiry that embraces comparisons cross-culturally.

But it is not just on political grounds that comparisons are necessary. An understanding of Judaism as a religious culture necessitates cultivating sensitivities that can only be developed through exposure to a variety of cultures in a wide range of contexts. This process of "enculturation" alerts interpreters to clues that would otherwise go unnoticed. A clue is a clue only for someone who already has suspicions about what to find. Like detectives, interpreters of historical cultures are better equipped to decipher cultural traces the more exposure they have to different kinds of cases. Like other interpreters, I would not have known what to make of the metaphor of "uncircumcised fruit trees" had I not been familiar with similar symbolism surrounding circumcision in other traditions. Nor would it have occurred to me that slicing an animal in half might have more significance than simply creating a covenant had I not read Evans-Pritchard's ethnography of the Nuer. The Nuer, as Evans-Pritchard suggests, perform similar kinds of acts to symbolize ruptures in their genealogies (chapter 6). Had I not learned from Lévi-Strauss that ritual sometimes remedies a situation by symbolically reversing it, I never would have understood the significance of intentionally producing male menstrual fluid to decontaminate a person from corpse pollution (chapter 7). Finally, knowing how important animal metaphors are in other religious cultures led me to look for their presence in Israelite literature. Despite my familiarity with this literature, I had never considered how abundant such metaphors were, let alone what their implications might be.

Comparative inquiry thus has a number of important functions above and beyond its political implications. It serves as a kind of substitute for native exegesis. Since we cannot ask ancient priests why they described juvenile fruit trees as "uncircumcised," we must imagine how they might have responded and what meanings they presupposed that they did not verbalize. One way of doing this is by seeing what others at other times and other places have said about related matters. This procedure, of course, cannot be falsified, but it is the only technique available to aid our imagination. The exposure to other cultures alerts interpreters to clues that might otherwise have escaped notice or been misinterpreted and provides interpreters with an awareness of what cultures are and how they work. That awareness makes them ask questions that have not been asked before and suggests answers that others may never have imagined.

In these various sorts of ways, the anthropological study of Judaism is an enterprise of cultural criticism. It takes as its premise that the sharp distinctions that once supported the dichotomy between Judaism and savage religions are problematic. That assumption allows similarities to savage traditions to emerge and the baser sides of Judaism to be explored. The analysis in turn validates the premises from which the inquiry springs. Furthermore, it makes the concept of culture, with all of its rich implications, central to interpretation.

The anthropology of Judaism thus radicalizes the critical role once assigned to the historical study of Judaism. In the nineteenth century, the subjection of Judaism to the historical gaze constituted a fundamental break with modes of perception that had previously dominated the tradition, and it unleashed a critique that had profound implications for how Judaism was conceptualized and practiced. As radical as the historical study of Judaism was and is, it pales in comparison to the anthropological study of Judaism. History, as the intervening centuries have shown, can make its peace with the privileging impulse that wishes to treat Judaism as unique but not other. After all, history as a mode of analysis has often been justified as an idiographic enterprise that captures the distinctive and nonrepetitive developments of some given people or tradition. Consequently, the historical study of Judaism did not contest the purported difference between savage religions and Judaism nor did it question the understanding of religion that associated it so closely with theology and other matters of high culture. For these reasons, anthropology releases a more savage critique. In addition to questioning the uniqueness of Judaism, it draws attention to the baser sides of this cultural tradition. Jews have frequently been presented as a "People of the Book." But it would be equally appropriate to describe them as a "People of the Body." The former description emphasizes the life of the mind and the importance of learning within the tradition. But at the same time it diverts attention from the fact that those books, which were of such obsessive interest, were deeply concerned about the body and other equally mundane matters. The anthropology of Judaism thus allows Judaism to be embodied even if its God is not.

Furthermore, this critique, which is generated by turning the anthropological gaze on Judaism, is fully at home in the postfoundational setting of contemporary discourse. At a time when the objectivity of the social sciences has been repudiated, when "the view from nowhere" (Nagel 1986) is regarded as unattainable (Foucault 1973b; Gadamer 1975 [1960]; Geertz 1973; Rorty 1982; Ricoeur 1981; Rabinow and Sullivan 1979; Rabinow 1983), when anthropology is simply a way, among other ways, of "writing culture" (Clifford and Marcus 1986), then the only justification for a discourse is its power to unleash a new reading or to act as a form of moral inquiry (Foucault 1973a; 1975; 1977; Haan et al. 1983; Rabinow 1983; Marcus and Fisher 1986; Taylor 1985). On these grounds alone, the anthropology of Judaism deserves an opportunity to develop and flourish. Indeed, without such a discourse it is simply premature to say, as Rabinow (1983) has suggested, that the relativist critique has run its course. Until the anthropological tradition turns its gaze more intensely on traditions of Jews and Christians, the differences that once supported the dichotomies between higher and lower, civilized and savage, will continue to operate, albeit in a disguised form, as they always have.

In conclusion, it is worthwhile pondering the fact that an obsolete spelling of the term "savage" is "salvage" (OED 1971, 2:69, 135). This linguistic accident summarizes the critical thrusts of this project. Savaging Judaism is a salvage operation. It is an attempt to salvage the Enlightenment critique of Judaism, which saw no fundamental differences between Judaism and savage religions, yet to temper that critique with the rehabilitated image of the savage developed in twentieth-century anthropology. The discovery of the savage in Judaism also salvages the lower orders of Judaism, which have been suppressed in the quest to make Judaism live *up* to expectations of what a higher tradition should be. In the end, it is my hope that the breakdown of the traditional dichotomies between primitive and higher religions, and between anthropology and the history of Judaism, which is really another form of the same opposition, will better reflect the truth that provides the foundation for a new discourse: the savage is within us all.

Abbreviations

B.	Babylonian Talmud	Hab.	Habakkuk	Matt.	Matthew	IQM	The War Rule
Ber.	Berakhot	Hag.	Hagigah	Mic.	Micah	Qid.	Qiddushin
Bik.	Bikkurim	Heb.	Hebrews	Miq.	Miqvaot	Rom.	Romans
B.M.	Baba Mesia	Hor.	Horayot	M.S.	Maaser Sheni	Sam.	Samuel
CD	The Damascus Rule	Hos.	Hosea			San.	Sanhedrin
		Hul.	Hullin	Neh.	Nehemiah	Shab.	Shabbat
		Isa.	Isaiah	Nid.	Niddah	Sheb.	Shebuot
Corin.	Corinthians	Jer.	Jeremiah	Num.	Numbers	Sot.	Sotah
Dem.	Demai	Judg.	Judges	Obad.	Obadiah	T.	Tosefta
Deut.	Deuteronomy	Kel.	Kelim	Oh.	Ohalot	Ter.	Terumot
Eduy.	Eduyyot	Ker.	Keritot	P.	Palestinian Talmud	Uqs.	Uqsin
Erub.	Erubin	Ket.	Ketubot			Yad.	Yadaim
Exod.	Exodus	Lam.	Lamentations	Par.	Parah	Yeb.	Yebamot
Ezek.	Ezekiel	Lev.	Leviticus	Pes.	Pesahim	Zech.	Zechariah
Gal.	Galatians	LR	Leviticus Rabbah	Ps.	Psalms		
Gen.	Genesis			Prov.	Proverbs		
Git.	Gittin	M.	Mishnah	IQS	The Community Rule		
GR	Genesis Rabbah	Makh.	Makhshirin				
		Mal.	Malachi	IQH	The Hymns		

Notes

Introduction

1. In this book I am primarily interested in the possible use of anthropology to study Israelite religion and ancient Judaism. The following writers have appealed to anthropology for this purpose: Andriolo (1973); Carroll (1977); Davies (1977); Donaldson (1981); Fiensy (1987); Feeley-Harnik (1982); Goldberg (1987); Hendel (1988); Jay (1985; 1988); Jobling (1984); Lang (1985a; 1985b); Leach (1969; 1976, 81–97); Leach and Aycock (1983); Long (1976); Marshall (1979); Oden (1987); Pitt-Rivers (1977); Prewitt (1981); Rogerson (1970; 1978); Soler (1979); Wilson (1980; 1984). For a more detailed bibliography, see Lang 1985a, 17–20. There is also a growing trend to subject modern forms of Judaism to anthropological inquiry. See, for example, Goldberg (1987); Kirshenblatt-Gimblett (1982); Kugelmass (1986; 1988); Myerhoff (1979); Prell (1989); Zenner (1988).

2. It is interesting to note that the field of biblical studies has more readily absorbed those anthropological theories that are anticomparativist and that preserve an opposition between Israelite religions and primitive religions. This is evident, for example, in the work of Sidney Hooke and his colleagues, who relied upon Hocart's idea of a ritual and myth pattern that diffuses from a cultural center (Leach 1982). Hooke and his followers postulated that ancient Babylonian, Egyptian, and Israelite religions all conformed to a single myth and ritual pattern. This theoretical perspective effectively ruled out all comparisons with noncontiguous cultures.

3. The history of the distinction between "Israelite religion" and "ancient Judaism" would constitute an interesting essay in its own right. It reflects historical judgments as well as theological claims. To begin with, the distinction is intended to mark the fundamental religious changes that occurred as a result of and in the wake of the Babylonian exile (sixth century B.C.E.). The forms of Israelite religion that emerged were fundamentally different from their predecessors and had important commonalities with the forms of Judaism that emerged only later. Furthermore, the distinction draws attention to the important fact that Judaism cannot be equated with the religion of the Old Testament. Since Judaism does not receive its "classical" formulation until the emergence of the rabbis (second–sixth centuries C.E.), it must be understood as the religion of the Hebrew Bible as refracted through the eyes of the rabbis. The mistaken identification of Judaism with the religion of the Old Testament has been quite common since the Enlightenment, and the above distinction is in part an attempt to rectify this mistake by recognizing the historical complexity of the tradition called Judaism.

Unfortunately, the distinction between Israelite religion and ancient Judaism has some difficulties. To begin with, it emerged from and reinforced a Christian polemic against Judaism. Christianity claims to inherit the prophetic tradition of the Hebrew Bible and to denounce "the law." The distinction between Israelite religion (which is often treated as early and identified with the 'ethical monotheism' of the prophets) and Judaism (which is viewed as 'late' and often identified with the priests who were concerned with law) thus encourages this Christian polemic (e.g., Wellhausen 1973 [1878]). Moreover, the claim that Judaism developed in the postexilic period was based on the assumption that the priestly writings, with their obsession with cult and law, were exilic or postexilic. But biblical scholars no longer accept a sharp dichotomy between prophetic and priestly forms of Israelite religion (Tucker 1985, 325–54). Moreover, there is some indication that the priestly writings may be much older (see chapter 6, note 4). If this is so, then "Judaism" is pushed back into the pre-exilic period and the distinction between Israelite religion (early) and ancient Judaism (late) collapses.

4. It may appear that Rogerson's work (1978) contradicts the thesis elaborated here. But that is not the case. Rogerson has focused on those biblical interpreters who have been influenced explicitly or implicitly by anthropological assumptions. I am asking a somewhat different question: Why is it that the mainstream interpreters of biblical Judaism have ignored anthropology and studies of non-Near Eastern peoples?

5. As Rogerson points out, it is generally nineteenth-century anthropological views that have entered twentieth-century discourse on Israelite religion. Twentieth-century biblical interpreters have generally ignored the work of anthropologists of their own generation. As I will suggest below, this is not accidental. Nineteenth-century anthropological views permit biblical interpreters to oppose ancient Israelite and savage religions, whereas twentieth-century anthropological theory undermines such an opposition.

6. In fact, linguistics has shown that on a formal level languages can be compared cross-culturally. This insight provides the foundation of Lévi-Strauss's structuralist perspective.

7. I fundamentally disagree with Edmund Leach (1961, 371–87; 1982, 73–93), who argues that the details Frazer considered were "not such as might be likely to arouse passionate debate among theologians, either Jewish or Christian." That Frazer's work did create controversy is amply documented by Ackerman (1987, 164–96).

8. Childs (1970) and Dever (1980) point out the influences of Protestant theology on biblical archaeology. The purpose of the present discussion is to consider the implications of that influence for the rejection of anthropology and the comparative method within biblical studies.

9. The role of comparison within the British tradition is more complex than I am making it out to be. Evans-Pritchard, for example, had reservations about the kind of comparative method favored by Radcliffe-Brown. Nonetheless, even Evans-Pritchard did not favor abandoning the comparative enterprise altogether (Evans-Pritchard 1965).

10. I do not consider the work of Max Weber on ancient Judaism to be an exception to the claim being made here. Weber, as a sociologist, did not compare Judaism with primitive religions. In fact, Weber's own work reflects the very assumption that this essay attempts to expose. Weber focused his work on "world religions," thus assuming that Judaism could not be compared to primitive religions.

11. For a traditional account of this change see Evans-Pritchard (1951) and Harris (1968). The understanding of this transition, however, is currently under revision. See especially Stocking (1983) and Strathern (1987).

12. The relationship between early anthropology and classics is very complex. For an introduction to the subject, see Kluckholn (1961).

13. Kuhn's own understanding of scientific practice was in part inspired by Polanyi's work which also argued that scientific thought constitutes a closed system of self-validating assumptions. Polanyi was influenced in his ideas by Evans-Pritchard's treatment of Azande witchcraft beliefs.

14. See note 1.

1. The Literature of Travel and the Enlightenment Critique

1. One could trace this opposition back even further. For the purposes of this inquiry, however, I am interested in the opposition between ancient Judaism and the "savages" of the "New World."

2. Apparently Garcia did not believe exclusively in the theory that the Indians were

descendants of the Jews. His work takes up each of the various theories for the Indians' origin and defends them all. As a curious note, Calancha recounts a story about someone who claimed that the Spanish words for Indian (Indio) and Jew (Iudio) were permutations of one another. If the "n" in Indio is inverted, the word Iudio is produced (Huddleston 1967, 85).

3. The quotations from Thorowgood's work are taken from chapters 2 and 3.

4. For a discussion of this exchange, see Glaser (1973, 40–42); Huddleston (1967, 133); Hyamson (1903, 665); Wasserman (1954, 466–67).

5. My account of the Enlightenment relies on a variety of primary and secondary sources. References to primary sources are cited in the text that follows. I am indebted to the following secondary sources for my general understanding of the Enlightenment: Cassirer (1951); Cragg (1964); Gay (1964; 1966; 1968); Hazard (1973); Manuel (1959); Orr (1934); Schwarzbach (1971); Stephen (1902); and Torrey (1930; 1931). The following discussions of the Enlightenment views of Jews and Judaism are also crucial for my own account: Ettinger (1961; 1964); Glassman (1975); Hertzberg (1968); Katz (1980); Manuel (1983); Meyer (1963); Schwartz (1981); Schwarzbach (1973); Wiener (1941).

6. Since the attack on Jews and Judaism was a weapon in the Enlightenment's critique of Christianity and revelation, it is difficult for scholars to determine whether a given Enlightenment figure is anti-Jewish or criticizing Judaism as a means of attacking Christianity and revelation. See, for example, the interesting interchange between Gay (1964, 96–107), Hertzberg (1968, 283–86), and Meyer (1963, 1176) on Voltaire's attitude toward Jews and Judaism.

7. In the vocabulary of the Enlightenment, "paganism," "heathenism," and "superstition" referred to those puerile and barbaric religious forms, both the modern and ancient, which reason and revelation both found offensive.

8. Throughout this chapter, I am focusing on the critical or secular deists who wanted to do away with Christianity and Judaism. Other deists equated Christianity and Judaism with the religion of reason. In their view, the unreasonable parts of these traditions represented corruptions of and deviations from the core, which they believed was reasonable. The views of these more moderate deists are discussed below in chapter 2.

9. Deists disagreed among themselves about whether the notion of reward and punishment in an afterlife could be derived from the use of reason.

2. Reviving the Opposition

1. There are some indications that Morgan believed in revelation. However, as Leland points out, Morgan effectively tried to demolish the possibility of discriminating between false and true revelations. For example, Morgan writes that "In a word, there can be no such Thing as divine truth upon human Testimony; and this absurd supposition has been the Ground of all the superstition and false Religion in the World" (Morgan 1738, 81–82). For this reason, I treat Morgan as a Christian deist who equates Christianity with reason.

2. It is true that in traditional Christian thought, the New Testament is regarded as superseding the Old Testament. But the development of truth in this case is the result of a divine intervention into history and is not the result of an internal religious development. See Troeltsch (1971 [1901], 5–53) on the similarities and tension between the orthodox Christian view and the evolutionary perspective.

3. See Manuel (1959, 10–57) for a discussion of other eighteenth-century thinkers who adopted a developmental perspective.

3. Romanticism, Relativism, and the Rehabilitation of the Savage

1. Healy (1958) has argued that the tendency to ennoble the savage was a consequence of Jesuit theology and the social conflict that developed between Jesuits and Jansenists.

2. My account of Herder relies on a variety of primary and secondary sources. Primary sources are cited in the text. Secondary accounts include Apsler (1943); Barnard (1959; 1965; 1969); Clark (1934; 1955); Ergang (1966); Frei (1974); Gillies (1945); Manuel (1968); Schütze (1920–1923).

3. A similar sort of relativism developed in American anthropology originating with Boas and his disciples. Broce (1973) in fact has suggested that the founders of this tradition, some of whom were German in origin, were directly influenced by Herder's work. I focus on the British tradition because the recent interest in the religion of the ancient Jews stems from this tradition.

4. In my judgment, the connection between Lévi-Strauss's structural anthropology and Radcliffe-Brown's social anthropology has been underestimated. To be sure, Lévi-Strauss repudiates the functional dimension of British anthropology. But his concept of structure and his idea that elements only have meaning within a system is already found in Radcliffe-Brown. Moreover, Radcliffe-Brown anticipated Lévi-Strauss in suggesting that one interprets practices the same way one interprets language. One determines the meaning of a practice by noting the different occasions on which that practice occurs. One can assume that its meaning must make sense in all those different situations (Radcliffe-Brown 1965 [1952], 146). Finally, Lévi-Strauss (1962, 83–91) acknowledges that Radcliffe-Brown's later understanding of totemism anticipated his own.

5. There is one important way in which some British social anthropologists did not embrace relativism. Radcliffe-Brown and some of his students conceived of anthropology as a science that would eventually discover social laws. Anthropology could and should be as objective as the natural sciences.

6. The desire to demonstrate the intelligibility of primitive thought is also evident in Evans-Pritchard's "The Problem of Symbols" (1956, 123–43).

7. I am aware of the fact that in *Purity and Danger,* Douglas argues that the category of primitive society should be retained. But this viewpoint is actually overshadowed by precisely the opposite tendency, namely, to overcome a number of the old dichotomies that previously had grounded the distinction between primitive and nonprimitive traditions.

8. Readers familiar with Douglas's work will note an interesting paradox. Douglas aims her criticism at Robertson Smith and Frazer, precisely the figures whom I have treated as exemplary in my Introduction. The difference in our accounts stems in part from the fact that Douglas and I have different objectives in providing a historical perspective. Douglas wants to locate the origins of twentieth-century anthropology and thereby challenge certain oppositions that have operated therein. My concern, by contrast, has been to follow the rise and fall of the opposition between ancient Judaism and primitive religions. From this perspective, Robertson Smith and Frazer are meritorious since they entertained the possibility of seeing resemblances between the religion of the Jews and savages. From Douglas's vantage point, they are responsible for various problematic oppositions that are coordinated with the larger difference of primitive and advanced.

It still seems to me, however, that Douglas condemns Robertson Smith and Frazer somewhat unfairly. Although they do use some of the oppositions that Douglas finds problematic, both were simply articulating views that already had a two-hundred-year history behind them. Indeed, the difference between magic and religion as articulated by Robertson Smith and Frazer is a repetition of the old theological distinction between Christianity and Judaism. My account, therefore, takes notice of what is innovative about the work of Robertson Smith and Frazer, while Douglas condemns them for what they merely inherited from their predecessors.

9. See Pace (1986) for an excellent and thorough treatment of this romantic impulse in Lévi-Strauss's work. Pace convincingly argues that this dimension of Lévi-Strauss's work cannot be dismissed as marginal to his enterprise.

10. I am aware of the "Virgin Birth" debate that Leach's essay has stimulated (see Spiro 1968; Monberg 1975; Barnes 1977; Delaney 1986). My intention here is not to side with Leach but simply to show how Leach's relativism led him to look at Judaism and Christianity.

11. It is interesting to note that Leach points to Radcliffe-Brown's work, among others, as responsible for undermining this portrayal of primitive thought.

4. Beyond Parallel-anoia

1. I can no longer sort out the influences on my own conception of comparison. The following essays, however, all contributed to the position I develop in this chapter: Eggan (1954); Evans-Pritchard (1951; 1965); Radcliffe-Brown (1958 [1951]); Smith (1978; 1982).

2. Interpreters who are open to comparison tend to be those who are also involved in the application of anthropological inquiry to Israelite religion and ancient Judaism. I have already cited this literature in the Introduction.

5. Israel in the Mirror of Nature

1. There is some question whether the name "Leah" does in fact mean "antelope" (see BDB 1975 [1907], 521).

2. Lévi-Strauss is a transitional figure in this paradigm change. He was first to systematically exploit the comparison of culture and language, but he still espoused a natural science model for the social sciences. In his view, the reason language serves as a good metaphor for understanding culture is because language is the one cultural artifact that has been reduced to universal rules and laws. But as the natural sciences ceased to be a metaphor for the activity of cultural analysis, cultural analysis itself changed.

3. Throughout this paper, I use the expression "Israelite religion" to refer to the beliefs and practices of those writers who stand behind the texts of the Hebrew Bible. Archaeological evidence indicates that there were other beliefs and practices in Israelite religion that were not reflected in the elite religion portrayed in biblical literature.

4. While the view espoused here derives from the work of Mary Douglas (1975), I am uncomfortable with the kind of language Douglas sometimes adopts to explain the homologies one finds between the social system and the society's views of nature. Douglas, for example, understands such homologies as communicating information (5–6). Thus she interprets attitudes toward animals as implicitly communicating information about proper sexual behavior. But this view is problematic because no one but the anthropologist recognizes the connection; therefore it simply cannot be understood as communication. In my view, the homologies one finds in culture do not necessarily communicate anything at all. The parallels between sexual behavior and food rules emerge only be-

cause individuals experience a satisfaction when various parts of the cultural system fit together. In other words, there is a sense of rightness when various parts of the cultural system cohere. This view is also found in Douglas's work, but it is sometimes overshadowed by the more problematic language noted above.

5. Gen. 49:24; Isa. 40:11; 53:6; 63:14; Jer. 12:3; 13:17; 23:2–3; 31:10; 50:19; 51:40; Ezek. 34:1–31; Hos. 4:16; Mic. 2:12; Pss. 23; 78:52; 79:13; 95:7; 100:3.

6. All quotations from the Hebrew Bible derive from the translation of the Jewish Publication Society of America (1962; 1978; 1982).

7. For a more comprehensive discussion, see Schochet (1984).

8. A number of these correspondences have been noted by Milgrom (1981), Douglas (1975, 267), and Soler (1979).

9. In dating the sources, I rely primarily upon Noth (1981). The rules about firstborn animals, Israelites, and first fruits all appear in the Book of the Covenant (Exod. 22:28; 23:17, 19). The J source (Exod. 34:19–20, 26), Deuteronomist (Deut. 15:19; Exod. 13:2, 12–13; Deut. 26:10) and Priestly source (Num. 8:16–18) each mentions all three prohibitions.

10. The law requiring Israelites and their animals to rest appears in the Decalogue (Exod. 20:9; Deut. 5:12–14) as well as in the Book of the Covenant (Exod. 20:9). The death penalty for animals and humans appears in the Book of the Covenant (Exod. 21:12, 28).

11. The rules about human and animal blemishes are found in Deuteronomy (Deut. 17:1; 15:21; 23:2) and the Holiness Code (Lev. 21:17; 22:19), as are the prohibitions against various kinds of mixtures (Deut. 7:3–4; 22:9; Lev. 19:19). The treatment of human corpses and animal carcasses as sources of impurity are specified in the priestly strand (Num. 9:7; Lev. 11:24). The homologies between the nazirite and unpruned grape vines (Num. 6; Lev. 25:5) and the uncircumcised boy and juvenile fruit tree (Lev. 19:23–25) derive from priestly sources.

12. It may be that before the rule appeared in writing, Israelites circumcised their male children on the eighth day. However, Exod. 4:25, which is an early source, suggests that circumcision may not always have been on the eighth day. In any case, it is still interesting that the rule about circumcising on the eighth day is articulated in writing later than the rule that prohibits sacrificing an animal before the eighth day after birth.

13. It is possible that the metaphoric equation of Israelites and animals with cloven hooves underlies a practice which subsequently develops in Judaism. According to one tradition, when the priests stand up before the congregation to bless the people, they divide the fingers of their hands into two groups, with the division taking place between the third and fourth fingers. This makes the hands resemble cloven hooves!

14. The rabbis were sensitive to the symbolic association between unclean animals and the unclean nations (Genesis Rabbah 65:1 and Leviticus Rabbah 13:5).

15. Douglas (1975, 305) gives a similar interpretation of the attitude to the pig in biblical religion. She argues that the pig had only one of the criteria that make it an insider (cloven hooves) and thus it is treated like a half-blooded Israelite.

16. The rabbis suggest a similar interpretation of the ass in the story of Abraham going up to Moriah to sacrifice his son (Gen. 22). When Abraham commands his servants to remain behind with the asses, the rabbis conclude that the servants are being equated with asses (GR 56:2).

17. After completing this essay, I discovered that Calum Carmichael (1985, 193–96) has given a very similar interpretation to this story. Carmichael views Israelite law as an embodiment of ideas contained in Israelite narratives. My approach is similar to his. However, I consider the connections between law and narrative to be less direct and less conscious. In my view, metaphor is the missing link between law and narra-

tive. Since the same foundational metaphors stand behind the laws and narratives, similar associations are found in each. Robert Alter (1981, 39) applies a similar kind of analysis to another biblical character's name, Eglon, which is related etymologically to the Hebrew word for calf. Alter concludes that "the ruler of the occupying Moabite power turns out to be a fatted calf readied for slaughter."

18. Absalom is also a product of mixed seed. His mother is Maacah, daughter of King Talmai of Geshur (2 Sam. 3:3). See also Cohen (1985) who offers a similar interpretation of mule imagery in later Judaism.

19. Lest one think that Milgrom's interpretation explains all the facts, it is important to realize that it is also subject to certain kinds of criticism. There are instances in biblical law that explicitly mix the categories of life and death. In order to purify oneself from corpse uncleanness, for example, a person must be sprinkled with a solution made from the ashes of a red heifer and "living" water (Num. 19). Here, a substance that is symbolic of life ("living" water) is mixed with a substance that is associated with death (ashes of a heifer). Moreover, if impurity represents death, it is difficult to understand how sprinkling oneself with ashes of a cow could effect purification. One would expect purification to occur via a substance that symbolizes life. Finally, if the purpose of the prohibition on the kid-goat was to establish a distinction between life and death, why is it only forbidden to cook it in its mother's milk? If it was cooked in the milk of another animal, would this not constitute mixing life and death?

20. I actually came to this conclusion independently and only subsequently discovered Soler's essay.

21. Robert Alter kindly pointed this out to me in a personal communication.

22. I owe this insight to Girard (1979, 5) although I by no means accept his view that primitive religion can be interpreted as an attempt to deal with the ever present possibility that violence will erupt.

23. When Jesse sends his son David to King Saul, he sends along a kid-goat, signaling that just as Saul would eat this kid, he would attempt to consume David (1 Sam. 16:20). Similarly, in the story in which Manoah and his wife are informed by an angel that they will shortly conceive a male son, they reciprocate by offering the angel a kid-goat (Judg. 13:15). The goat also figures prominently in the story in which Joseph's brothers sell Joseph into slavery. In this case, it is not a "kid" but a male goat. The brothers dip Joseph's coat into the blood of the goat in order to convince their father that Joseph was attacked by a wild animal. Again, the goat serves as a symbolic replacement for the boy. When Jacob sees the coat he exclaims, "Joseph was devoured by a wild beast," when in fact it was the goat that was devoured by the beasts who were Joseph's brothers.

24. Jay (1988) drew my attention to the role of sacrifice in symbolizing patrilineal descent in this story. My contribution is to note the opposition of sacrifice and boiling.

25. Driver (1895, 32), Noth (1981, 271), and Eissfeldt (1965, 200) assign this source to the J strand. Haran (1979, 33) assumes this is part of the Book of the Covenant.

26. In a personal communication, Milgrom has objected to this interpretation because the phrase "her offspring" is asexual and thus can include male offspring. I do not regard this objection as particularly damaging to my thesis. To begin with, it is difficult to determine the gender of fledglings. Consequently, if a correspondence is to emerge between rules applying to capturing birds and capturing women, as a purely practical matter the gender of the birds might have to be ignored. Moreover, there is a larger theoretical question at stake here. If the rules governing animals are not precisely parallel to those governing social relations does that mean that the correspondence is not operative? I would argue against Milgrom that simply showing a number of similarities is sufficient to make their correspondence plausible. The reason I hold

this view is because, as noted at the outset of this essay, I do not regard these correspondences as manufactured intentionally by the actors. Rather, interconnections between various cultural rules emerge haphazardly and without the conscious awareness of the participants. To expect a precise parallel in all cases is to assume a more conscious model of how social rules develop.

27. For the sake of simplicity, I am not distinguishing here between the Holiness Code and Leviticus. I am assuming that the authors of chapter 18 had in hand the Holiness Code and that therefore one can speak about them as a unit.

28. It is possible that the rule against sacrificing an animal and its offspring on the same day also corresponds to the prohibition against sexual relations between a man and his daughter-in-law, a prohibition also found in Leviticus but not in Deuteronomy. If one looks at the rules about sacrificing the animal from a woman's standpoint, she is commanded not to have a male animal and its male offspring sacrificed on the same day. This would parallel the prohibition against a woman having intercourse with her father-in-law or her stepson. One might object that I have no grounds for introducing a woman's perspective. However, one has to remember that for unintentional violations and for rites of purification, women were required to bring animals to the Temple. Consequently, the prohibition against sacrificing an animal and its offspring on the same day is also directed to women.

29. An objection to the view presented here might be raised based on the work of Jacob Milgrom (1971; 1976a; 1976b) on the biblical notions of sacrifice. Milgrom argues that the so-called "sin-offering" is not a sin-offering at all but a "purificatory offering" that cleanses the altar of impurity. By the same token, Milgrom suggests that the "guilt-offering" is in fact a "reparations offering" which constitutes repayment for misusing property of the Deity. Milgrom's understanding of these offerings might seem to undermine the view that animals are substitutes for humans. For if the offering does not atone for a person's sin or guilt, in what sense is it meaningful to say that the animal is a substitute for human life?

Milgrom's interpretation of these sacrifices, however, is compatabile with the understanding offered here. In fact, the interpretation I am suggesting answers a question that Milgrom's thesis leaves open, namely, why sprinkling the blood of the animal effects purification. I suggest that the reason the animal's blood has such effects is because the death of the animal and the spilling out of its life force serves as a substitute for the person on whose behalf it is brought. The person who has defiled the sanctuary, for example, owes God his or her life. But rather than take human life, God takes animal life instead. The same argument can be made with respect to "reparations offerings." The death of an animal serves as reparation for trespassing on divine property, because God ultimately has the right to take the person's life but has agreed instead to accept the death of an animal.

The interpretation I am offering is very close to that of Levine (1974, 61). In analyzing the notion of *kôper* ("atonement") in noncultic contexts, Levine concludes that this term, which means

"ransome, expiation, gift," is a case in point . . . [it is] a payment made for the purpose of erasing or "wiping away" guilt incurred by the offense. . . . As a concession, one may in certain situations of limited responsibility redeem his life (Hebrew: *pādāh*) by paying a *kôper* (Exodus 21:30), where, according to the theory of Israelite law, actual forfeiture of one's life would have been required. In other situations, where, for example, premeditated murder was involved, no *kôper* may be substituted for the death penalty (Numbers 35:31–32). Similarly, when one's time to die has come, no *kôper* is possible, (Psalm 49:8). The *kôper* is thus a substitute for a life (Exodus 30:12; Isaiah 43:3), one's own or another's (Proverbs 21:18).

Levine argues that the biblical cultic writers alter this conception somewhat by making the sacrifice a prerequisite activity for expiation. "As a result of the performance of certain rites, God grants expiation or atonement. In such instances, expiation, forgiveness, etc. are not the direct physical effects of the rites performed. Such acts are prerequisite, but not causational. It is God who grants the desired result!" (1974, 65–66). Finally, Levine argues that blood is a cleansing agent because blood can serve as a substitute for life (1974, 68).

30. This view closely resembles that put forth by Levine. See previous note.

31. De Vaux (1965, 455) and Wenham (1979, 27) anticipate this view to some extent. This idea is similar, moreover, to Girard's. Girard argues that sacrifices are displaced objects of violence. But sometimes "the mechanism of substitutions had gone astray, and those whom the sacrifice was designed to protect became its victims" (1979, 40).

32. For an example of how kinship relations can be expressed in a theological idiom, see Harman (1985) on the role of kinship metaphors in the Hindu pantheon.

33. Quotations of the New Testament derive from the RSV (1971) translation.

6. The Fruitful Cut

1. Reviews of this literature on Israelite circumcision can be found in Bryk (1970 [1930]), Morgenstern (1973), van Gennep 1960 [1908], 73), Weiss (1962).

2. Articles in the *Jewish Encylopedia* and *Encylopedia Judaica* barely allude to cross-cultural studies of circumcision.

3. It is unclear precisely when Israelites began circumcising on the eighth day. Only priestly sources (7th–5th centuries) specify the eighth day as the proper day for the ceremony. The J source (Exod. 4:25) suggests that Moses's son was circumcised sometime shortly after birth, but it is not clear how old he was. Other sources indicate that circumcision may have taken place at marriage, but these sources deal with the marriage to those outside the Israelite community. For a summary of this issue, see Morgenstern (1973).

4. A review of this issue can be found in Wenham (1979, 9–13). The view that P is postexilic was argued in detail by Wellhausen in his *Prolegomena to the History of Israel* (1973 [1878]) and has remained convincing to many scholars (e.g., Cross 1973). However, Kaufmann (1972 [1937–56]), Hurvitz (1974), and others cite evidence for dating P earlier. The dating of P turns out to be irrelevant to the interpretation of circumcision that follows, which is applicable whether P is pre- or postexilic. This is one of the advantages of this interpretation over its competitors.

5. The only sources that explicitly link circumcision with the covenant derive from priestly circles. Circumcision was practiced by Israelites before this time. In earlier sources, circumcision is treated as a mark of ethnic identification and a rite of protection (see Kosmala 1962). At some point, however, circumcision became a sign of the covenant. The earliest source to explicitly understand circumcision in this way is the priestly source written sometime between the seventh and fifth centuries B.C.E. Nevertheless, such an association may have been in place earlier. For example, both Jeremiah and the author of Deuteronomy speak of a circumcised heart as a requirement of the covenant with God. These sources seem to presuppose a connection between circumcision and covenant.

6. I am not the first to argue for these interpretations of Israelite circumcision. Helpful reviews of the various interpretations of Israelite circumcision can be found in van Gennep (1960 [1908], 73) and Morgenstern (1973).

7. It is important to note that circumcision has a similar range of meanings among other peoples such as certain Australian aborigines (e.g., Meggitt 1962), and related themes often appear in initiation practices that do not involve circumcision (Herdt 1987; Strathern 1970). But not all circumcision ceremonies involve the themes developed below.

8. Other passages in which the priestly writer uses the word *'ōt* to mean "symbol" include Exod. 8:19 which discusses the plague of insects God brings against the Egyptians. This plague is a symbol "that you may know that I the Lord am in the midst of the land." Num. 17:3 deals with the aftermath of the Korah rebellion. The fire pans of Korah and his supporters are hammered into sheets which serve as a symbol for the children of Israel. They have a metonymic relation with the sin of Korah and his followers and hence serve as a powerful symbol of warning for Israel. Other writers sometimes use *'ōt* to mean "sign," as does the J writer (Gen. 4:15; Exod. 3:12; Exod. 4:8=J).

9. I am here following the terminology of de Saussure (1966) who treats a "sign" as unmotivated and a "symbol" as motivated. In American anthropology, the terminology is sometimes reversed (Sahlins 1976, 59).

10. This interpretation understands the expression "being cut off from one's people" as parallel to the expression used by the Deuteronomist: "so his name will not be effaced in Israel" (Deut. 25:6). Rashi (ad loc.) adopts the interpretation offered here and Ibn Ezra (ad loc.) presents this interpretation as one possible alternative.

11. Many translators and commentators understand the verse *wa- 'ăralĕtem 'orlātô 'et-piryô* to mean "you shall regard its fruit as uncircumcised." An alternative reading is "you shall regard its fruit as its foreskin." By this understanding, the tree is regarded as uncircumcised and its fruit is its foreskin. This translation is supported by the Vulgate (BDB 1975 [1907], 790b), Ibn Ezra (ad loc.), and Noth (1977, 137), and is considered a less preferable interpretation by BDB (1975 [1907], 790b). My colleague Jo Ann Hackett was kind enough to explain in technical terms why this reading is a plausible one: "*'orlātô* is a cognate accusative (Gesenius et al. 1976 [1910], 117p-r) and probably serves merely to reinforce or clarify the idea of the verb. Gesenius (1976 [1910], 117r) does not mention Lev. 19:23 where he discusses the extension of the strict sense of cognate accusative to those cases where the verb is denominative and derived from the noun in question. But this verse is similar to 2 Kings 4:13 which he does mention and which also has a definite cognate accusative.

"The lack of the accusative marker *'et-* before the defined *'orlātô* is perplexing, but is perhaps a sign that this word, although defined, is not strongly definite (Andersen 1970, 33). That is to say, the lack of the accusative marker perhaps signals that this word should be translated as less definite (i.e., '*a* foreskin of its [the tree's]') rather than interpreted as referring to a particular foreskin. It is also possible that as a body part "foreskin" does not take the accusative marker, as in the common phrase, 'reach out his hand' *(šālah yādô)*.

"The plural *'ărēlîm* in the next clause can refer to 'trees' even though 'trees' appears in the singular (collective) in the preceding clause. Collectives in biblical Hebrew are construed as either singulars or plurals. The verb *yihĕyeh* appears in the masculine singular because it agrees with the singular 'any tree' *(kol- 'eş)* earlier in the passage, but the plural predicate adjective indicates that the collective is at that point being regarded as plural. The ambivalence between verb and predicate adjective in the same sentence is unusual, and there may be other explanations for the apparent plural, but it is not impossible as it stands" (Jo Ann Hackett, personal communication).

12. Goor and Nurock (1968) directed my attention to this source.

13. As I indicated in notes to chapter 5, the sages were also alive to the way in which animals served as metaphorical human beings in Israelite literature. In this respect, the rabbis were less alienated from the symbolic language of Israelite religion than its modern interpreters.

14. I am following Bright's (1965, 84) translation here which interprets *"bĕlaḥĕmo"* as "in its sap."

15. On the importance of metaphor in structuring conceptual domains, see Lakoff and Johnson (1980).

16. I am incorporating a JPS emendation here.

17. Parts of this chapter may derive from E (Speiser 1964, 113).

18. Reviews of the relevant literature can be found in Speiser (1964, 113) and Sarna (1970, 126).

19. The only other reference in the Bible to cutting an animal in two is Jer. 34:18–19. It is possible that a similar interpretation can apply to this occurrence. According to this passage, King Zedekiah made a covenant with the Israelite people to emancipate Hebrew slaves in the seventh year "so that no one should hold his fellow Jew in bondage" (Jer. 34:9). But the people changed their minds and enslaved the men and women they had set free. In response God says, "I will hand over [to their enemies] the men who violated My covenant, who did not fulfill the terms of the covenant which they made before Me, by cutting in half a young bull and passing between the pieces" (Jer. 34:18). In this case, we are not dealing with a situation where kinship ties are being severed. Nonetheless, an inappropriate relation between kin (i.e., Israelites and their Hebrew slaves) is being undone. The covenant ritual of cutting an animal may dramatize that the relationship between the two categories of persons (owners and slaves) is severed.

20. Jensen (1960) in his "Beziehungen zwischen dem Alten Testament und der nilotischen Kultur in Africa" anticipated the argument I am making here. In this essay, Jensen draws attention to the similarity between the biblical covenant of cutting an animal in half and similar practices by Nilotic peoples, such as the Nuer, Dinka, Bari, and Nuba. Jensen concludes that the culture of ancient Israelites was historically connected to that of the Nilotic culture of northeast Africa. While I agree with Patai (1962) in rejecting the assumptions of cultural diffusion presupposed in Jensen's argument, I am not content with Patai's conclusion that the Israelite and African practices are not comparable. In his haste to reject the idea of diffusion, Patai missed the deep similarities in these practices. This is an example of how such similarities can exist between cultures separate in time and place (see chapter 4).

21. I am following Cross (1973, 293–325) in assuming that the priestly writer did not write a complete narrative paralleling the JE narrative, but rather expanded and supplemented it. If this is so, one must consider why the priestly writer felt compelled to write a whole chapter about the covenant when JE had already developed that theme (Gen. 15). On other topics, the priestly writer was content with just supplementing JE. One must assume, therefore, that the priestly author was unhappy in some way with the earlier conception of the covenant.

22. Wenham (1979, 255) arrives at a similar analysis. "Foreign to our way of thinking is the idea that a wife's nakedness is her husband's nakedness and vice versa. In other words, marriage, or more precisely marital intercourse, makes the man and wife as closely related as parents and children. In the words of Gen. 2:24, 'they become one flesh.'"

23. This point was suggested to me by Sarah Pike, a graduate student at Indiana University.

7. Menstrual Blood, Semen, and Discharge

1. I will consider below why the prohibition on sexual relations with a menstruating woman is not listed along with the rules concerning her impurity.

2. I have not attempted to deal with Freud's general views on the motivation of the menstrual taboo. This subject could constitute an independent essay. In addition to the reasons given here, Freud suggests three other possible reasons for menstrual taboos. First, he argues that a child's sighting of blood on the bed sheets (an event Freud regards as a common experience) is regarded as proof that his father is attacking his mother, and therefore "much of the otherwise inexplicable 'horror of blood' shown by neurotics finds its explanation from this connection." He also suggests that the special helplessness on the part of the menstruating woman stimulates male desire. The taboos, therefore, help temptation be resisted. Finally, Freud argues that in the dawn of human history menstrual blood performed the function of sexually arousing men. As visual stimuli subsequently assumed that function, a taboo on menstrual blood came into being as a "defense against a phase of development that had been surmounted" (Freud 1953, 9:222; 13:33; 21:99).

3. In ways that I can no longer reconstruct, the following part of my analysis, which attends to the symbolization of gender differences, has been influenced by feminist criticism and gender analysis of the past two decades. Particularly influential for me have been the essays in Rosaldo and Lamphere (1974) and Ortner and Whitehead (1981). In an earlier version of this essay that was never published, I completely missed the importance of gender as a symbolic concern. I thank Riv-Ellen Prell for originally calling my attention to this serious lacuna. However, as my analysis makes clear, gender concerns do not totally control the symbolism of body emissions.

4. In this passage, Israel is metaphorically a woman, a metaphor which sets up the accusation of harlotry in the rest of the chapter.

5. I have been anticipated to some extent by Rachel Biale (1984, 147–74).

6. I will return to the difference between menstrual blood and circumcision and sacrificial blood in another context.

7. I am perplexed by the fact that P does not explicitly proscribe masturbation. Below, I speculate as to why this might be the case.

8. See also Powers (1980) for the connection between menstruation, fertility, and fruit trees among the Oglala, a native American tribe.

9. It would be illuminating to know the likelihood of death in childbirth, a factor that might also contribute to the association between death and blood from the birthing process.

10. It would be interesting to know whether Israelites used human excrement for fertilizer. If so, then excrement might have an association with fertility rather than "waste" or "death."

11. I do not mean to imply that a man has total control over semen, for semen is sometimes ejaculated at night during a dream. Relatively speaking, however, semen is controllable, at least in comparison with nonseminal discharges, over which a man has no influence whatsoever. Moreover, because semen is ejaculated (even while a man is asleep) it represents a muscular event and hence the discharge is associated with more human control than is the release of nonseminal fluids. Consequently, semen is a less powerful contaminator than nonseminal fluids. On the other hand, semen is considered less controllable than urine. Consequently, semen can contaminate the body for one day, while urine is not a conveyor of impurity at all.

12. Milgrom (1971; 1976a) has argued that the sacrifices purify the altar rather than the person. While this seems correct, one still must consider why each person must

present his or her own animals for sacrifice. If the only issue is the purity of the Temple, why can't the priests simply sacrifice animals continually on the altar? It appears therefore that sacrifice is also part of the individual's purification process.

13. Since the Israelite God did not have other gods with whom to interact, the relationship between God and Israel is often thought of as analogous to the relation between husband and wife. But these metaphors have some obvious limitations: in what sense could such a marriage be understood to involve sexuality and reproduction?

14. This problem leads Bird (1981) to argue that the idea of humans being made in the divine image and likeness did not imply a resemblance in form. Even von Rad (1976, 60) who argues that it does imply a resemblance in form admits that "man's procreative ability is not here understood as an emanation or manifestation of his creation in God's image." Thus according to either interpretation sexuality and the division of the sexes poses a problem to the idea that humans are made in God's image.

8. The Status of Impurity

1. See Rodney Needham's (1963, xv–xvi) critique of Durkheim's and Mauss's essay. Durkheim has also been criticized for postulating that it was the organization of society which originally gave humans the idea of classification. Durkheim argued (against Kant) that the ability to classify is not inherent in the mind but arose as people reflected on social groupings. As Gehlke noted, the ability to classify had to exist before the recognition that society itself was classified (Needham 1963, xxvi–xxvii; Hallpike 1979, 49). Moreover, as Hallpike has recently argued, society is not in fact classified in a logical way and hence probably could not provide a model for classification (Hallpike 1979, 212–24). In my view, Bärbel Inhelder and Jean Piaget (1969) have provided the most convincing explanation of the origin of the classificatory ability. According to their account, this ability arises in the child through internalization of action.

2. Moreover, as Lévi-Strauss has argued, social structure is itself a form of classification. Like other forms of classification, it represents a community's attempt to impose order on complex social relations.

3. To be sure, in most groups both ascription and achievement play a role in determining status. Furthermore, ascription and achievement may vary in importance from subgroup to subgroup within a larger community. For example, while it might be the case that achievement is crucial for defining male status, women may be excluded from all sorts of roles simply by virtue of their gender. So it is crucial to ask for which community of people in particular does a given symbolism speak.

4. I am oversimplifying matters here. As noted in chapter 6, there was debate about the genealogical line from which priests actually emanated.

5. I have discussed the rabbis' ambivalence toward the priests elsewhere (Eilberg-Schwartz 1986, 197–99). See also [Avery]-Peck (1981, 2–3) and Jaffee (1981, 1) on how the sages take up a perspective outside that of the priests in interpreting priestly laws.

6. Excrement is the only body product that does not fit with this interpretation. Although excrement is released from an orifice, it has no role in the system of impurity. This appears to contradict the idea that muscular orifices are themselves symbolic of control. Since it is released through an orifice, we would expect it to be treated like urine or ear wax, which are also released through an orifice and subject to human control. If so, then like these bodily discharges, excrement should make food susceptible to impurity. But it does not.

It is not clear why the Mishnah does not treat excrement as a source of impurity. It completely ignores the rule in Deuteronomy which commands Israelites to defecate outside the camp in order to preserve its sanctity (Deut. 23:13–15). This ruling could easily have been a basis for the judgment that excrement is contaminating, which would have further established a connection between impurity and control. Closer inspection reveals the reason for this apparent discrepancy. According to the Mishnah only fluids have the power to make food susceptible to impurity (M. Makh 1:1; 6:4–5). The Mishnah regards ear wax and not excrement as a fluid (M.Makh. 6:4–6).

9. *Creation, Classification, and the Genealogy of Knowledge*

1. J. Z. Smith (1978, 99, 129–45, 162–71) shows how societies sometimes rebel against the accepted cosmogony. This insight initially led me to consider the way in which the creation story is not paradigmatic for Israelite religion.

2. A number of thinkers anticipated Eliade on the importance of cosmogony in religious systems, for example, Durkheim (1965 [1915], 420, 423) and Frazer (1919). Due to the constraints of space it is impossible to provide an extensive list of the numerous articles and books on the subject of cosmogony. See, for example, R. Pettazoni (1954), H. Bauman (1964 [1936]), and most recently Lovin and Reynolds (1985).

3. Eliade uses the term "ontology" in this less technical sense. As I understand it, in Eliade's writing ontology refers to the significance or meaning of objects or events. Therefore, those things endowed with significance or meaning Eliade labels as "real." Reality, here, is not a metaphysical category as much as a statement of people's concern. See Eliade (1963, 3–5, 34) and J. Z. Smith (1978, 92–93).

4. Similar conclusions were arrived at independently by Jean Soler (1979, 24–30). Like Douglas, he argues that the animals that are anomalous are the ones deemed unclean. However, the presuppositions of Soler's analysis are quite different from Douglas's. Ultimately, Soler (1979, 28) is a structuralist who wants to understand the dietary laws as well as the creation myth as "a taxonomy in which man, God, the animals, and the plants are strictly defined through their relationship with one another in a series of opposites."

5. J. Z. Smith (1978, 150) was the first to point out the relationship between Douglas's analysis and the work of Eliade.

6. I realize that Genesis 1 does not actually distinguish between clean and unclean animals. In fact, according to the priestly tradition, the distinction between pure and impure was not revealed until Sinai (Pfeiffer 1941, 193; Speiser 1964, 52). However, according to Douglas's argument as I understand it, the criteria by which pure and impure things would subsequently be distinguished were established at creation. Thus God created only some animals with fins and scales. Similarly, some of the animals God created chew the cud and have split hooves and others lack these traits. According to the priests, at Sinai God revealed the significance of creation by indicating which animals are to be clean and which unclean.

7. Douglas's views have been accepted by some biblical scholars (Milgrom 1981a, 4–6; Porter 1976, 84), as well as by interpreters of religion (J. Z. Smith 1978, 137, 148; Alter 1979, 46–51). In addition, her theory has been applied successfully in the discussion of other cultures (Tambiah 1969, 424–59; Löfgren 1985, 184–213; Bulmer 1967, 5–25).

8. Fishbane (1985) does not discuss the particular passages to which I refer, but his work on intrabiblical exegesis provided the suggestion for the analysis which follows: The precise relationship between Leviticus 11 and Deuteronomy 14 has been a long-standing question in biblical scholarship. Four positions have been articulated: First, Deuteronomy 14 represents an abbreviation and summary of Leviticus 11. Second, Le-

viticus 11 represents a reworking of Deuteronomy 14. Third, there is a dialectical relationship between two passages, each influencing the other. Fourth, both passages derive from a common source. A good review of this issue is found in Moran (1966, 271–77).

The first view has, in my mind, been convincingly rejected by Moran. I favor the second view, for reasons which I spell out below. However, it is important to note that my own position—that Leviticus 11 represents a reworking of the dietary restrictions in light of the priestly cosmogony—is not contradicted by the third or fourth alternatives. The third view explicitly allows for the possibility that Leviticus 11 represents a modification of Deuteronomy 14 in light of the creation account. By the same token, if both sources derive from a common source, then Leviticus 11 represents a revision of that common source in light of the priestly cosmogony. My own contribution to this discussion, therefore, is to suggest an explanation for why the framers of Leviticus 11 revised Deuteronomy 14 in the ways they did.

9. Lev. 11:24–26 refers to large domesticated animals *[běhēmâ]*, 11:27 refers to wild (or small) animals *[ḥayyâ]*, and 11:29–31 refers to things that swarm on the earth *(šereṣ)*. This scheme parallels Gen. 1:24–25 which also distinguishes between three kinds of land animals. In fact, Leviticus 11 uses two of the three terms that are used in Genesis 1 to describe land animals. Significantly, Deuteronomy only recognizes one category of land animal. See von Rad (1976, 57), Speiser (1964, 6–7), and Hoffman (1976 [1905–6], 225).

I would argue, moreover, that the desire to distinguish among three categories of land animals explains two further differences between the formulation of these rules in Leviticus and Deuteronomy. First, it explains why Leviticus deletes the list of permitted animals recorded in Deuteronomy (14:4–5). It does so because this deuteronomic list represents a confusion of two categories of land animals: domesticated and wild. This presents a problem for the authors of Leviticus who wish to follow Genesis 1 and differentiate among the various types of land animals. Consequently, in reworking Deuteronomy 14 they drop this list.

For the same reason, the authors of Leviticus modify the introductory formula to the dietary laws as recorded in Deuteronomy. Deuteronomy introduces the laws as follows: "These are the animals *(běhēmâ)* you may eat." Leviticus, by contrast, introduces the laws this way: "These are the creatures *(ḥayyâ)* that you may eat from among all the land animals" *(běhēmâ)*. In adding the word *ḥayyâ*, the framers of Leviticus signal their desire to preserve the linguistic distinction found in Genesis 1 between *běhēmâ* and *ḥayyâ*.

10. As noted by von Rad (1966, 101), the structure of Deut. 14:3–20 does not follow the order of creation. While the passage in Leviticus parallels the one in Deuteronomy (compare Lev. 11:2–20), it supplements it with additional material (11:21ff). I am suggesting that the additional material in Leviticus brings the discussion of the dietary laws closer to the structure of the Genesis account. Specifically, Leviticus contains a discussion of (1) large domesticated animals (Lev. 11:24–26), (2) nondomesticated (or small) animals (Lev. 11:27–28) and (3) things that swarm on the land (Lev. 11:29–31). Commentators on Leviticus note that the reference to large domesticated animals appears out of place. Logically, it should appear after verse 8 (Driver 1898, 75; Noth 1977, 92; Porter 1976, 90; Snaith 1967, 86). Consequently, the suggestion has been made that these verses derive from an independent tradition which was inserted here (Porter 1976, 90). But even if this is the case, it is difficult to understand why it was not added at 11:8 where it logically fits. I would argue, rather, that the framers of this passage purposefully inserted the reference to land animals at Lev. 11:24 in order to make the discussion follow the order in which wildlife was created. According to Genesis 1, the order of creation was fish, birds, then land animals (Gen. 1:20–25). By inserting the discussion of land animals at Lev. 11:24, the discussion of wildlife now

follows the order in which they were created: Lev. 11:9–12 discusses water animals; Lev. 11:13–23 discusses flying things; Lev. 11:24–31 discusses land animals.

11. A number of writers have drawn attention to the role of human intention in classifying things: Neusner (1981, 270–83; 1983, 72–80); [Avery]-Peck (1981, 3); Jaffee (1981, 4–5); Mandelbaum (1982, 3); Newman (1983, 17–19). My own study (1986, 95–143) systematically examines the role of intention in the Mishnah. The study at hand sets this discussion into a broader perspective by linking the emphasis on intention to changing conceptions of cosmogony, and by understanding such changes as a result of sociological factors.

12. It is interesting that in other instances Leviticus goes to great lengths to enumerate the criteria that will be used in classification (Lev. 11:2–20). It is possible that the priests failed to provide a definition of "useful" things because they wanted to downplay the role of humans in the classification scheme. To define what is useful would presumably involve appealing to human actions or perceptions. Such a view would be in tension with the overall thrust of the priestly system, which seeks to link its taxonomy to creation. Consequently, by not spelling out what is useful and useless, the priests mask what would otherwise represent a challenge to their system.

13. Alternative interpretations of this passage are discussed in Eilberg-Schwartz (1986, 123).

14. I have already discussed this point at some length elsewhere (Eilberg-Schwartz 1986, 103–8). Here, let me briefly mention the references in the Mishnah to the priestly creation story. First, the Mishnah refers to this story of creation in contemplating the obligation of Israelites to procreate (M. Yeb. 6:6), and in attempting to clarify the meaning of the biblical prohibition against sacrificing an animal and its offspring on "one day" (Lev. 22:28 [M. Hul. 5:5]). The influence of the priestly story of creation on mishnaic theology is evident in the types of blessings which the Mishnah requires Israelites to say over the food they are about to eat. Significantly, the substance of these blessings refers to creation and indicates that the sages of the Mishnah expect Israelites to routinely reflect on the act of creation (M. Ber. 6:1–3). Another example of how the creation story shaped mishnaic theology is the famous passage in Sanhedrin which discusses the moral implications of the fact that Adam was created alone (M. San. 4:5).

15. After developing this argument, I learned that Goldberg (1987, 107) had anticipated me. Goldberg develops a similar point through an analysis of certain traditional practices. My argument makes the contribution of showing how this symbolism is already underway in early rabbinic Judaism and how that symbolic process is absorbed in a radically altered way from the priestly system.

16. I realize that the term "rabbi" may have been used as a term of respect before its use in rabbinic circles. See the debate on this issue between Shanks (1976) and Zeitlin (1976). I am not claiming that the emergence of this term was in any way connected to its potential association with reproduction. Rather, I am suggesting that the rabbis who stand behind Avot interpreted their own title in this way.

Conclusion

1. I am here influenced by Bakhtin (1984). Neusner (1979) also anticipates me in seeing anthropology as useful in this regard. The distinction between low and high culture should not be confused with the distinction between elite and nonelite cultures. Although cultures of the elite might be more likely to develop themes of high culture, elites also have low culture: theories about the body and its emissions, etc.

References

Aberbach, M.
    1976   "The Relations between Master and Disciple in the Talmudic Age." In *Exploring the Talmud.* Vol. 1. Ed. Haim Z. Dimitrovsky. New York: Ktav Publishing House.

Ackerman, Robert
    1987   *J. G. Frazer: His Life and Work.* Cambridge: Cambridge University Press.

Adler, Margot
    1986   *Drawing Down the Moon.* Boston: Beacon Press.

Adler, Rachel
    1973   "Tum'ah and Toharah: Ends and Beginnings." *Response* 18:117–24. Reprinted in *The Jewish Woman.* Ed. Elizabeth Kolton, 63–71. New York: Schocken Books.

Albright, W. F.
    1942   *Archaeology and the Religion of Israel.* Baltimore: Johns Hopkins University Press.
    1964 [1940]   "How Well Can We Know the Ancient Near East?" In *History, Archaeology and Christian Humanism.* New York: McGraw-Hill.

Allegro, J. M.
    1956   *The Dead Sea Scrolls.* Baltimore: Penguin Books.

Allison, Henry S.
    1966   *Lessing and the Enlightenment.* Ann Arbor: University of Michigan Press.

Alter, Robert
    1979   "A New Theory of Kashrut." *Commentary* 68 (2):46–51.
    1981   *The Art of Biblical Narrative.* New York: Basic Books.

Altman, Alexander
    1983   Introduction to *Jerusalem,* by Moses Mendelssohn. Ed. Allan Arkush. Hanover: University Press of New England for Brandeis University Press.

Andersen, Francis I.
    1970   *The Hebrew Verbless Clause in the Pentateuch.* Nashville: Abingdon.

Anderson, G. W.
    1951   "Hebrew Religion." In *The Old Testament and Modern Study.* Ed. H. H. Rowley. Oxford: Oxford University Press.

Andriolo, Karin
    1973   "A Structural Analysis of Genealogy and Worldview in the Old Testament." *American Anthropologist* 75:1657–67.

Apsler, Alfred
    1943   "Herder and the Jews." *Monatshefte für deutschen Unterricht* 35:1–15.

Astley, H.J.D.
    1929   "Biblical Folklore." In *Biblical Anthropology Compared with and Illustrated by the Folklore of Europe and the Customs of Primitive Peoples.* London: Oxford University Press.

Atkinson, Geoffroy
    1924   *Les relations de voyages du XVIIe siècle et l'évolution des idées.* Paris: E. Champion.
Bakhtin, Mikhail M.
    1984   *Rabelais and His World.* Trans. Hélène Iswolsky. Bloomington: Indiana University Press.
Barnard, F. M.
    1959   "The Hebrews and Herder's Political Creed." *The Modern Language Review* 54:533–46.
    1965   *Herder's Social and Political Thought: From Enlightenment to Nationalism.* Oxford: Clarendon Press.
    1969   Introduction to *J. G. Herder on Social and Political Culture.* Cambridge: Cambridge University Press.
Barnes, J. A.
    1977   "Genetrix:Genitor::Nature:Culture?" *The Character of Kinship.* Ed. Jack Goody. Cambridge: Cambridge University Press.
Barr, James
    1959   "Theophany and Anthropomorphism in the Old Testament." *Vetus Testamentum.* Supplements. 7:31–38.
Bauman, H.
    1964 [1936]   *Schöfung und Urzeit des Menschen in Mythus der afrikanischen Völker.* Berlin: Reimer.
BDB
    1975 [1907]   *A Hebrew and English Lexicon of the Old Testament.* Ed. Francis Brown, S. R. Driver, and C. A. Driver Briggs. Oxford: Clarendon Press.
Beidelman, T. O.
    1974   *W. Robertson Smith and the Sociological Study of Religion.* Chicago: University of Chicago Press.
Berger, Peter, and Thomas Luckmann
    1967   *The Social Construction of Reality.* Garden City: Doubleday.
Betts, C. J.
    1984   *Early Deism in France.* The Hague: Martinus Nijhoff Publishers.
Biale, Rachel
    1984   *Women and Jewish Law.* New York: Schocken Books.
Bird, Phyllis A.
    1981   "Male and Female He Created Them." *Harvard Theological Review* 74 (1):129–60.
Bissell, Benjamin
    1924   *The American Indian in English Literature of the Eighteenth Century.* New Haven: Yale University Press.
Black, J. S., and G. W. Chrystal
    1912   *The Life of William Robertson Smith.* London: A. and C. Black.
Blenkinsopp, Joseph
    1983   *Wisdom and Law in the Old Testament.* Cambridge: Cambridge University Press.
Boas, Franz
    1940 [1896]   "The Limitations of the Comparative Method." In *Race, Language, and Culture.* 270–80. New York: Free Press.
    1940 [1920]   "The Methods of Ethnology." In *Race, Language, and Culture,* 281–94. New York: Free Press.

1940 [1930]   "Some Problems of Methodology in the Social Sciences." In
              Race, Language, and Culture, 260–69. New York: Free Press.
Brandes, Stanley
    1981   "Like Wounded Stags: Male Sexual Identity in an Andalusian Town."
            In *Sexual Meanings*. Ed. Sherry Ortner and Harriet Whitehead. Cam-
            bridge: Cambridge University Press.
Bright, John
    1965   "Jeremiah." *The Anchor Bible Commentary*. Garden City, New York:
            Doubleday.
Broce, Gerald Lloyd
    1973   "Herder and the Genesis of Cultural Relativism." Ph.D. diss., Univer-
            sity of Colorado. Ann Arbor: University Microfilms.
Bryk, Felix
    1970 [1930]   *Sex and Circumcision*. Reprint of *Circumcision in Man and
                  Woman*. North Hollywood, Calif.: Brandon House.
Buckley, Thomas, and Alma Gottlieb
    1988   "Introduction: A Critical Appraisal of Theories of Menstrual Symbol-
            ism." In *Blood Magic: The Anthropology of Menstruation*. 1–54. Ed.
            Thomas Buckley and Alma Gottlieb. Berkeley: University of California
            Press.
Budapest, Z.
    1986   *The Holy Book of Women's Mysteries*. Vol. 1. n.p.
Bulmer, R.
    1967   "Why Is the Cassowary Not a Bird?" *Man* 2 (1):5–25.
Burrow, J. W.
    1970   *Evolution and Society: A Study in Victorian Social Theory*. Cambridge:
            Cambridge University Press.
Carmichael, Calum
    1985   *Law and Narrative in the Bible*. Ithaca: Cornell University Press.
Carroll, Michael P.
    1977   "Leach, Genesis, and Structural Analysis: A Critical Evaluation."
            American Ethnologist 4:633–77.
Cassirer, Ernst
    1951   *Philosophy of the Enlightenment*. Princeton: Princeton University Press.
Cassuto, U.
    1969   *The Book of Genesis* [Heb.]. Part 1. Jerusalem: Magnes Press.
Chandler, William H.
    1950   *Evergreen Orchards*. Philadelphia: Lea and Febiger.
Childs, Brevard
    1970   *Biblical Theology in Crisis*. Philadelphia: Westminster Press.
Chinard, Gilbert
    1911   *L'exotisme américain dan la littérature française au XVI siècle*. Paris:
            Hachette.
    1913   *L'amérique et le rêve exotique dan la littérature française au XVII et au
            XVIII siècle*. Paris: Hachette.
Christ, Carol P.
    1987   *Laughter of Aphrodite*. San Francisco: Harper and Row.
Chubb, Thomas
    1978 [1730]   *The Comparative Excellence and Obligation of Moral and Positive
                  Duties*. New York: Garland Publishing.

1978 [1731]   *A Discourse Concerning Reason.* New York: Garland Publishing.
Clark, Robert T.
1934   "The Noble Savage and the Idea of Tolerance in Herder's *Brief zu Beförderung der Humanität." Journal of English and Germanic Philology* 33:46–56.
1955   *Herder: His Life and Thought.* Berkeley and Los Angeles: University of California Press.
Clifford, James
1988   "On Ethnographic Authority." In *The Predicament of Culture,* 21–54. Cambridge, Mass.: Harvard University Press.
Clifford, James, and George E. Marcus, eds.
1986   *Writing Culture: The Poetics and Politics of Ethnography.* Berkeley: University of California Press.
Cohen, Shaye J. D.
1985   "The Matrilineal Principle in Historical Perspective." *Judaism* 34 (1):9–14.
Collier, Jane, and Michelle Z. Rosaldo
1981   "Politics and Gender in Simple Societies." In *Sexual Meanings.* Ed. Sherry Ortner and Harriet Whitehead. Cambridge: Cambridge University Press.
Collingwood, R. G.
1958   *Principles of Art.* Oxford: Oxford University Press.
Collins, Anthony
1976 [1724]   *A Discourse on the Grounds and Reason of the Christian Religion.* New York: Garland Publishing.
Condit, Ira J.
1947   *The Fig.* Waltham, Mass.: Chronica Botanica.
Conybeare, John
1732   *A Defense of Reveal'd Religion.* Ann Arbor: University Microfilms.
Cook, Stanley
1902   "Israel and Totemism." *The Jewish Quarterly Review* 14:413–48.
Cragg, Gerald P.
1964   *Reason and Authority in the Eighteenth Century.* Cambridge: Cambridge University Press.
Cross, Frank Moore
1973   *Canaanite Myth and Hebrew Epic.* Cambridge, Mass.: Harvard University Press.
Culler, Jonathan
1982   *On Deconstruction: Theory and Criticism after Structuralism.* Ithaca: Cornell University Press.
Culley, Robert C.
1985   "Exploring New Directions." In *The Hebrew Bible and Its Modern Interpreters.* Ed. Douglas A. Knight and Gene M. Tucker, 167–89. Philadelphia: Fortress Press.
Daube, David
1949   "Rabbinic Methods of Interpretation and Hellenistic Rhetoric." *Hebrew Union College Annual* 22:239–64.
Davies, Douglas
1977   "An Interpretation of Sacrifice in Leviticus." *Zeitschrift für die alttestamentliche Wissenschaft.* 89:387–99.

Delaney, Carol
    1986   "The Meaning of Paternity and the Virgin Birth Debate." *Man* 21 (3):494–513.
    1988   "Mortal Flow: Menstruation in Turkish Village Society." In *Blood Magic: The Anthropology of Menstruation,* 75–93. Ed. Thomas Buckley and Alma Gottlieb. Berkeley: University of California Press.
de Vaux, Roland
    1965   *Ancient Israel: Religious Institutions.* Vol. 2. New York: McGraw-Hill.
Dever, William G.
    1980   "Biblical Theology and Biblical Archaeology: An Appreciation of G. Ernest Wright." *Harvard Theological Review* 73 (1–2): 1–14.
Donaldson, Mara E.
    1981   "Kinship Theory in Patriarchal Narratives: The Case of the Barren Wife." *The Journal of the American Academy of Religion* 49 (1):77–87.
Douglas, Mary
    1966   *Purity and Danger.* London: Routledge and Kegan Paul.
    1973   *Natural Symbols.* New York: Vintage Books.
    1975   *Implicit Meanings.* London: Routledge and Kegan Paul.
Douglas, Mary, and Baron Isherwood
    1979   *The World of Goods.* New York: Basic Books.
Downie, R. Angus
    1970   *Frazer and The Golden Bough.* London: Victor Gollancz.
Driver, S. R.
    1895   *International Critical Commentary on Deuteronomy.* New York: Charles Scribner's Sons.
    1898   *The Book of Leviticus.* New York: Dodd, Mead and Company.
    1906   *The Book of Genesis.* New York: Edwin S. Gorham.
Durkheim, Emile
    1965 [1915]   *The Elementary Forms of the Religious Life.* Trans. Joseph Swain. New York: Free Press.
    1968 [1895]   *The Rules of Sociological Method.* Trans. Sarah A. Solovay and John H. Mueller. New York: Free Press.
Durkheim, Emile, and Marcel Mauss
    1963 [1903]   *Primitive Classification.* Trans. Rodney Needham. Chicago: University of Chicago Press.
Eggan, Fred
    1954   "Social Anthropology and Controlled Comparison." *American Anthropologist* 56:743–63.
Eilberg-Schwartz, Howard
    1986   *The Human Will in Judaism: The Mishnah's Philosophy of Intention.* Atlanta: Scholars Press.
    1987a   "Who's Kidding Whom? A Serious Reading of Rabbinic Word Plays." *Journal of the American Academy of Religion* 55 (4):765–88.
    1987b   "When the Reader is in the Write." *Prooftexts* 7 (2):194–208.
    1989   "Witches of the West: Neo-paganism and Goddess Worship As Enlightenment Religions." *Journal of Feminist Studies in Religion* 5 (1):77–95.
    1990   "Myth, Inference, and the Relativism of Reason: An Argument from the History of Judaism." In *Myth and Philosophy.* Ed. Frank Reynolds and David Tracy. Albany: State University of New York Press.

Eissfeldt, Otto
　　1965　*The Old Testament: An Introduction.* Trans. P. R. Ackroyd. New York: Harper and Row.
Eliade, Mircea
　　1954　*The Myth of the Eternal Return.* Trans. Willard R. Trask. New York: Pantheon Books.
　　1963　*Myth and Reality.* Trans. Willard R. Trask. New York: Harper and Row.
Eliot, John
　　1671　*A Brief Narrative of the Progress of the Gospel amongst the Indian in New England in the Year 1670.* London: n.p.
Ergang, Robert R.
　　1966　*Herder and the Foundations of German Nationalism.* New York: Octagon Books.
Ettinger, Shmuel
　　1961　"The Beginnings of the Change in the Attitude of European Society Towards the Jews." *Scripta Hierosolymitana* 7:193–219.
　　1964　"Jews and Judaism As Seen by the English Deists in the 18th Century." [Heb.]. *Zion* 29:182–207.
Evans-Pritchard, E. E.
　　1933　"The Intellectualist Interpretation of Magic." *Bulletin of the Faculty of Arts* 1 (2):282–311.
　　1934　"Lévy-Bruhl's Theory of Primitive Mentality." *Bulletin of the Faculty of Arts* 2:1–27.
　　1951　*Social Anthropology.* London: Cohen and West.
　　1956　*Nuer Religion.* Oxford: Oxford University Press.
　　1960　Introduction to *Death and the Right Hand,* by Robert Hertz. Glencoe: Free Press.
　　1965　"The Comparative Method in Social Anthropology." In *The Position of Women in Primitive Society,* 13–36. Glencoe: Free Press.
　　1976 [1937]　*Witchcraft, Oracle and Magic among the Azande.* Abrdg. Eva Gillies. Oxford: Clarendon Press.
Everett, Thomas H.
　　1981　*The New York Botanical Garden Illustrated Encylopedia of Horticulture.* Vol. 3. New York: Garland Publishing.
Fairchild, Hoxie Neale
　　1961　*The Noble Savage: A Study in Romantic Naturalism.* New York: Russell and Russell.
Feeley-Harnik, Gillian
　　1982　"Is Historical Anthropology Possible?: The Case of the Runaway Slave." In *Humanizing America's Iconic Book.* Ed. Gene M. Tucker and Douglas A. Knight, 95–126. Chico, Calif.: Scholars Press.
Feldman, Emanuel
　　1977　*Biblical and Post-Biblical Defilement and Mourning.* New York: Yeshiva University Press.
Feliks, Jehuda
　　1976　*Plant World of the Bible* [Heb.]. Ramat Gan: Masada.
Fenton, William N., and Elizabeth L. Moore
　　1974　Introduction to *Customs of the American Indians Compared to Primitive Times,* by Joseph François Lafitau. Toronto: The Champlain Society.

Fernandez, James W.
    1972   "Persuasions and Performances: Of the Beast in Every Body . . . and
            the Metaphors of Everyman." *Daedalus* 101 (1): 39–60.
    1974   "The Mission of Metaphor in Expressive Culture." *Current Anthropol-
            ogy* 15 (2): 119–33.
    1977   "The Performance of Ritual Metaphors." In *The Social Use of Metaphor*.
            Ed. David Sapir and Christopher Crocker. Philadelphia: University of
            Pennsylvania Press.
    1982   *Bwiti: An Ethnography of Religious Imagination in Africa*. Princeton:
            Princeton University Press.
    1986   *Persuasions and Performances*. Bloomington: Indiana University Press.
Feuerbach, Ludwig
    1959 [1841]   *The Essence of Christianity*. Trans. George Eliot. New York:
                   Harper Torchbooks.
Feyerabend, Paul
    1975   *Against Method*. Norfolk: Thetford Press.
    1978   *Science in a Free Society*. Norfolk: Thetford Press.
Fiensy, David
    1987   "Using the Nuer Culture of Africa in Understanding the Old
            Testament: An Evaluation." *Journal for the Study of the Old Testament*
            38:73–83.
Fisch, Harold
    1971   *The Dual Image: The Figure of the Jew in English and American Litera-
            ture*. New York: Ktav Publishing House.
Fischel, Henry, ed.
    1977   *Essays in Greco-Roman and Related Talmud Literature*. New York: Ktav.
Fish, Stanley
    1980   *Is There a Text in This Class?* Cambridge, Mass.: Harvard University
            Press.
Fishbane, Michael
    1985   *Biblical Interpretation in Ancient Israel*. Oxford: Clarendon Press.
Fohrer, Georg
    1972   *History of Israelite Religion*. Trans. David E. Green. Nashville: Abingdon
            Press.
Foster, James
    1731   *The Usefulness, Truth, and Excellency of the Christian Revelation*. 3rd ed.
            London: n.p.
Foucault, Michel
    1973a   *Madness and Civilization: A History of Insanity in the Age of Reason*.
            Trans. Richard Howard. New York: Vintage.
    1973b   *The Birth of the Clinic*. Trans. A. M. Sheridan Smith. New York:
            Vintage.
    1973c   *The Order of Things: An Archaeology of the Human Sciences*. Trans. A.
            M. Sheridan Smith. New York: Vintage Books.
    1977   "Nietzsche, Genealogy, History." In *Language, Counter-memory, Prac-
            tice*. Ed. Donald F. Bouchard. Trans. Donald F. Bouchard and Sherry
            Simon. Ithaca: Cornell University Press.
    1979   *Discipline and Punish: The Birth of the Clinic*. Trans. Alan Sheridan. New
            York: Vintage.

Fox, James
  1971 "Sister's Child As Plant Metaphors in an Idiom of Consanguinity." In *Rethinking Kinship and Marriage*. Ed. Rodney Needham. London: Tavistock Publications.

Frankfort, H.
  1951 *The Problem of Similarity in Ancient Near Eastern Religions.* Oxford: Clarendon Press.

Frankfort, H., and H. A. Frankfort
  1971 [1946] "The Emancipation of Thought from Myth." In *Before Philosophy: The Intellectual Adventure of Ancient Man.* Ed. H. Frankfort et al., 237–64. Baltimore: Penguin Books.

Frantz, R. W.
  1967 *The English Traveller and the Movement of Ideas: 1660–1732.* Lincoln: University of Nebraska Press.

Frazer, J. G.
  1900 *The Golden Bough.* 2d ed. 3 vols. London: Macmillan.
  1919 *Folklore in the Old Testament.* London: Macmillan.
  1967 [1894] "William Robertson Smith." In *The Gorgon's Head and Other Literary Pieces,* 278–90. Freeport: Books for Libraries Press.

Frei, Hans
  1974 *The Eclipse of Biblical Narrative: A Study in Eighteenth and Nineteenth Century Hermeneutics.* New Haven: Yale University Press.

Freud, Sigmund
  1953 *The Complete Psychological Works of Sigmund Freud.* Standard Edition. Trans. James Strachey. London: Hogarth Press.
  1974 "The Taboo of Virginity." In *Sexuality and Psychology of Love.* Trans. Joan Riviere. New York: Collier Books.

Friedl, Ernestine
  1975 *Women and Men: An Anthropologist's View.* New York: Holt, Rinehart, and Winston.

Gadamer, Hans-Georg
  1975 *Truth and Method.* New York: Crossroad.

Gardner, Victor R., F. C. Bradford, and H. D. Hooker
  1952 *Fundamentals of Fruit Production.* New York: McGraw Hill.

Gay, Peter
  1964 *Party of Humanity: Essays in French Enlightenment.* New York: Alfred A. Knopf.
  1966 *The Enlightenment: An Interpretation.* New York: Alfred A. Knopf.
  1968 *Deism: An Anthology.* Princeton: D. Van Nostrand.

Geertz, Clifford
  1973 *The Interpretation of Cultures.* New York: Basic Books.

George, Katherine
  1958 "The Civilized West Looks at Primitive Africa, 1400–1800: A Study in Ethnocentrism." *Isis* 49:62–72.

Gesenius, W.
  1976 [1910] *Gesenius' Hebrew Grammar.* Ed. E. Kautzsch and A. E. Cowley. Oxford: Clarendon Press.

Gildon, Charles
  1976 [1705] *The Deist's Manual.* New York: Garland Publishing.

Gillies, Alexander
 1945 *Herder.* Oxford: Basil Blackwell.
Girard, René
 1979 *Violence and the Sacred.* Trans. Patrick Gregory. Baltimore: Johns Hopkins University Press.
Glaser, Lynn
 1973 *Indians or Jews? An Introduction to a Reprint of Manasseh Ben Israel's "Hope of Israel".* Gilroy: Roy V. Boswell.
Glassman, Bernard
 1975 *Anti-Semitic Stereotypes without Jews: Images of the Jews in England 1290-1700.* Detroit: Wayne State University Press.
Gluckman, Max
 1949 "The Role of the Sexes in Wiko Circumcision Ceremonies." In *Social Structure,* 145-67. Ed. Meyer Fortes. Oxford: Clarendon Press.
Goldberg, Harvey, ed.
 1987 *Judaism Viewed from Within and from Without.* Albany: State University of New York Press.
Goldenberg, Naomi
 1979 *Changing of the Gods.* Boston: Beacon Press.
Goody, Jack
 1956 "A Comparative Approach to Incest and Adultery." *British Journal of Sociology* 7:286-305.
Goor, Asaph, and Max Nuroch
 1968 *The Fruits of the Holy Land.* Jerusalem: Israel Universities Press.
Gottlieb, Alma
 1988 "Menstrual Cosmology among the Beng of Ivory Coast." In *Blood Magic: The Anthropology of Menstruation,* 55-75. Ed. Thomas Buckley and Alma Gottlieb. Berkeley: University of California Press.
Gottwald, Norman
 1979 *The Tribes of Yahweh.* Maryknoll: Orbis Books.
Gould, Steven Jay
 1982 *The Panda's Thumb.* New York: W. W. Norton & Company.
Graupe, H. M.
 1978 *The Rise of Modern Judaism: An Intellectual History of German Jewry 1650-1942.* Trans. John Robinson. Huntington: Robert E. Krieger Publishing Company.
Haan, Norma, Robert N. Bellah, Paul Rabinow, and William M. Sullivan, eds.
 1983 *Social Science As Moral Inquiry.* New York: Columbia University Press.
Hallo, William
 1980 "Biblical History in Its Near Eastern Setting: The Contextual Approach." In *Scripture in Context: Essays on the Comparative Method,* 1-26. Ed. Carl D. Evans, William W. Hallo, and John B. White. Pittsburgh: Pickwick Press.
Hallpike, C. R.
 1979 *The Foundations of Primitive Thought.* Oxford: Clarendon Press.
Hambly, Wilfrid D.
 1935 "Tribal Initiation of Boys in Angola." *American Anthropologist* 37:36-40.

Hanke, Lewis
    1951 *Bartolomé De Las Casas: An Interpretation of His Life and Writings.* The Hague: Martinus Nijhoff.
    1965 *The Spanish Struggle for Justice in the Conquest of America.* Boston: Little, Brown and Company.
    1970 *Aristotle and the American Indians: A Study in Race Prejudice in the Modern World.* Bloomington: Indiana University Press.

Haran, Menahem
    1979 "Seething a Kid in Its Mother's Milk." *Journal of Jewish Studies* 30:23–35.

Harman, William
    1985 "Kinship Metaphors in the Hindu Pantheon: Siva as Brother-in-Law and Son-in-Law." *Journal of the American Academy of Religion* 53 (3):411–30.

Harris, Marvin
    1968 *The Rise of Anthropological Theory.* New York: Harper and Row.

Hayes, E. Nelson, and Tanya Hayes, eds.
    1970 *Claude Lévi-Strauss: The Anthropologist As Hero.* Cambridge, Mass.: MIT Press.

Hazard, Paul
    1973 *European Thought in the Eighteenth Century.* Gloucester, Mass.: Peter Smith.

Healy, George
    1958 "The French Jesuits and the Idea of the Noble Savage." *William and Mary Quarterly* 15:143–65.

Hempel, Carl
    1968 "The Logic of Functional Analysis." In *Readings in the Philosophy of the Social Sciences.* Ed. May Brodbeck. New York: Macmillan.

Hendel, Ronald
    1988 "The Social Origins of the Aniconic Tradition in Early Israel." *Catholic Biblical Quarterly* 50 (3):365–82.

Herbert of Cherbury
    1937 [1624] *De Veritate.* 3rd ed. Trans. Meyrick H. Carré. Bristol: J. W. Arrowsmith.
    1944 [1645] *De Religione Laici.* Trans. Harold L. Hutcheson. New Haven: Yale University Press.

Herder, Johann Gottfried
    1969 [1774] "Yet Another Philosophy of History." In *J. G. Herder on Social and Political Culture.* Ed. F. M. Barnard. Cambridge: Cambridge University Press.
    1969 [1784–91] "Ideas for a Philosophy of the History of Mankind." In *J. G. Herder on Social and Political Culture.* Ed. F. M. Barnard. Cambridge: Cambridge University Press.
    1980 [1782–83] *The Spirit of Hebrew Poetry.* Trans. James Marsh. Ann Arbor: University Microfilms.

Herdt, Gilbert
    1987 *Guardians of the Flutes: Idioms of Masculinity.* New York: Columbia University Press.

Hertz, J. H.
   1961 [1935]   *The Pentateuch and Haftorahs.* London: Soncino.
Hertzberg, Arthur
   1968   *The French Enlightenment and the Jews.* New York: Columbia University Press.
Hodgen, Margaret
   1936   *The Doctrine of Survivals.* London: Allenson and Company.
   1964   *Early Anthropology in the Sixteenth and Seventeenth Centuries.* Philadelphia: University of Pennsylvania.
Hoffman, D.
   1906   *Das Buch Leviticus.* Vol. 2. Berlin: Poppelauer.
Hoffman, Lawrence
   1987   *Beyond the Text: A Holistic Approach to Liturgy.* Bloomington: Indiana University Press.
Holdredge, Claire Parker, and Kimball Young
   1927   "Circumcision Rites among the Bajok." *American Anthropologist* 29:661–69.
Horticultural Crops Group
   1982   *Date Production and Protection: With Special Reference to North Africa and the Near East.* Rome: Food and Agricultural Organization of the United Nations.
Huddleston, Lee Eldridge
   1967   *Origins of the American Indians: European Concepts 1492-1729.* Austin: University of Texas Press.
Hume, David
   1956 [1757]   *The Natural History of Religion.* Ed. H. E. Root. Stanford: Stanford University Press.
Hurvitz, Avi
   1974   "The Evidence of Dating the Priestly Code." *Revue Biblique* 81:24–57.
Hutcheson, Harold L.
   1944   Introduction to *De Religione Laici,* by Lord Herbert of Cherbury. New Haven: Yale University Press.
Hyamson, Albert
   1903   "The Lost Tribes, and the Influence of the Search for Them on the Return of the Jews to England." *Jewish Quarterly Review* 15:640–76.
Hyatt, J. P.
   1976   "Circumcision." *Interpreter's Dictionary of the Bible Supplement.* Ed. Keith Crim, 629–31. Nashville: Abingdon.
IB
   1953   *The Interpreter's Bible.* Ed. George A. Buttrick. Vol. 2. New York: Abingdon.
Inhelder, Bärbel, and Jean Piaget
   1969   *The Early Growth of Logic in the Child.* Trans. E. A. Lunzer and D. Papert. New York: W. W. Norton and Company.
Isaac, Eric
   1964   "Circumcision As a Covenant Rite." *Anthropos* 59:444–56.
Jaffee, Martin S.
   1981   *Mishnah's Theology of Tithing.* Chico, Calif.: Scholars Press.
Janick, Jules, and James N. Moore
   1975   *Advances in Fruit Breeding.* West Lafayette: Purdue University Press.

Jay, Nancy
 1985 "Sacrifice As Remedy for Having Been Born of Woman." In *Immaculate and Powerful.* Ed. C. W. Atkinson et al., 283–309. Boston: Beacon Press.
 1988 "Sacrifice, Descent, and the Patriarchs." *Vetus Testamentum* 38 (1):52–70.
Jensen, Ad. E.
 1960 "Beziehungen zwischen dem Alten Testament und der nilotischen Kultur in Afrika." In *Culture in History.* Ed. Stanley Diamond. New York: Columbia University Press.
Jobling, D.
 1984 "Lévi-Strauss and the Structural Analysis of the Hebrew Bible." In *Anthropology and the Study of Religion.* Ed. R. L. Moore et al., 192–211. Chicago: University of Chicago Press.
Johnson, Barbara
 1980 *The Critical Difference: Essays in the Contemporary Rhetoric of Reading.* Baltimore: Johns Hopkins University Press.
Josephus
 1978 *Jewish Antiquities.* Vol. 1. Trans. H. Thackeray. Cambridge, Mass.: Harvard University Press.
JPS
 1962 *The Torah.* Philadelphia: Jewish Publication Society of America.
 1978 *The Prophets.* Philadelphia: Jewish Publication Society of America.
 1982 *The Writings.* Philadelphia: Jewish Publication Society of America.
Junod, Henri A.
 1962 [1912] *The Life of a South African Tribe.* New Hyde Park, N.Y.: University Books.
Kadushin, Max
 1952 *The Rabbinic Mind.* New York: Bloch Publishing Company.
Kamenka, Eugene
 1970 *The Philosophy of Ludwig Feuerbach.* New York: Praeger.
Kant, Immanuel
 1960 [1794] *Religion within the Limits of Reason Alone.* Trans. Theodore M. Greene and Hoyt H. Hudson. New York: Harper Torchbooks.
Katz, Jacob
 1980 *From Prejudice to Destruction: Anti-Semitism, 1700–1933.* Cambridge, Mass.: Harvard University Press.
Kaufmann, Yehezkel
 1972 [1937–56] *The Religion of Israel.* Trans. and abrdg. Moshe Greenberg. New York: Schocken Books.
Kennedy, J. H.
 1950 *Jesuit and Savage in New France.* New Haven: Yale University Press.
Kirshenblatt-Gimblett, Barbara
 1982 "The Cut That Binds: The Western Ashkenazic Torah Binder As Nexus between Circumcision and Torah." In *Celebration: Studies in Festivity and Ritual.* Ed. Victor Turner. Washington: Smithsonian Institute Press.
Kluckholn, Clyde
 1961 *Anthropology and the Classics.* Providence: Brown University Press.
Kosmala, Hans
 1962 "The 'Bloody Husband.'" *Vetus Testamentum* 12:14–27.

References

Kroeber, Alfred
  1935   "History and Science in Anthropology." *American Anthropologist*
          37:539–69.
Kugelmass, Jack
  1986   *The Miracle of Intervale Avenue: The Story of a Jewish Congregation in
          South Bronx*. New York: Schocken Books.
Kugelmass, Jack, ed.
  1988   *Between Two Worlds: Ethnographic Essays on American Jewry*. Ithaca:
          Cornell University Press.
Kuhn, Thomas S.
  1970   *The Structure of Scientific Revolutions*. 2d ed. Chicago: University of Chi-
          cago Press.
Lafitau, Joseph François
  1974 [1724]   *Customs of the American Indians Compared to the Customs of
          Primitive Times*. Ed. and trans. William N. Fenton and Elizabeth
          L. Moore. Toronto: The Champlain Society.
Lakatos, Imre
  1970   "Falsification and the Methodology of Scientific Research Program-
          mes." In *Criticism and the Growth of Knowledge*. Ed. Imre Lakatos and
          Alan Musgrave. Cambridge: Cambridge University Press.
Lakoff, George, and Mark Johnson
  1980   *Metaphors We Live By*. Chicago: University of Chicago Press.
Lang, Bernhard, ed.
  1985a   *Anthropological Approaches to the Old Testament*. Philadelphia: Fortress
          Press.
  1985b   "Non-Semitic Deluge Stories and the Book of Genesis." *Anthropos*
          80:605–16.
Leach, Edmund
  1961   "Golden Bough or Gilded Twig." *Daedalus* 90 (2):371–87.
  1969   *Genesis As Myth*. London: Jonathan Cape.
  1976   *Culture and Communication*. Cambridge: Cambridge University Press.
  1982   "Anthropological Approaches to the Study of the Bible during the
          Twentieth Century." In *Humanizing America's Iconic Book*. Ed. Gene
          H. Tucker and Douglas A. Knight, 73–93. Chico, Calif.: Scholars Press.
Leach, Edmund, and D. Alan Aycock
  1983   *Structuralist Interpretations of Biblical Myth*. Cambridge: Cambridge
          University Press.
Leland, J.
  1798   *A View of the Principal Deistical Writers*. 5th ed. Vol. 2. London: n.p.
Lescarbot, Marc
  1914 [1611]   *History of New France*. Vol. 3. Trans. W. L. Grant. Toronto: The
          Champlain Society.
Leslie, Charles
  1828 [1723]   *A Short and Easy Method with the Deists*. London: C & J
          Rivington.
L'Estrange, Hamon
  1652   *Americans No Iewes, or Improbabilities That the Americans Are of That
          Race*. London: n.p.
Levine, Baruch
  1974   *In the Presence of the Lord: A Study of Cult and Some Cultic Terms in
          Ancient Israel*. Leiden: E. J. Brill.

Lévi-Strauss, Claude

    1962   *Totemism.* Trans. Rodney Needham. Boston: Beacon Press.

    1963   *Structural Anthropology.* Trans. Claire Jacobson and Brooke Grundfest Schoepf. New York: Basic Books.

    1966   *The Savage Mind.* Chicago: University of Chicago Press.

    1973   *From Honey to Ashes.* Trans. John and Doreen Weightman. New York: Harper and Row.

    1975   *Tristes Tropiques.* Trans. John Weightman. New York: Atheneum.

    1978   *The Origin of Table Manners.* Trans. John and Doreen Weightman. New York: Harper and Row.

Lévy-Bruhl, Lucien

    1985 [1910]   *How Natives Think.* Princeton: Princeton University Press.

Lewis, Gilbert

    1987   "A Lesson from Leviticus: Leprosy." *Man* 22 (4):593–612.

Licht, Jacob

    1958   "An Analysis of the Treatise of the Two Spirits in DSD." *Scripta Hierosolymitana.* Vol. 4. Ed. Chaim Rabin and Yigael Yadin. Jerusalem: Magnes Press.

Lieberman, Saul

    1950   *Hellenism and Jewish Palestine.* New York: The Jewish Theological Seminary of America.

Lightstone, Jack

    1988   *Society, the Sacred, and Scripture in Ancient Judaism.* Waterloo, Ont.: Wilfrid Laurier University Press.

Linton, Ralph

    1936   *The Study of Man.* New York: Appleton-Century-Crofts.

Llewelyn-Davies, Melissa

    1981   "Women, Warriors and Patriarchs." In *Sexual Meanings.* Ed. Sherry B. Ortner and Harriet Whitehead. Cambridge: Cambridge University Press.

Locke, John

    1967 [1695]   *The Reasonableness of Christianity.* Ed. I. T. Ramsey. Stanford: Stanford University Press.

    1967 [1706]   *A Discourse on Miracles.* Ed. I. T. Ramsey. Stanford: Stanford University Press.

    1975 [1690]   *An Essay Concerning Human Understanding.* Ed. Peter H. Nidditch. Oxford: Clarendon Press.

Löfgren, Orvar

    1985   "Our Friends in Nature: Class and Animal Symbolism." *Ethnos* 50 (3–4):184–213.

Long, O.

    1976   "Recent Field Studies in Oral Literature and Their Bearing on OT Criticism." *Vetus Testamentum* 26:187–98.

Lovejoy, Arthur O.

    1936   *The Great Chain of Being.* Cambridge, Mass.: Harvard University Press.

Lovejoy, Arthur O., and George Boas

    1965   *Primitivism and Related Ideas in Antiquity.* New York: Octagon Books.

Lovin, Robin W., and Frank Reynolds

    1985   *Cosmogony and Ethical Order.* Chicago: University of Chicago Press.

Lukes, Steven

    1985   *Emile Durkheim: His Life and Work.* Stanford: Stanford University Press.

Malinowski, B.

    1929 *The Sexual Life of Savages.* New York: Harcourt Brace Jovanovich.

    1954 [1925] "Magic, Science, and Religion." In *Magic, Science, and Religion.* Garden City: Doubleday.

    1959 [1926] *Crime and Custom in Savage Society.* Patterson, N.J.: Littlefield, Adams.

    1961 [1922] *Argonauts of the Western Pacific.* Prospect Heights: Waveland Press.

    1978 [1935] *Coral Gardens and Their Magic.* New York: Dover Publications.

Mandelbaum, Irving

    1982 *A History of the Mishnaic Law of Agriculture.* Chico, Calif.: Scholars Press.

Manuel, Frank E.

    1959 *The Eighteenth Century Confronts the Gods.* Cambridge, Mass: Harvard University Press.

    1968 Introduction to *Reflections on the Philosophy of the History of Mankind,* by Johann Gottfried von Herder. Chicago: University of Chicago Press.

    1983 *The Changing of the Gods.* Hanover: University Press of New England.

Marcus, George E., and Michael M. J. Fischer

    1986 *Anthropology As Cultural Critique: An Experimental Moment in the Human Sciences.* Chicago: University of Chicago Press.

Marett, R. R., ed.

    1966 [1908] *Anthropology and the Classics.* New York: Barnes and Noble.

Marshall, Robert

    1979 "Heroes and Hebrews: The Priest in the Promised Land." *American Ethnologist* 6 (4):772–90.

Martin, Emily

    1987 *The Woman in the Body: A Cultural Analysis of Reproduction.* Boston: Beacon Press.

McCauley, Robert N., and E. Thomas Lawson

    1984 "Functionalism Reconsidered." *History of Religions* 23 (4):372–81.

McLennan, J. F.

    1869–70 "The Worship of Plants and Animals." *Fortnightly Review* 12:404–27; 13:194–207.

Mead, Margaret

    1977 [1935] *Sex and Temperament in Three Primitive Societies.* New York: Routledge & Kegan Paul.

Meeks, Wayne

    1977 "In One Body: The Unity of Humankind in Colossians and Ephesians." In *God's Christ and His People: Studies in Honour of Nils Alstrup Dahl.* Ed. Jacob Jervell and Wayne A. Meeks. Oslo: Universitetsforlaget.

    1983 *The First Urban Christians.* New Haven: Yale University Press.

Meggit, M. J.

    1962 *Desert People: A Study of the Walbiri Aborigines of Central Australia.* Chicago: University of Chicago Press.

Meigs, Anna

    1984 *Food, Sex, and Pollution: A New Guinea Religion.* New Brunswick: Rutgers University Press.

Mendelssohn, Moses
  1983 [1783] *Jerusalem: Or On Religious Power and Judaism.* Trans. Allan
                Arkush. Hanover: Brandeis University Press.
Mendenhall, George
  1961 "Biblical History in Transition." In *The Bible and the Ancient Near East.*
          Ed. G. E. Wright. Garden City: Doubleday.
Merton, Robert K.
  1967 "Latent and Manifest Functions." In *On Theoretical Sociology,* 73–138.
          New York: Free Press.
Meyer, Paul H.
  1963 "The Attitude of the Enlightenment Towards the Jew." *Studies on Vol-
          taire and the Eighteenth Century* 26:1161–1205.
Myerhoff, Barbara
  1979 *Number Our Days.* New York: E. P. Dutton.
Milgrom, Jacob
  1971 "Sin-Offering or Purification-Offering?" *Vetus Testamentum* 21:237–38.
  1976a "Israel's Sanctuary: The Priestly 'Picture of Dorian Gray.' " *Revue Bib-
          lique* 83:390–99.
  1976b *Cult and Conscience: The Asham and the Priestly Doctrine of Repentance.*
          Leiden: E. J. Brill.
  1981a "An Investigation into the Meaning of 'Unclean' in Our Culture."
          Direction Oct.:4–6.
  1981b "Kashrut is an Instrument to Perpetuate and Sustain Life." *Direction*
          Nov.: 7–8.
  1985 "You Shall Not Boil a Kid in Its Mother's Milk," *Bible Review* 1
          (3):48–55.
Miller, Patrick
  1970 "Animal Names As Designations in Ugaritic and Hebrew." *Ugarit For-
          schungen* 2:177–86.
Modder, Montagu Frank
  1960 *The Jew in the Literature of England to the End of the Nineteenth Century.*
          Philadelphia: Jewish Publication Society.
Monberg, T.
  1975 "Fathers Were Not Genitors." *Man* 10 (1):34–40.
Montaigne, Michel Eyquem
  1984 [1580] *Essays.* Trans. J. M. Cohen. New York: Penguin Books.
Moore, O. K., and David Olmstead
  1952 "Language and Professor Lévi-Strauss." *American Anthropologist*
          54:116–19.
Moran, W. L.
  1966 "The Literary Connection Between Lev. 11:13–19 and Deut. 14:12–
          18." *Catholic Biblical Quarterly* 28:217–77.
Morgan, Thomas
  1738 *The Moral Philosopher in a Dialogue between Philalethes a Christian Deist
          and Theophanes a Christian Jew.* London: n.p.
Morgenstern, Julian
  1973 *Rites of Birth, Marriage, Death and Kindred Occasions among the Semites.*
          New York: Ktav.
Nagel, Thomas
  1986 *The View from Nowhere.* New York: Oxford University Press.

Neusner, Jacob
    1973 *The Idea of Purity in Ancient Judaism.* Leiden: E. J. Brill.
    1978 "Comparing Judaisms." *History of Religions* 18:177–91.
    1979 "Anthropology and the Study of Talmudic Literature." In *Method and Meaning in Ancient Judaism.* Missoula: Scholars Press.
    1981 *Judaism: The Evidence of the Mishnah.* Chicago: University of Chicago Press.
    1983 *Ancient Israel after Catastrophe.* Charlottesville: University Press of Virginia.
    1986 *Judaism in the Matrix of Christianity.* Philadelphia: Fortress Press.
    1986b *The Oral Torah: The Sacred Books of Judaism.* San Francisco: Harper and Row.
Newman, Louis E.
    1983 *The Sanctity of the Seventh Year.* Chico, Calif.: Scholars Press.
Newton, Michael
    1985 *The Concept of Purity at Qumran and in the Letters of Paul.* Cambridge: Cambridge University Press.
Nietzsche, Frederick
    1974 [1873] "On Truth and Falsity in Their Ultramoral Sense." In *The Complete Works of Frederick Nietzsche.* Ed. Oscar Levy. Trans. Maximilian A. Magge. New York: Gordon.
Noth, Martin
    1977 *Leviticus.* Revised Edition. Philadelphia: Westminster Press.
    1981 *A History of Pentateuchal Traditions.* Trans. Bernhard Anderson. Chico, Calif.: Scholars Press.
Oden, Robert
    1987 *The Bible without Theology.* San Francisco: Harper and Row.
OED
    1971 *The Compact Edition of the Oxford English Dictionary.* 2 Vols. Oxford: Oxford University Press.
Oesterley, W.O.E., and Theodore H. Robinson
    1937 *Hebrew Religion: Its Origin and Development.* New York: Macmillan.
Orr, John
    1934 *English Deism: Its Roots and Its Fruits.* Grand Rapids: Wm. B. Eerdmans.
Ortner, Sherry B., and Harriet Whitehead
    1981 *Sexual Meanings: The Cultural Construction of Gender and Sexuality.* Cambridge: Cambridge University Press.
Otzen, Benedickt, Hans Gottlieb, and Knud Jeppesen
    1980 *Myths in the Old Testament.* Trans. Frederick Cryer, London: SCM Press.
Pace, David
    1986 *Claude Lévi-Strauss: The Bearer of Ashes.* London: ARK Paperbacks.
Pagden, Anthony
    1982 *The Fall of Natural Man: The American Indian and the Origins of Comparative Ethnology.* Cambridge: Cambridge University Press.
Paige, Karen Ericksen, and Jeffrey M. Paige
    1981 *The Politics of Reproductive Ritual.* Berkeley: University of California Press.

Parsons, Talcott
    1951   *The Social System.* New York: Free Press.
    1968   *The Structure of Social Action.* Vol. 2. New York: Free Press.
Parsons, Talcott, and Edward Shils
    1951   "Values, Motives, and Systems of Actions," in *Toward a General Theory of Action.* Ed. Talcott Parsons and Edward Shils. Cambridge, Mass.: Harvard University Press.
Patai, Raphael
    1959   *Sex and Family in the Bible and Middle East.* Garden City: Doubleday.
    1962   "The Ritual Approach to Hebrew-African Culture Contact." *Jewish Social Studies* 24:86–96.
Pearce, Roy Harvey
    1967   *Savagism and Civilization: A Study of the Indian and American Mind.* Baltimore: Johns Hopkins University Press.
Peck, Alan [Avery]-
    1981   *The Priestly Gift in Mishnah.* Chico, Calif.: Scholars Press.
Penner, Hans
    1971   "The Poverty of Functionalism." *History of Religions* 11 (1):91–97.
Pepper, Stephen
    1942   *World Hypotheses.* Berkeley: University of California Press.
Petazzoni, R.
    1954   "Myths of Beginning and Creation Myths." In *Essays on the History of Religion.* Leiden: E. J. Brill.
Pfeiffer, Robert H.
    1941   *Introduction to the Old Testament.* New York: Harper & Brothers.
Philo
    1971   *Questions and Answers on Genesis.* Trans. Ralph Marcus. Cambridge, Mass.: Harvard University Press.
Pitt-Rivers, Julien
    1977   *The Fate of Schechem.* Cambridge: Cambridge University Press.
Plaut, W. Gunther
    1974   *The Torah: Genesis.* New York: Union of American Hebrew Congregations.
Polanyi, Michael
    1958   *Personal Knowledge.* Chicago: University of Chicago Press.
Poliakov, Léon
    1975   *The History of Anti-Semitism.* Vol. 3. *From Voltaire to Wagner.* Trans. Miriam Kochan. New York: Vanguard Press.
Popenoe, Paul
    1973   *The Date Palm.* Miami: Field Research Projects.
Popenoe, Wilson
    1920   *Manual of Tropical and Sub-Tropical Fruits.* New York: Macmillan.
Porter, J. R.
    1976   *Leviticus.* Cambridge: Cambridge University Press.
Powers, Marla N.
    1980   "Menstruation and Reproduction: An Oglala Case." *Signs* 6:54–65.
Prell, Riv-Ellen
    1989   *Prayer and Community: The Havurah in American Judaism.* Detroit: Wayne State University Press.

Preuss, Samuel
 1987 *Explaining Religion: Criticism and Theory from Bodin to Freud*. New Haven: Yale University Press.
Prewitt, Terry
 1981 "Kinship Structures and the Genesis Genealogies." *Journal of Near Eastern Studies*. 40:87–98.
Rabinow, Paul
 1983 "Humanism As Nihilism: The Bracketing of Truth and Seriousness in American Cultural Anthropology." In *Social Science As Moral Inquiry*. Ed. Norma Haan et al. New York: Columbia University Press.
Rabinow, Paul, and William M. Sullivan
 1979 "The Interpretive Turn: Emergence of an Approach." In *Interpretive Social Science*, 1–24. Ed. Paul Rabinow and William M. Sullivan. Berkeley: University of California Press.
Radcliffe-Brown, A. R.
 1958 [1931] "The Present Position of Anthropological Studies." In *Method in Social Anthropology*, 45–85. Ed. M. N. Srinivas. Chicago: University of Chicago Press.
 1958 [1951] "The Comparative Method in Social Anthropology." In *Method in Social Anthropology*, 108–29. Ed. M. N. Srinivas. Chicago: University of Chicago Press.
 1965 [1952] *Structure and Function in Primitive Society*. New York: Free Press.
Reardon, Bernard M. G.
 1977 *Hegel's Philosophy of Religion*. New York: Barnes and Noble.
 1985 *Religion in the Age of Romanticism*. Cambridge: Cambridge University Press.
Ricoeur, Paul
 1974 "Structure and Hermeneutics." In *The Conflict of Interpretations*. Ed. Don Ihde. Evanston: Northwestern University Press.
 1981 "The Model of the Text: Meaningful Action Considered As Text." In *Hermeneutics and the Human Sciences*. Cambridge: Cambridge University Press.
Ringgren, Helmer
 1963 *The Faith of Qumran*. Philadelphia: Fortress Press.
 1966 *Israelite Religion*. Trans. David E. Green. Philadelphia: Fortress Press.
Robertson Smith, William
 1880 "Animal Worship and Animal Tribes among the Arabs and in the Old Testament." *Journal of Philology* 9:75–100.
 1903 [1885] *Kinship and Marriage in Early Arabia*. London: A. and C. Black.
 1927 [1889] *Lectures on the Religion of the Semites*. 3rd ed. New York: Meridian Books.
Rogerson, J. W.
 1970 "Structural Anthropology and the Old Testament." *Bulletin of the School of Oriental and African Studies* 33:490–500.
 1978 *Anthropology and the Old Testament*. Atlanta: John Knox Press.
Rorty, Richard
 1982 *Consequences of Pragmatism*. Minneapolis: University of Minnesota Press.
Rosaldo, Michelle Z., and Louis Lamphere
 1974 *Woman, Culture, and Society*. Stanford: Stanford University Press.

Rossi, Ino, ed.
  1974 *The Unconscious in Culture: The Structuralism of Claude Lévi-Strauss in Perspective.* New York: E. P. Dutton.
Rotenstreich, Nathan
  1953 "Hegel's Image of Judaism." *Jewish Social Studies* 5:33–52.
Roth, Cecil
  1945 *A Life of Menasseh ben Israel.* Philadelphia: Jewish Publication Society of America.
RSV
  1971 *The New Oxford Annotated Bible.* Revised Standard Version. Ed. Herbert G. May and Bruce Metzger. New York: Oxford University Press.
Safrai, Shmuel
  1987 "Oral Tora." In *The Literature of the Sages.* Part 1. Philadelphia: Fortress Press.
Sahlins, Marshall
  1976 *Culture and Practical Reason.* Chicago: University of Chicago Press.
  1981 *Historical Metaphors and Mythical Realities.* Ann Arbor: University of Michigan Press.
  1985 *Islands of History.* Chicago: University of Chicago Press.
Sandmel, Samuel
  1962 "Parallelomania." *Journal of Biblical Literature* 81:1–13.
Sapir, David, and J. Christopher Crocker, eds.
  1977 *The Social Use of Metaphor.* Philadelphia: University of Pennsylvania Press.
Sarna, Nahum
  1970 *Understanding Genesis.* New York: Schocken Books.
Sasson, J. M.
  1966 "Circumcision in the Ancient Near East." *Journal of Biblical Literature* 85:473–76.
  1976 "Ass." In *The Interpreter's Dictionary of the Bible. Supplement.* Ed. Keith Crim. Nashville: Abingdon Press.
Saussure, Ferdinand de
  1966 *Course in General Linguistics.* New York: McGraw Hill.
Sayce, A. H.
  1889 "Review of William Robertson Smith's *Religion of the Semites.*" In *Academy* 36 (Nov. 30): 357–58.
Schapera, Isaac
  1955 "The Sin of Cain." *Journal of the Royal Anthropological Institute* 85:33–34. Reprinted in *Anthropological Approaches to the Old Testament.* Ed. Bernhard Lang. Philadelphia: Fortress Press.
Schiffman, Lawrence
  1983 *Sectarian Law in the Dead Sea Scrolls.* Atlanta: Scholars Press.
Schleiermacher, Friedrich
  1958 [1821] *On Religion: Speeches to Its Cultured Despisers.* Trans. John Oman. New York: Harper and Row.
  1976 [1830] *The Christian Faith.* Ed. H. R. Mackintosh and J. S. Stewart. Philadelphia: Fortress Press.
Schochet, Elijah J.
  1984 *Animal Life in Jewish Tradition: Attitudes and Relationships.* New York: Ktav Publishing House.

Scholte, Bob
  1987   "The Literary Turn in Contemporary Anthropology." *Critical Anthropology* **7** (1):33–47.
Schorsch, Ismar
  1975   Introduction to *Heinrich Graetz: The Structure of Jewish History*. New York: The Jewish Theological Seminary.
Schütze, Martin
  1920–23   "The Fundamental Ideas in Herder's Thought." *Modern Philology* 18:1–15, 57–70; 19:113–30; 20:361–82; 21:29–48, 113–32.
Schwartz, Leon
  1981   *Diderot and the Jews*. London: Associated University Presses.
Schwarzbach, Bertram
  1971   *Voltaire's Old Testament Criticism*. Geneva: Librairie Droz.
  1973   "The Jews and the Enlightenment Anew," *Diderot Studies* 16:361–74.
Shanks, Herschel
  1976   "Is the Title 'Rabbi' Anachronistic in the Gospels?" and "Origins of the Title 'Rabbi'." In *Exploring the Talmud*. Vol. 1, 164–71, 177–82. Ed. Haim Z. Dimitrovsky. New York: Ktav Publishing House.
Shore, Bradd
  1981   "Sexuality and Gender in Samoa: Conceptions and Missed Conceptions." In *Sexual Meanings,* 192–215. Ed. Sherry B. Ortner and Harriet Whitehead. Cambridge: Cambridge University Press.
Simmons, Alan E.
  1972   *Growing Unusual Fruit*. New York: Walker.
Skinner, John
  1910   *Genesis*. International Critical Commentary. Vol. 1. New York: Charles Scribner's Sons.
Smith, Jonathan Z.
  1978   *Map Is Not Territory*. Leiden: E. J. Brill.
  1982   "In Comparison a Magic Dwells." In *Imagining Religion,* 19–35. Chicago: University of Chicago Press.
Snaith, Norman H.
  1944   *The Distinctive Ideas of the Old Testament*. London: Epworth Press.
  1967   *Leviticus and Numbers*. London: Thomas Nelson and Sons.
Soler, Jean
  1979   "The Dietary Prohibitions of the Hebrews." Trans. Elborg Forster. *New York Review of Books* 26:10 (June 14):24–30.
Speiser, E. A.
  1964   *Genesis*. The Anchor Bible Series. Garden City: Doubleday.
Spencer, Paul
  1965   *The Samburu: A Study of Genrontocracy in a Nomadic Tribe*. London: Routledge and Kegan Paul.
Spiro, Melford
  1966   "Religion: Problems of Definition and Explanation." In *Anthropological Approaches to the Study of Religion*. Ed. Michael Banton, 85–126. New York: Frederick A. Praeger.
  1968   "Virgin Birth, Parthenogenesis and Physiological Paternity: An Essay in Cultural Interpretation." *Man* 3:242–61.
Starhawk
  1979   *The Spiral Dance: A Rebirth of the Ancient Religion of the Great Goddess*. New York: Harper and Row.

1982 *Dreaming the Dark: Magic, Sex, and Politics*. Boston: Beacon Press.
Stephen, Leslie
1902 *History of English Thought in the Eighteenth Century*. Vol. 1. 3rd ed. London: Smith, Elder & Co.
Stocking, George W.
1983 "The Ethnographer's Magic: Fieldwork in British Anthropology from Tylor to Malinowski." In *Observers Observed*. Ed. George W. Stocking, 70–120. Madison: University of Wisconsin Press.
Strathern, Andrew
1970 "Male Initiation in New Guinea Highlands Societies." *Ethnology* 9 (4):373–79.
Strathern, Marilyn
1987 "Out of Context." *Current Anthropology* 28 (3):251–81.
Sykes, Arthur Ashley
1740 *The Principles and Connexion of Natural and Revealed Religion*. London: n.p.
Talmon, S.
1977 "The Comparative Method in Biblical Interpretation: Principles and Problems." *Vetus Testamentum, Supplement* 29:320–56.
Tambiah, S. J.
1969 "Animals Are Good to Think and Good to Prohibit." *Ethnology* 7 (4):423–59.
Taylor, Charles
1979 "Interpretation and the Sciences of Man." In *Interpretive Social Science*. Ed. Paul Rabinow and William M. Sullivan, 25–72. Berkeley: University of California Press.
1985 "Social Theory As Practice." In *Philosophy and the Human Sciences: Philosophical Papers*. Vol. 2, 91–115. Cambridge: Cambridge University Press.
Thorowgood, Thomas
1650 *Iewes in America, or Probabilities That the Americans Are of That Race*. London: n.p.
Tillich, Paul
1974 *The Construction of the History of Religion in Schelling's Positive Philosophy*. Trans. Victor Nuovo. Lewisburg: Bucknell University Press.
Tindal, Matthew
1730 *Christianity As Old As Creation*. London: n.p.
Torrey, Norman
1930 *Voltaire and the English Deists*. New Haven: Yale University Press.
1931 *Voltaire and the Enlightenment*. New York: F. S. Crofts.
Trachtenberg, Joshua
1943 *The Devil and the Jews*. New Haven: Yale University Press.
Troeltsch, Ernst
1971 [1901] *The Absoluteness of Christianity and the History of Religions*. Trans. David Reid. Richmond: John Knox Press.
Tucker, Gene M.
1985 "Prophecy and Prophetic Literature." In *The Hebrew Bible and Its Modern Interpreters*. Ed. Douglas A. Knight and Gene M. Tucker. Chico, Calif.: Scholars Press.
Tucker, John T.
1949 "Initiation Ceremonies for Luimbi Boys." *Africa* 19:53–60.

Turner, Victor
    1962   "Three Symbols of Passage in Ndembu Circumcision Ritual." In *The Ritual of Social Relations*. Ed. Max Gluckman. Manchester: Manchester University Press.
    1967   *The Forest of Symbols: Aspects of Ndembu Ritual*. Ithaca: Cornell University Press.
    1969   *The Ritual Process*. Ithaca: Cornell University Press.
    1974   *Dramas, Fields, and Metaphors: Symbolic Action in Human Society*. Ithaca: Cornell University Press.
Tylor, Edward
    1958 [1871]   *Primitive Culture*. New York: Harper and Brothers Publishers.
Urton, Gary, ed.
    1985   *Animal Myths and Metaphors in South America*. Salt Lake City: University of Utah.
van Gennep, Arnold
    1960 [1908]   *The Rites of Passage*. Chicago: University of Chicago Press.
Vermes, Geza
    1975   *The Dead Sea Scrolls in English*. New York: Penguin.
    1977   *The Dead Sea Scrolls: Qumran in Perspective*. Philadelphia: Fortress Press.
Voltaire
    1962 [1762]   *The Sermon of the Fifty*. Trans. J.A.R. Sequoin. New York: Ross Paxton.
    1962 [1764]   *Philosophical Dictionary*. Trans. Peter Gay. New York: Basic Books.
von Rad, Gerhard
    1966   *Deuteronomy*. Philadelphia: Westminster Press.
    1976   *Genesis*. Philadelphia: Westminster Press.
Vriezen, Th. C.
    1967   *The Religion of Ancient Israel*. Philadelphia: Westminster Press.
Wasserman, Maurice
    1954   "The American Indian As Seen by the Seventeenth Century Chroniclers." Ph.D. diss., University of Pennsylvania. Ann Arbor: University Microfilms.
Weiss, Charles
    1962   "A Wordwide Survey of the Current Practice of Milah (Ritual Circumcision)." *Jewish Social Studies* 24:30–48.
Welch, Claude
    1972   *Protestant Thought in the Nineteenth Century*. New Haven: Yale University Press.
Wellhausen, Julius
    1973 [1878]   *Prolegomena to the History of Ancient Israel*. Gloucester, Mass.: Peter Smith.
Wenham, Gordon J.
    1979   *The Book of Leviticus*. Grand Rapids: Wm. B. Eerdmans.
Westermann, Claus
    1984   *Genesis 1–11*. Trans. John J. Scullion. Minneapolis: Augsburg Publishing House.
White, C.M.N.
    1953   "Notes on the Circumcision Rites of the Balovale Tribes." *African Studies* 12 (2):41–56.

White, Hayden
    1978   *Tropics of Discourse.* Baltimore: Johns Hopkins University Press.
Whitney, Lois
    1965   *Primitivism and the Idea of Progress: In English Popular Literature of the Eighteenth Century.* New York: Octagon Books.
Wiener, Max
    1941   "John Toland and Judaism." *Hebrew Union College Annual* 16: 215–42.
Wilson, Monica
    1954   "Nyakyusa Ritual and Symbolism." *American Anthropologist* 56 (2):228–40.
    1957   *Rituals of Kinship among the Nyakyusa.* London: Oxford University Press.
Wilson, Robert
    1980   *Prophesy and Society in Ancient Israel.* Philadelphia: Fortress Press.
    1984   *Sociological Approaches to the Old Testament.* Philadelphia: Fortress Press.
Winch, Peter
    1959   *The Idea of a Social Science and Its Relation to Philosophy.* London: Routledge and Kegan Paul.
    1970   "Understanding a Primitive Society." In *Rationality.* Ed. Bryan Wilson, 78–112. Oxford: Basil Blackwell.
Wolf, Lucien
    1901   *Menasseh Ben Israel's Mission to Oliver Cromwell.* London: Macmillan.
Wright, G. E.
    1950   *The Old Testament against Its Environment.* Chicago: Alec R. Allenson.
    1957   *Biblical Archaeology.* Philadelphia: Westminster Press.
Yadin, Yigael
    1977   *The Temple Scroll* [Heb.]. 2 vols. Jerusalem: Israel Exploration Society.
Zeitlin, Solomon
    1976   "A Reply" and "The Title Rabbi in the Gospels Is Anachronistic." In *Exploring the Talmud.* Vol. 1, 172–76, 183–87. Ed. Haim Z. Dimitrovsky. New York: Ktav Publishing House.
Zenner, Walter P.
    1988   *Persistence and Flexibility: Anthropological Perspectives on the American Jewish Experience.* Albany: State University of New York Press.

Index of Sources

General Index

HOWARD EILBERG-SCHWARTZ teaches in the Department of Religion at Temple University. He serves as editor of the SUNY Press series The Body in Culture, History, and Religion. He is author of *The Human Will in Judaism: The Mishnah's Philosophy of Intention* as well as numerous articles on the anthropology of Judaism.